AF322788

Endorsements

The discussion about manhood and men's roles on achieving gender equality in the US and internationally is too often stuck in polarized debates. Gayle Kimball set out to listen to the various sides and comes to clear-eyed conclusions about what it takes to find a way forward that is feminist, inclusive, and compassionate toward men. The result is accessible, fascinating, and urgent.
Gary Barker, CEO, Promundo-US

I've been helping men and their families since our first son was born in 1969. When I began working in the field there were very few voices that address topics of masculinity and what it means to be a good man in today's world. Now there are many more men and women in the field. Gayle has done a great job in bringing together many diverse voices. You won't agree with the views of everyone, but this book will open your eyes, your mind, and your heart.
Jed Diamond, Ph.D., LCSW, author of *The Irritable Male Syndrome* and *12 Rules for Good Men*

A breakthrough book for a female feminist with a history in the male feminist community to begin to incorporate the contributions of experts on men's issues who resist feminist definitions of men and masculinity as oppressors and part of "the patriarchy." May Kimball be opening the door to increasingly male positive discussions of men and boys, with the understanding that we are all in the same family boat so that when either sex wins, both sexes lose.
Warren Farrell, Ph.D., author of The *Boy Crisis* and *The Myth of Male Power*

In a world of polarization, suspicion, and hostility, Gayle Kimball offers us the chance to occupy middle ground and talk about difficult gender stuff, a great job in putting the two sides (and more) of the debates in ways that promote discussion rather than polarize. The first step in realizing this goal is to begin to talk across a gender ideological divide as deep as the cold war. There's nothing like dogma to produce in-fighting and intolerance! I recommend this book as that first step.
Robert Morrell, Ph.D., a pioneer of Critical Masculinity Studies in South Africa

This dialogue features men who have done so much on behalf of boys and men throughout the world. Their different backgrounds and approaches indicate a shared love and concern for males, both young and old.
Mark Sherman, Ph.D., Professor of Psychology, Emeritus, SUNY, New Paltz

This global dialogue about masculinities has sounded the trumpet call to wake up and face up to men's issues worldwide. The book embraces the long untouchable challenges of masculinity.
Dr. **George F. Simons**, Creator of diversophy, France

I maintain a unique online library of over 4,683 books on men. Kimball's is the first book I'm aware of that gives guidance from such diverse experts on the issue of men and masculinities. An extensive read about this challenging topic.
Gordon Clay, Menstuff.org

Books by Gayle Kimball

50/50 Marriage
50/50 Parenting
Happy Marriages

Calm: How to Thrive in Challenging Times
Calm Parents and Children: A Guidebook

Mysteries of Reality: Dialogues with Visionary Scientists
Mysteries of Healing: Dialogues with Doctors and Scientists
Mysteries of Knowledge Beyond the Senses: Dialogues with Courageous Scientists
Essential Energy Tools: How to Develop Your Clairvoyant and Healing Abilities illustrated with 3 videos and 2 CDs

Women's Culture
Women's Culture Revisited
Brave: Young Women's Global Revolution (2 vols.)
Climate Girls Saving Our World

The Teen Trip: The Complete Resource Guide
How to Survive Your Parents' Divorce
Answers to Kids' Deep Questions in Photos
Your Mindful Guide to Academic Success: Beat Burnout
Everything You Need to Know to Succeed After College
Quick Healthy Recipes: Literacy Fundraiser

Ageism in Youth Studies: Generation Maligned
How Global Youth Values Will Transform Our Future
Resist! Goals and Tactics for Changemakers

A Global Dialogue on Masculinity

33 Men Speak Out

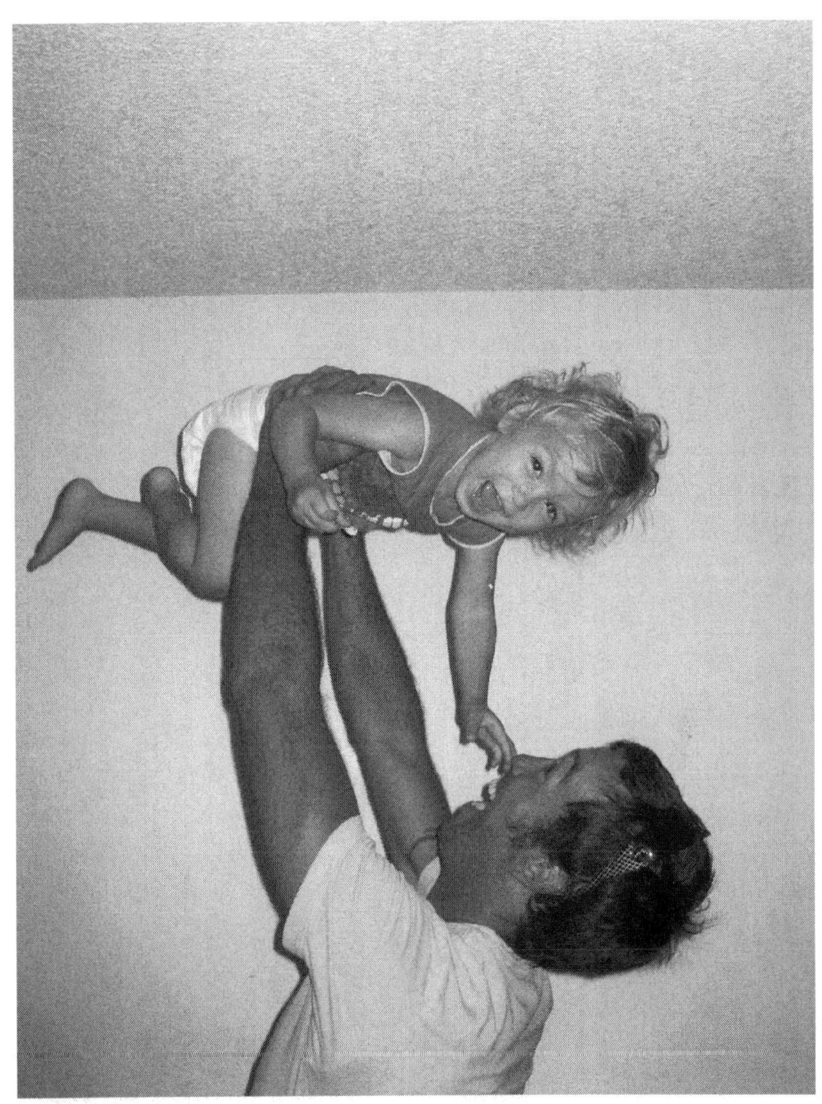

Gayle Kimball, Ph.D.

Equality=Press

earthhavenchico@hotmail.com

https://globalyouthbook.wordpress.com

https://greenlocalsolutions.wordpress.com/

Library of Congress Catalogue Subject Headings:
HQ1075-1075.5 sex role, HQ1088-1090.7 men, HM831-901 social change, HM701 social systems, HM711-806 groups, HQ801-801.83 relationships, HQ503-1064 Family, HQ767.8-792.2 children, H1-99, social sciences

Cover design by Miles Huffman

Photo of the author's son and grandson on the title page.
This book is dedicated to Jed and Soren.

Print ISBN: 978-0-938795-11-7
Ebook ISBN: 978-0-938795-10-0

Printed in the United States of America
First Printing, 2022

Table of Contents

Introduction

Today, social conditioning still tells boys not to be like girls or express their vulnerabilities, but boys and young men today are more open to a wider range of emotional expression. Boys I know don't think girls have cooties or are lesser people. But the high rate of divorce initiated by women and high rates of domestic violence indicate that intimate communication between men and women is still problematic. Daniel Ellenberg reported about his therapy clients, "Women often feel like guys don't listen." The hazards of the masculine role for men need to be examined, such as risk-taking, competition, not asking for help, inhibiting emotional expression, and the fear of being labeled feminine.

I was fortunate to participate in an era of women's and men's liberation movements during a pivotal time. After I joined the Religious Studies faculty at California State University, Chico, students in my first Women Studies classes taught me feminist vocabulary and methodology. Since then, I've had the privilege of interviewing trailblazing men and women. The most recent changemakers for gender equality are featured in this book.

An unusual perspective on gender liberation movements was gained by being active in the National Organization of Men Against Sexism (NOMAS) as a member of the Men and Women's Task Group, along with Gordon Clay* and Randy Crutcher.* Men and Masculinity (M&M) conferences in Seattle, Hartford, and Pittsburg and a father's rights conference in Denver were informative and fun. Recently I interviewed the thoughtful men featured in this book as well as others who commented on drafts. I've also learned from my father, Tom; my brother, Greg; my son, Jed; and my grandson, Soren.

Serving as Coordinator of Women's Studies for decades led me to attend many feminist conferences including the National Women's Studies Association (NWSA) and National Organization for Women (NOW). I organized conferences at California State University-Chico (CSUC), including a large three-day conference on "Feminist Visions of the Future," which resulted in a video of the same title. Many other conferences on changing gender roles resulted in videos in 1987, including *Men's Changing Roles, Women and Men,* and *Dual-Earner Families*--available on my YouTube channel. Six of the men featured in this book are included both in the earlier videos and in our 2021 video interviews.

The men in this book debate if gender is constructed more by nature or nurture, genes or socialization, and who is most oppressed. Feminist men, led by academics and psychologists, emphasize men's behaviors that harm women and children--mainly violence. They critique how men are socialized into dominator roles, which led John Stoltenberg* to title one of his books *Refusing to Be a Man.* Some of these pro-feminists seem to assume a zero-sum game approach fearing that men's gain is women's loss, as Gary Barker* and Daniel Ellenberg* pointed out. That is, if they acknowledge men are harmed by traditional gender roles they worry it detracts from the harm women experience from male dominance and violence. Yet, to acknowledge that we can all gain from being fully human strengthens the equality movement with different perspectives.

A major issue in the men's movement is that some of the male feminists refuse to dialogue with the men's rights leaders, specifically mentioning Warren Farrell* who first gained fame as a feminist working with NOW. Psychologist Daniel Ellenberg* reported, "I've recommended some dialogues with Warren and I got routinely turned down: 'We don't talk to people like that.'" However, Farrell doesn't identify with men's rights but rather as an "advocate of gender liberation who believes in the liberation of both sexes from the rigid roles of the past, toward more flexible roles for the future." Several feminist men told me they were reluctant to be in this book because it includes authors like Farrell* and Jack Kammer,* who refers to himself as a counter-feminist.

These contests over political purity are characteristic of most progressive groups I've been involved with. This contrasts with the US right-wing's consistent and unified focus on abolishing abortion, access to guns (even for the certified-mentally ill), and economic benefits for the rich such as tax breaks.

To discover changes and progress in achieving equality, in 2021 I did extensive interviews with 33 men (four decided not to include their entire interviews) and 10 shorter exchanges.

The men represent a wide range of viewpoints: feminist, equalist, mythopoetic (as initiated by poet Robert Bly), fathers' rights, men's studies, and men's support groups. The latter is currently the most popular approach of the men's movement.

I included men from Generations Silent to Z, from various ethnic backgrounds, men from 12 countries (although still US-centric), and men with various sexual orientations. Two of the men had been married to women and are now married to men.

What motivated these men to think about and work to change men's roles--and for many of them to go into helping professions that require higher education? The most prominent influence was their relationship with their father. Like the men I interviewed for *50:50 Marriage* and *50:50 Parenting*, their father being a very positive or very negative example was most impactful, especially the latter:

His father died when the boy was young: Branch, Ellenberg, Mbewe, Tello.

His father was absent due to divorce: Diamond, Glosby, Kaveladze, Smiler, Zhang.

His father was away due to long work hours: Clay, Kammer, Marcus.

His father was too authoritarian: Bliss, Ellenberg, Farrell.

Versus:

He had a nurturing loving father: Barker, Crutcher, Hodgson, Kinote, Messner, Simons, Straton, Stoltenberg, van de Ven.

Many in the group with optimal fathers are feminists with activist compassion for women, perhaps something they learned from their kind dads. This makes the point that father involvement should be taught and enabled by social support systems like parental leave as they have in Nordic countries and other industrial nations. Boys need instruction in emotional literacy, called social and emotional learning--many resources are available.[1]

The interviews were done on Skype and posted unedited on my YouTube channel, available to view. The men's social media links are listed on the YouTube post and in their short biographies seen online.[2] The transcripts were edited by me and the interviewees and many people associated with men's studies were invited to critique a draft and some added comments to the overview chapter. The six chapters are organized by the focus or goal of the men's activism and writings.

An asterisk by a man's name indicates he's an interviewee. I asked about astrological signs, although that is not at all scholarly, as a quick way to discuss the man's personality. The most common were Gemini (7, communicators) and Sagittarius (6, ask deep questions); this is not a random distribution of the 12 signs and therefore significant. (Interestingly, in my interviews for a visionary scientists' trilogy, Sagittarius was the most common of the 65 interviews.)

This book raises questions and answers some of them. How do we encourage boys to attend college at the same rate as girls now that they're less likely to graduate than their female peers? How do we make STEM and caregiving professions more available to all? How do we teach boys that it's human to express vulnerability in ways other than humor or anger and to ask for help? How do we replace blaming discussions of toxic masculinity with instructive "tonic masculinity"? Gender liberation is about allowing a full range of expression and experience and equal opportunity for all of us.

Chapter 1: Men's Changing Roles

The Hazards of Precarious Masculinity

"When I got into men's work, I was stunned by the male deprivation that most of the guys I was working with had experienced growing up," observed George Simons,* who was one of the fortunate minority of our changemakers who had intimate bonds with male relatives. Updating his observation from France, where he now lives, he commented, "I lecture in Finland and other countries, and, generally, at least half the students are from all over the world. What I see is that the guys are not doing very well." Owen Marcus* agrees, "Guys are lost, they don't have anyone to connect to, anyone to explain it to them. They feel trapped because they don't see a way out" of what's called the man box. He observes, "Young men are hungry for what they never got--models and direction."

It's not enough to just have a male body, as masculinity is seen as precarious. As Ashanti Branch* said about being a teenager, "You're always in that space of questioning yourself. Are you man enough?" The Boy Scouts were founded (in 1908 in the UK and in 1910 in the US) to "re-masculinize teen boys" and these youth groups spread quickly around the world. A former Eagle Scout observed, "You might even call scouting 'Masculinity for Dummies,' but only for heterosexual boys." [3] However, over 60,000 former Scouts sued over sexual abuse by adult scout leaders and reached an $850 million settlement in 2021, the first of many such lawsuits. [4]

Poet Robert Bly popularized the critique of American men as too soft and feminized in his 1990 book, *Iron John: A Book About Men.* His approach sparked the mythopoetic men's movement and his book spent 62 weeks on the best-seller list. Bly said men need to recover their inner strength to be nurturing fathers and mentors and was concerned about boys growing up without their fathers.

More recently, other popular writers spread the same message to "man up." International best-selling author and Canadian Jordan Peterson tells men in *12 Rules for Life* to "Toughen up." [5] He told boys to be more boyish and stated that male oppression of women is a myth. He warns, "If men are pushed too hard to feminize, they will become more and more interested in harsh, fascist political ideology." [6] And, "If you think tough men are dangerous, wait until you see what weak men are capable of." His YouTube channel has more than four million subscribers and almost 500 videos.

In 2021, Missouri Senator Josh Hawley made one of his campaign themes the crisis of "the decline of traditional masculinity" (defined as being independent and assertive).[7] He blamed "the Left" and Hollywood for a deliberate attack on masculinity which he claims led to "the deconstruction of American men." Hawley states that this plot caused men to withdraw into video games, pornography, idleness, and substance abuse, as well as to avoid fatherhood and suffer from mental health problems. He calls on young men, in particular, to get a job and "be who you were meant to be," while simultaneously opposing job bills like the Build Back Better Act.

On the other side, Ronald Levant, Ed.D., (co-author of *The Tough Standard: The Hard Truth about Masculinity and Violence*) argues that masculinity is harmful to us all and that "What we need to learn--and teach our children--is how to be a man without masculinity." [8]

Femininity is seen as dangerous to precarious masculinity. Tucker Carlson, the most-watched US cable news host, said (December 7, 2021, on his Fox News show) about British Prime Minister Boris Johnson, "Somebody who knows him told me. . .that getting Covid emasculated him, it changed him, it feminized him, it weakened him as a man."[9] When my son was a baby, people got upset if he was dressed in pink onesies handed down from friends with girls. Brazilians call President Jair Bolsinaro the Trump of the Tropics; he revealed in 2017, "I've got five kids but on the fifth, I had a moment of weakness and it came out a woman."[10] (His daughter Laura.) From Kenya, Jeffer Kinoti* reported, "Femininity or any sign of weakness is regarded as very negative. You're supposed to be this uptight, no emotion-showing kind of an animal, not to show any form of emotional weakness like crying."

Emails from Raiders football coach Jon Gruden surfaced in 2021, in which he uses words such as "faggot" to disparage men who disagreed with him, labeling then-Vice President Joe Biden a "clueless pussy."[11] He also shared photos of almost naked women. Donald Trump said of French President Emmanuel Macron, "He's a wuss guy," made fun of his height (5'8"), and called Senator Marco Rubio "Little Marco." [12]

All too common are shooting rampages by boys and men in the US and Canada, which adds to the anti-male rhetoric about toxic masculinity. Some in the men's movement trace the heavy criticism of men to the period after World War II and the continuing warfare in Korea, Vietnam, Iraq, and Afghanistan. Some elements of the Second Wave of the woman's movement in the '60s and '70s criticized "male chauvinist pigs." Some separatists said men weren't necessary as in the slogan, "A woman needs a man like a fish needs a bicycle." Theologian and former Catholic nun Mary Daly told me during a conference that men are a mutation as seen in their smaller Y chromosome, a pseudo-theory put forth by Valerie Solanas in her book, *The S.C.U.M. Manifesto,* published in 1968, the year she shot and wounded Andy Warhol. [13]

The incontrovertible facts are that men generally die earlier than women, are more likely to commit suicide, take more risks, and more often commit and receive violence. [14] It's ironic that the most advantaged groups can also be disadvantaged, like wealthy celebrities with drug problems and divorces, or men as a group. Because we live in a patriarchy where a relatively small group of men controls governments and finances, a natural assumption is that they have more power in all aspects of life. Most men probably don't feel very powerful as they work hard to provide for their families. When they're not able or needed to protect and provide for women and children, where do they find traditional male identity and men's power and privilege?

In his book *Is Masculinity Toxic?,* Andrew Smiler,* Ph.D., concludes the answer to the title's question is "yes" because gender beliefs are hazardous for men's health. Miles Groth and others advocate "tonic masculinity" to build on positive traits such as "creative risk-taking,"[15] and men's support groups emphasize dedicating a mission to serve others. Perry Garfinkel explained in our interview, "What we're really trying to gain is understanding of the beauty of man power, the life-giving aspects of that male power, rather than the destroying aspects of it." George Simons* also emphasizes traditional male virtues such as protectiveness and hard work, as do the weekend trainings for men discussed in this book.

On the other side, former Major League baseball player Aubrey Huff wrote, "I support Toxic Masculinity" on his Twitter biography. He also is against "bullshit" requirements to wear masks during the pandemic. Brazil's President Bolsonaro agreed that "masks are for fairies," before he contacted Covid.[16]

The traditional masculine belief system is limiting. Sociologist Walt Schafer defined the limitations in our interview; "You can show the joy of succeeding or anger, but you don't dare show vulnerability or weakness or self-doubt. A key belief is that if you're not struggling, you're probably not making it. Your self-worth is determined by your achievement."

Fred Hayward* explained, "Our roles are basically competitive, in a way that the female role is not, which inhibits intimate friendships and nurturance among men. Homophobia is a particularly potent fear that keeps men too distant from each other," as seen in recent studies of boys by Niobe Way and Peggy Orenstein (discussed later). Gordon Clay* agrees that homophobia "put us in an incredible box and keeps us apart as men."

Being in the "man box" limits men's range of expression,[17] one of the reasons robots like Sophia and virtual assistants like Siri, Alexa, and Cortana are portrayed as female to convey helpfulness. In a meta-analysis of five studies, Professor Sylvie Borau discovered that women are perceived as more human than men![18] Therefore, we may be more upset when women soldiers are killed than when their male comrades are sent home in body bags, although they're equally human.

Limiting our range of emotion and behaviors to stereotypes of proper masculinity or femininity cuts off the full range of human expression and achievement, as shown in research based on Sandra Bem's Sex Role Inventory. The test measures include nurturant and instrumental traits (and neutral). She found that androgynous people who score high on both are more flexible and mentally healthy than people who score traditionally--with especially better mental health than those who score low on both, called "undifferentiated."[19]

Naming these hazards of being male, as psychologist Herb Goldberg titled his 1976 book, helped spark the men's movement (his subtitle was *Surviving the Myths of Masculine*

Privilege). Seeing the problems facing boys and men, one would expect a men's movement as lively and influential as the Second Wave of the women's movement, which began in the 1960s when Betty Friedan named the problem that had no name--sexism, but it's not prominent. Despite their internet presence, when was the last time you heard about men's rights, fathers' rights, mythopoetic, pro-feminist, masculinities studies, or men's inner work?

Relationships and Sexuality

We hear a lot about "toxic masculinity," (Shepherd Bliss* is credited with coining the term), as personified by former President Donald Trump. He infamously said his wealth and status allowed him to be a "chick magnet" and molest women. Despite Trump's admitted lack of respect for women, as he told radio host Howard Stern,[20] a majority of white women voted for Trump in 2016 and 2020. This vote is "validation that many women (and men) are attracted to 'bad boys' or rich men, or expressions of powerful masculinity," states Canadian Robert Samery (active in the Canadian Centre for Men and Families[21]). Professor and co-author of books about misandry, Paul Nathanson adds that women still prefer to "marry up," as portrayed in romance novels written by and for women. How will this expectation play out as globally more women than men achieve college educations?

About 25% of women (more so for women of color and LBGTQ+ people) and 10% of men have been victims of violence or stalking by a partner, according to Amy Butcher in *Mothertrucker*.[22] Samery cites data that finds a range of 10% to 55%.[23] In the country with the world's highest incarceration rate, 93% of the US Federal Bureau of Prison inmates are male.[24] Samery points out that men don't often see male mental health providers, partly because in 2019 70% of US psychologists were female and the gap is increasing yearly.[25] He reports that most male suicide victims didn't receive a mental health diagnosis or treatment.

Expectations for men to initiate relationships with women can also be burdensome and intimidating. Fred Hayward* reported, "My job is to figure out what she wants in a man and show her that I'm better than other guys, up to her standards." Physiologically, men are more likely to feel swamped and to shut down during emotional disagreements with women, as found in psychologist John Gottman's research in what he calls the "Love Lab." A common pattern is the woman presses for more closeness, the man pulls away, the woman gets angrier, and he retreats further. Both of them feel frustrated and lonely (these attachment patterns are discussed by psychologist Sue Johnson's Emotionally Focused Therapy and in my book *Happy Marriages*). Studies show that men in the US are more lonely than in Europe because of our definitions of masculinity: The Survey Center on an American Life found that 15% of men have no close friendships.[26]

In all the English-speaking countries, women are much more likely to initiate divorce. In the US, women are more likely than men to ask for divorce (70% overall and 90% of college-educated women initiate the divorce) according to an American Sociological Association study.[27] Also, divorced women are more likely than men to blame their ex-spouse (64% of women blamed them compared to 44% of the men in an Avvo study).[28] I was surprised to learn from the recent interviews that many men feel disadvantaged in relationships with women, saying that women have superior verbal and emotional skills. This can be explained by the way we raise boys to fear being like girls and perhaps due to some physiological differences discussed later.

Sex, sports, and earning money are other areas where men often face pressure to perform. Over a third of US adults surveyed report having experienced some type of sexual dysfunction (43% of women and 31% of men in one study).[29] Fewer young adults are having casual sex than they did a decade ago, partly because they are now more likely to live with their parents (43% [30]). Women in their 20s in the US are more likely to reject exclusive heterosexuality than men, perhaps linked to some feminist arguments against what Adrienne Rich called "compulsory heterosexuality."[31]

Male sexuality, including addiction to pornography, is explored by researchers like Justin Lehmiller (*Tell Me What You Want* and *The Science of Human Sexuality)* and David Ley (*Ethical Porn for Dicks*). Some young men substitute video games for relationships and are doing less "partying."[32] In a

2021 survey, 28% of US men between ages 18 to 30 said they hadn't engaged in sex during the past year.[33]

Psychologist Herb Goldberg observed, "We have created this fantasy of a sex life when there is no such thing as a sex life; there is our sexual response. Masters and Johnson reinforced that mechanistic orientation." (Note that this famous couple is part of the divorce statistics.) He advocated that instead of men thinking of their penis as a performance tool, somehow separate from their feelings, that they should pay attention to the "wisdom of the penis" in the context of relationships. His solution was to understand that:

> *Both masculinity and femininity are psychological disorders in the sense that they're defensive strategies against certain inner experiences. I think one of the best things that can happen to men, if they could accept it, would be feminism. If they could expect equal responsibility and equal privilege, and no longer feel guilty when things go wrong, that in itself would be tremendous.*

The narrator of our *Men's Changing Roles* video, Randy Crutcher* explained, "Men are faced with confusing images about masculinity, split between Rambo on one side and the wimp on the other." Randy and I led workshops with college students where men said that women tend to be attracted to tough guys rather than to nice guys. The male students expressed appreciation for women initiating relationships.

A man who critiqued this chapter suggested adding what it means to have a male body, so I asked him. Dan Clifford is a Gen X therapist:

> *As part of a generation where male was interpreted as a dominating force to overthrow and humble, I grew up confused. I was not marginalized by sexuality, gender, or race in a day when those marginalized were necessarily highlighted and celebrated. I was often one of the smartest, strongest, loudest people in the room, all of which was frowned upon because as a white male, I was privileged, and in the eyes of culture it was*

time for that privilege to end. Not knowing it was a cultural aspect, I took it personally and diminished myself in order for others to feel comfortable. I learned that, metaphorically, my penis was the antagonist in most everyone's victim story and that any assertion of my hopes, needs, or wants was an infringement upon their rights. As a white male, I was a scary person to most and eventually embodied that projection internally without ever knowing it.

The pressure to be masculine is associated with the fear of being seen as queer or feminine, which causes many boys to feel lonely in adolescence, as Niobe Way describes in *The Crisis of Connection*. Peggy Orenstein also interviewed boys and reported in *Boys and Sex* that her subjects were eager to talk to her because "nobody talks to boys, nobody listens to boys." For example, they only get about 10 minutes of sex talk during their adolescence, mostly from their mothers, so they learn about sex from peers and pornography.[34] (Her website provides guidance for parents.[35]) As Ashanti Branch* said, "I learned more sex ed in the back of 9th-grade Algebra class than anywhere else."

Orenstein found that just as girls are cut off from their bodies (as in feeling insecure about their attractiveness), boys are cut off from their hearts by not being allowed to express vulnerability. They told her, "I trained myself not to feel," and "All I'm allowed is happiness and anger," etc. They were afraid to be seen as unmasculine or gay; for example, it would be seen as gay to have a female friend, although they weren't homophobic. Orenstein concludes that we're 25 years behind assisting boys with the kind of support that we give to girls. Many of the men featured in this book would agree.

These social pressures to achieve and perform are stressful for young people. Studies indicate that youth anxiety and depression are increasing, especially for young women. A 2021 Harvard poll of people between 18 and 29 reported that 27% of men and 28% of women had suicidal thoughts and 48% of men and 54% of women had felt depressed in the previous two weeks.[36]

A consequence of masculinity training is that men are less likely to seek help, and more likely to take risks, and drink and smoke heavily, which are all behaviors that can lead to illness and to dying sooner than the average woman (76 vs. 81 years in the US). A recent example is women are more likely to get vaccinated against the Covid virus than men and less likely to die from it. Men are more likely to be Republicans and to more often hear warnings that vaccine and mask mandates interfere with their autonomy and masculinity.

Boys' Disadvantage in Education

With major consequences for their families, boys are less likely to go to college around the world, except in sub-Saharan Africa.[37] Between 1959 and 2021, the number of male students for every 100 women fell by 62%. An alarming fact is that young men make up only 40.5% of US college students (as of June 2021) and more women complete their degrees. This gap has slowly widened since the 1970s and, if the trend continues, two women will earn a degree for every man. The implications are broad since educated men are more likely to earn high salaries and to stay married, which correlates with well-being for the adults and their children. Blacks are the only US ethnic group that has more married men than married women.

I interviewed Andi for a future book on young feminists, a college senior in New York City (seen on YouTube). She said when she was in secondary school, it was clear that the teachers didn't like the boys because they were troublemakers. Her girlfriends said to each other, "I hate boys," unless they were dating one. Tristan Glosby* had a similar observation about his school teachers favoring girls and reported, "In my social circles, men and women generally do not get along and stick to their own gender. I generally find that women tend to be more verbal but less direct, while men tend to be more direct but less verbal." Perhaps this correlates with boys being only 30% of high school valedictorians.

Boys are also more likely to have learning disabilities such as ADD/ADHD, including 13% of boys in the US and 7% of girls.[38] Males also comprise about one-third of eating disorder cases. [39] Nathanson noted, "The ADD diagnosis itself, however, is somewhat controversial. Teachers--mainly female ones--are troubled by the unruly behavior of boys in class. But those boys are not necessarily 'sick.' That kind of behavior is natural for boys." For the boys of color whom Ashanti Branch* works with in the San Francisco Bay Area, and that Jerry Tello* works with in Los Angeles and nationally, it's often uncool to get good grades. This is scorned as acting white and not masculine. (The Asian "model minority" is different, as Lee Mun Wah* explains.)

MIT Economics Professor David Autor addresses this issue of boys' education problems and their "cloudy future," especially as low-skill workers.[40] He reports that in almost every industrialized country, women are about 30% more likely to get a college degree than men, partly because women face fewer barriers than before. He's concerned about the loss of jobs for uneducated men and the resulting instability experienced by children in low-income single-parent homes. Education is the best way to promote economic mobility, but the US faces increasing inequality between children in less-educated and minority households.

Autor finds it's particularly disadvantageous for boys' education in resource-poor, single-mother families--but not for girls when single mother households have doubled in the past 50 years.[41] Mothers tend to spend more time with their daughters and feel closer to them. Important evidence is that in families where the father is present and has some college education, boys and girls are about equally likely to complete college.[42] Thus, the formula is: loss of earnings for uneducated men leads to single-parent families, which inhibits boys' education and thus future earnings and stability. This of course influences the women and children in their lives.

Jon Marcus explains that men are the minority of college students in the US because boys are more concerned about making money right after they graduate from high school, college is expensive, boys in low-income areas don't have role models of successful college graduates, girls get more encouragement, and worldwide girls are better readers beginning in kindergarten.[43] "I've had male students tell me their first week in college they were made to feel like potential rapists," reported Jim Shelley, manager of the Men's Resource Center at an Ohio community college.

To encourage students who identify as male, Professor Miles Groth formed a research center and arranged for groups and retreats for male undergraduates at Wagner College. He taught a "Psychology of Boys and Men" course for many years and founded two peer-reviewed journals on male studies.

Nathanson believes that boys and men are subjected routinely to "identity harassment," by mockery and denunciations of boys and men that damage their collective identity. "Identity protection cognition" occurs when people dismiss facts that challenge their beliefs and cultural identity. An example is 56% of men surveyed by Pew Research don't believe that gender biases make life more difficult for women, despite facts like women's salaries are less than men's globally and that "the motherhood penalty" in the workforce is not experienced by fathers.[44] Men were more likely than women to believe Judge Brett Kavanaugh's denial of assaulting Christine Blasey Ford when they were teens. Women opposed his nomination to the Supreme Court by 20 points, while men supported him by four points more than women.[45]

Global studies report that the main reason (79%) employees quit their jobs has less to do with earnings and more to do with lack of recognition or appreciation, which indicates how important identity can be.[46] Writing in the online newsletter *Medium*, Colter Whitlock charged, "Modern society is destroying young men. . . they are made to be ashamed to be male."[47] What they need, he says, is encouragement. Another *Medium* writer, Jason Helton observed, "We've ruined society" by telling men they are toxic.

Literature contributes to disparaging men. Leslie Fiedler pointed out in *Love and Death in the American Novel* that US classic fictional heroes are boys who avoided being civilized rather than men who relate to women--like Huck Finn, Tom Sawyer, and Ishmael.[48] Yet, these fictional young men often have close male friends, including the hobbits in *Lord of the Rings* like Merry and Pippin and Frodo and Sam. A.O. Scott argued more recently that, "All American fiction is young-adult fiction," as are popular TV shows about "bro culture" or monstrous men.[49] He calls the men in TV shows like *The Sopranos, Breaking Bad,* and *Mad Men* the last of the patriarchs, but with regret; "It seems that, in doing away with patriarchal authority, we have also, perhaps unwittingly, killed off all the grown-ups."

Cross-Cultural Socialization

Felix Mbewe,* in Zambia, reports that his community praises men's stewardship (considering women the weaker sex although they do the majority of hard work on farms) and watches out for him and his wife. They selected watchful mentors to help long-term with his new marriage and will send a relative to live with them for months after they have a baby. This form of mentorship is a lifelong commitment. However, Jeffer Kinoti* said that in Kenya there's growing concern that "we have started losing the boy child in the process of empowering the girl."

From South Africa, Professor Robert Morrell was a pioneer of Critical Masculinity Studies in South Africa.[50] His path to the study of men and masculinities began in 1989 when he was teaching feminism to Education students at the University of Natal (now UKZN) in Durban. He said this started a journey of exploration and discovery which ended with opening up a new field in research in South Africa.

Morrell observed, "Where Africa comes up in its own right, it generally is to identify the exception of Sub-Saharan Africa as not following global trends regarding, for example, improved female performance." He summarizes African debates on men and masculinity.[51]

The lived reality of men in Africa varies a great deal. Among the determining factors are wealth and employment and connections with value systems that predate colonialism, which still exercise influence on understandings of gender roles and norms. In Southern Africa, where an industrial economy emerged on the basis of diamond and gold mining in the late 19th century, a racialised labour market emerged with black African men often drawn into badly-paid wage labour. White settlers (varying from 17th century colonizers from the Netherlands and France to 19th century immigrants from the UK) developed an urban, waged lifestyle retaining close ties with Europe.

While the black middle class grew, its growth was stunted by apartheid and it has only been since 1990 (when the ANC was unbanned and steps towards democracy were taken) that a substantial black middle class emerged. It is among the educated (black and white) middle classes that feminism has had the strongest influence, which stimulated a women's movement in South Africa. Black African women have been involved in political protest for over a century while some white women supported the Suffragette Movement in the early 1900s.

This background explains the emergence and success of gender organisations in the 1990s that began to take men's issues seriously and research on men and masculinity in South Africa was undertaken. These two forces supported one another and meant that Sonke Gender Justice, one of the largest gender NGOs in the world (founded in South Africa but with work across the sub-continent), was a founding member of MenEngage. In fact, the story of MenEngage can be told as a story of South-South collaboration between Brazil (Gary Barker and Promundo) and South Africa (Sonke Gender Justice).*

Profeminist gender work in South Africa has been embraced by government but this is not the only approach to gender in South Africa. Large parts of the population do not support feminism and draw on indigenous understandings of gender to make sense of intimacy, marriage, child-rearing, etc. We see convergence on some issues such as the recognition of widespread gender-based violence and a society-wide commitment to reduce levels of violence.

To see if masculinity is as precarious in India as in the US, I interviewed Jayesh Tombe, 33, who grew up in an educated family in Mumbai and came to the US for graduate school when he was 28. He heard a few "don't be like a girl" comments in elementary school if a boy complained when he was injured playing sports, but didn't hear anything like that during his teen years. Homophobia isn't a driving force keeping boys from close friendship; Indians are accustomed to seeing village men--who come to the city to work--walking hand-in-hand. In contrast, he was advised when dating in

California not to order a fruity sweet drink for fear of being seen as feminine.

In both India and the US, Jayesh found that women want to marry a man with higher incomes and that having an expensive car adds to his appeal. Women are respected as deities like Lakshmi and Durga (their images are on taxis, in stores, in homes) and mothers: Jayesh would reach for both parents' feet to ask for a blessing before exams. However, traditional Hindus rely on the oldest son to perform important rituals, such as funeral ceremonies, and grandparents are more likely to live with a son than a daughter. Street harassment of women, bride burnings, rape, and domestic violence are common. Perhaps it's obvious that men have more power so it doesn't have to be proven. (See Ashanti Branch's* observation after spending eight months in India.).

The men's rights movement spread to India where it's called "Meninism," to protest problems like false accusations of rape or child custody issues after divorce (which is uncommon). Thus, in Jayesh's observation, masculinity in India isn't threatened by what a man drinks but men are "success objects." Single women still advertise themselves on marriage sites as "homely" meaning domestic, and light-skinned, as well as stating their education level.[52]

In the UK, Members of Parliament formed a group to study boys' and men's issues (similar to problems they face in the US) because "areas of male disadvantage" are ignored or hidden and masculinity is too often viewed as negative.[53] They pointed out the ill effects of father absence, as found in various studies showing children do better in two-parent homes.[54] Their report focused on the need for positive male role models and developing programs to alleviate educational underachievement, crime, and health and mental health problems.

The Canadian Association for Equality identified similar issues in their 2021 Momentum Conference: the boy crisis, workplace problems, men's health, fathers' rights, violence, and cultural and academic misandry.[55] Looking at 20 pages of masculinity book titles available on Amazon, I found the main themes are how to nullify toxic masculinity, ethnic and national masculinities, history, Christian men, and how to attract women.

These pressures help explain why many men don't feel privileged or powerful. In a World Bank 2013 survey of gender norms in 20 countries, focus groups of 4,000 adults reported the women felt their power was surging while men said they were "stagnating or sliding backward."[56]

Demonstrating further lack of progress, in the fall of 2021, the Chinese government started a campaign against "sissy men," celebrities said to be too effeminate or "girly" and "morally flawed." However, men dominate government, as seen in the fact that only one woman is represented on the powerful 25-member Politburo.[57] Beijing states that the "masculinity crisis" stems from "effeminate" entertainers with "abnormal aesthetics" that are corrupting a generation. A rule prohibited their appearance on TV and video streaming sites. Previously, Beijing had banned images of men kissing and holding hands with each other.

In South Korea, groups of young men launched an anti-feminist campaign in what's called gender wars, calling women protesters "ugly feminist pigs," while making pig sounds and chanting "Stop the misandry."[58] They use social media and demonstrations to pressure the government and businesses to roll back gender equality programs. In Kenya, Jeffer Kinoti* reports that on Twitter's #MasculinitySaturday "men express all sorts of toxic masculinity sentiments towards women."

Without male mentoring, boys turn to peers and media superheroes to learn about masculinity, including animated video fathers, or action films about fathers rescuing their adult children, as played by actors Liam Neeson and Jackie Chan. Others turn to gangs, fan clubs, and fraternal or religious organizations for support. Programs like Big Brothers need to be multiplied and gender issues included in teacher education. Denmark, one of the happiest nations, teaches programs like the Step by Step, My Circle, and the CAT-kit to children as early as preschool. They learn to identify emotions, empathy, problem-solving, and self-control, as explained in *The Danish Way of Parenting* by Jessica Alexander and Iben Dissing Sandal.

Definitions of Masculinity

How exactly is masculinity defined? In the 2021 film *The Tender Bar*, the boy called J.R. learns about being a man from his uncle (played by Ben Affleck). He emphasizes it's about how to relate to women: hold doors open for women, don't hit women even if they come at you with scissors, and take care of your mother. A man should also know how to change tires.

Robert Brannon and Samuel Juni developed the Brannon Masculinity Scale in 1984: avoid femininity (no sissy stuff), conceal emotions, be the breadwinner, be admired and respected (a big wheel), be tough (a sturdy oak), be a male machine (don't ask for help or show weakness), and go for violence and adventure (damn the torpedoes and some team sports). When boys and men violate these unspoken rules, they may be told to "man up," or "grow a pair," resulting in boys learning fewer social skills. This problem is discussed in books like *Raising Cain: Protecting the Emotional Life of Boys* by Dan Kindlon and Michael Thompson and *Boys Adrift* by Leonard Sax. Most reasonable people would agree that it's advantageous to help boys to develop positive male identities.

Honor is associated with masculinity, so that in many cultures if a woman is raped, the main offense is to her father's or husband's honor. Men fought duels over offenses to their honor until the 19th century, especially in the US South. The families of US soldiers who die are honored (*e.g.,* Gold Star families of dead soldiers). Since honor seems to be a major value for men, especially those with a military background, I interviewed a Marine named Jeremy Starkey. His father taught him a man's word is his bond; you shake hands, look a man in the eye, and give him your word.

Starkey also learned about honor from comic book superheroes (as other men reported in *Redefining Masculinity* by Davidson Hguyen Hang) and from being in the military. He reported the three values drummed into Marines were honor, courage, and commitment; plus duty to God, Country, and the Corps--not necessarily in that order. He explained that honor means having the self-discipline to serve others, be chivalrous, and know the difference between right and wrong in order to be able to win the battle of your emotions (note the military approach).

Starkey believes the hardest job in the world is being a good person. This code of ethics, plus his knowledge of combat, enables him to hold his head up high and be proud. He believes that enemies shudder when they think of fighting Marines and this identity will always be part of him.

George Simons* and colleagues surveyed over 700 adults from 70 countries about gendered values, reported on in *Culture Detective: Men and Women.* [59] They found men are believed to value being protective, productive, logical, brave, honorable, and competitive. Women are believed to value nurturing relationships, aim to be inclusive and helpful, and are less direct (as seen in questioning or qualifying speech like *perhaps* and *don't you agree?*)

These views of masculinity haven't changed much: A Pew Research Center poll in 2017 asked adults what traits society values most for men: honesty, financial success, leadership, and toughness.[60] For women: physical attractiveness, kindness, intelligence, and honesty. The Millennial men surveyed were much more likely than older men to report feeling pressure to fight, to talk with other men about women disrespectfully in a sexual way, and to brag about having many sexual partners, indicating the staying power of old definitions of masculinity.

Is Gender Fluid or Essential?

Some academics emphasize gender fluidity versus essentialism. Jed Diamond* and Nathanson argue that men have essential or distinctive physiologies that influence their behavior. On a spectrum of gender identity, some people are gender diverse, non-binary, queer, or trans, while less than two percent of babies are intersex anatomically. Gender refers to cultural norms and social roles, so that masculinity and femininity vary across cultures, while sex refers to our physiology as male or female. Some professors use the term "Male Studies" rather than "Men's Studies" to highlight the importance of our bodies. "Sex and gender are more complex than previously assumed," concluded American Medical Association board member Dr. William E. Koble in 2018.[61]

Essentialism is the belief that there are intrinsic qualities of being male or female *e.g.,* a trans woman always retains her XY sex chromosomes. The often-quoted Professor Judith Butler maintains in her theory of "gender performativity" (see *Gender Trouble)* that gender identity is established through various behaviors or performances. Therefore, it's changeable and fluid and is not an essence. John Stoltenberg* favors this viewpoint, as do most men's studies scholars. When I checked with him, he concurred, "My concept of gender identity as an ethical construction, *i.e.,* not inscribed by biology."

Some essentialist feminists believed in what I called the "women are wonderful" approach in my two books on women's culture. This theme was recently repeated by many of the Gen Z climate activists interviewed for *Climate Girls Saving Our World* (2021). These Boomer to Gen Z women believe that women and mothers are closer to nature and her cycles and therefore more caring and peaceful than men. Many of the young women also believe they're braver than their male peers in speaking up against climate change. The debate is how much of gender role is socialized and how much is due to having male or female bodies, but none of the men featured in this book consider men superior.

An essentialist issue, a major controversy for UK and US feminists, is whether to include transwomen in women's groups, as Stoltenberg* and Barker* advocate. Gender-essentialist comedian Dave Chappelle's "The Closer," an October 2021 special show, stirred up a storm when he said, "gender is a fact" and he's "team TERF." This refers to trans-exclusive radical feminists like author J. K. Rowling. She doesn't believe that trans women should be accepted as women; "If sex isn't real, the lived reality of women globally is erased. I know and love trans people, but erasing the concept of sex removes the ability of many to meaningfully discuss their lives." [62]

If masculinity is not biologically determined, it's possible to create "a new way of being," states Davidson Nguyen Hang, the editor of *Redefining Masculinity.* One of his solutions is to encourage intimate conversations with other men.[63] Stephen Whitehead argues in *Toxic Masculinity: Curing the Virus,* that "collapsed masculinity" is harmful but we have ways to make men "smarter, healthier, safer." [64] He sees the solution as becoming feminists, meaning embracing gender equality, similar to what Herb Goldberg advocated.

Professor Robert Jensen agrees with them, finding that, "Feminism is a threat to holding on to normal guyness, a gift to us."[65] He emailed that, as a young, skinny, nerdy guy, he thought he wasn't man enough, and other men were doing fine. "Doing my best to be a normal guy, I dated, told sexist jokes, and used pornography," until he discovered self-acceptance through feminism, as explained in his TED talk.

Masculinity is an ideology, defined as a series of beliefs that groups buy into, according to Todd Reeser in *Masculinities in Theory*.[66] He explains that if gender is not binary, it's always changing, so "there is no masculine being, but only a series of becomings." Norms change like views towards male intimacy in ancient Greece or in the Middle East. The editors of *Constructing Masculinity* agree that masculinity is not a "monolithic entity," because it's "always ambivalent, always complicated, dependent on the exigencies of personal and institutional power."[67] Academics look at gender through the lens of power relations.

Some indigenous tribes recognize a third gender, usually biological men who identify as female. An internet poll of more than 19,000 people of various ages in 27 countries reported that Gen Z is more likely than people over 40 to identify as gender-nonconforming--18% compared to 9% of all respondents.[68] Fashion designers reflect this trend with clothes presenting "gender fluidity or gender neutrality or dual-gender hybrids," such as men wearing skirts.[69] Some have called ours a post-gender era and think that gender has been over-emphasized and the influence of our bodies neglected in terms of their influence on our attitudes--such as men being protective about external genitals.

Influential Australian sociologist R.W. Connell emphasized the importance of using the plural *masculinities* to indicate there are many ways to be a man, as explained in her 1995 book of that title and her blogs.[70] She also developed the concept of *hegemonic masculinity*, meaning male dominance reinforced by homophobia and physical force, which is mutable and changing. Subordinated and marginalized masculinities refer to low-income men and men of color.

(Connell transitioned to becoming a woman in her 60s, from Robert to Raewyn.)

Recently, *toxic masculinity* is frequently discussed. Changes in *hybrid masculinities* are explored by scholars such as Tristan Bridges to challenge systems of inequality (he's also researching homes with "man caves," mass shootings, and men's images in advertising).

Regarding terminology, Daniel Ellenberg* explained that "men's roles" is not a term that Critical Studies of Men and Masculinities would use these days, and that they research "precarious masculinity," meaning the belief that it can be lost and has to be proven (the linchpin of what harms men). Nathanson thinks misandry is the current problem due to what he calls "identity harassment," which is the fallout from feminist and "woke" ideology (refers to a slang word advocating being alert to injustice, especially racism). "Men's Studies" and "Masculinity Studies" are terms that have been debated for some while and in many contexts rejected in favor of "Critical Studies on Men." Feminists aim for "non-normative masculinity" leading to equality.

Branches of the Men's Movement or Men's Work

Men's Peer Support Groups
Some say there isn't a men's movement as men of various ages are increasingly turning to peer-led men's groups to find support in expressing a range of feelings and enhancing positive male qualities, such as leading community service. These groups evolved from feminist consciousness-raising groups and from the Jungian mythopoetic viewpoint. This branch of the men's movement was led by Shepherd Bliss,* poet Robert Bly (author of *Iron John: A Book About Men)* who advocates Zeus and Wildman energy,[71] and others who help men find their "deep masculine." They emphasize the importance of fathers in the development of boys' and men's ways of communicating side-by-side but are criticized by other men for lack of political activism.

Examples of these organizations featured in this book are The ManKind Project, EVRYMAN, National Compadres Network (and its curricula for boys and for fathers), and Ever Forward Club. The Oakland Men's Project developed trainings for boys. The Good Men Project was founded in 2009 by Tom Matlack to provide a space for men to tell stories about their lives and define "enlightened masculinity."[72]

Evangelical Christian men's groups include the Promise Keepers who filled stadiums with large numbers of men. Barker* reports, "Promise Keepers are a much smaller movement than they were once were partly because of the push toward militaristic, muscular Christianity, but it's staging a modest comeback, as described by *Jesus and John Wayne* by Kristin Kobes Du Mez."

Men's Sheds started in Australia during the 1980s with a national clearinghouse and spread around the world to provide support groups with a focus on men's health. Their motto is, "Men don't talk face to face, they talk shoulder to shoulder," as Shepherd Bliss taught.[73] Participants are called "shedders." (There's also an Australian Institute for Male Health and Studies.) Lee Mun Wah,* Chinese American counselor, author, documentary filmmaker, and diversity trainer,[74] led the first Asian men's group in the San Francisco Bay Area, which he describes in Chapter 6.

Online groups include an app called Whoop used by about 85,000 teams to keep track of each other. One of the team members reported that if he sees on the app that his friend is sleeping only three hours a night, he contacts him and says, "Hey, want to get a beer?"[75] (Beer and bars/pubs seem to be a major lubricant for male friendship.) A website called Self-Himprovement was founded by Blake Reichenbach who observed that as men struggle with isolation, these support groups are increasing around the world.

Some young men get support from other online communities, including mental health support forums like Reddit's r/Anxiety, as Benjamin Kaveladze* discusses. A carpenter named John who participated in men's groups and gatherings for years told me they talked about their relationships in their group but were most likely to feel free to cry over the deaths of their dogs. In contrast, Gordon Clay* said his decades-old group doesn't often discuss relationships, and Crutcher* said his group often talks about work/life balance. Nathanson commented that these groups don't address "the relentless barrage of misandry and the institutionalized preoccupation with only women's problems. No personal or group therapy can solve that problem."

"There's a lot of very progressive, appropriately politicized pro-feminist men's work that looks on the inner work of such men's groups as almost blasphemous," said Barker.* He adds, "On the progressive, political side we can often get into this precious mode of saying it's all structural and systemic." Jack Straton* advocates, "more bonding together to try to figure out: how do the most activist men find a better center and how do those most interested in centering find more activism?"

Men's Rights

The men's rights branch is fueled by fathers, like Fred Hayward,* who feel the courts discriminated against them in custody arrangements. However, women don't do well in family courts when they allege domestic violence, especially when the father charges her with "parental alienation."[76] The British author of *Sex Differences Explained* and *The Woman Racket,* Steve Moxon disagrees with this conclusion, "You misrepresent 'men's rights' in saying it is all through male divorce experience, but it's through a whole range of inter-related topics." A critic of feminism, his research finds biology is the basis of gender roles, as he explains on my blog. [77]

The men's rights activists focus on the harms to boys of father absence after divorce or due to long work hours. Gordon Clay* calls this absence "the father wound." It's common sense that children of both sexes benefit from positive fathering. Gerhard Amendt, German Sociology Professor, thought the importance of mothers' influence should be added to this chapter. He's in the men's rights branch.[78]

> *Boys are formed by their identification and interaction with mothers as much as by their fathers. I have researched the mother-son relationship for 20 years. Neither the public nor the scientific community was "delighted" by my research findings since the victim-perpetrator dichotomy would have gone down the drain!*
>
> *One of my major findings was that mothers often try to shape their sons as a better version of their*

husband, or try to make the sons into an idealized version of what they consider to be good manhood. This perspective turns the widespread opinion of gender relations (i.e., that how boys develop depends mostly on how their fathers raised them) upside down. My two volumes of research have been published in German, translated as How Mothers See Their Sons *and* Yearning for the Father.

Perry Garfinkel, author of *In a Man's World*, told me, "In solving the issues of how men can relate better to each other, we have to first resolve our relationship with our fathers and then move forward into the relationships with other men from that." From our fathers, our primary male role models, Garfinkel said, "Men learn about lack of communication, lack of expression of feelings, and about competition, power, hierarchy, and territoriality." He reports this leads to a feeling of inferiority to other men.

Rather than father absence, Boysen Hogson* traces uncertainty to the fact that "In the last 200, or the last 20 years, we're doing things that human beings have not done in our entire conscious history. It's a massive social experiment we're doing on ourselves," so it's not surprising some are floundering. Since the end goal is the same for our changemakers, dialogue seems both reasonable and helpful. Crutcher* refers to *The Third Alternative*, by Stephen M. Covey, to see multitudes of examples where people in different groups came up with solutions together that were better than either group could do on their own.

Men's rights activists reject the concept of a patriarchy where men have privilege and emphasize instead how traditional gender roles harm men's physical and mental health. (The concept was developed by Karl Marx and Max Weber to explain women's subordination and unpaid labor.) Hayward* explained his disagreement with my statement that we live in a patriarchy:

The feminist perspective misses the complexity of what we are really dealing with, such as a woman with eight children by different fathers has one family, but a man with two children with two different women has two families. Male politicians and business executives have to appeal to the mostly female electorate [10 million more women voters in recent elections[79]] *and customers* [women control or influence 85% of US consumer spending[80]]. *I see men and women as equally powerless and having equally numerous and serious problems.*

He added, "You and I are like those couples who each feel they do most of the housework. (Fortunately, my partner, Barbara, has no trouble acknowledging that I do.) You feel I have more power and I feel you have more power, but the important thing is that it leaves us equally motivated to end all double standards and bring real equality to humanity." What fair person couldn't agree with this goal?

Feminists

When egalitarian social supports such as family leave are provided, fathers spend more time with their children. For example, Canadian fathers average 14 hours a week on caring for their children, compared to only eight hours averaged by US fathers.[81] Out of the 40 weeks of Canadian parental leave since 2019 five weeks are reserved for dads. Their studies show that taking parental leave is good for marriages and for children. Although the richest countries offer an average of eight weeks of paid paternity leave, the US offers none.[82]

Scandinavians are in the forefront of policies encouraging gender equality and work-life balance, which results in being one of the happiest nationalities.[83] Sweden was the first country to provide paid parental leave to fathers. Currently, 90 days of the total 480 leave days are reserved for each parent. This national policy of balance and enjoyment of life is called *lagom* by the Swedes, *hygge* by the Danes and Norwegians, and *sopivasti* by the Finns. It results in the highest scores on World Happiness Reports.[84]

Feminist men, such as pioneering Professor Michael Kimmel (author of *Guyland*, etc.), aim to alleviate problems caused by patriarchy, such as violence. (Mentors in Violence Prevention was co-founded by Jackson Katz. For domestic violence prevention see Ingólfur Vilhjálmur Gíslaso* and Crutcher.*) Some feminists are reluctant to be associated with men's rights leaders. An Australian feminist academic said about this chapter, "Having looked briefly at the text you sent has reinforced that reluctance, as much of that text seems to repeat a series of problematic 'men's rights' claims about male disadvantage."

After reading the list of men included in this book, feminist co-chair of NOMAS (National Organization of Men Against Sexism), Moshe Rozdial emailed:

> *I have a problem with any discussion of masculinity that does not address deep-seated misogyny and sexism: That masculinity is embedded in a male supremacist/entitled ideology relative to the disrespect, oppression, and degradation of the feminine. Most of the men's movements, other than the pro-feminist, are different versions of men's rights/violence and are not invested in the future of the human male, but rather in protecting the privileged supremacist role of the MAN of the past and present.*
>
> *Our feminist analysis understands that men pay a price for collusion in the patriarchal supremacist ideology, but are NOT disadvantaged by them. Men, as a group, benefit from maintaining the system. I also believe that as long as masculinity is defined, by that construct, as the misogynistic opposite of woManKind, that there is no such thing as healthy masculinity, no matter how much one tries to massage the definition.*
>
> *Any attempts to promote a distinction between female and male traits, other than those defined by biology, are collusion with the sexist male supremacist ideology. In fact, other than my deep respect for John Stoltenberg,* I am uncomfortable in the presence of so many men who are working hard to maintain patriarchy and white straight male supremacy.*
>
> *I urge you to read Allan Johnson's* The Gender Knot: Unraveling Our Patriarchal Legacy *and Caroline Perez'* Invisible Woman: Data Bias in a World Designed for Men, *as well as the APA guidelines on masculinity.*[85]

One of the feminist academics I asked to critique this chapter highlighted some controversial areas of disagreement among different branches of men's work (choosing to remain anonymous):

There are many analyses of the "boy crisis" in education, where some say that it's because female teachers, using a feminized curriculum, alienate boys, while others point out that it's only boys of color who are "missing" in school. The "father absence" literature is equally controversial, with correlations bandied about as if they were causal and less attention to boys' resilience than to problematic behavior. And even the supposed "cause" of father absence itself: Is it feckless fathers or feminist mothers pushing the men away? It's a minefield. You're reluctant to take a position yourself, which may leave the reader without a clear focus, and ill-prepared to come to a conclusion.

My position is that I encourage dialogue based on research and the common goal of equal opportunity. When I advocated for including men's rights spokespersons at an early M&M conference in Hartford, I was criticized and asked if I would include anti-ERA advocate Phyllis Schafly in a feminist conference; I said I would love to debate her. However, I would see no reason to debate Incels full of hate with no common goals. They're part of what Laura Bates calls a terrorist movement in her 2021 book *Men Who Hate Women.* My observation is that traditional gender role limitations harm us all, which is why I wrote this book, but it seems obvious if we look at leaders and power brokers that we do live in a patriarchy where some men have more power, control, and privilege.

Some feminists argue that all white males experience some privilege, seen in men's more assertive speech patterns, which seems difficult for some transwomen to emulate. When male faculty at CSUC saw a group of us women faculty talking together, they'd joke, "Oh, oh, they're up to something." When we saw groups of men in suits talking, that was the norm and not a joke--we women were what Simon de Beauvoir called "the Other."

Pro-feminist NOMAS' first Men and Masculinity Conference was held in 1975. Lyrics of the songs of the pro-feminist men's movement provide insights into their approach.[86] Other pro-feminist groups include the Achilles Heel Collective in Britain, Men against Sexual Assault in Australia, and MenEngage's international conferences drawing from members in 70 countries, which began in 2021. From South Africa, Robert Morrell, Ph.D., commented on the global influences on our learning, "Dean Peacock, co-founder of MenEngage with Gary Barker,* is a South African showing how these kinds of connections have fed into activism and debate. Similarly, the fact that Australian R. W. Connell was lecturing at Harvard and at the University of California has influenced her work, as well as influencing the ways that profeminism emerged in the US."

Masculinities Studies

Barker* described Promundo's research for global equality:

> *I think it's fair to say that Promundo has been key, along with NGO research centers like the International Center for Research on Women, to building a science of intervention with boys and men within a feminist framework and measuring results of such programmatic approaches in terms of women's well-being, improved gender relations with benefits for men and boys themselves.*
>
> *Promundo-US is a research-focused NGO that has taken a feminist approach to studying masculinities cross-culturally, both with our International Men and Gender Equality Survey, carried out with the UN in more than 45 countries, and our Man Box survey, in more than five countries. We've also conducted numerous randomized-control level trials with interventions called "gender transformative" in that they seek to transform inequitable and harmful aspects of gendered norms and gender relations.*
>
> *We follow the rigor expected in academic circles, including doing psychometric testing of attitude scales, having IRBs* [review boards], *following standard*

survey methodology, and the like. Our website has self-published reports and reports published in peer-reviewed journals.

Pro-feminist research-oriented groups in the US include The American Men's Studies Association.[87] Also pro-feminist, The American Psychological Association (APA) Division 51 Society for the Psychological Study of Men and Masculinities is currently led by Daniel Ellenberg.* He stated on their website, it's an "uphill struggle of changing masculinity." Both organizations publish journals.

The APA Division 51 states on their website that they're at "the very beginning of constructing a new psychology of men" based on understanding the "socially constructed nature of masculinity."[88] They explain "the ideal, dominant masculinity is generally unattainable for most men," although generally, males have more social and economic power in a patriarchal society. They aim to do more research on men of color, men with disabilities, and men with various sexual orientations. They agree that children benefit from positive fathering. Boys and men of color may construct their own standards of masculinity, such as joining gangs, inventing dress styles, looking down on being studious, and being "cool."

Men's Studies courses tend to be feminist but are much rarer than Women's Studies courses. They grew out of Women's Studies, just as that grew out of Black Studies. Masculinity Studies courses tend to be feminist and thus emphasize the intersectionality of power influences on gender roles, but are much rarer than Women's Studies courses. They're usually housed in Gender Studies programs. In the '70s and '80s, the men's studies programs drew from feminist theory and Queer Studies, which provides about half of the influence, according to Professor Michael Kimmel.[89] He explained that the latter provides theory about power relations among men.

Judith Kegan Gardiner observed that masculinity studies agrees with the poststructuralist approach of fluidity rather than essentialism or "static binary views of victims and oppressors, difference and dominance, and hegemonic and alternative masculinities," such as those demonstrated by men of color and queer men.[90] She points out that both masculinity and femininity are fantasies and myths about power, the former seen as a crisis due to a lost nostalgic past and the latter about an ideal future. Her goal is "reformulating gender" and "meaningful collective action in the struggle for gender justice."

Men's Studies instructors report that women students are much more likely to enroll in them because men don't think they need to learn to be men. Joan Korenman lists over 900 programs called women's, gender, sexuality, or feminist studies--which means there are many more courses in those majors and minors.[91]I couldn't find a similar list for men's studies, but the XYonline.net website, led by Australian feminist Michael Flood, includes 18 masculinities courses from 2001 to 2021 (in the US or Australia). The site includes bibliographies and many other resources.[92] Flood's own 2021 syllabus for "Engaging Men" includes an extensive bibliography.[93]

The American Men's Studies Association (AMSA) began in 1983 as a task group of the National Organization for Men against Sexism (NOMAS).[94] Men's Studies pioneers included Shepherd Bliss,* Michael Messner,* Harry Brod, etc. Their first conference was held in 1989 as part of the 14th M&M conference. AMSA became independent in 1991, despite opposition from NOMAS, and rejected being guided exclusively by feminist principles, seeing their organization as "pluralistic," although men's studies often focus on "hegemonic masculinity." Andrew Smiler* suggested the split was between academics and activists. He guesses there are as many as 150 offerings of an Introduction to Men's Studies course at maybe 75 to 100 universities across the U.S and Canada in any given academic year.

These are the few men's studies programs I found in an online search: Leeds Beckett University in the UK (along with a Centre for Men's Health), and the Queensland University of Technology in Australia. A minor in Men's Studies is offered at Hobart and William Smith College[95] and a master's degree at New York University at Stony Brook was started in 2019 by Michael Kimmel (founder of the Center for the Study of Men and Masculinities).

Courses are offered at Canada's University of Calgary Masculinity Studies program, which explains, "Masculinities

Studies research operates from a pro-feminist standpoint. . . feminist theories addressing gender identities. Specifically, masculinities scholars argue that masculinities are fluid, socially constructed and that the ways in which boys and men take up 'projects of masculinity' are connected to power relations."[96] Professor Jon Bradley, McGill University, emailed that Canada doesn't have a national men's studies organization but The Canadian Centre for Men and Families is one of several groups that focus on men's health and relationships.

Bradley added that an emerging Canadian topic is First Nations; the vast majority of First Nation teachers are female, as they are in the nation as a whole. He raises the question: Is there such a thing as a "gendered learning environment"? He's concerned that male teachers get stereotyped as pedophiles or gay and falsely accused of sexual crimes (in the UK, a group called FACT supports victims of false allegations).[97]

Anti-Feminists

British anti-feminists include Steve Moxon, introduced earlier, and Mike Buchanan who leads an annual International Conference on Men's Issues (The first ICMI conference was held in Detroit in 2014). In 2013 Buchanan helped to organize a British political party called Justice for Men and Boys, "to campaign for the human rights of men and boys, and the only resolutely anti-feminist one." He also formed the Anti-Feminist League and Men Shouldn't Marry. He wouldn't agree to be interviewed when I told him I was a feminist.

The most extreme men's groups are the InCels (Involuntary Celibates), part of the misogynous internet "manosphere," which believes men are oppressed by women's denial of sex, except to alpha males.[98] Mass killings in Canada and the US were carried out by self-proclaimed InCels.[99] Groups of women InCels tend to blame themselves and not commit violence.[100]

Similar misogynous groups are Pickup Artists who teach how to seduce women, Red Pillers who believe a feminist conspiracy runs society, and Men Going Their Own Way, which advocates that men separate themselves from women and a society corrupted by feminism. The Southern Poverty Law Center categorizes male supremacist groups as fundamental to the racist "alt-right."[101]

Does Nature or Nurture Shape Gender Roles?

The US public is split on whether gender differences are due to biology or social expectations. Gender differences surfaced in a Pew Research Center 2018 survey of parents: 66% of the mothers, but only 31% of fathers believed in the importance of socialization over biology in shaping their parenting styles.[102] John Gray, Ph.D., helped popularize the emphasis on our physiological differences and hormones in over 20 books building on *Men Are from Mars, Women Are from Venus,* published in 1993. He claims to have sold over 50 million books in 50 languages. In his blog, he explained,

> *Men need 10 times more testosterone than women to feel calm, capable, confident, and romantic. But when he connects with you, his estrogen levels will go up, which lowers his testosterone even more. So, on a biological level, he needs to have distance, disconnection, and detachment in order to rebuild his masculine hormones.*[103]

Thus, his advocacy of a "man cave" where a man can retreat, which became a popular meme. *Medium* writer Carlyn Beccia calls Gray's book the one that most harmed feminism with its "neurosexism."[104]

Two trans couples interviewed for my *Happy Marriages* book reported the main difference they experienced after taking hormones was to whom they were sexually attracted. (A transman said he could no longer admire strangers' babies, seen as deviant behavior for a man).

Therapist Jed Diamond* is interested in physiological differences that influence our behavior. He believes the male brain is more likely to be wired for building systems, while the female brain is more likely to be wired for empathy, as explained in *The Pattern Seekers* by Cambridge psychologist Simon Baron-Cohen. However, Diamond says he is more empathetic than systematic, so these tendencies vary widely among individuals and most researchers agree the average sex differences are small.

An anti-essentialist radical feminist approach to gender is that it's mainly nurture rather than nature, socially constructed rather than genetically determined. This is portrayed in Marge Piercy's novel *Woman on the Edge of Time*, where physiology has absolutely no influence. (Earlier in 1870 Annie Denton Cridge envisioned a society where sex roles were reversed.[105]) In her book *The Gendered Brain*, Dr. Gina Rippon argued for the role of nurture over nature. She emailed, "Feminist neuroscience acknowledges the entangled nature of biology and society (*e.g., see* Anne Fausto-Sterling)." She added that she and Dr. Lise Elliot "take a systems biology approach, in that different social forces (such as stereotypes) impact differently on different biologies."

A meta-analysis of 30 years of brain research by Lise Eliot, Professor of Neuroscience, didn't find significant differences between women and men.[106] Dr. Eliot emailed,

> *There is no solid science behind any of these claims about the neural or hormonal basis of behavioral sex difference. It's basically all cherry-picked because it sounds right and fits evo-psych stereotypes. You will be doing a disservice to both women and men if you recycle this trash. There is tremendous plasticity in gendered behavior, and power/status explains a lot more than sex for most group-level male/female differences. It's true that women are diagnosed two times more often than men with depression, but again, there are life circumstances contributing to this (poverty, abuse, lack of agency; and depressed men turn to substance abuse two times more than women), as well as diagnostic bias based on how depression is defined in the* DSM. *Please see my book* Pink Brain Blue Brain. *My studies are infinitely more rigorous than what you're citing but it doesn't tell the fun, sexy story.*

In *The Male Brain*, Louann Brizendine, MD, argues for real sex differences. This evolutionary psychology approach is also seen in David Buss' books *The Evolution of Desire: Strategies of Human Mating* and *When Men Behave Badly: The Hidden Roots of Sexual Deception, Harassment, and Assault*. Marianne Legato, MD, founded the Partnership for Gender-Specific Medicine at Columbia University. In *Why Men Never*

Remember and Women Never Forget she describes sexual differences. I summarize Dr. Legato's findings online because it's a significant controversy, she cites research, and it's possible that evolution would select for different responses from hunters and childrearers and gatherers--which accounts for over 95% of our existence.[107]

Human History of Equality

In addition to the hazards of male privilege, another irony is that we seem to have gone backward in terms of gender equality. For over 95% of human history or 150,000 years, we were egalitarian gathers and hunters, like living hunter-gatherer bands. Female fertility figures, such as the Venus of Willendorf fertility statue, were made around 28,000 years ago. Although *homo erectus* appeared about two million years ago, patriarchy only appeared around 10 to 12 thousand years ago. Marxists think its purpose was to establish a dominance hierarchy to control women's fertility, so that property was passed on to the father's heir. Invading warrior tribes brought male domination to the Mediterranean and the domination of warrior male gods like Zeus, Thor, and Yahweh.

For most of human history, we traveled in leaderless small bands following the game and food sources. One sex was not considered superior, although our ancestors valued the protein in meat contributed by male hunters. Respect was earned by exhibiting high skills by either sex. There was no such thing as rape and divinity wasn't seen as male, as explained in an account of living with small bands of the Kalahari San Bushmen by Elizabeth Marshall Thomas in *The Old Way: A Story of the First People.* The band helped care for children, although of course mothers carried and nursed their babies. (Videos of the Hazda tribes in Tanzania show living hunters and gatherers.[108])

A similar description of Neolithic society, *Forgotten World* by Raymond Barnett, reports on egalitarian villages, peaceful and matrilineal. He relates that around 7500 BC, urban centers developed in the "Fertile Crescent" in Mesopotamia. They lasted for 10,000 years until around 2,500 BC until the rise of cities, patriarchy, warfare, and exploitation of the environment.

Earlier, drawing on Marija Gimbutas's work, Riane Eisler describes in *The Chalice and the Blade* that matrifocal Neolithic societies thrived around the Mediterranean without warfare, such as in Crete's Bronze Age Minoan civilization. Archeologist Ian Hodder confirmed that in the archeological discoveries of Çatalhöyük, a large Neolithic site in what's now Turkey (thriving around 9,000 years ago with 2,000 houses), gender equality existed with no sign of warfare for over 1,000 years.[109]

Hodder's excavations revealed few differences between men's and women's work, what they ate, and how they were buried. They hunted and gathered as well as domesticated animals and crops. They created elaborate art, including goddesses like a naked woman sitting on leopards, her hands resting on their heads. Much of the art, however, was about male virility, such as bulls and stags with erect penises.

Other peaceful egalitarian and early cities are described in *The Dawn of Everything* by anthropologist David Graeber and archaeologist David Wengrow. For example, from 4100 to 3300 BC, prehistoric cities in Ukraine and Moldova were planned in circles divided into districts with assembly meeting buildings. Despite our human roots in gender equality (plants also cooperate and share[110]), our written history is about wars and political power struggles. Graeber and Wengrow advocate another urban revolution along those peaceful and democratic prehistoric patterns.

Will The Future Return to Equality?

The hopeful news is that Generations Y and Z are well known for their comfort with diversity of all kinds. I found no significant gender differences when I surveyed and/or interviewed over 4,000 Gen Y youth from 81 countries for a series of books about global youth.[111]

Youth, like the seven young men included in this book, are comfortable with diversity, including gender fluidity, some are influenced by the globally popular K-pop South Korean boy bands. In the US, a majority of people under 18 classify themselves as people of color according to the 2020 census. This is reflected in comics where the new Aquaman is a gay black man. DC Comic's new Superman, Jonathan Kent, the son of Clark and Lois, is bisexual and kisses his friend Jay.

However, young men aren't very involved in the traditional men's movement, observed Owen Marcus,* because although they're interested in equality and diversity, they don't want to be told what to do (such as how to be a particular kind of man), which is what the men's movement thought was needed.

Gen Z is also much more likely than older generations to speak out on behalf of LGBTQ+ people, like a college student named Jimbo who identifies as non-binary and queer (seen on a YouTube video of college students' personal identity stories.[112]) Jimbo self-describes as they/them and as a "faggot freak, nonconforming, functioning in the middle of masculinity and femininity, gender fluid." They is also an advocate for black transwomen.

My 10-year-old grandson, Soren, doesn't differentiate by gender or skin color; it's a non-issue for him and his friends. This attitude was preceded by fictional children like Tom Sawyer, Huck Finn, and Jean Louise Finch in *To Kill a Mockingbird.* Soren reads about Greek goddesses as well as gods in novels about Percy Jackson but plays a lot of video games where the object is to blow up a target. When I asked him what pronouns he preferred, he said "dragon."

At a friend of Soren's appointment to get his stitches out after a skateboard accident, Loran's mother told me that the nurse warned them to keep an eye on the wound because "Boys tend to get dirtier with their rough and tumble behaviors."

Loran: "What does that mean?"

Nurse: "Just that you are a boy and like to play hard in the dirt."

Loran: "You don't know me and what I like to do."

Nurse: "Well, I know you're a boy!"

Loran: "That doesn't mean anything about how I like to play. Anyway, girls can be and do whatever they want and so can boys."

Youth in the Western world are increasingly resisting rigid gender roles. This indicates that the limiting impact of patriarchal gender roles is changing, with more freedom. However, many of the men represented in this book think progress is too slow in encouraging boys and men to be all they can be as human beings. We need many more support groups for boys and men, like those developed by our changemakers.

Chapter 2: What We Teach Boys about Masculinities

I was born in Oakland, California to a single mother. My father died before I was born in December 1974. *As a Sagittarian, do you think of yourself as adventurous and asking deep questions?* I do, and I love taking the young people in our program on outdoor adventures. We just created a game called Ever Forward Club: The Adventure.

My father had gone to Little Rock, Arkansas for his own father's funeral. He planned to come back to Oakland and pack up his barbershop and move to Arkansas, to get away from some of the chaos in Oakland. In one of those last nights of partying, someone laced marijuana with a drug and his heart couldn't handle it. Instead of them taking him to the hospital, his "friends" took him to my grandmother's house and he passed there before the ambulance could arrive.

You majored in civil engineering at Cal Poly San Luis Obispo, one of the best technical schools in California. How did you get there being raised without male role models to tell you to succeed? When I was in high school I was in a program called MESA (Mathematics, Engineering, and Science Achievement). A man came to a camp who was an engineering major at Cal Poly and I got to meet him. I felt like he was a poet with the power of words, he knew his history.

When I was a junior in high school, there were two seniors in my calculus class who were going to Cal Poly and I thought, "I'm going to Cal Poly." I took a tour there and I got off the bus; it was a rainy, a gloomy, an ugly day, in San Luis Obispo and I'm like, "This is where I'm going to go to school?" When I got to Cal Poly, there wasn't a lot of diversity, not a lot of people who looked like me.

You say in one of the videos on your website that, for the boys that you taught as a math teacher, it was not cool to get A's, not considered a manly thing to do. Why didn't you ⊹ fall into that trap? Now, if girls were getting good grades, it was cool because that's what they were supposed to do. If you were okay being a nerd, then it was okay to be smart; but for the guys I hung out with, smart wasn't cool. My friends were like, "You think you're smarter than us?" It was almost as if acting smart was a threat to other young men in my circle. Peers might call you an Oreo, black on the outside/white on the inside, if you act white, talk white. It's like you're trying to be fancy because, in this community, we are not fancy, so you must think you're better than us.

My strategy was not to let them see how smart I am and pretend not to be doing my work. I would do really good in math because math was easy for me, so people thought my report card was a mistake or I was cheating. Why do you have C-, C-, D, and then a B+ or an A on math? School was like a break from my night job of taking care of my siblings. I didn't go home and just chill and work on homework, I had to cook, clean, wash dishes, and fold clothes.

I was the oldest of four. I had a sister who was four years younger who could help me when she got older, but I was still responsible for them. I had to make sure they did their work; if I gave them chores to do, I had to re-fold the clothes because my mom's standards are high. My mom got married when I was 12 or 13 and had a son by that man. I thought I was getting a father, but I got a very mean person instead. His son experienced a father who was loving and took him places, but we didn't get that. I was told by my uncle at seven years old, "Ashanti, you're the man of the house," so I knew my role was to take care of my siblings the best way I knew how. When my stepfather came and treated us kind of badly, I just kept loving them and taking care of them like I was obliged to do by my uncle.

My mom and I had a lot of arguments because she took his side a lot of times. My grandfather played the mediator role sometimes, telling me that's her husband now, so she has to agree with him. I'm like, "Look, I've been here since the beginning. How's she going to take his side? How are you going to believe him over me?" There was a lot of animosity and emotional baggage but luckily we survived. I survived it enough to get to college and move into the dorms as soon as I could.

Did your mom, a teacher, encourage you to get good grades? That's an amazing story in that my mom actually never told me I had to go to college. I remember watching *The Brady Bunch* episode where Greg said, "I'm going to go join a band when I finish high school," and his parents said, "No, you're going to college." "After that episode, I went to my mom's room and said, "I'm mad at you. Why didn't you ever tell me I have to go to college?" She said, "Are you going to go to college?" When I said yes, she replied, "Well, I guess I didn't have to tell you." She never told me I had to be a teacher like her; she was pretty hands-off. Once I got my act together after middle school, I didn't need any guidance from her around school.

I had arguments with her about finishing paperwork when I applied for Upward Bound, a program that helps first-generation students go to college when I was around 14 so I asked her to fill this application out. They turned me down because I wasn't first-generation since my mom went to college; that was the first time I knew that my mom went to college. I thought if we're this poor, what's wrong with her? I decided that day that I was never going to be a teacher when we had so little money that I have holes in my shoes and when it rains my feet are soaking wet. She and my stepfather were always arguing about money and I'm like: "Who wants a lifestyle like that?" I wanted to be rich.

Young men that I've interviewed in their early 20s say when they were in middle school or earlier, they started hearing what it is to be a man--not be feminine. What did you hear? Since my uncle told me I was supposed to be the man of the house at seven years old, I already thought I was a man, given the responsibility of taking care of my siblings. I didn't make any kids, I didn't even know what that meant, but I knew I was the man of the house. I thought being a man was being responsible, taking care of people around you, with a lot of duties and chores and responsibilities. No one really cares about what you think or what you feel.

When I left the house for school, the rules changed. Being a man was being tough, strong, dominant, having all the answers, but being too smart wasn't it. Answers in the classroom were not really where your points were, they were on the playground. When I got to high school, I didn't really care what people thought was cool because I knew there was no way I'm going to get out of Oakland unless I go to college. That is how the journey began for me.

You said that math saved your life? Is that because it got you to college and professional work? Yes, it was my ticket in middle school when I was doing badly in every other class and I was doing good in math, so my math teachers would see that I would finish my work super-quick; like, I got it! I loved math but every other class I didn't really care about. It wasn't until I got my act together in my ninth-grade year that it all turned around. An English teacher, whose class I didn't like, changed my life. She asked me, "Why are you acting like you're not smart? You're always goofing off and playing around." She said, "I know your father died before you were born but don't use it as an excuse. Life gives us what we get and we've got to make the most out of it."

It changed my life. It was like I'd been using my father's death as a reason why I should be angry. Sadness wasn't accepted in my community so anything that could be seen as sad, you turned into anger. I considered myself to be very angry about my father's death because I didn't have anyone who would even care about my sadness. She changed my life.

My peers were talking about sports; knowing all the facts and data and having all this knowledge was seen as important. No one cared if you knew the facts of any history or whatever. There was a lot of dominance like, nobody backs down and don't let anybody take advantage of you. My experience with trying to prove my coolness began in fourth grade, around eight years old. I was sexually assaulted and it was a really rough experience since I couldn't talk about it because if I'm the man of the house, how could I let this happen to me, right? How are you a man at all if you let somebody take advantage of you? It happened in the dark at night at a camp and I thought I could never tell anybody. It disappeared from my memories until I started doing this emotional work with other men and learning what happened to them.

I think I was always questioning, am I man enough? I have no money and no job, but I have a whole lot of responsibilities as a very domesticated man of the house. I knew how to take care of a home, I knew how to prepare any meal. Middle school became the time where boys in my circle started talking a lot about sex. I learned more Sex Ed in the back of Algebra class than anywhere else. Calvin was like the biggest of all middle schoolers and had a story every Monday morning about what he did over the weekend. One of the boys in the circle said, "Ashanti, you don't know anything about this." I lied, " Of course I do," like it wasn't an option not to be sexually active.

I had to defend my manhood, my masculinity, in front of these boys who were saying you're not a man because you ain't never seen this or touched this or that. I'm spinning because at 13 I'm not at an age where I was interested in it at all. I didn't want to be in this conversation anymore because they wanted evidence. I was learning from other teenagers because there was no man in my house teaching me any of this stuff, learning some unhealthy stuff and sometimes inappropriate stuff. "Are you man enough?" You're always in that space of questioning yourself.

The first time I had sex I was 18 years old, a sophomore and I was like "Whoa!" It was a wild experience but I still didn't tell anybody because I felt ashamed that it was so late, because everybody in most of my circles had started way before. I felt like I had to pretend I had been doing it all my life. *A book by Peggy Orenstein about boys and sexuality reports parents average 10 minutes talking to boys about sex. So they learn from peers and porn, which is really sad.* Really sad.

After Cal Poly, did you work as a civil engineer? Yes, I worked for about five years doing a lot of building design. I wanted to see things being built, I wasn't really into sitting in a cubicle designing. Then teaching called me but I ran from it. The first time somebody said I should be a teacher was when I was in college but I felt insulted because I felt, how dare you insult me as an engineering student? I'm going to be rich.

Later I was a tutor at Mills College in Oakland after a buddy of mine asked me to tutor for Upward Bound on Saturday mornings. I told him, I don't even know what Saturday morning looks like. I thought as an engineer who makes good money, I would be happy all the time but I wasn't. I journeyed to every Happy Hour I could find in the Bay Area. I told him I need my Friday night fun because it's the only time I'm really enjoying life. He said, "Give me two months to find a new teacher but I need somebody right now." I said okay and that's how the calling happened.

A kid named Damon walked in late to tutoring, saying hello to everybody like he was Norm from *Cheers* or the mayor of this class. I told him, "Listen, don't walk in my class a half-hour late and then start talking to everybody." I was clear about my standards so when he went to the back to the back of the room and goofed off, I made him sit next to me in the front. I'd drive home thinking I can't wait till next week. The second call was tutoring at the Huntington Learning Center where there are not a lot of black people and no other black mentors or teachers. I took the job because all I did when I left for home from work was play video games. My life was kind of empty, working all day and then going home and doing nothing.

I think this kid, Lucas, was wondering how this big dude with dreadlocks was going to help him with his algebra test. When I showed him how to solve the problems, I saw a rainbow and flowers and heard a humming sound that was like, yes! It was also scary because I realized this is like teaching and teachers don't make money. So the next day I quit that job, thinking you're not sucking me into this. I knew what was happening internally was a fight between who I believed I was supposed to be and who this calling was going to make me be.

I got a new job making more money in engineering in San Jose. I had to drive from my house an hour and a half every morning and evening although I never knew why people would do that. I found out my building burned down while I was in Mexico. I could have kept my job, but at that time a buddy of mine invited me to apply to Mills College to earn a credential and masters in education.

When you were teaching math, you saw one of the barriers to boys of color doing well was "it's not cool to be smart," so how did you change that attitude? I was teaching ninth-grade Algebra. I can't do it in the classroom by pointing you out in front of everybody, so I started the Ever Forward Club. I wanted to bring them to a space where they could be their best self. I told them I want you to be your best self, be like a rooster, crowing and sharing how amazing you are. This is not a place to play small. I had to make a special space for them until society is ready for our boys to be able to be full emotional beings. I demonstrated that your full self matters here.

In organizing in general, food gets people out. You told the boys: "Come on Thursday at noon and I'll have food for you." I told them, "In exchange for lunch, I want you to teach me to be a better teacher." Something was missing in the translation between me trying to teach them math. Ever Forward became a safe space to be yourself and figure out: Who do you want to be? Who are you dreaming of being? What's in the way? How can we support you? They began to really build community with each other. It was beautiful to watch some of those 13-year-olds who are still friends in their 30s who are connected in a brotherhood they created. It's almost indescribable and also really beautiful. It started off with a group of eight to ten young men and grew to a club of over 75 students in the first two years. I didn't know what I was doing but those in those circles, we were a brotherhood.

I don't care what prowess you have to prove with midnight stories but in this room truth is sacred. No one was questioning their authenticity, a break from a space where everyone is always testing you. A lot of them were amazing young men who had not found their way of being themselves.

We didn't tolerate putting anybody down. If you didn't jump to a meeting, we went to find you because you don't miss a meeting, it's almost like family. I treated them like they were five years older than they were but I expected them to act like they were five years younger. So, if you're 13, I'm expecting that a lot of time you'll act like you're eight. It really helped them to learn how to communicate and gave them vocabulary and emotional language they could navigate.

When the club started in 2004, did the girls say, "We want a club too?" Yes, the girls were upset with me because every Thursday lunch I would send them out of my room; people were in my room all the time. The following year, we found a teacher who was willing to run The Young Women's Club. We had Chicas for young girls and Siempre Allende for the newcomers. A lot of immigrants to the US were getting recruited by gangs and I was seeing really good kids getting sucked in, so I created a co-ed club for them.

You said that most of the kids who were in the club went on to college? Yes, 93% go to college, military, or trade school with a post-secondary plan. The idea was if you are in a space where high expectations are the norm, creating an academic family, we're going to support you in your growth and we need you to give your best. We asked them, "What do you want to do with your life? How are you going to get there?" We took them on college tours but it wasn't me saying you must go, although I knew how college had made my life so much richer, but you're going to be ready if you choose to go.

The emotional toolkit that you taught them is giving them the safe space and the vocabulary to say there are other emotions besides anger and pride in succeeding. It's okay to talk about how my girlfriend dumped me and I feel sad. That's right. I told them most times I saw young people with two tools--a hammer and a tickler--so if you're not laughing about it, you're angry about it. We have a whole lot more emotions than those two; I helped them navigate what they were really feeling, like being angry because a girl wouldn't give me her number, but deep down why am I mad at her? Five minutes ago I wanted her number and now I hate her and she's all kinds of bad names? We need help in navigating feelings, especially with these young loves.

Do you have a way for people to duplicate the program? Yes, we created a program so people can bring it to their schools and we also created the Taking Off The Mask: The Box. Our organization can train them to run a club and they can order a kit. I'll show you the links about how to run our signature workshop in their schools without us there because some schools don't have the resources to bring us in. *You left teaching to do the Ever Forward Club full-time?* Yes, in 2016 after I left the Fellowship at Stanford, I came on full-time as the director with only three months of revenue, plus a program officer and a COO. October is my fifth year anniversary: I think it's time for a sabbatical.

Do you have kids? I don't, I think about that a lot because I raised my siblings and three godsons. I think about legacy, the end of me on this family tree, and feel really sad about that. I just don't have the energy to raise kids. I want kids but I'm not willing to do all the work it takes to raise them. Maybe I'll adopt. *Your legacy is with thousands of kids that you've helped so the actual genetics is not that important.*

You went to India, what did you learn there cross-culturally about what they teach their boys about how to be men? I saw that smart was absolutely cool, the Class Topper is the one who people cheer for. I did a Fulbright Fellowship there for eight months. They don't have the hyper-sexualized communities there. The young men know that they won't get married till their mid-20s and their parents are going to arrange the wedding. I was always curious as to how they focused so much on education and how they created so many professionals and stay focused. I asked some 24-year-olds, "How is it that you don't think about sex or girls"? I was in the southeast which is very much more traditional and cultural.

They said you think about it and put it out of your mind. It's easier than when you're in a community where the men around you are talking about prowess and conquering and sex. Because no one's getting married until they're 25, you go to college, and then your parents will find you a wife. Behind the scenes, there's some dating happening, which looks very different. But now they have access to porn on their phones

I learned there's a lot more room for boys to have intimate friendships so they're not always looking for comfort from a woman. *I've been to India too, where some women told me it's such a relief not to have to date because women feel they have to kind of dumb down, and flirt to get male approval. They're more straightforward and it's cool for girls to be good in math.*

In Canada, I led a camp for boys of color and learned they all call themselves Canadians, rather than Black Canadians or Indian Canadians. *What about Mexico, what did you learn there?* I lived in a village there for several months but there is a lot more of the machismo, a lot more of "you better prove it," there's a lot of dominance around "are you gay or straight?" There's a lot of testing it out, questioning you, a lot of jokes, and people make fun of you. You have to prove how much of a man you are even when you're just a little boy. Homophobia exists in many cultures but I saw a lot of it in machismo culture. The village doesn't experience it, but you see the difference in the city in Oaxaca. *I thought that girls aren't supposed to go on dates without a chaperone, like their brother?* Mexico City is a big city, so there's a lot of dating. They meet on the subway, on the metro, under the clock. You just say, "Meet me at the clock."

What branches of the men's movement do you think are doing good work? I've done weekend retreats with a lot of organizations: MDI (Mentor Discover Inspire), the ManKind Project, Sacred Sons, EVRYMAN, and others. If you don't have a good marketing plan, you're not going to attract men to the space to talk about feelings, when people say that men shouldn't talk about feelings. So I think part of that work is a deep dive around that. I'm trying to figure out how we get more young men in those spaces so that they have a space to talk about what they're going through in a really heartfelt way.

We were in a documentary called *The Mask You Live In* about how this hyper-masculine narrative of being a man is hurting our boys. We created a campaign called the Million Mask Movement where we invite people all over the world to make masks. I want to invite people to make a mask and go to the website (100Kmasks.com) to see the masks. We see that men all over the world, of all ages, have so much more in common behind the mask.

I was born in March of 1983 in Edinburg, Texas, part of the Rio Grande valley. I mostly grew up down by the Mexican border. *As a Pisces, do you feel like a sensitive, caring, occasionally indecisive kind of person or not?* I've been told that from time to time, something about water signs, but partly it has to do with growing up in the borderlands and being aware of the culture, the community. *How many generations of your family lived in Texas?* On my father's side, my father was born in Texas, his mother was born in Texas and her parents immigrated from Northern Mexico. My father and his mother were all born on the farmworker trail, traveling up north to follow cotton crops.

My mother was raised in Nuevo Leon, Mexico and as a teenager, she came to the states to work. She traveled to California to work with grapes for several years, so both my families are farmworkers. Even though they were born and lived in Texas, it was quite a different lifestyle than folks who stuck around in one place and had the ability to grow in one direction. They followed the crops throughout the country.

It used to be among the Chicanos that I knew that the emphasis was, you work for la familia *rather than go to college but that's changed.* When Chicanos in Texas were fighting for equality in education, just about everyone with a Spanish surname was forced to repeat the first grade a couple of times. My dad lived through that, so at the age of 15, he was still going to Travis Elementary. He was part of that generation where he had to work before school and after school. Upon his father's early death he had to work more, so he might have made it to the eighth grade.

The little village where my mother grew up in Nuevo Leon only had school up to fourth grade. Their whole life was always about work. Fortunately, though, my parents always pushed education on my older sister and me. Not going to college wasn't an option for us. My sister Yesenia became a school teacher and I never left college. I got my bachelor's degree, then I pursued a master's degree and Ph.D. because they were huge proponents of us becoming educated.

When you were a child were they following the crops? I was lucky because my dad worked the cotton fields for the season in West Texas up to about when I was four years old. My mom had a full-time job at the Hagers factory in Edinburg. When I turned three, mom quit the factory and opened up a daycare at home and dad found a job as a custodian at the local high school. We weren't making more money but dad didn't have to leave the family for a couple of months. This was quite different from the rest of my family who were all seasonal farmworkers.

During the summer months the crops die off because of the heat and people have to leave South Texas, so a lot of my family worked in West Texas, Memphis, and Florida. This meant that we started and finished the school year in the same school, as opposed to some of my *primos* and *primas* (cousins) who would leave in May and then sometimes wouldn't be back until September or October and have to start the school year in Colorado or wherever.

In terms of terminology, do you prefer: Latinx, Latino, Hispanic, Chicano, Mexican-American? I identify with the term *Chicano*. My father grew up during the Chicano movement but he didn't share much with me, a real shy guy. He would take me to my school every morning that had more white students than my previous elementary school. He told me, "Mijo, you're a Chicano," one of the few times that my dad was aggressive about anything. Later in life, I really became interested in the Chicano movement and history and realized he was trying to convey the pride and acknowledgment of who you are as a person. The more I move out of Texas and be around folks from other parts of Latino America, the term *Latino* gets thrown around, but I'm fine with Chicano or Mexican-American.

The stereotype I see often in practice, portrayed in the 1997 film, Fools Rush In, *is that kids in Chicano families grow up with extended families that get together often with influence from grandparents, aunts, uncles, and cousins. How fair is that stereotype?* In my household, my home was the hub because my maternal grandmother stayed with us. My mother never wanted my grandmother to be on her own even though she had her own house till the day she passed away. It was a block away from us so, as my sister got older, she'd go stay with her so she wouldn't spend the night by herself until eventually she would stay the nights with us. I would spend the afternoons with grandma, walk her over to the house, but on the weekend she would stay with us so this meant that my *tias, tios, primas,* and *primos* would visit grandma at our house.

I did grow up having those connections to the extended family so you grow up knowing that there's more than the immediate family. My father's family was different, because of the farmwork lifestyle. I had aunts and uncles in San Antonio, Idaho, New Mexico, and West Texas. As they traveled, my aunts and uncles fell in love and got married on the farmworker trail, so his family was all over the place.

The recent books about American boys by Naiobe Way and Peggy Orenstein report that teenage boys are lonely. They give up close friendships with other boys because people might think they were queer and get taught to shut down their feelings. Is that not so true for extended Latinx families? It's hard to be lonely but we learn gender roles from our family and, to a certain extent, there's truth to that.

When I was a kid, I was heavily influenced by my uncles on my mother's side. I had an uncle who really embraced these negative attributes of machismo; for instance, he told me that men aren't supposed to smile in photos--only clowns and queers smile. As a kid, I thought, "He's my uncle; he must be right." For a very long time, I didn't know how to smile. It does create some social anxiety or loneliness where you're restricted to certain behaviors. A very common one as a kid growing up in the '80s is that *los machos no lloran*, boys are not supposed to cry. That did have an impact on boys of my generation.

Do you think that you got more guidance about what it was to be a man than a boy growing up in an Anglo family in South Texas? We had double the work to do adjusting to cultural norms coming from a Chicano household in the US and had to adjust to some of those social norms. By the time that I was growing up in the '80s, white flight had taken place in South Texas, so I grew up in a society that was 95% Mexican-American.

As someone who grew up in Texas, what are Chicano voters currently doing about the Republican attempts to limit voting? Whenever a group of people is losing power, they will do all they can to maintain it. We see this with the rise of the Ku Klux Klan post-Civil War, the rise of strong nationalism in the 1920s and 1930s, and right now *with the Trumpites.* White Americans who see these changing demographics are extremely fearful of what's going to happen. In Spanish, we have a saying, "The lion feels that everyone is of his condition" and what does the lion do? What did white Americans do for a very long time against people of color? The fear is that the Latinx population is going to arise to oppress white folks.

You could stop migration right now but the Latino population will continue to grow because Latinos are a very young population. Every 30 seconds a Latino in the US turns 18, so a large number of Latinos still can't vote in Texas because of their age.[113] The Republicans are trying to curb what they can before this age group jumps up to the age where they can vote. *There are about the same numbers of Anglos and Latinx in Texas.* Also, the way districts are gerrymandered in Texas is insane. I lived through a lot of that.

Governor Greg Abbott was hit by a tree when he was jogging and I wonder if that influenced his mental abilities because his anti-abortion law encouraging vigilantes seems so bizarre. Absolutely, this is the most restrictive law against women in 50 years. What people like Abbott have going on, along with governors like Ron DeSantis in Florida, and some extreme right-wingers, is effective propaganda. They make up boogeymen and culture wars because none of their policies are forward-thinking. Their policies are extremely backward, like how they've handled Covid. Texas and Florida have been brutalized by Covid, but the governors stick to their anti-mask and anti-vaccine mandates.

They want to be these tough macho men who are standing firm in these cultural wars, like Texas allows carrying guns without a permit. They pick on the undocumented folks, women, and communities of color. DeSantis picked on the immigrant community time and time again on how they've been these spreaders of Covid. However, the Cuban community in Florida has historically been politically to the right of the rest of the Latino population nationally.

Do they believe a real man doesn't wear a mask? Abbott ended up having Covid after being vaccinated but has access to a lot of the drugs that aren't available to you and me. Those people live in a very different reality. Trump was making fun of Joe Biden one week about wearing masks and five days later Trump had Covid himself. There's a false sense of manliness that means you take risks because you're a man, and I think we've seen that during the pandemic. *It's true that women and Democrats are more likely to get vaccinated than men and Republicans.*

Since we're talking about machismo, you wrote three books: From Death Valley to the Río Grande Valley: World War II and Korean War Prisoners of War (2006); I'm Not Gonna Die in this Damn Place: Manliness, Identity, and Survival of the Mexican-American Vietnam Prisoners of War (2013); *and* Mexican-American Baseball in South Texas (2016). *What got you interested in prisoners of war and baseball?* My graduate adviser suggested I look at Mexican-Americans in the military. I began to identify POWs who were living, and those who had passed; in the newspapers at the time it was incredible how much coverage they gave to POWs. I found few scholarly works on veterans and especially POWs so I thought this was a nice niche. I began interviewing these men and their families and wrote a master's thesis on them. Texas Tech University has the largest archive in the world on the Vietnam war, so it made sense to expand to Vietnam for the doctoral dissertation.

I saw a huge difference between the POWs in the three wars. The Vietnam war group was not diverse at all, compared to the previous wars. The large majority of POWs in Vietnam were white officers, the John McCain-types shot down on their missions over North Vietnam. I wanted to see what was pushing Latinos towards the military and, of course, I used manliness as one of these factors.

Did you find any differences between Chicano, Black, and Anglo POWs? There are only about 10 Mexican-American POWs and 16 African-Americans in Vietnam where the number of POWs in Vietnam was about 600 to 700 POWs, compared to the thousands in the previous wars. A lot of the Latinos came from farmworker backgrounds, kids working the fields in the Depression Era when a lot of them went to bed hungry. *They were used to hardship and adversity.* Yes, similar to some of the African-American POWs, especially the guys coming out of the South. North Vietnamese camps were very much similar to a formal prison in the States where officers quickly set up a rank system and these senior POWs were white. There was a huge difference between the POWs who were in North Vietnam as opposed to the guys in the South.

I went in-depth on these POW manly ideals. It's not that they wanted to prove their toughness in the battlefield or get as many kills as they could. A lot of them wanted training, to be able to come back home and get a nice job. They were so afraid of being drafted that they thought, maybe if we volunteer and we pick our specialty, we'll have input on where we're going to end up. In their Cold War mentality, they were being told that in the middle-class American family, the father-husband has a decent job to enable the wife to stay at home where she could be the caretaker. They wanted to partake in this booming economy of the Cold War and come back to a society where they could grow and prosper.

For a lot of these men coming out of the southwest from extreme poverty, the military could offer some of that social mobility. *The military has more men and women of color than their population percentage, but whites are still a majority of active-duty enlisted people.*[114] Today the figures are almost reflective of the population at large. Unfortunately, it doesn't always transition to moving up the military hierarchy. When we're looking at people of color and women, the number of these folks transitioning to the three-star rank and above is limited.

Is it due to prejudice and structural barriers or is it that they're not as educated? It's a little bit of both. During Vietnam, when the rate of African-Americans and Mexican-Americans were extremely disproportionate, folks began to say these men were volunteering for dangerous jobs because the bonuses that airborne divisions were offering were of interest to soldiers from a lower socioeconomic status. This speaks not only to the system in the military but social system that leaves these people out to dry. The other thing to look at is how many African-Americans and Latinos went to the military academies.

What did you find about Mexican-American baseball in South Texas? I was looking at masculinity in Chicano neighborhoods and saw a few behaviors that stood out connected to manliness--fighting and sports. Fighting was connected with the military and sports was used as a way of social mobility. My friend Omar Rivera's brain is so full of all these potential topics; he told me about a team in 1962 in Hidalgo County that won the Colt League World Series. They were 15 and 16-year-olds who won the World Series in Shawnee, Oklahoma but nothing has been written about it. I was trying to write a community history of what was going on in South Texas in the '60s.

This baseball team was divided down the line, with eight Mexican-American boys and eight white boys, in a time where South Texas had a good number of white folks in the area, which was segregated. I was expanding on that aspect of masculinity and spoke to some of their "manly ideals." A lot of men coming back from World War II and Korea developed baseball leagues throughout South Texas so about every town had a semi-professional team. It was a form of distraction or a coping mechanism for them to deal with their Combat Stress Disorder. For Mexican-Americans in South Texas, sport was a way of becoming integrated in the community and becoming Americanized, while, especially for my generation, soccer was still seen as an immigrant sport. Whether it's about the military or about baseball, I showed how Latinos have been involved in these two worlds and how underrepresented they are in academic work.

To understand masculinity, I went back to the Pueblo natives of the Southwest and how they were impacted by the Spanish conquistadors and missionaries who transformed their whole notion of masculinity. Manliness in Pueblo society was associated with the hunter as the provider and protector in warfare. I investigated how Mexican writers looked at machismo, back to writers of the 1920s and 1930s, people like Samuel Ramos and Vicente Mendoza who articulated what it meant to be a man.

Mendoza identified two forms of machismo. One embraced being the provider, having responsibility to the family, making sure that the children were disciplined, and making sure that they grew up with all that they needed to become successful. They valued traits like stoicism, more positive than negative. He also identifies a negative form of machismo, which is in the mainstream, such as the womanizer and dominance.

You said the conquistadors changed the gender relations in the pueblos. Is that because before it was matrilineal and women were important and honored? Yes, in the pueblo a young man gained his rites of passage through hunting trips, *going to the wilderness alone.* When the Spaniards brought Christianity, the Corn Mothers went away. For every native that a Spanish killed, they were sexually entitled to a native woman. According to Ramon Gutierrez, this eventually translated to native men doing the same, in that masculinity was tied to sexual conquest, very different from before.

There's also the concept of caballerismo, *an old Spanish knight and chivalry honor concept.* The code of chivalry is a positive aspect of macho with an honorable way of treating women, children, and the elderly, which Facundo Valdez wrote about. He wrote a piece on *verguenza,* shame. One of the worst things that they could tell you growing up is that you're a *sin verguenza,* you're shameless, lacking a code of ethics and honor.

Part of the code of honor is that your word means something. It's one of the positive attributions to manliness taught by people like Jerry Tello.* He has this concept of *un hombre noble,* the noble man, very engraved with caballerismo's traditional ways of behaving. *Did you hear those concepts when you were growing up?* Absolutely. You're never supposed to hit women, you're to take care of your sister even though she's older than you, you never curse in front of women, you provide, and you open the door for children, for women, and for elderly.

The more we progressed in society, the more that negative images took over some of those positive traits of being a macho. Gloria Anzaldua looked at gender relations in rural South Texas and talked about some of those positive macho traits she saw growing up, like the father as *caballero* (gentleman). Sometimes we can't even have these conversations as people look at some of these negative aspects of machismo and don't look at some of the positives, as I did in my book. There were different ways of viewing machismo for folks from a rural area like I came from, to inner-city people like in Mexico City.

In cities, that means gangs? To a certain extent yes; when I was in Michigan I did some work in the prison system. I went to a couple of prisons there, starting off when I gave a talk for Cinco De Mayo, then one of the groups called LASSO (Latin American Spanish Speaking Organization), invited me to become their sponsor. Those young men really wanted to learn more about their heritage, so I would go to the prison in Jackson Cooper Street Facility twice a month and attend their meetings. They grew up with this idea of embracing all these falsehoods about machismo.

Being in this gang world, sometimes you have all these crazy ideas that you can't be a man unless you father X amount of children, you're out there with all types of women, drinking and doing drugs. These young men grew up with the mindset that you had to embrace all these very dangerous lifestyles to be considered a man in the barrio. I'm currently writing a piece on my experience working with these young men.

I interviewed a Chicano, seen on my YouTube channel, who spent a lot of time in California prisons and he said that among the Latino convicts, it's not okay to have sex with men. They have a strict code of ethics. LASSO would not permit drug users to consume drugs in the prison and their bylaws frowned upon sexual relations among prisoners as well.

Marianismo and the influence of the Catholic church mean women are supposed to be like Virgin Mary. A girl is supposed to have a chaperone on a date until she's married. My family was quite untraditional in that my mom was the disciplinarian in the household and the one who decided things. My father went along with everything my mom suggested, so if we wanted to do something we asked mom. My dad was totally fine with that, he was always there for us but he deferred to mom. She was pretty much the brains of the operation.

I was a chaperone for my sister well into my teenage years. She was in college and I would still tag along when she went out with her boyfriend and that was totally a thing in my family. I'd be stuck at a dance just sitting there because I was a chaperone. Mexican families tend to keep a close grasp on what our women are doing while we give young men the liberty of being out in the streets, which often leads to them getting into trouble.

Is it fair to say still that most Hispanics are Catholic and observant although there's a growing evangelical wave? What's the role of Catholicism in shaping gender roles? I grew up Methodist with a lot of Catholic traditions. The majority of the students in my elementary school were Catholic and we grew up with all those traditions, especially during Lent and Christmas. The Catholic church, from a surface level, does portray those gender divisions where young girls are expected to keep their virginity until marriage. However, in the last two decades, we've seen tremendous growth of Protestantism among Latinos and the Mormon church is one of the fastest-growing in Latin America. (Felipe Hinojosa wrote *Apostles of Change: Latino Radical Politics, Church Occupations, and the Fight to Save the Barrio.*)

A big thing for Latina girls is a quinceañera *when they're 15, the coming of age celebration. Is there anything like that for boys' initiation into manhood?* There are quinceañeros for boys. I have an aunt who would always give us something for our 15th birthday. For young men sometimes it's a hunting or fishing trip to get their first kill. Quinceañeras used to be family affairs where the family would do the cooking and the arrangements, while nowadays families are spending $20,000 to $30,000. *It's like a wedding.* It speaks to not only consumerism but its appeal to the Latino community, like keeping up with the Garcias. The rule in my family was at 15 a girl can dance with boys and wear makeup.

A major global issue for boys is they're not going to college as much as girls, except in Sub-Saharan Africa. What do you see in your students? We've seen a shift going back 40 to 50 years when the majority of the students were males. Young men of my generation in Texas, especially once the oil boom began in the early 2000s, saw that there wasn't a need to go to college. They thought, "I'll be making much more money and I'll be doing manly work." My second cousin, unfortunately, died on one of these job sites where a lot of these men were doing risky jobs. It speaks to the gender division of labor and also to some of these masculine ideals that attracted some of these men. I'm at a teaching university that attracts a great number of first-generation students, a lot of whom want to go into the STEM fields, as opposed to going into the humanities and arts that have taken a huge hit in the last two decades.

An increasing number of young people are anxious and depressed.[115] *Is your college paying attention to those mental health issues and do you see them among your students?* Yes, I think all universities are looking at this. We see the expansion of services as these talks have definitely grown in the last two decades. For this generation of college students, technology and social media have a tremendous influence. They live with so many pressures compared to when I was a kid when your school world and your personal world were isolated from one another, except for visiting some friend's home like for a birthday party. This lack of boundaries leads to confrontations outside the classroom.

Do you let your students use their phones in your classroom? I try not to and I even have a limitation on laptops since studies show that the student learns more when they're writing down things. *I saw a video of a big Midwestern college lecture class from the back where you could see the students' laptop screens playing games and emailing.* This country hasn't started treating internet use as an addiction, although it's an extreme addiction. *China just mandated kids can only watch three hours of video games a week.* A decade ago the Chinese were treating internet addiction.

Because of your interest in gender, are you interested in branches of the men's movement? This reminds me of something out of a sitcom out of the 1990s, *Married With Children*. Al Bundy has a group of men form this misogynistic group called "No MA'AM." The reason why it was hilarious is because a lot of men felt that way and we're seeing that today where there's a backlash. To a certain extent, conservative women have embraced this type of mentality. *Like the Promise Keepers and Oath Keepers.* Right, and Proud Boys. To me, it really speaks to the insecurities in society that some of these men have. The president of my university is a woman and some faculty members are intimidated by that and feel it's a problem.

What do you teach? I coordinate the minor in Latino and Puerto Rican studies. I teach "Intro to Latino Studies," Puerto Ricans and Latinos in the United States, Latinos and Civil Rights, Oral History, and Community and Public History on Race and Ethnicity. *Is there an active women's studies program on campus?* Yes, and I'm going to their next meeting. There's a divide when you look at gender issues and cultural issues and I've had people at conferences confront me about this, especially when I was looking at the positive notions of machismo. A Latina confronted me, saying, "Latinos do oppress Latinas," which can be true. But we need to be open to grow and learn about gender dynamics and have these discussions.

It's awkward because the term *machismo* is often used by society to neutralize the Latino as oppressors. Once we shut down, it stops us from really growing and learning. When discussing gender relations, there needs to be an avenue for acceptance and discussion. *Every liberal progressive group I've known ends up with factions and divisions as to who's the most politically pure.* Absolutely, it becomes about who's more progressive. In contrast, the right-wing has three beliefs: Jesus, guns, and lower taxes, as opposed to folks on the left with all kinds of issues.

Our former president used simple words, like bad guy or good guy, like talking to a four-year-old. *He said bad hombres come from Mexico and rape women.* When Trump was elected, a lot of us realized that our country was never going to be the same again and this is not something that you fix in four years, even though Americans have such a short attention span. The Russians wanted to create a division in society and were very successful in doing that.

They made up news stories that really strike at America's heart and are responsible for a lot of the social anxiety and social divisions, similar to the divisions that existed during the Civil War Era and abolitionism, as well as in the 1950s and 1960s. Today these differences have divided families and households. *What's interesting to me is how effective Russia was in aggravating the divisions and probably got Trump elected although their economy isn't bigger than California's.* Yes, and America has interfered in so many elections abroad. The only reason we got Barack Obama elected was because of the blunder of George W. Bush years, starting two insane wars without any direction. People who make money off of this bank on these divisions. It's a wild time we're living under.

Daniel Ellenberg, Ph.D.
President of the Society for the Psychological Study of Men and Masculinities

I was born in December 1953 in New Jersey, or at least that's what I was told. I don't remember too well. *That makes you a Sagittarian.* That is correct, finally, we got to the most important detail about my entire life. *So are you adventurous, forward-looking, outspoken? They ask deep questions and they're willing to take on the establishment.* It does sound familiar.

When you were growing up in New Jersey, what messages did you get about being a man? My brother Marc, who is five years older than me, was called Marcy by my father--who died when I was in the fourth grade, of a heart attack. That's part of what brought me into the field of men and masculinity. Certainly, there were messages like don't be a girl and a lot of negative messages including fear of getting cooties from girls. The instructions are to be tough, to take no prisoners, don't be a cry baby, don't show emotion, and don't be vulnerable.

The great irony is that being vulnerable helps us to connect on a human level, but early in life boys learn to not be relational. I think the belief is "recursive," a term engineers use to describe something that recurs and keeps turning back on itself. The belief that boys are not relational, are not interested in emotional connection and are more individualistic and independent, leads parents and teachers to treat them differently.

That belief pattern or expectations, what psychologists call "schemas," lead to behavioral interventions that reinforce the belief itself. A classic study showed that when teachers are told a certain class of kids is really exceptional, despite the fact that the class was random, it led teachers to treat them as if they were exceptional. And the students did significantly better based on being treated with higher regard. The same pattern of treating boys as if they are not relational leads them to become less relational.

When your father died, did you have another father figure or how did you learn about being an adult man? The truth is that I'm still learning at 67. It certainly didn't happen when I was young. My mother remarried when I was 13. She and my stepfather, Bernie, had a very good marriage. He was a very nice guy, but not much of a father figure. I've pieced together learnings from various men over my life. I've made my way through the land of male role models with some successes and some disappointments. I've become a role model to a good number of men over the years.

Guys are generally not learning about masculinity through a particular role model; instead, they learn from movies, videos, games, books, athletics, music, and especially social media these days. I'd like to see a world of gender transcendence where gender isn't the first portal that we see. Historically we've believed boys and men are supposed to be masculine, the warrior, the hero, the soldier, or the fireman. Historically, men have learned to be very instrumental and not be like women are supposed to be--very emotional and expressive. Denying and downplaying the emotional, relational aspects of life is just not cutting it. Today the world is increasingly interconnected and relational skills are more important now than ever. If guys don't develop more of a relational mindset and skillset, they're going to keep falling behind.

As a leadership coach involved with leadership research, I can see where women are scoring significantly better than men in terms of leadership effectiveness because of their relational skills: their willingness and ability to mentor, to be emphatic, and to create caring connections. *I'm thinking of the effectiveness of women heads of state dealing with Covid like in New Zealand and Germany.* That's not historically part of the traditional male role, which we need to expand. If we're going to be resilient and get with the times, we need to expand our mindset and skill set as males. Girls and women are expanding, but sometimes not in the best ways because they start emulating some of the elements of so-called masculinity where they get cut off more from their feelings. Evolution is not a straight line. I think about the words of Gandhi: "Be the change you want to see in the world."

Do you think this is changing with young kids? It's such a big beast that it doesn't change overnight. I started getting involved with men's work in the heyday of the men's movement, back in the '80s--particularly in the San Francisco Bay Area. I, and many of the people involved, thought we were going to be a lot further along than we are right now. Yes, there is much more emphasis on gender fluidity, there are changes and with change comes pain, often because there is resistance. That drag factor keeps pulling on people in a multitude of different ways and it's quite confusing.

Trump is a perfect example of that resistance to change; if I'm a man I can do whatever I want. Do you think he exacerbated the situation? He definitely exacerbated it--he's the poster child of negative masculinity. I purposely didn't use the word toxic, which is used in the press a lot. I'm President of the American Psychological Association division that focuses on men and masculinity. We never use the word "toxic." Rather, we research traditional masculinities or precarious masculinity, involving the belief that being masculine is something that must be earned and can be easily lost, so you have to keep proving it on some level. I think that's the linchpin, the harmful belief we have to prove masculinity, which unfortunately involves denying vulnerabilities.

Those beliefs can get in the way of relationships and as someone who believes that the core of human life is about our connections with ourselves and with other people, those beliefs are anti-health. It's part of why men die five years younger on average. The times are changing and a lot of men aren't, partly because Trump was saying you can double-down on being hostile and aggressive.

It seems to me that the largest branch of the men's movement today is apolitical peer-counseling groups that provide support and initiation as a man. (This topic is discussed on YouTube.[116]) The men's movement is not one movement. The men's rights activists are certainly involved with legislative actions and see how men aren't being treated fairly in custody arrangements. One of the challenges is that we men tend to see things in terms of zero-sum, like, if girls and women are being lifted up, boys and men are being pushed down. I'd like to live in a world where we're helping to lift each other up. As someone who's involved in the land of gender, it's really hard to have these conversations. It's remarkable how many smart, professional people, people who are involved with legislative actions, seem to think it's an either/or game. I think it's both/and. Until we change our mindset about it, we're still going to be at war.

Warren Farrell calls it gender liberation and if one sex isn't liberated the other one isn't either.* Warren is somebody who's seen as a men's rights activist (*he rejects that label*) and as an either/or but I know him and I wouldn't say that's the case. *I think he's a feminist who wants to have liberation for all.* In my division, he's not well regarded, he's seen as a men's rights activist. It's a very complex political and psychological territory that tends to trigger a lot of vitriol from different folks. I've recommended some dialogues with Warren and I got routinely turned down; "We don't talk to people like that." To me it's ignorance and I've said it to their face.

I believe that healthy arguments, in the Greek sense, are vital and valuable. If you don't agree and you have a better argument, why wouldn't you dialogue? The Israelis and the

Palestinians need to talk with each other. The Harvard Negotiating Pact aims to get to yes, so you start off with what you agree on and then you move from there, but that's not the way most people do it. They immediately start off on what they perceive as disagreement. I think sometimes there is more agreement than is realized but people aren't even trying to find the places of intersection. Human beings are the rationalizing species driven by confirmation bias, seeing what we seek to see. *To me, the most extreme example of that is people who say, "God tells me you're sinners and I should kill you in a holy war."*

As boys spend many hours a day in front of video games, what is the message besides blowing things up? Win at all costs. I work with some people in the video industry who are trying to change these dynamics with socially conscious games. How do you tap into a perhaps biological or certainly conditioned orientation of guys to be the hero for a good, prosocial cause, not simply self-aggrandizement? That's what I'd like to see. *Like a video game with Gandhi, Martin Luther King, Susan B. Anthony, Mother Teresa, or Mandela to help them win their battle for justice.* Exactly, we need to change this idea of winner-take-all competition, treating other people as objects instead of I-thou relationships, starting early in life. A lot of boys are treated as objects, not touched as much as girls, not spoken to as much, treated in more roughhouse ways. We keep handing down some of the messages from the past that don't work.

For 98% of human history, we were hunters and gatherers who lived in egalitarian bands. It seems like our DNA is wired for cooperation because they had to cooperate as small bands to make it. The potential for human beings to be the greatest saint imaginable and the worst sinner imaginable is all packed into the DNA code. When you think about epigenetics, our genetic code is vast and what gets activated is the relationship with our environment. For example, Fred Trump was a tyrant who told his son Donald that there are winners and losers in life; you've got to be a winner. Take no prisoners; lie, cheat, and steal your way to the top. If he had a different father, he would not have been the tyrant he is. *His mother was sick a lot and he didn't get that feminine nurturance as well.*

What led you to be a psychologist? Certainly, my father's death was key. I was very aware that when I was playing basketball that other kids had their fathers in the stands while I didn't. I decided not to go out for football in high school, although, as a pretty good athlete I was expected to don the helmet but I decided to go into the band. Before ninth grade I ran into the star athlete and he yelled at me, "Ellenberg, you're going out to the football team, aren't you?" I said, "No, I'm going to the band" and he yelled at me "You pussy!" He was a decent guy, trapped in his own male conditioning. I still remember the moment over 50 years later. It was shaming. We don't address the power of shaming males into confined masculinity nearly enough.

Another influence was when I was struggling with a college major, my mother, who was not super tuned into my psyche, had some surprising insight, "Why don't you study psychology? You've always been interested in what makes people tick." It hit me like a light bulb went off and I've never doubted it since she suggested this when I was 20. I was someone who was very disconnected earlier in my life, but I'm pretty connected now with a lot of great friends and a sense of community. I see that the big problems on this planet are problems of disconnection. No one goes to war because they feel too emotionally connected. Much of my work has focused on helping people develop greater connectedness within themselves and in relation to others.

Where were you an undergraduate and graduate student? Boston University undergraduate and I got my master's at JFK University and my Ph.D. at California Institute of Integral Studies where I ended up doing a little teaching and was on the board of directors for a while.

Why did you leave the East Coast for California? It was the dream, California dreaming. I met a California hippie when I was living in Boston and he told me lots of stories about San Francisco. There was always a part of me that dreamed of going to California. After graduation, I got in my car and drove 14,000 miles over four months, arriving in San Francisco in the summer of 1977.

How has your initial lack of connection affected your marriage--you've been married a long time? I think about my father and his profound verbal abuse of my mother which I witnessed daily and relentlessly. Clearly, my parents were not well connected. Although I was never as unkind as my father, I still carried some of the defensiveness I witnessed in him. Not surprisingly, early in our relationship with my wife, I'd be nasty and critical. Fortunately, I didn't marry someone who I could run over. She was and is quite formidable. Unconsciously, I looked for someone who could stand up to me, particularly when I was behaving poorly. Shall we say, she gave me lots of feedback.

Also, I've done a lot of therapy as a client and, aside from leading men's groups for 38 years, have been in one for 34 years. I've listened to feedback I've received from various people; for example, that I could be sarcastic and mean-spirited when I thought I was simply being funny. I'm someone who's learned from feedback and that involves connection and trusting people. That's a lot of what my work with people is about, even my work in organizations; you don't have to be a jerk to do well.

Now that he's 32, what did you learn from being a father about how to raise a boy with options? He went to a Waldorf-inspired school, which is about the imagination. He grew up in a very different environment than I did so without much of a focus around gender. My wife would play more of the male role because she was the one who did more discipline and she was dealing more with finances, so he didn't grow up with those kinds of gendered beliefs. He's married and treats his wife very well.

When you work with couples in your private practice, what issues do they come to you with and why is it that women initiate more of the divorces? Yes, usually it is women who initiate coming to couple's counseling in the first place. Understandably, women eventually get tired of asking for something and not having an empathetic reaction. They are more likely to take action and to reach out for a therapist. So, if I ask a man and woman how they see the relationship on a scale of zero being terrible and ten being awesome, usually women will scale it about three or four points lower than men. Women often feel like guys don't listen.

It seems like one of the things women are most angry about is sharing family work because studies show that when they're both employed, she still does a lot more childcare and housework. A Lean In survey in 2021 found employed women are five times more likely to be responsible for most or all of the childcare and housework, so 42% of women said they're burned out, compared to 35% of men.[117] *How does one resolve that dilemma?* It's often sadly through the threat, *I'm going to leave you if you don't shape up.* Yes, and there are a lot of guys who are doing much more household work and doing more childcare. *They're doing more than their dads for sure.* Yes, I think it's important to note that there are changes and celebrate at least the small successes. There tends to be a threat reactivity in relationships because couples may not see themselves as allies all the time. *Psychologist Sue Johnson's attachment therapy finds often the woman pushes for more intimacy, he backs off, and she pushes harder in a downward spiral.*

I think about the metaphor of the ping-pong table with the balls being behaviors like you didn't pick up your clothes, you didn't pick the kid up on time. . . you didn't, you didn't, you didn't. What we don't talk about are the bowling balls underneath the table slamming up against the ankles, symbolizing the invisible self-concept issues. We argue about the ping pong balls of behavior when it's the bowling balls of beliefs that cause the greatest emotional damage. For example, the fact that I've asked you to do dishes and you don't do it is triggering a belief that I don't matter, that I'm insignificant or I'm not lovable. It doesn't mean that I don't want you to do the dishes; it's just that the emotional reactivity relates to larger issues.

Generally, these self-concept issues are unconscious; like the water to the fish, these beliefs are invisible. It means that the added charge to the emotional reactivity is fueled by these unconscious beliefs about ourselves, like the bowling balls activating the ping-pong balls. Part of the work is to become aware of your triggers and why is that so painful to you? Getting to a deeper level tends to evoke much more compassion than reactivity, so I like to emphasize that awareness. Also, what is true partnership? My wife (a therapist) and I wrote *Lovers For Life* in the late '90s. I had to challenge a belief in myself about the male dominator paradigm. I had to learn to shift that paradigm to see what's getting in the way of what I want in my marriage. A lot of times couples bicker about the ping-pong balls, but the real issue is the bowling balls. The acronym WAIT (Why Am I Talking) can be helpful here. I've suggested to a lot of clients that they let go of the small stuff. That certainly wasn't my go-to position. I used to really believe in total candor and transparency, but I've come to ask, is it worth it? It's part of my mindfulness practice, to let go of perfection or having things be exactly as I want them to be and accept things as they are.

On the other hand, if you gunny sack then the last straw happens and the person explodes. The partner asks, "Why are you so upset over one wet towel on the floor?" So a balance is necessary. Absolutely, we all have our own individual fates that we must work with in terms of how we turn them into our destinies. From a mindfulness perspective, I can recognize how easy it is to react. Am I in a very chill place or super-reactive part of me? I'm a strong believer that we are complex beings, divided in certain ways, and the more we can step back and say, "That's a part of me" and I can look at my wife and recognize, "That's part of her." How can I bring out more of this part of her that I enjoy rather than blame her for being different from what I want? *Yes, Hal and Sidra Stone's Voice Dialogue work teaches that I need to be aware of what part of you is speaking now and what part of me is up. If I know if it's your adult, your child, your inner critic, or your judge, I can react accordingly.*

You are president of the APA's men and masculinities division. What issues are Division 51 and its journal The Psychological Study of Men and Masculinities *currently exploring?* We explore ways to help males expand beyond old, archaic beliefs about how males should be. As males, we can be kind and direct, compassionate and decisive, rational and emotional. In other words, we aim to help males become full, prosocial human beings.

We're very guided by overcoming racism, sexism, and generally lifting people up who have been pushed down. The woman who was president in 2020, Wizdom Powell is an African-American woman whose presidential initiative was lifting up boys and men of color and overcoming their health disparities. We're looking at different research such as what happens with Asian-American men when they're seen as less "masculine." To learn more, I highly recommend our journal, and our website (https://www.division51.net).

Regarding Farrell's The Boy Crisis *book, I don't think they'd find anything to disagree with.* The major disagreement is the major conclusion that "It's father deprivation that's leading to the boy crisis," while that's not a universally accepted conclusion at all. (*Feminist Michael Kimmel discussed his view of the boy crisis in a TED talk and there's a Facebook page about the crisis.*[118]) *Do you agree that fathers are the main problem or not?* I don't know enough, but I think that research can be very murky. We know that there is a replication crisis in social sciences, where you can have two different research teams doing the same experimental design and getting different results. *It's a problem that needs to be addressed because of the high divorce rate and men's long hours at work and lacking examples of how to be a nurturing father.* I agree because we need to find ways to work together.

How are psychologists addressing the boy crisis, raising boys who have more options? Niobe Way's research found boys are super vulnerable and relational when they're younger and then they wind up giving that up as adolescents. We have a Boys' Task Force focusing on how boys are falling behind in education and creating fact sheets about this. There are some biological differences, although that's going to be sacrosanct in my division sometimes, saying that anything is biological. *Fluidity versus essentialism.* There are some differences and I think we need to account for them. If you think about boys not learning about relational skills and being in school in where you're supposed to sit there with your hands folded, not getting to exert some of your kinetic energy, there can be problems right off the bat, although a lot of schools are cutting back on physical education these days.

How does the Men's Studies Journal *compare with the APA journal?* They tend to be a little more academic and much more about teaching gender studies in universities. *What's happening with Men's Studies?* Generally, I see an ongoing curiosity about gender and gender fluidity. I've had two clients whose children have had sex changes. We're living in a very different time and it's causing all kinds of political reactivity. It even connects with mask-wearing and vaccine-taking.

On the APA site, you wrote, "We are still at the very beginning of constructing a new psychology of men, there's an uphill struggle of changing masculinity, we need to expand to men of color, different cultures men with different disabilities, GLBT." Could you say a word about a new psychology of men? The division used to be called, "The Society for The Psychological Study of Men And Masculinity" (singular) and it was changed in 2017 to "Masculinities" (plural). That is a huge difference right there, designating there's no one way to be masculine, including being gender fluid. I would like that to be the case rather than the ideal of brave, stoic, individualistic, tough, "take no prisoners" masculinity.

Falling short triggers shame, hiding, unworthiness, and feeling unlovable and incompetent. There's a little boy in every man who wants more affection, connection, and care. If you happen to have the physique, the voice, and whatever characteristics deemed more traditionally masculine, it can put you in a bigger "man box" if inside you're very different. It's a trap for everyone and it's a box that we need to escape.

What I hear from young men is that women like nice guys for friends but they're attracted to tough guys. Absolutely, but I also think that some guys can be nice guys defensively, appeasing, placating, "Are you okay? Can I help you out?" that frankly isn't that attractive. A lot of young people are looking at the difficulties in the world and wondering if they want to bring children into this world and what can they count on? They are the first generation in American history in the last 150 years that have it worse off than the generation before. They're not making as much money in general, they're in debt, and there's climate change; so what do they have to look forward to? What can they trust? They feel anger toward Boomers and despair at the heart of it all. Making hookups here and there or not deeply connecting is understandable, at the same time a lot of Gen X and Millennials are really interested in connecting in relationships.

Your emphasis in your work is on teaching resilience and how to thrive. You and your wife developed a resilience program for NASA. What are some of the core concepts about how to thrive? The first one is, start where you are, as Buddhist teacher Pema Chadron reminds us. Ernest Hemingway stated, "Life breaks us all; some of us become strong in the broken places." We talk about post-traumatic growth. Fate is the hand you're dealt like a car accident, but how do you play that hand? Do you go into a cave? That doesn't mean jumping into action;

the first step is, start where you are. All resilience begins with some type of disruptive unwanted change; as John Lennon said, "Life is what happens when you're busy making other plans."

When you think about resilience through the lens of male psychology, when you're handed a fate that you're not supposed to reveal pain or cry, how do you move through grief, which is really at the core of resilience? Tears contain cortisol, a stress hormone, so crying is one of nature's ways of de-stressing us. A lot of guys haven't cried in decades, which is inhuman but part of the masculinity standard.

Questions to ask after a challenge are: What and who are my resources? Where do I want to get from here? What resources do I have within myself? How do I develop my resources to be able to mitigate and metabolize life stressors and how do I turn my particular fate into a positive destiny? One of the best ways to grow is to give, although at those times when we feel resource depletion it seems a bit paradoxical to give. When you share things with others, you get stronger through the power of care and connection.

Part of resilience is also around self-compassion because a lot of people are wired to be self-critical. If you think about a zebra being chased by a lion and it gets away, then what does it do? *It shakes off the stress physiologically.* But what do human beings do when they get away from the metaphorical lion? Most tend to find countless ways to criticize themselves. There's a lot of research about self-compassion as a major antidote to self-criticism; for starters, to be kind to yourself and to others. We can ask, "How can I develop a growth mindset from this experience," which is certainly at the core of thriving. As my friend, Rick Hansen, would say, "Turn positive states into positive traits." *To me, that's the key so when I make a mistake I ask what can I learn from this and do differently next time?*

Teens in the western world increasingly present with anxiety and depression, especially girls. Why? Social media for sure. We know that from the research that people who spend more time on Facebook tend to be more depressed and more anxious. I've thought about why that would be the case. We post a nicely curated images of ourselves but we view it through our shadow self, which triggers natural jealousy, feeling less than. Negative social comparison can trigger anxiety and depression. Not to mention some of the bullying that goes on, so the fear of being exposed triggers an ongoing anxiety in a lot of younger people. Boys tend to have more acting-out behaviors that would not be designated in a DSM-5(R), such as guys tend to drink more, drive faster, do more dangerous things, have more physical accidents, rather traditional ways that depression and anxiety have been understood. *Some say boys are not as affected by social media because they're doing the video games or they're not as judged by their appearance.* I'm sure there's truth to that.

Rats who are given even (predictable) shocks are significantly less neurotic than rats that are given uneven shocks. Part of what the brain does is prediction, particularly around pleasure and pain, i.e., threats to survival. If you're constantly checking what's happening right now on your social media, should we be surprised?

What's happening in the men's movements today? The major three areas are mythopoetic, (Robert Bly, Michael Mead, James Hillman) and the feminist men's movement that's the undergirding of my APA division. The Men's Rights tends to be more around men's legal and legislative rights. There are a lot of support groups, you could say that were feminist-inspired.

The counseling organizations, like EVRYMAN and ManKind Project, see themselves as coming out of the mythopoetic movement, so maybe you could say that mythopoetic is the biggest branch? I've been involved with feminist-oriented and mythopoetic but don't know how I would ever define myself, frankly. I've been leading weekly interpersonal men's groups for 38 years, but when I look at these groups, I don't say they're mythopoetic, or feminist *per se*. I don't even know what that means anymore. We have to deeply define our terms because even in feminism there are four waves of feminism and a lot of feminists disagree with each other.

I'm a supporter of feminism but at the same time, when I hear that guys need to get in touch with their feminine side, I think that's bad branding. As a very emotional man who can cry quite easily, I never think that I'm getting in touch with my feminine side when I feel emotional. I also don't think when women are being assertive or even aggressive that they're in touch with their masculine sides. Ideally, we can get over genderizing the whole gamut of human emotions and experiences as male or female.

How have those groups that you've been running for over 37 years changed? The theme of getting in touch with their masculine or feminine sides still isn't central to my groups. It's ironic in that all this stuff about the importance of gender may not be the most relevant aspect of life. If you get down to what people really want, they want to feel safe, some satisfaction in life, and to feel connected.

Anything else that you would like people to think about in terms of men's changing roles? Don't give up on guys, don't give up on women, especially since there's a lot of pessimism in the world and a lot of hopelessness. I get disheartened at times, but I think about the Japanese saying, "Fall down seven times, stand up eight," which is what resilience is about. How can I keep seeing the best in people but not be naïve and stupid, being as respectful and pro-social as possible even in the midst of intense negative reactions. As John Milton said, "The mind is his own place and in itself can create a heaven of hell or a hell of heaven." I will end with the words of Zen Teacher Suzuki Roshi who said, "You're perfect and you could use some improvement."

Tristan Glosby
Gen Z Artist

I was born in Guam in September 1999, because my dad was in the Navy. *I think of Virgos as loving, talkative, and sensitive; does that apply to you?* I'm not very talkative but the other ones generally apply. I was in Guam for about two years and then we moved to San Diego, then to Monterrey, then back to San Diego. I went to high school in northern Virginia. *Monterey is a language school, was your dad studying*

Mandarin? Yes, he's currently working in Laos. My mom and dad got divorced when I was 11.

Warren Farrell's book The Boy Crisis *says that boys are not doing as well as girls in terms of education or mental health. He focuses on problems due to not having dads involved. How did it affect you to have your parents divorced?* I primarily was in my mom's house because my dad moved to Singapore a year and a half after they got divorced, so there was a span of five years that we lived on opposite sides of the planet. I'm not super sure how it affected me, but there was definitely a lack of father figures in my life, especially between the ages of 12 and 15. I think that definitely had a negative impact on my life, like I wasn't doing super well in school. *Did your mom remarry?* No, my mom's still single, so I had some male teachers that filled that role a little bit.

Do you have siblings? I have two younger brothers. I'm 21, the middle one is 19, and the youngest is 13. The middle one is very into cars, rebuilding the engine of his old Miata, while the youngest one is still coming into his own. He plays a lot of video games.

In your preface to Jack Kammer's book for boys, Heroes of the Blue Sky, *you wrote, "In middle school, there's really a very clear message to be a man don't. . . don't be like a girl, don't be a sissy, don't be weak, don't be vulnerable."* Don't be emotional and don't be vulnerable because those things are seen as weaknesses by a lot of men and by women. It's a very clear message starting when you're eight or ten. There's a specific point in second grade where one of my teachers ceased to treat me as a child and treated me more like a male adult, which was shocking to me. It was almost a traumatic moment of sorts in my psyche as I had a very clear memory of that happening. It was a moment of being too emotional, with the teacher saying stop crying, figure it out, and do something about it. It kind of continues to happen as you grow up.

That's something every child needs to learn at some point, that the way forward is to do something about the problem in front of you, but there's an emphasis on suppressing the emotional side, suggesting that your emotions are not productive and not going to get you anywhere. To a certain extent, I don't think that advice is wrong, since my emotions don't get me anywhere in society. *Did girls get that message to keep a stiff upper lip, don't cry, do something?* No. *So there really was a gender difference?* Absolutely.

What did you do after high school? I've gone through some college. I spent about a year after high school working with other ceramic artists in the area, doing some studio tech work at studios, loading and unloading kilns, and mixing glazes. Then I went to school in North Carolina about two years ago, which didn't pan out, but I'm still living in Asheville. The professor and I didn't have a positive relationship and she was the professor for half of my classes. *Were you majoring in studio art?* Yes, and I have applications out to other schools, so I'm looking to go back to school.

I'm an apprentice for a potter in this area so I work for him two days a week and I have a ceramic studio. I work for three other artists as well. *How did you fall in love with ceramics? Was it offered as a course in high school?* Yes, but I started making pots the summer before my sophomore year in a weekly class outside of school. By the time I was a senior, half of my high school courses were in the ceramic studio. It slowly consumed my life and still kind of does. *If someone wants to look at your creations, where can they see them?* The best place is my Facebook page "Tristan Glosby, Artist."[119]

What are you seeing in your peer groups in terms of dating practices? Do people experiment and hook up here and there but not make a commitment? In a lot of my straight friends, I see a bit more commitment. I should preface this: I'm bisexual, so I have lots of friends all over the sexuality spectrum. It's interesting because I see these gender dynamics from both sides because I'm attracted to both men and women, an interesting position to be in. I find that there's a decent amount of commitment but it's not super long-lasting--like there will be an intense amount of commitment for say six months and then it breaks off. There's not a lot of relationship building. It's like there's a lot of basic instinct attraction that wears off and fizzles out so there's not a whole lot of active partnerships being built. I don't foresee my peers getting it together and getting married. That's not something that I'd even advocate for because I don't see traditional long-term monogamy being a vast success in my generation.

Is that because you're young and that's natural or is it because values have changed? I think it's both, it's partially us being young, but I don't think that's going to change and that those values are going to hold. *Marriage rates are down, as are divorce rates, and people are getting married later. If your peers are not looking for commitment and working through personal growth issues, are they just looking to have fun?* Fun is definitely an aspect of it. I think there's a lot of blowing off steam as well since there's a lot of stress in everyday life and sex is a good outlet for that. I'm not opposed to long-term relationships but I'm not actively looking either. I accepted that I don't embody what society values in the man's role in a long-term relationship. That's okay and I don't have a problem with that.

Does that mean that you're probably not going to be a rich potter? What are other aspects of being non-traditional? I've opted to take a life path that's not going to make me very financially well off, that's for sure. I also don't want kids and I have no real desire to get married, but not because I'm opposed to commitment. I can easily see myself being with one person for the rest of my life but I don't accept the need for marriage with a religious institution or the state to stamp my relationship as official. Many people would say, "He's afraid of commitment," but I'm not.

Do you see any differences in how you behave if you're in a relationship with a man or with a woman? Courtship, for lack of a better word, or the act of wooing someone, *flirting,* exactly, seems to be more important for women. I find that relationships with men are easier in the sense that you're attracted to me and I'm attracted to you and that's clear. We don't need to let go through all of this BS to prove it to each other; we see it, and it is what it is. In relationships with women, it seems to be like there's a lot more flirting and courtship and more build-up. *Which can be fun.* Yes, it's double-edged. *What's double-edged, the work?* Yes, I don't derive more payoff from it.

Some men say that it's easier to talk to a woman about their intimate feelings or vulnerabilities than it is to a man. Do you find that or not? No, actually in the context of relationships, I find it easier to talk to a man I'm in a relationship with than a woman. *Because he understands where you're coming from?* That's part of it but, in my experience, there's a lot of judgment that comes from women when you try to express your feelings, especially when you're her partner. That's been an ever-present theme, which has turned me off from being overly expressive to female partners in my life. I think that women often underestimate how much emotional labor they generate in the context of relationships, or outside them. Men share a great bit more emotional content with one another than we get credit for. It just doesn't happen in the same ways that women share.

There's a meme that men are emotionally stubborn and underdeveloped. What I find, however, is that it's not that men are incapable of expressing their emotions within the context of relationships, it's that they choose not to as a result of past experiences. Many men in heterosexual relationships that I have talked to have said something to the effect of, "My partner has very little patience for my emotions that don't suit her needs." Men are often used as emotional receptacles for women. There is a reason why there is a stereotype where a woman walks into the home from work and immediately starts unloading all the day's happenings onto her partner. This in turn means that there is very little room for men's emotions within the context of the relationship. Men's negative emotions (*e.g.*, sadness/depression, anxiety) are often shamed heavily.

Contrary to popular belief, shaming usually doesn't come from other men. I have both experienced and have seen other men experience partners who push us to open up and then when we do, they get upset because it is not the emotion that they wanted us to have. So, we learn a lesson very early on that displaying any emotion other than the one that is expected of us is a surefire way to cause a fight. This is a self-perpetuating problem on a societal level. Men experience no advantages to expressing their emotions and as they stop doing so at a relatively young age.

As a result, many women don't have lots of experience with emotive male partners and don't know how to handle that. This in turn creates a dynamic in which the takes up all of the emotional space. This comes full circle and prevents men from feeling like the relationship is a safe space to be emotive in the first place. Even my most understanding female partners have occasionally said something to the effect of, "You need to stop being depressed because it's inconvenient to me."

Men may not be having lots of emotionally charged conversations with one and other, but when it comes to having emotionally vulnerable conversations without fear of judgment, a male friend is nearly always a better bet than a female partner. These conversations between men are not often talked about because they happen less often and less publicly than women have them; they usually never see the light of day. They are private conversations that once they're resolved, are often never talked about again. In my experience, men tend to opt not to have emotionally vulnerable conversations unless they are near a breaking point of some sort, but by the same token, most men are not apprehensive about having those conversations should they feel the need to. They just choose to be introspective when possible.

Can you think of an example where you said something to a woman and felt judged? I strongly struggle with anxiety and depression. There was a point when I was with a woman, going through a rough time, and she asked, "What's wrong? What's wrong? What's wrong?" She wanted me to tell her I was okay, kept pushing me and pushing me. I eventually told her what was happening and you could see it in her eyes, an immediate switch to, "Oh! You're no longer that stoic brick wall that I've been looking at." It was like, "You're weak." It's definitely something that's happened numerous times with different women. *The old stereotype of John Wayne that men should be stoic and always strong is alive and well.* Yes, absolutely.

Do you see any changes in the media as to how men are portrayed or do you see that the strong man image still prevails? I think it takes different forms as culture changes but I don't think it's fundamentally different. *I read about ads that showed men as jerks or dumb, like a Super Bowl ad for Doritos. A couple was at an ultrasound for the pregnant woman and the dad was just focused on eating Doritos. That's a weird juxtaposition because the bumbling idiot man is somehow supposed to be competent, strong, and be the problem solver. That's very confusing.* Yes, absolutely.

So, you feel more comfortable with men because they don't impose that macho image on you? I think they generally impose it on me less. I've made the conscious decision that I'm going to be who I'm going to be. I make a conscious effort to not bend to the pressures that society puts on me. I'm going to be who I'm going to be and be comfortable with that. *What pressures do you feel subtly coming at you besides breadwinner, money maker?* Moneymaker is a big one, not even because of providing for a family, although that'd definitely be part of it. But it's this attitude that if you're not upwardly mobile as a man you're a failure. If you're stagnant, you're a failure, not providing value to society.

As a bi-man, often I'll be flirting with a woman having a fine time until she finds out that I'm bi. It's not something that I try to hide and they're immediately turned off. They go, "You're gay?" No, but the perception is like if you're not purely obsessed with women and you are also attracted to men then you must be gay. *So it's not just sexism that's still alive, homophobia is still alive.* Yes, absolutely, but it's not generic homophobia that you normally see. It's only specific to bi-men and how they interact with straight women. A wonderful study was done by Neil Gleason on perceptions of dating and having sex with bisexual people.[120] He found straight women on average find the same man less attractive if they think he is bi, while straight men (and gay men) did not find bi people (men or women) more or less attractive on average than their straight counterparts.

Increasing numbers of US teens are gender questioning, gay, trans, thinking about what pronouns to use, etc. Why are so many young people questioning their gender? Funny enough, this is going to sound like an oxymoron, but I think it's two things simultaneously and they're polar opposites. On one hand, the door has been opened so there is a little more room (especially within peer groups) to explore that sort of thing. Also, there is a lot of pressure to be the idealized version of men and women. A lot of people see those stereotypes and those pressures and try to find a way to escape them. If you identify as queer, although you mainly identify as male within broader society, it's a way of sidestepping all of those pressures that are placed upon men and women because you're no longer squarely in that box.

At the same time, there's an increase (I'm not suggesting they have anything to do with each other) in anxiety and depression in young people, especially with girls. I wonder if that's simply because boys aren't given permission to say they're anxious and depressed because, as you say, it's seen as a weakness. I think young people, in general, are stuck in this analysis paralysis of sorts from having an over-abundance of options about what they're going to do with their lives. In terms of what's expected of them, it's stressful. What I saw a lot in high school is the only thing that matters is your GPA, how many AP classes you're taking, and what college you're getting into. It's like if you don't have a 4.2 GPA, you're a failure. *It's a lot of pressure and I agree it's a major cause of anxiety.*

There's an increased emphasis on going to college but one of the things that happens when everyone goes to college is the value of a college degree goes down--a shocker. *But people with degrees do earn more on average.* You end up with lots of people who have been incredibly stressed for their entire lives, and then they go to a college to do, let's say pre-med, and end up with a $100,000 and more student loan debt. So you have this intense need to do well in order to be the most successful, in order to get to the next best place, and eventually, that drops off because there is no next best place. It's just the real world and that leaves a lot of people wondering what to do.

Academics like Jean Twenge say there's more anxiety and depression because of social media, but I think the main reason for anxiety is people are pressured to get into a good college. But, you know you're going to have a huge debt and have to have a good job to pay it back. There are more people now, but not more high-level universities, so there's more competition. It's broadly more difficult to be successful in today's world. It seems as if, in order to get to a place that is comfortable, there's a lot more work involved than what my grandfather did. That's not to say that my grandfather didn't work hard but he didn't graduate from high school, so there's certainly a difference there.

You went to Washington, DC to see The Red Pill *documentary about the men's rights movement. Why did you want to see it and what are your thoughts about the different branches of the men's movement?* I was 17, in my senior year of high school. I'm part of the Men's Brand subreddit and found out online. I was interested in gender and how it interacts in society, but not especially in a men's movement. I've always been a little bit of a nerd, like in 10th grade I was reading psychology papers on my phone during chemistry class. I always go deep into a rabbit hole and read all that I can on something.

I had gone on some deep radical dive when I found some random YouTuber and wondered, "Who's this person?" I was interested in seeing *The Red Pill* because I wanted to see how someone who wasn't associated with the men's movement would portray it because I've seen a lot of character assassinations of people within that movement over the years. I was curious to see how that documentary portrayed the men's movement, which has its productive spaces and has its unproductive ones.

Is a particular branch of most interest to you? I don't actively follow any of it, just casually glance over it sometimes. I don't think the mythopoetic aspect is all that productive, but by that same token, I'm also a proponent of people doing whatever works for them as long as it doesn't hurt anyone else. I tend to lean towards the father's rights camp; it's definitely something that I followed for a long period of time and still tend to follow a little bit. Also, I'm interested in a specific genre that advocates for male bodily autonomy (anti-circumcision, the push for male birth control, etc.)

Did your father have to struggle with custody? My father said to my mother that he wanted custody but wasn't going to fight her for it. *Do you wish that he had fought?* No, I think it would have been ugly and the results would have been the same. *Sometimes in single mom households the oldest son ends up being the substitute dad figure. Did that happen with you?* Yes, to a certain extent.

Was that a burden or was that something you were willing to take on? It was definitely a burden; it was not something I would have had imposed on me at that age. I was often a babysitter although not the disciplinarian. There was a phrase that people would often say to me that always stuck with me that you shouldn't be saying to a 12-year-old. Whenever you get to a family gathering or something like that, as we were leaving someone would always say, "Take care of your mother." *My son heard that too and also heard, "Big boys don't cry."*

In terms of anxiety and depression, studies show that meditation and exercise are the best remedies. What have you found that helps you cope? I do meditate and find it helpful.

I'm not in a position right now where I can easily exercise as far as the space around me but I do find it to be helpful. I also have been on antidepressants and at various points in my life they were helpful. *If you were talking to a 13-year-old boy who told you, "I'm really anxious, I'm depressed" what would you suggest to him?* It's a good question and a hard one because at that age you don't have a whole lot of control so anxiety oftentimes is justified. I know that as a 13-year-old I was an incredibly anxious individual and that's not something that has remedied itself well to this day. It's not something that really rounded up in any meaningful fashion until I was a little older and had a little more control in my life.

Do you think the anxiety had anything to do with the divorce? That was definitely part of it, but pressure to do well in school, generally, was more significantly stressful for me. I also had ADHD so I didn't do super well in a classroom environment and so from sixth grade to graduating, it was a roller coaster. I would sometimes be doing okay and sometimes not, but it wasn't because I didn't understand the material, it was just I wasn't suited to a school environment. *Some kids with ADHD turn to video games, which supposedly make their dopamine go up as a remedy. Were video games part of your coping?* Yes, definitely. I don't game as much as I used to but it was definitely a significant part of my high school experience.

Your dad was in the military with its distinct notion of masculinity, honor, strength, and duty; did he convey those definitions of masculinity to you? No, my dad was actually very flexible and understanding. From the time I was little, he told me to do what makes me happy and that he will be happy so long as I'm happy, so I've been fortunate to have that. *Have you visited him in Laos?* Yes, it's really hot and humid but it's absolutely beautiful. I spent about a week there and did a bunch of other traveling on that trip before I moved to Asheville. I went to New Zealand, Australia, Singapore, and Laos.

I want to go back to boys and education, since around the world except for sub-Saharan Africa, more girls graduate from university. Why do you think that's happening? It probably has something to do with the fact that women over the last 20 to 30 years have had more encouragement and assistance in going to university. *In your high school did girls get more support and encouragement to excel?* They certainly got more time from teachers and were generally praised more for their positive work and chastised less for their outbursts. *It used to be that there was more dialogue and interaction and encouragement for boys but that's not your observation when you were in high school?* No.

If you think about your grandfather and your father, would you say there have been big changes in what it is to be a man or not? I don't think stereotypes have changed massively in terms of what society expects of you as a man. A change is that my grandfather was a successful businessman and he didn't go to school past the age of 12. That was a viable path for him to become successful, while if I had left school at the age of 12, there's no way that was going to happen. So there's more pressure in the sense that it is more difficult to achieve the same goals but I don't think that the goals are different. *That leads to the depression and anxiety?* Yes, absolutely.

Do you see anything changing with your little brother? I don't think too much will change, except things may get more polarized. I find that in my social circles, men and women generally do not get along. I find that in people of my age, men generally associate with other men and women generally associate with other women. Like they love each other but they don't like each other. *So the opposite sex is just for sex?* Right, and I think that's part of the whole promiscuity thing, the lack of desire to be in a long-term relationship with the opposite sex. because I think that men and women often generalize about each other's tendencies in a negative way. *So they say men are jerks and women are bitches?* Something along those lines.

A lot of that breaks down into fundamental differences in communication styles. People don't want to do the work that comes with communicating with someone who doesn't communicate in the same ways that you do. I think we have definitely seen that people around my age stick to their own gender more often than not. I generally find that women tend to be more verbal but less direct while men tend to be more direct but also less verbal. I'll often watch a couple in my friend group and the woman will be hinting at something, trying to get him to something, non-stop for hours on end. She finally gets upset but she didn't verbalize the thing that she wanted and that happens a lot.

I interviewed a mom who has two boys and two girls and she said with the teenage boys, they would mostly grunt yes, no, and then tune her out. If I was doing something in my room and my mother was trying to get me to do something, I would probably get distracted before she finished two paragraphs. You're going to lose them if you don't do it succinctly. *What I hear from couples of any age is the moment the wife says, "How is your day?" he says fine or not good, while she goes through a narrative of all the emotional interactions and exchanges.* Yes, absolutely. I've definitely had that in my own relationships. *It's like the John Gray approach that men are from Mars and women are from Venus. But we're human beings who should be able to talk to each other.* Yes.

Benjamin Kaveladze
Psych Grad Student

I was born in New York City, June 1996. *Do you feel like a Gemini with multiple interests and personalities, and communicative?* I do feel that; I was sort of raised by my grandma, hearing a lot about astrological science. She pounded it into me; although to be honest, I don't really buy into it from a logical perspective. I do see the value in thinking about yourself in different ways and seeing where that takes you.

How did you get from New York to our alma mater UC Berkeley? My family and I moved when I was seven to Los Angeles where I went to community college for a year and then transferred into Berkeley. I wasn't a very impressive candidate out of high school, so I didn't get into any of the colleges that I wanted to go to. In community college, I gained a different appreciation for learning in a college setting and became a much better student, so I ended up having a pretty solid application as a transfer. I had a bunch of AP credits and I took a bunch of units in my year at a community college so I was able to enter as a junior.

Did you major in psych? Yes, I've been into psychology for a really long time. I was 14 years old when I read some of Sigmund Freud's introductory lectures about psychoanalysis and from then on I was really into it. My mom had some books she shared with me and my grandma also had a bunch of cassette tapes on old psychological theories and I would listen to those a bunch. *May I ask what professions your parents were in and did that influence you?* My mom's a psychiatrist so that's definitely an influence. My dad is a businessman. *Did your mom psychoanalyze you when you were growing up?* She didn't strike me as having a psychoanalytic perspective; she seemed a normal person to me, being in the moment and a passionate strong-willed individual.

Do you have siblings? Yes, a big brother and a little sister. *The stereotype is that the middle children are peacemakers and sometimes don't get as much attention from their parents.* I'm a little bit quieter at home than my siblings who are both very expressive people.

High school is the time when young people are most segregated; like during lunchtime, you can see the jocks, the cheerleaders, the preppies, the nerds, and this ethnic group is here and that one there. Was it like that in your high school? My friend group in high school didn't necessarily fit into any of those categories; we were not socially terrible or terribly skilled in athletics or terribly smart, but sort of smart. *Did you have boys and girls as friends?* In high school, I didn't, but in college, my best friend all throughout was a woman.

Tristan Glosby said when he was in middle school there were really strong injunctions to "be a man" which means don't be like a girl. I recently heard a father say, "toughen up" to a crying nine-year-old boy.* Middle school is a period where you learn in an intense and painful way about all of those norms, but through high school, the intensity of those roles loosens. In college, especially in Berkeley, that's not even a concern. Certainly, middle school is a time where I felt I had to change myself a lot to meet those kinds of standards of a man. It's a general toughness and engaging in the competition for hierarchy with other boys in the class and that sort of continues.

That's one of the differences between friendships between two males and between a male and a female. If you have a friend of the opposite gender, there's less of that jockeying for position, whereas, with a male friend, I have to be sensitive that I'm not stepping on his ego and there's a constant battle for who is the head of this relationship. *The linguist Deborah Tannen found that girls tell each other secrets, while boys jockey for dominance hierarchies and share how-to information. So, in romantic relationships, the girl is used to telling secrets and the guy is used to solving problems; it takes a while to harmonize that. Do you think that's still true?*

In my core group of close friends, maybe we're weird, but all we did in high school was sit in a parking lot and talk in my friend's car. We mostly talked about our feelings or hopes-- emotion-focused discussions. I think that concept of gender differences is changing unless we were outliers and most men are still talking about those things. *An interesting study would be what do teenagers talk about in same-sex groups today.*

Girls talk to me about "drama," which I think means who is talking about who behind who's back and romances. Perhaps boys don't get involved in drama the same way because they're not as interested in emotional nuances. Seeing my sister growing up, the amount of interpersonal conflict within those girl groups is nuts, it's a constant turmoil for the entire period of adolescence. *The turmoil is we're five friends but now it's these two against these three or this one's left out. Is that the conflict?* Exactly.

Now that you're in graduate school with people in their mid-20s, what do you find in terms of how men and women graduate students relate to each other? I feel gender is playing less of a role than it has in other times in my life because everybody has such similar interests. I don't really think about gender much when I'm interacting with different members of my cohort or in my classes. *What about hanging out to get coffee after a class?* I would have similar conversations with any of them because we are on the same page about what is acceptable and not acceptable to talk about. It changed a lot in grad school.

It seems like dating is almost an old-fashioned concept now, as people hook up casually or go out in groups. No, people still date for sure. It's definitely a thing in a lot of college campuses where people are interested in monogamous relationships. I feel a lot of people are passively looking to see if one of these people they hook up with could turn into a relationship. That's how a lot of relationships start. People might meet on a dating app and think that it's something casual until it blossoms into something different.

What are your pronouns and what do you think of that identification? My pronouns are he, him. It's interesting that that has changed in the past few years as there's a whole different way of looking at gender. I think it's a cool thing that people are being applauded or are encouraged to express different parts of themselves that they would want to hide in the past.

What are you finding in your research of adolescent support communities online? I did one study where I surveyed people from different mental health support communities online--many are teenagers. I asked people to indicate their genders and there were a fair amount of people who were gender questioning or didn't identify as cisgender. They are a unique population of people who seek mental health support online, so it's certainly not representative of the general population.

I wonder if it's part of a typical adolescent rebellion? The adolescent's job is to question the roles imposed on them to create their own identity. Gender questioning is a phenomenon but I also think that there were a lot of forces in the past that are not as strong now so people can try out expressing different parts of themselves. For example, the stereotypes about transgender people in the past were really severe and harsh.

I'm thinking about decades-long traditions of popular singers like Boy George who present as feminine, which gives men permission to wear makeup, high heels, and jewelry, etc. Yes, that's part of that cultural trend of more acceptance of different ways of presenting. *What I find that distinguishes Generation Y and your Generation Z is they're comfortable with diversity and don't care what your color is or your gender or your ethnicity.* I think that it's impossible to not care about those aspects of people, however, we at least try hard not to let that influence our perception of people. We're trying to build a world in which people feel they have equal opportunities to live full lives despite various backgrounds.

The men's movement makes the case that young men are disadvantaged, less likely to graduate from university around the world, more likely to commit suicide, more likely to die earlier than women. Do you agree with that analysis or not? That's a really bold claim. I think my initial reaction is that that is a ridiculous claim given the history of patriarchy in the world. Maybe there's some truth to it as we move into a more modern world when some of the things that were advantageous for men historically, like physical strength, are becoming less and less advantageous. But at this current time to say that men are disadvantaged in society seems a stretch. *Men run the corporations and the governments and they're the billionaires.*

Do you have any ideas about why women are more likely to graduate from university? I'm sort of stumped, but maybe there are certain male jobs that don't require a college degree. What have you heard about it? *Tristan Glosby, age 21, said that girls got more support and encouragement throughout secondary school. Studies used to show that a girl would say something in class and the teacher would say "uh-huh" and the boy would say something and the teacher would say, "Tell me more about why you made that conclusion." But his experience was that the teachers were more supportive of the girls.* I haven't noticed that gender difference but I believe him. As a psych major in my undergrad, I was usually one of five males in a class of about 50. *UCB and UCR are about even in terms of female and male undergrads.*

Adolescents report increasing rates of anxiety and depression. Professor Jean Twenge says that it's because of social media--is it? I've heard a lot of different arguments about that from researchers like Twenge and Jonathan Haidt, and podcaster Joe Logan talks about how social media is dangerous. I think at some level there are dangers of getting addicted to social media and everybody in my generation--including me--is appalled at how much time we spend scrolling through Twitter and stuff that in retrospect is not meaningful to us. Also, what Twenge reports about teenagers obsessing about what they post and having these really intense experiences watching what comes into their post and all that validation, it's certainly an emotionally salient experience. However, the evidence has not shown that social media is linked to mental health deterioration. There have been attempts to show that, but in general, the evidence is not there.

Twenge analyzes thousands of surveys of high school seniors and college freshmen and concludes that the anxiety and depression rates correlate with cell phone use and access to social media. I've seen those charts but the problem is correlation of one variable and another variable going over 10 years because there are so many variables. It's true that social media and smartphones are probably one of the greatest variables that have changed in people's lives, but studies that tested for causal associations between social media use or digital technology use and mental health have not found it. There are many interesting questions about the impact of social media that I want to research.

Dr. John Gray thinks that video games generate dopamine like heroin where you need an ever more violent, more exciting video game. As someone who grew up playing video games, that doesn't strike me as being true. I wasn't seeking out more and more intense games but there are certainly aspects of my own video game use when I was growing up that had emotional salience. I experienced that dopamine craving to get on RuneScape and crew more of these weird video games that I still enjoy. I don't know about that more intense cycle and my own interest in video games fizzled out as I found different things to get into. I don't think it was that serious for me.

Do you agree that they can be addicting? For sure, I think a lot of people are low-level addicted. People definitely are addicted to their phones. I'm addicted to getting regular exercise in some ways. So addiction may be part of the human condition at a certain level.

What other explanations can you think of as to why anxiety and depression rates have gone up, especially for girls? Maybe people are more aware about mental health issues and therefore more interested in getting help or seeking a diagnosis. *There's more pressure on young people now because it's harder to get into college, it's more expensive, and you should look good on your Instagram posts or Twitter. Pressure from every direction can be anxiety-producing.* Yes, at least for some people that is a real cause of anxiety. I certainly was stressed a lot about what is going to happen after college all throughout my college years, Now I'm not that stressed, even though I probably should be stressed about the future a bit more. I've picked up some more coping skills like doing yoga now so I don't worry as much.

Do you know your dissertation topic? I'm still second year, so I have more time to figure out exactly what I want to do. I'm thinking about an intervention for mental health that can be done in an online context, tailored to the needs of online community members. I'm working with a computer scientist to try and design an artificial intelligence system that can respond to mental health questions. The idea is that we train this system with data from actual online support communities, so we will poll a bunch of questions and responses that people post on an online community to collect a real person's response and a real person's answer. Then we'll try and train this AI system to create new responses to new questions based on what it has learned.

Have you heard of the android Sofia who has those kinds of capabilities?[121] A lot of different conversational bots or agents can have those kinds of interactions, but there are still challenges in having someone perceive that this agent is being empathetic towards you or able to provide meaningful advice. It's still not something that has been perfected, so there's a lot of room to develop. *By the way, it's interesting that androids and AI helpers like Alexa and Siri are all females, and females are seen as more human, more helpful.* At least in our evolutionary environments, most interpersonal threats of violence probably came from men. But why are women viewed as more pleasant to talk to?

What else are you finding from these online support communities? The central purpose of these communities is mostly to ask questions and get advice from other people. In some mental health communities, there's a lot of venting to express their feelings, and then people will respond and provide emotional support. They're really complex, rich dynamics in each of those different spaces. *What do you see in terms of gender usage?* In the mental health ones, the people who responded to my survey were around 60% female and

40% male. In other communities, it can be 99% male. *What are some of the male majority groups?* For more mundane topics, boxing forums or MMA forums. I used to go to a bodybuilding forum when I was a teenager, mostly males talking about man things like physical strength, women, sports, and general competition for social status.

There were a few females but it seemed sort of an abrasive experience to be a female in that space because you would get so much attention from all the other members and a lot of it was negative. They're always weird subsets of individuals who have extreme beliefs but I think the majority of gamers don't really worry about gender and are less severe. I definitely don't feel it's a general characteristic of gamers to be sexist.

Thinking about your grandfather, your father, you, your brother, do you see changes in how they think of themselves as men? I was mostly raised by my mother, and to some extent by my grandmother. I didn't have strong male influence so I don't really think about it. Nothing really stands out to me as different in the way that we present our masculinity between me or my dad or my grandparents.

Do you think of yourself as a feminist? I definitely think of myself as a feminist, defined as wanting to ensure that all people have access to opportunity, at least under the law, with some level of equal opportunity to do what they want to do.

What are your thoughts about becoming a father? I'm excited about it. I'm not really close to it since I'm single but I'm optimistic. *I wrote* 50-50 Marriage *and* 50-50 Parenting *in the '80s when, if a man was with a kid in a park, people would either think he's a deviant or how nice, he's babysitting for his wife. Now men are with little kids everywhere and people don't think it's weird.* Interesting.

What else are you observing about gender? *I have a grandson who's ten and so I hang out a lot with 10-year-olds. When he's with boys they talk about Percy Jackson novels about Greek gods and magical powers and if you had this weapon, how would you kill this other person who was after you? When I take the boys hiking, they make guns out of wood and take their weapons with them on the hikes and the girls do not.*

He has a good girl friend and one of their conversations was about setting up a café and what roles their friends would play. She decided they were engaged and going to get married--and a year later she decided they were unengaged. It was so stereotyped with the relationship discussion vs. the power hierarchy. I can think of a lot of examples of girls being into superheroes and girls being more aggressive or caring more about power in some situations. *Studies show their aggression is just more indirect.*

Meta-analyses of studies of brain differences find they're minimal, although hormones do affect behavior. Boys don't think of girls having cooties like when I was growing up and they're more comfortable being friends. Interesting, I was always confused by cooties when I was growing up; I never really bought into that. *Did you hear that the other sex had cooties?* I definitely heard that but I feel it was adults mentioning that and laughing; it always seemed absurd to me.

Jeffer Koome Kinoti
Growing Up in Rural Kenya

I was born January 30, 1992, in central Kenya. I have an elder sister, myself, and my younger sister. *Some people say middle children get kind of lost.* In our culture men and boys, in particular, are cherished while ladies and girls are cherished within a family. Being the only son and the eldest boy in our larger extended family, there was a lot of attention towards me coming from all directions.

Did your cousins live around you in an extended family? Yes, that's how people live in my community. If your grandparents have a big piece of land, the sons subdivide it among themselves. Girls are married off so there's no point in subdividing it for them. The children then have their families, so your grandparents are a stone's throw away and your uncles are across. Then the land is subdivided into very small portions. For example, if there are four or five kids in an acre, you can imagine the fraction each son will get.

How many uncles lived around you? I had three uncles. Since my school principal grandfather was the more educated one, he bought land away from where he grew up because his land was very small. He went away with two of his younger brothers and settled with their families on land big enough to subdivide among themselves. We didn't have family gatherings until we were in high school when we started knowing about them. Also, there were conflicts among the brothers, some not willing to associate with the other part of the family. However, children will always be children, so when my cousins saw us gathering and they smelled food, they came around. Time has broken the cycle of grudges of our parents and our grandparents.

What kind of games did you play as kids? There was hide and seek. I grew up in a very hilly tea-zone area with a lot of vegetation so someone could look for you for two hours. Children have a way of making other children unhappy; for example, if one child has a bold personality or doesn't have low self-esteem issues, they can make the other children who are not outspoken feel inferior and not participate in games or volunteer to lead in anything, which was common among my cousins and brought conflicts.

Duff mpararo is a game where you pour water on a hill on the farm and the boys would slide the farthest they could. It used to get us into trouble because we would have torn clothes and be very dirty when we got home. The boys used to compete using car tires cut very thin in a hoop to pedal around the farm. We also climbed trees, especially during the fruit season when we had a competition about who was going to get the most ripe fruit from the farthest branches. We would have a lot of excitement about it. Another game was *kati* where you have two people on different sides and then someone in the middle and a ball made of cloth that you throw from one end to the other. The one in the middle makes sure the ball never hits them; if it does, they switch.

Did the girls do all of that or have their separate games? There were girls who were very handy about getting into our boys' games, although there were things that girls were not supposed to do, especially the hoop game was purely for boys and girls going up the trees was taboo. Girls used to dig a small hole in the ground and get a few stones or nuts or fruits, especially the macadamia nuts which are very smooth to be able to work with. They toss and catch them, adding two or three pits per toss. *We call that jacks.*

Another girl's game around the world is two girls making designs with strings between their hands. Yes, they were making letters of the alphabet where you weave a letter like W, or R, A, or B. I remember it very well because girls would laugh at me since I couldn't weave a letter, but girls were very fast in doing it.

Did the girls have dolls? When I was growing up there were plastic dolls but they were very rare and maybe the privileged or the financially stable families would buy them from town for their daughters, but it was not something that you would expect to see. If your parents went to town, the only thing they would bring back is clothes or shoes. However, boys were known to get more toys, like small German toy cars, but nowadays dolls are everywhere.

In your family house, did the kids have to gather firewood? When I was growing up the vast majority of the community did not have electricity, only two households owned by government officials did. Now you pay around $150 to get the connection and the wiring because there is a government initiative to connect people with electricity. However, back then the cost would go as high as $1500 to have a power line brought to your house and you had to know people in high places for that to happen. I was introduced to electricity when I went to high school, so we used to use kerosene lamps, which produced a very dark smoke and weren't healthy.

What did people cook on? Purely firewood because people had trees on their farms and the Mount Kenya forest is close by and that was the time when people could get into the forest unrestricted. There was a lot of damage done because most of the indigenous trees were lost. The deforestation at the time was mainly to make poles with the hardwood trees for exportation, especially to Asian countries and South Africa. There was a lot of corruption; not that it's any better now but there was less accountability back then.

Traditionally in developing countries, girls are the ones who gather firewood and fetch water which means they have less time than boys to go to school. My grandfather was very keen for his grandchildren to go to school. He did not see any sense for the grandkids to go fetch water rather than go to school. Also, we live in a place where there's a lot of rivers, so families used pipes to get water near the houses which made it easier to fetch. In some instances, you would find two or three rivers on your farm. For firewood, girls would do it with their mothers especially over the weekend or in the evenings after school when they're helping out to prepare dinner.

I would say compared to some other parts around the country, we had it easy. You'd hear stories where girls have 10 to 15 miles to go fetch water, then prepare breakfast for the family while the boys go to graze the cows. Then she has to walk to school. However, the area is not safe for her to walk through because of cattle rustlers and bandits. For my household, the boys were tasked with feeding the cows and other farmwork. My sisters used to help out in the kitchen and bring us food in the afternoon and go back to do more house chores. It was a tea zone so you can imagine from 8:00 am you're hand-picking the tea leaves, standing the whole day. It was tough but I wouldn't compare it to some of the other areas I heard stories about.

For the outhouse, what happened when it filled up? Something that was introduced when I was around seven or ten years old is a pit latrine. Though we had one, pit latrine diggers became a booming business for people to build latrines. At the time there was a cholera outbreak so it was mandatory for each household to have one or more pit latrines, no more going to the bushes. They helped a lot and when it filled up, some families would fill it up with soil and plant a banana tree and dig another.

How far was school for you and your sisters? Not far, particularly for me and my siblings. We used to walk to school with my mum because she was a teacher at my school. As you know, boys become big-headed and I would sneak sometimes and follow other students to feel like a part of them as it looked fun walking alone without their parents. Sometimes in the morning, I would sneak out and even leave my shoes because most of the kids didn't have a pair of shoes and I felt very odd wearing them. As soon as I left the family compound, I would hide them and make sure during the day my mother wouldn't see me because there would be some explanation to do.

About how many pupils were in primary school because I hear stories of 100 kids and one teacher in a classroom. That's something very serious in our education system, all tied to corruption. The area where I grew up was considered a green zone and there were a lot of community-based projects around education, so you'd find communities wanted a school within their zone and that led to so many schools within a radius of maybe 20 km.

One thing that kept some students walking long distances to school was the school-clustering system for the best performing schools in the district or where teachers were considered to be doing well in schools. The clustering went from the local schools all the way to the national schools, therefore parents felt compelled to take their children to those high-performing schools without being mindful of whether the child would be walking longer. This is why some kids would walk past two schools to go to another one almost 10 kilometers away.

In most classes, we were between 35 to 45 pupils in primary school classes and those numbers would change with each term due to high dropout, especially for the boys and the senior girls in class Six to Eight who were married off or due to family wrangles. Most of those boys went to work in the family farms but later a government initiative mandated that every child has to get at least a high school certificate. However, there were areas in the country with 60 to 70 children in a class with one teacher. In some instances, they were makeshift classes with just the roof and pillars with no walls. These areas are prone to cattle rustling or flooding, resulting in no school for the next two or three weeks.

In some areas, you find a teacher combining a number of classes, for example, Class One and Class Two. The principals posted there by the government will tell you they are working with what they have. It was very messy until at some point it was addressed through community initiatives or government intervention in some cases, but for some students, their future was lost.

I visited a rural school in Tanzania with no glass in the windows and just a blackboard with no books. They sat three or four kids on a bench (photos are on my global youth webpage). Where I grew up, Catholic missionaries were very big and a lot of them brought books and simple basic classroom utilities, so sometimes you'd get free storybooks. When it came to textbooks, parents bought them, so you'd find a book shared between four to five kids. Each school would get a number of books for each class, and it was up to the school principal and the teachers to rearrange the timetable for various classes to allow the rotation of the books. After every lesson, the books were collected and taken to the staff room, so there were a lot of problems in getting quality education as you only had what you wrote down during the lesson.

Secondary school was a bit different in that students were asked to buy books as a mandatory way of getting admission, because there were not many day secondary schools back then as most of the schools were full-board. Part of the admission on your admission letter was to provide those particular books. They're left within the school system and therefore, after a few years of accumulation, you would find there was a good number to go around.

Did your family have to pay for primary school fees as well? Yes, education was paid for 100% by the parents with no government supplements. If you can't afford to pay, you're expelled so there was a lot of trauma among kids. Some students' lives were ruined because their parents were unable to pay the fees. During lunch break, some students would ask you to share your lunch with them, but back then kids were so used to problems that staying hungry during the day wasn't a big deal.

Education is considered free now, according to the government, but there are hidden costs like some schools have shady projects that they force parents to contribute to them. Parents complain as to why they are charged close to $100 extra when you're told education is free. To arm-twist parents to give in, in some instances schools will withdraw some services or privileges the students were enjoying in order to force parents to contribute.

Do you still have to pass an exam to get into high school and is high school free now? Yes, there is an exam to get into high school but the government is subsidizing school fees now. The government wants a 100% transition from primary school to high school to increase the literacy levels. They have increased the number of tests in the new curriculum introduced in the last two years. Previously you did the exam in class 8 and got a pass-mark which determined which school you will be posted to, regardless of your choice. That system of school placement was also very unfair to kids.

In high school, you also have to do the Form Four Exam with a grading system that gives you the opportunity to join a public university from a particular cut line of either a C+ or a B-. *So if you get a C+ on the test you can go to university?* Yes, you are actually among the students who can get into government-sponsored programs. Anyone can get into university and you can start from a parallel program as a private student and still graduate but if you have a C+ and above you can be enrolled in a course--not necessarily what you choose.

What's the percentage of males and females who go to university? The new push to have most students get to high school has really evened the numbers. Previously it was dominantly boys who were the majority in college and university. Before, parents were struggling to raise school fees for high school which was full board but going to the next level of education is almost even right now. A lot of chartered universities have come up to take in the government-sponsored students. Before there were about five universities in the whole country now we have close to, if not more than, 60.[122]

Polytechnics have been chartered to take up degree programs and each community is supposed to have a university, which has increased the number of girls accessing higher education in some communities. However, getting to university is easier nowadays, but the course or career path you will major in is up to the government to determine in most cases. There was a time when the government was accused of arm-twisting students to study to become extension officers or field officers.

You can imagine if you have an A- and you expect to get into a very good course of your choice, but you get an invitation letter to a university you don't even know existed, to a course you have no idea what it is about. To make it to the course you wanted to study, you have to apply as a private student and not a government-sponsored student. This will require you to pay close to KSH 80,000 (equivalent to $800) a trimester to attend the course of your choice. Things are changing now when there are so many courses, but you are still not sure which course you'll be selected to join.

I was selected to study a bachelor's degree in something I didn't like and hadn't heard of, which didn't sit well with me. Students get depressed over this but I was very lucky my parents self-sponsored me to pursue IT. Watching movies and shows from our small TV added to my desire to try to understand the mystery behind them. *But it's been very hard for you to find an IT job.* It's very difficult. The job market itself can't absorb the many students graduating so as a graduate you are hungry and can't even meet your basics, so you get into whatever job is available. Companies looking for employees want experienced people so most students end up taking up different career paths. In Kenya right now there's a lot of unemployment. It's crazy, especially for the last ten years, with the highest numbers of seriously educated people but no jobs.

Did your sisters go to university and what did they study? My elder sister did accounting. She started in banking and was very lucky because many banks were coming up and they needed clerks and accountants. Later on, there were issues with retrenchments and financial crisis in banks which forced her into tourism and that's where she has been since then. My younger sister studied something to do with health but now she's a businesswoman.

Going back to your boyhood, Jomo Kenyatta wrote in Facing Mount Kenya *that youth age groups were guided by the adults who initiated teens into adulthood.* I wouldn't say that most of it now has been eroded, but it was at its peak when I was growing up when I saw the best and the worst of it. You are told this initiation is part of who you are and your identity. You're made to subscribe to it through fear because people who are older than you have gone through this doctrine that I find crazy now and very backward. It's very hard for you as a 10 to 14-year-old to fight them. I don't know where you could have gotten the energy to say this is wrong and I'm not going through with it. I feel that part of me was taken away during the initiation period.

Growing up I was that kid who could have a father-son conversation and even with my mum and my sisters. However, in this stage of initiation, you are introduced to another side of the universe of people who don't subscribe to whatever you thought was sane when you're growing up. Part of the initiation, especially where I came from, was so hardcore that some of the children would die during the process, or some of them would get crippled due to punishments and radicalism.

There was beating after circumcision to the extent some kids died or were injured. You were taken away for up to a month where circumcision took place and you're being indoctrinated on how to be a man, pulling down all the walls of what you believed and knew from a small boy. *Like you shouldn't talk with women?* Yes, and the ladies include your mum and that's the worst part of it because growing up, I could talk to my mum and ask her anything. Although she punished me once in a while, I knew it was because I made a mistake, but there was love that came from a mother so you forgot everything else.

We were told you can't share a seat with your mum whether it's within your house or anywhere. There's no hugging them or sharing a light moment with your mum. You're told if you walk past your mum, you are supposed to pass from the left side. You can't ask questions; you're just told what to do with no explanation. You have to move to a separate house and the women have to bring you food at a distance and then leave, then you go pick it up since they can't enter your house. Imagine in the event you left the house and went to meet up with other guys and you come home late at night, they will have to wait for you to pass you the food regardless of what time of the night; it's outrageous.

When you built that little hut, was that permanent? That's permanent, there was no going back. *How old were you?* 12 years. Immediately after you finish Class 8, after circumcision, that's it, you have your own house until you get married. It was very worrying because some boys now had the freedom to do whatever they have always wanted which includes involvement in criminal activities and their parents have no control over them.

Could you go to your family's house and have dinner with them? I broke a few rules; I won't lie. I would go and talk with my dad because he understood me and he encouraged me to get involved with them a lot more. I could go talk with him, sit within the homestead in a three-legged stool under a tree, and have a chat. Mum would bring a cup of tea or porridge and get into the conversation. As time went by I felt I needed to let go of some of the traditions after going to university and seeing how things are different. It was clear I couldn't continue holding onto some of those traditions. If you found yourself in urban centers holding to all these traditions, you would have a very miserable life as you would be an outcast to everyone.

Did girls have female circumcision as part of their initiation? Growing up, FGM was rampant in some communities, especially the pastoral areas where girls as young as eight years would go through the ritual. In other communities, like the Samburu and the Maasai, they had traditions on how they molded their girls to be women, which included circumcision. To eliminate FGM, the government, together with the NGOs, played a big role in influencing that decision to outlaw FGM. Some of these NGOs found it very backward and very dangerous health-wise for the girls, with the trauma girls have to go through.

The government felt the pressure because the NGOs played an important role in terms of community programs when the government was doing virtually nothing. There were ultimatums from NGOs to make changes, especially in legislation, or the donor funding would be withdrawn. Local politics was really a problem because some leaders did not buy the idea of banning FGM because how can you go against the people who elected you and it's what they've done their entire lives. NGOs started creating centers for girls to escape. This encouraged girls to get education in these areas, even in communities that believed a girl is supposed to be married off.

In some communities, you heard stories that if they have more than two girls and there is no boy, they will kill the next girl born to stop the curse. These stories are very shocking but they used to happen, especially in pastoral communities that were so obsessed with having boys. The NGOs and some of the community-based programs saw that to resolve the FGM problem, you need to involve the boys by teaching them they can marry someone who has not undergone circumcision and still make a beautiful wife. Make them understand the trauma of why an eight-year-old girl shouldn't be married off to a 50-year-old man with four other wives, and the community started to change with time. There are a lot of big changes within those communities.

When you had the initiation ceremony at 12, what were the other messages you got about what it is to be an adult male? Femininity or any signs of weakness is regarded as very negative, especially where I come from. You're supposed to be this uptight, no emotion-showing kind of an animal, not to show any form of emotional weakness like crying. No matter what comes your way, face it like a man. Two or three of your peers in initiation are believed to have the power to resolve anything because you poured blood together.

You're told how to interact with women related to you. If you were found interacting with a female who is not related to you, there were beatings because your peers said you were embarrassing them to the other generations because you haven't gotten to an age where you can be allowed to date or talk to the opposite gender.

When I got to high school, we had students who had performed well in the Kenya Certificate of Secondary Education (KCSE) and would teach during the holidays at local school centers because everyone wanted to emulate their achievement. You paid a small fee to be part of the class. These interactions may spill over into the streets and this is where it gets crazy because these guys in your age cohort are waiting to see who slips by talking to a girl. There were a lot of conflicts and people started rebelling against the culture they were supposed to be upholding and cherishing because of the treatment. Some of those radical beliefs were diluted over time and now someone can choose what they want in life.

In the US, the universities have sororities and fraternities that do hazing, where the pledges go through "hell week." There were schools here where hazing was crazy. The local slang is "monolization," a demeaning word for the first years of high school. When you get to schools--especially in community-based schools and some district schools--you find guys who have repeated classes maybe two or three times and don't have anything to lose in life. In boarding schools, you're under the care of older students called "fathers" who give you guidance around the school compound. Some students will hijack everything you have, so you may end up with nothing but the clothes you are wearing during school reporting, but you find ways of survival from other students.

Some of these "fathers" will make you do all their chores, like washing their clothes, or picking up their meals, singing them a lullaby at night as they go to sleep, using your shoe as a telephone to call home. It was very traumatizing and some student deaths were reported, so it was crazy.

Did the girls do the same things? Yes, even in girls school you could hear stories of girls asking others to do things with their used sanitary towels, a girl being asked to breastfeed someone, others being asked to walk naked around the hall as the other ladies cheered. To arrest the situation the school administration started suspending or expelling some of the students involved. Nowadays students have other ways to rebel like burning schools, using drugs, and high numbers of rape as students have bottled up feelings since they were assaulted or sodomized when young and had no counseling.

What about religion? Kenyans are either Christian, Muslim, or animist? Yes, Hindus are also a very big religious group within Indian Kenyans. When I was growing up there was no space for you to think on your own on which religious direction to take. It was one of those areas that you can be cast out easily. I still see the fear in my friends who come from the same area as I do, because when they go back home every Sunday morning they have to be in church with the family. If you ask any child, say four years old, what happens if you don't go to church, they say you will go to the devil. Even after initiation, if you don't go to church, girls don't want to associate with you and some of these stereotypes can get under your skin.

Reading my interviews with couples in the US for the Happy Marriages *book, what are your impressions?* The people in these interviews have a deep understanding of their feelings and emotions, how every little thing that happens has a meaning to it and is understood deeply. In my country, I can resoundingly say we have little or no understanding of what a relationship should entail and mean to a person. The issue I hear couples in Kenya raise about their relationship is they don't know how to tap into their emotions to have a better understanding of dealing with their partner. This results in the high femicide and gender-based violence in our society. Divorce is not common among most cultures as disputes are resolved customarily but it's a growing trend in urban areas.

On the issue of gender rights, growing up and to the present, there is a lot of emphasis on girl child development, which I totally support. Some of our communities had really neglected the girls and subjected them to early marriages and to the woman belongs in the kitchen" mentality. However, there is a growing concern among youths and men in particular that we have started losing the boy child in the process of empowering the girl. This is very evident in social media in Kenya with the #MasculinitySaturday on Twitter. Men, in particular, express all sorts of toxic masculinity sentiments towards women in regards to how a man is supposed to carry themselves in a relationship. It's really becoming a worrying trend if what they Tweet is actualized.

Does your family expect to find a partner for you? Nowadays, it is left to an individual to find a partner. However, when my mum and dad were growing up, for some communities, someone who is senior to you introduces you to someone, indirectly implying this is the person I want you to marry. The society in Kenya has gone rogue, in that the dating scene should be a case study because there is a lot of foreign influence from western movies and a "Keeping up with the Jones" mentality. People want to belong to the group of people who are seen to be doing well, but there is a disregard of morals and relationships have been commercialized a lot.

Female empowerment is something that should be valued and encouraged, but we have a generation that is disregarding that. Right now dating is like an exchange program, sex for money or money for sex. Our parents' generation has accumulated wealth but among young people, there are no jobs, so older ones are taking advantage of the young people and girls in particular. If a young man tries to date a lady of the same age group and there is an older wealthy guy pursuing her, she will automatically go for the older man because of the opportunity that comes with it. So the young men are feeling inadequate and it's creating a social conflict. I don't know what needs to happen for this to change, especially in urban areas and now it's getting in the rural areas in that whoever has money has their way.

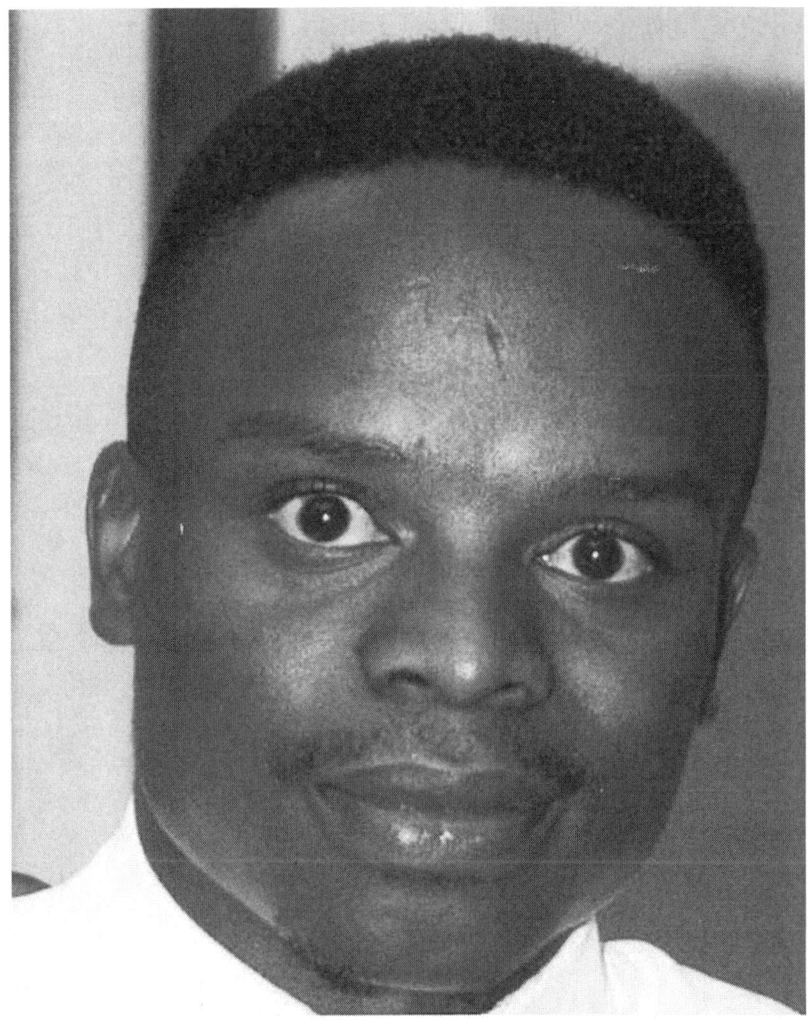

I was born in Lusaka in 1990 on the 7th of January. *I think of Capricorns as hardworking, grounded, close to the earth, and they can be stubborn. Does any of that apply to you?* That's very true. I've been doing research looking at where people were born and how that affects their behavior. I'm really hardworking, I love nature, and I'm an introvert. I'm a person who does what I feel is right and my mind is hard to change when I believe in something with a deep conviction.

Your father passed on when you were really young. I was raised by a single mom with eight of us, seven guys and one lady. Right now we have five graduates in my family, two more guys to go. I was the first one to have a BA degree, and now a Master's of Science in project management, all from the University of Zambia. We managed to get through school because of the support from my mother who used to sell fast food on the streets of Lusaka.

It wasn't easy but boys are easy to raise and we were raised to be very hardworking guys, very responsible and we're able to look after mom now. We're the middle class of Zambia although I was born in the lower class and hoping in a few years to get to the first class. *Are you the firstborn?* I'm the second but first among the guys.

How were you were able to afford university? We still have the loan or the bursary system here in the education system, so if you're among the students who get distinction after high school, you're given the chance to go to university for free though you pay back after you finish. I was able to pay back for the other two, and I still pay for the younger gentlemen.

Did your sister graduate from university after you? No, my sister, who is our firstborn, went up to 11th grade until she became pregnant, got married, and today she has five boys.

Why did you study in university? I come from a Catholic background and I've been largely influenced by religious teaching, though later on, I discovered a lot of things to do with what it means to be a spiritual person. When I went to university I had one thing in my mind. Because of the background I had with a lot of struggle, I wanted to study poverty.

I went straight into Development Economic Center and was given the chance to do a double major degree with philosophy. With that Catholic background, I knew so much about Plato and those Greek philosophers, so it was easy for me to blend in. I'm curious; I'm a very inquisitive person but not nosey. I really love to find out what is out there and what's new. University was very rigorous with a lot of math, statistics, and a lot of reading in philosophy, but I managed because of who I am.

What is the influence of your tribal background? My dad wasn't much like my grandpa, he wasn't so traditional. Generally, Zambia is not a very cultural country, especially for those of us brought up in the city where we are more exposed to a Western culture, though at the same time our culture has a lot of influence on us. It's not about passing on how to become men, since most of it has to do with language, food, and social relations.

At home we were always told to look after women, to look at them as the weaker gender who needs our help. It's been easy to look after my mum because of that mindset which embedded in me that I'm stronger than women. On the flip side, we used to do a lot of home chores like doing dishes. Neighbor girls would laugh at us because we fetched water, cleaned the house, did the washing, and I put my young brothers on my back. In our community, people looked at us like we were like girls.

I read that in Cuba, the most embarrassing thing for men was to hang laundry outside; men didn't want people to see them do that. Here, the most embarrassing task is when ladies see you put water on your head fetching water or cleaning the house or sweeping the yard; they'll definitely laugh at you. *Is that changing?* In places like where I grew up, it's still a laughable matter. But now in some areas, like where I am today, people look at it as a normal thing. Deliberate government policy is to encourage boys to be treated the same way as girls, so slowly that is changing.

Did you have an initiation ritual? No, actually there is only one tribe I know in Zambia that follows that old tradition of circumcising boys when they're about to become men. It is mostly found in the western side of Zambia, which is less than one percent of the population. For the rest of the tribes, we don't go through any initiation ceremonies except certain cultural dances when they reach a certain age. My tribe, the Chewas, is mostly found in Zambia, Malawi, Mozambique, and parts of Angola. We have cultural dances where boys of a certain age dress up in masks and people consider them to be men when they join those dances. However, my father and I didn't go through that, unlike those cultures where you need to be circumcised to be considered a boy or you're looked at as a weak man.

Did men in your tribe look out for you, especially after your dad passed on? Even before he died, culturally all my dad's siblings are not uncles or aunties, but are called dad or mom and my cousins are my sisters and brothers. So, there was nothing like an orphan because your uncles are your parents by default. They assigned my dad's younger brother to look after us, not to marry my mum or inheriting us, just to be there for us.

My uncles taught us about culture and language because my dad comes from the eastern side of Zambia and my mom comes from the northern part, so they speak different languages. It's a must that you should know your father's language. It was mainly the duty of my uncles to teach me the language and they made sure I knew my culture and our tradition, more than what I know from my mother's side. When I was getting married a few months back, they played a critical role and taught me stuff I didn't know for this important event in your life.

What are some of the philosophical teachings you learned from your tribe? Women are more respected in our matrilineal culture, with ancestral spirits viewed as part of the gods. The prophetess and the priestesses are all women who manage the shrines and all. The mother of the king or the chief is a more important person than the chief himself in my culture. When someone passes on, they go back to join the ancestors and people still pray during traditional ceremonies, like when there is a drought they still talk of ancestors. *How is a chief chosen?* The children of the chief's sister automatically become the chief.

Now we have a hybrid where people have merged Christianity with our culture, so those people worship ancestral spirits at the same time they say those spirits are the Christian God. They sing a lot of songs, do drumming, and appease the spirits by using different kinds of alcohol. *They pour libations of liquor to the ground to give to the ancestors?* Yes. I've only witnessed that because of visiting my village, as my parents were strong Christians, like my grandpa who was a Christian but a little bit more traditionally cultured than my parents. I've not had a lot of influence from my culture except we still use herbs, believe in taboos, and our traditional medicine. I have no problem using roots, leaves, or shrubs when I'm sick.

What else did you learn about what it was to be a man besides protecting women? In Africa, there is a very clear distinction between a man and a woman; you are taught what to do from childhood. You're told as a man you're more powerful than a woman, so as a man you need to hunt or find food and look after your family. As a man, you need to protect women; as a man, you're in charge. Ladies are told to prepare food at home, to clean their house, to look after babies, to help out their mothers at home, and to be submissive to men.

No one should call me a sissy because I don't do certain things that women do. It's really emphasized in our culture that men feel more powerful by virtue of their biology. *A common picture is African woman carrying a big load of firewood on her shoulders or a heavy water can on her head.* I work with the farmers in the villages to train farmers in conservation and organic farming. What I see is when it's time to do the actual farming, the tilling of the land, and plowing, more than 85% of the farmers are women. Those that don't have animals use their hands, but when you harvest, men show up to sell the produce although mostly women do the actual hard work.

If me and my wife were to go to work in our fields in the village, when she comes back--whether she's pregnant or she's got a baby on her back--she has to go straight into making a fire, starting to cook, and preparing food for me even if we were working together. I'll probably be seated resting while she is doing all that. There are very few instances where you see men helping out. Mostly men would drink beer or chat with their male counterparts.

Is there any kind of movement for change? A lot of civil society organizations advocate for gender balance and change of roles. In urban areas, people I know share work; like my wife and I both work, and I'm able to help her out, we prepare dinner, we help each other. I know she is tired, I'm tired too, but that is not the same story in the rural areas I go to.

In my organization, Love for Humanity Foundation, we teach farmers about conservation and that in-home management no one should be superior to the other. If you work together, you can make more money, you can be more productive than when it's only a woman and the kids doing much of the work. There's been slow, minimal change to men accepting being equal to women; it's good progress, but it's quite slow.

What percent of people graduate from high school? Education is free from the first grade to ninth grade, so we have more than half of Zambians who can read and write, can speak good English and some speak Mandarin because there are a lot of Chinese here. Of the people between the ages of 14 to 35, more than 75% of us can read and write. Our population is about 18 million people with two to three million degree holders. Around three-quarters of the rest have craft certificates, but most of those people are men.

When you go to the villages do the parents want their kids in school or to work on the farm? I go with graduates from the University of Zambia who volunteer in our program and they're able to speak very good English and speak our language fluently, so people get moved, especially when we give testimonies to inspire them about what we went through. Most volunteers are women from different colleges, which has changed things as role models are really powerful.

When you're teaching conservation, what are you asking them to do differently? When I was in my final year at university, an idea came to me on how I can contribute significantly to humanity. I struggled to have food while going to school, the major challenge that people have. Most of our farmers, more than 85% of them, don't have access to equipment or proper seeds. Most of the land is depleted because of overusing chemical fertilizers, plus, with climate change, people can no longer produce the same amounts of corn as they used to 10 years back.

In our organization at the University of Zambia, I had friends from all the faculties so we met together brainstorming to find the simplest and cheapest methods. We did pilot studies, demonstrations, and met with an organization based in the US and South Africa, teaching "Farming God's Way." We volunteered by going into villages to teach them about the model where we use ashes and compost manure to restore soil fertility and increase yields. We have good production from last year's farming season; I do this work despite working full-time. I've worked for Unilever since college in business intelligence and analysis so I audit numbers. On weekends and holidays, I get to travel and teach these farmers. It's a passion and I've been able to link them to government agencies and NGOs that believe in conservation.

I can say out of 100 farmers, less than 10 are fully practicing conservation farming, so it's still a long way to go. I've posted videos on YouTube where I explain the methods. You can search for Films Mbewe or Love for Humanity Foundation. *How is the Foundation funded?* I started the Village Improvement Market. I tell rich people if they buy land, I can farm for you then we share profit 35%/65% and most of them agreed and that's how I started. I grow high-value crops like strawberries, lettuce or Chinese cabbage, spinach, broccoli, and English cucumbers that fetch me a lot of money. When those people saw the passion that I have and my Facebook posts, the government, NGOs, UNDP [UN Development Program], and companies came on board--a blessing. It took me over five years to build the market until the municipal council in Lusaka gave me a space where we can trade farm produce and more. To teach 100 farmers in four days, I need between $1000 and $1500 dollars because I have to travel for more than a thousand kilometers.

Water scarcity and drought is a big problem. What do you find in terms of boreholes and wells drying up? We include water conservation under our program because we've seen a lot of droughts. When I was young we would have rains for more than four or five months, but today, it's three months only. When we dig a hole for a plant, we put grass at the bottom, then soil, then manure, ashes, and dry grass again, and more soil, then plant on top. We cover the soil with dry leaves or grass again, so when it rains enough moisture is captured inside there.

In villages, do they have solar for electricity or do they still rely on kerosene lamps? They don't have electricity but there is a drop in kerosene use because the Chinese brought in very cheap solar panels, the size of a small notebook, powered by a small battery and an inverter. People use them for lighting and to charge their phones. For cooking, there's still the use of firewood. *That's problematic because then they denude the forest which makes the climate more arid and less rain.*

We came up with a biogas stove, which costs around $250, but people live on less than a dollar a day. It's still a work in progress for us but other people maximize pressure cookers using charcoal or cow dung. Most people have animals or can use human fecal matter to power biogas stoves, except it produces methane which you need to control because it's dangerous for the environment. But, it's in small quantities compared to carbon monoxide produced by charcoal. I think it's a necessary evil for now, better than what's being practiced.

Former President Ellen Johnson Sirleaf is fearful about the growing Chinese influence in Africa, but it sounds like in Zambia it's been positive with solar batteries. I feel their development model does not translate into real practical knowledge because whatever they bring comes as the finished product and most of their technology is cheap, like the solar panels have to be replaced after two to three months. The Chinese brought a very big debt crisis by building large projects like dams, not just to Zambia, but Africa in general. They expect to have the loans paid back.

You emphasize that African solutions need to be honored, you can't just impose ideas from abroad, so what is particularly African that you're teaching now? In our model, its about African aid to Africans with local entrepreneurs and innovators. If what I learned in university can't be applied, then that's nothing for me. *You question the western idea of democracy as imposed on Africa. What's your feeling about good governments?* I look at it as good and bad. In Africa, people view society as a collective thing, rather than individualism. Do the people want a president to serve four years? Do they want the chief? A king? A group of many people? If that is respected by international agencies we can head somewhere but if you tell us we want you to do a,b,c,d, it becomes problematic. I feel the best leadership here is what defines us and what we feel is right.

It seems like the main problem is leaders elected democratically throughout Africa find ways to extend their terms which violate the constitution so democratic countries are in the minority. What could be done to change that or do you want to change it? I was born in the democratic society of Zambia where our first president ruled for 27 years and the current president now was elected. The only countries that are democratic like us are Botswana, South Africa, *and Rwanda.* No, their president has been there for over three terms. *What about Kenya?* Yes, Kenya is more democratic, as is Ethiopia and Malawi. Botswana has a group of technocrats, independent of political influence. If we can have that system adopted across Africa, we would not have issues with presidents changing the constitution.

It's kind of like Plato's philosopher-king. Exactly. *But who picks the technocrats?* They're like a civil servant. The coming of democracy scrapped almost everything that had to do with socialism, so we have a huge population of disgruntled people, especially people of my age.

To switch topics, congratulations on your marriage. How did you meet your wife? My wife was my neighbor back at home in the suburbs, when I was in sixth grade. My wife is very intelligent. I didn't go to college straight away from high school because I had to look for work and help out the family but she went to university before me and studied demography and development studies. We started the dating thing when she was in her final fourth year and I was in my third year. She later on went to do a master's in Finland. She works for our consultant's company and for the university, very innovative.

What changed to move from being friends to a romantic relationship? I was a little bit scared and young because women tend to mature faster than guys. Even when we were growing up together, she was always ahead of us. I thought she was on a different level and I started dating someone else but it didn't work out. I was convinced that she would be my wife and I made sure when I went to university to get closer to her.

You initiated the dating? Yes, I did. I think my wife was more extroverted than me. I'm more of a reserved person, I love my peace, my space to myself, so approaching that kind of outgoing girl was a bit of a challenge, but I had to man up and started going on dates with her. We had a lot of stories to talk about our childhood and the challenges we've been through.

We got married traditionally, not a white wedding or an English wedding. In Zambia and commonly in Africa, marriage is three or four parts. First, you take your dowry (money, cows, animals) with your uncles and grandparents, and her family accepts you and those gifts, and then she becomes your wife. Since we're from an urban area without animals, we went with money, wine, bedding, and other gifts. I was assigned a traditional person to take me through marriage and the bride has a months' long process. The lady's family comes to me with all kinds of foods and they do traditional dances. They show me what my wife will be preparing for me.

Secondly, they celebrate you as a man for marrying in their family and we have a "kitchen party," like a bridal shower to celebrate the woman. Some people do a church wedding which involves going to a priest or a pastor to bless you, which I've not done yet.

When you had instruction about marriage, what were the principles that you were taught? My wife was assigned another woman from her family, and I was assigned an elderly person from the side of my family who later on assigned somebody neutral. We're given someone who's an outsider but usually from your tribe. For my wife, the outsider is someone who should understand my culture and my tradition, so they have to look for someone from my tribe who's going to teach my wife about our culture.

For me, I was taught how to look after my wife and her family, how to respect her, how to look after my own family, and our boundaries, our independence, our oneness as a couple. I was taught if I want to buy a shirt, for instance, I should first buy my wife at least three dresses. Also, a woman has more needs in terms of hygiene, and I was told that I'm biologically stronger therefore I should take my wife as a helper. If I wasn't making money then I wasn't eligible to marry; she needs to come and help me build it.

I was taught a man should be logical, not emotional, and don't have tantrums, because you don't have all these hormones. You are a straight line but women have fluctuations in terms of their behavior because of the hormonal imbalances that they go through. That's a really big thing because sometimes I would look at her when she was moody and I understood it came from biology. I know now when to give her space, but before I didn't know.

What did they tell you about how to resolve conflicts? The first step is to try to resolve it. If you can't, we can always go to our patrons who mentor us on how to resolve our issues. It's not the job of our families, it's those neutral people. They act like our marriage counselors. *They stay with you through the course of your marriage?* Throughout your life. The person they picked for me was a close friend of my dad, who's known me from childhood. It's easy for me to talk to him about anything. *Did they teach you how to have satisfying sex?* Most definitely, although I was trying to avoid that. They teach you about sexual needs and how to fulfill them and how to satisfy your wife.

What did they advise you about becoming parents? We are told to have as many kids as possible if we're able to feed them, and that our kids don't just belong to us, they belong to the community. I was told to never give your children everything they need to teach them a mindset of fending for themselves, so they don't have an entitlement mindset. They should have a caring heart, be able to look after each other. In Africa, we believe in big communities rather than nuclear families. I'm okay with two or three kids because I have nieces and nephews, plus the kids I meet in the work that I do.

In Africa, usually, there are two things that happen when you get married. They give you a minimum of a year for the two of you, then they will give you an elderly person or girl to help you look after your wife because, by that time, she should be pregnant. Our elders may say you need to have this person or not, and that person will come, it could be my mother or her mother or her auntie. After six months or so they'll leave you.

Do some people have plural marriage? Zambia is a culturally diversified country with more than 72 tribes, each with its distinct behaviors. Only about two follow polygamy; you can't see the wives quarrel or argue, because they give each other respect. *Do some of the villages that you work with have polygamous families?* A lot of them. *It seems human to be jealous if your husband is giving more attention to the new wife.* That does happen and usually before the man takes a second or third wife he has to consult the first wife. You can't just do it.

Hillary Clinton quoted the Africans saying, "It takes a village to raise a child" and that's true. Yes, in my community if I do something wrong like fighting or insulting, a stranger is allowed to slap me, they can beat me up. If I'm walking anywhere and find kids fighting, I can stop a fight and their parents will be so grateful for that.

Do you personally honor your ancestors, like giving offerings, and were they included in your marriage ceremonies? Our marriage was a typical Christian marriage, plus traditions like my wife went through the initiation ceremony to become a wife and the other rituals that have to do with the ancestral condition. What happens is as people grow, they tend to lose touch and change. I've been switching from Catholicism to, not Pentecostal *per se*, but to real spirituality where I need to discover who I am as a person and my relationship with my environment and the universe. It's not about reciting the rosary; it's beyond that for me. It's a personal relationship with my creator.

I feel with a very strong objective mind, that in marriage people can learn a lot from the Biblical principles and the Christian advice about marriage, which doesn't make a man superior to a woman. The man is the head, the woman is a helper and you need to have some knowledge to help somebody. Women are powerful, their influence cannot be ignored. In less than a year with this person, I've seen amazing change because my wife understands her role. I don't understand why women fight for equality when they're in charge in the home. My wife tells me we need this and that and she can multitask: cooking, watching TV, on the phone with her friends, sending WhatsApp messages to her mother. But if I'm on the phone I can't do two or three things at a time.

In the villages that I go to, a woman may be busy preparing food, bathing a baby, and more--these women are so talented. If someone were to ask me who is superior, women are more gifted except that our society has elevated men falsely when actually women have more ability than men. Biblical principles about marriage have worked out for me and my mum and dad. It's not a servant and master relationship; the leader is the servant, so as the man in the house you have a bigger role to look after those people.

Andrew Smiler, Ph.D.
Therapist and Researcher in Male Development

I was born in Philadelphia in October 1968. I'm a Libra on the cusp of Scorpio. *Libras tend to like balance, fairness; is that true for you?* Yes, that's a pretty fair description of me.

Growing up, what messages did you get about how to become a man? I don't remember anything specific or particular; nobody ever took me aside and said, "This is what guys are supposed to be like." There was a lot of implicit content; it's in the air we breathe, so to speak. But to the extent that anybody did take me aside, it would usually be another kid from school or summer camp saying, "guys don't do that," or "you're such a girl," or "only girls do that." There was a little bit of "don't be a fag" but in the '70s and '80s when I grew up, that was not nearly as common as it was in the early 2000s.

What were examples of behaviors that were considered girly? Being too concerned about appearance. As a boy in the '80s, whether or not you could wear a pink shirt was a big deal, but it was also a period when guys started to wear earrings.

Depending on who you asked, only gay guys wore earrings, or straight guys could wear one but only in their right ear, or whatever, but this changed while I was a teenager. In the '70s you could be a guy and have long hair and I did eventually have a mullet.

Long hair signaled being a hippie. Right, a kind of counterculture or protest, which certainly wasn't mainstream. I was a big sports fan growing up and I still am. There were no professional football players who had hair long enough to come out under their helmets when I was growing up, but some rock stars had long hair. Today, athletes do have the freedom to have long hair, including football players like Clay Matthews and Troy Polamalu. *And Colin Kaepernick.*

Peggy Orenstein and Niobe Way report in their books about teen boys that the fear of being considered gay keeps boys from having close friendships in their adolescence. Yes, the psychology jargon is "impression management." A lot of teen boys have real concerns about being too emotionally open with their male peers, even a best friend because they are concerned about how he might respond and whether that's too much. In the 2000s the expression "no homo" was often used to clarify that, "I'm not gay but I have to tell you about how I'm feeling or about how good your body looks or something that might make you think I'm gay because I'm violating the stereotype of how straight guys act." That expression "naturally occurred" within male culture with no parallel in girls culture where girls would say "no dyke" or "no lesbo." Boys felt this pressure to make sure that everyone understood that they were straight; no one insisted they say "no homo."

You wrote Dating and Sex: A Guide for the 21st Century Teen Boy. *How would you summarize that if you were talking to a teen boy? One thing that I'd like boys to know is if you pay for a date, it doesn't mean that you're owed a kiss at the door or whatever.* Yes, I talk about fairness and equality and I talk about the pros and cons of splitting costs 50/50 or taking turns. I talk a lot about respect and people's reputations. The vast majority of sexual activity for most guys, from kissing to coitus, occurs within a romantic relationship or a wannabe romantic relationship. I talk a little bit about hookups with strangers in the book, but they are pretty rare for high schoolers.

A TV series on Netflix called "Never Did I Ever" is about an Indian-American teenager. It surprised me that in the first program she approaches a jock and asked him to have sex with her and he says okay but I can't tonight. I don't know any 15-year-old girls who would be so direct and the median age for first sex is 16. I certainly hear about stuff like that from some of my male high school and college students, talking about being approached by women just for sex but it's rare. In the book, I talk about how guys can stall for time to think about whether or not they want to say yes or no to question like, "Will you go out with me?" or "Do you want to have sex?" In general, American culture does a bad job of teaching boys how to react if someone else tries to initiate sexual or romantic contact with them.

It's not a thing that we teach boys. As far as I can tell, my book is the first one strictly for boys that talks about how to think about whether or not you want to say no. If you're a girl reading almost any book or magazine, like *Seventeen* or *Cosmo Girl*, about relationships or sex there's text in there for you in the articles or dating and sex advice columns, but boys don't get that. *What messages did you get as a teen?* Like most guys, I didn't get any advice on what to do if someone else asks me out or initiates sexual contact.

Advice books for women about how to get a man (like The Rules *series by Ellen Fein and Sherrie Schneider and many others) teach that men like a hunt and you have to be hard to get and make him chase you so he feels like he's conquering.* Yes, absolutely, but that describes the minority of men. In the Harry Potter series, you see how difficult it is for Harry and Ron to ask a girl to the Yule Ball (during the year of the Tri-Wizard Tournament). Those fictional boys do not try to "hunt." Harry, who by this time has defeated Voldemort and saved the world three times, can barely ask Cho Chang out to the dance. When he finally does, it's incredibly awkward. By the end of the series, Ron and Hermione are a couple and it's very clear that Hermione likes Ron before he likes her. *Do they have any sexual contact?* In the books and the movies, nothing goes beyond kissing. *So many young people around the world have read that influential series.*

What's the theme of your book Challenging Casanova: Beyond the Stereotype of the Promiscuous Young Male? That's my book for grown-ups with the database about what we know about boys' romantic and sexual development. It was my effort to set the record straight. The stereotype that says boys just want sex and aren't interested in relationships became dominant in the '70s and '80s. That describes 10% to 20% of older teen boys and young men, a minority of men, although many people believe this is the norm.

What led you to be a therapist who works with males? I went to Virginia Tech and got a degree in psychology and another in mathematics. I earned a degree in clinical psychology in '93 at Towson University. I went through undergraduate not having a career in mind. I started off as a math major and I did finish that degree, but I picked up psychology. Introduction to Psychology was the first course I took as a Gen Ed that really interested me and where I was actually willing to do the homework. I took more psychology courses and they kept being more and more interesting. And I was one of the people that friends would talk to me when they had really difficult stuff going on.

I got to senior year and I didn't know what I wanted to do except I didn't really want to stay in mathematics. People seem to pull that supportive side from me, so I became a therapist. I worked for the next five years in the Philadelphia suburbs. I wanted to work with teenagers and I had some experience doing that during my graduate program. I realized that in probably 70% of the kids or families that I worked with, a teen boy was the focus of my work, and I seemed to naturally understand them. I didn't want to do therapy forever so I went back and I got a Ph.D. in Developmental Psychology with the goal of being a professor. I was fortunate to get into the University of New Hampshire, where the Ph.D. Program in Psychology also trains its graduate students to teach. I then did a postdoc at the University Of Michigan and I taught in the New York State system for a while.

During that time, I started dating a woman (who is now my wife), also an academic. The two of us finding positions in the same city became quite an ordeal. I do research on the normative aspects of sexual development of boys and on definitions of masculinity, neither of which are research priorities anywhere, like for the NIH. We landed here in Winston-Salem, where my wife works for the Wake Forest

University School of Law. I stayed in academia for a few years and eventually moved into private practice, focusing my practice on teen boys and adult men seemed obvious given all I'd learned about them. Along the way, I also wrote a few books.

Tell us about Men's Studies courses. Men's studies hopes to be a distinct kind of interdisciplinary program, the contours of which are somewhat ambiguous. The two primary academic organizations are the American Men's Studies Association (AMSA, founded in 1991) and the Society for the Psychological Study of Men and Masculinities (SPSMM), which is Division 51 of the American Psychological Association (APA). AMSA grew out of NOMAS, the National Organization Of Men Against Sexism, which dates back to the late '70s. My understanding is that essentially there was a split between the academics and the activists; the latter stayed in NOMAS and the academics formed AMSA. SPSMM, where I'm a past president, is about equally split between full-time academics who publish research and full-time clinicians, all trained as psychologists. Many of the academics in both organizations identify as doing men's studies.

Did you teach Men's Studies? I got to teach a course in gender development. As a developmental psychologist trained in child and adolescent development, we talked about how males and females grow up and how they differentiate. Students were about three to one female to male, which matched my department's female to male ratio. In general, more women than men major in psychology.

Observers say academia is very petty with more infighting than the business world. What I observed is in meetings men would take terms talking to be heard, while women would want to get the job done. Maybe these guys were not the popular jocks in high school so it's their chance to be the alpha males. Do you think any of that is fair? One of my faculty members in my doctoral program was very fond of a Henry Kissinger quote the said something like "only in academia are the fights so bitter when the prizes are so small." I didn't have the experience that you're talking about. It's really the only industry where, because of tenure and relatively few positions open, the way you can advance is so limited. If I were in banking, there's always another bank in town and that other bank might be looking for a new branch manager. That rarely happens in academia.

Also, my experience of academics, all the Ph.D. folks, is that they're good at learning how the system works and "playing the game" and most of them are not particularly interested in taking risks or creating change. When I was on faculty, I saw that anytime we made a change to policy it had to be grandfathered in across four different years of students, so even a small change occurred slowly. There are people for whom that works, but I'm not one of them.

The Masculine Self *is the book you'd use as a men's studies text?* Yes, I wrote the textbook with Christopher Kilmartin for that intro course. First, we would talk about "what does it mean to be a man?" and "what is the definition of manhood or masculinity?" The text spells out some broad frameworks around diversity or intersectionality, frameworks about what it means to be a man, power, and macro theories of learned influences and culture--the nurture side.

An updated chapter on biological influences will be in the seventh edition, including research on testosterone and other physiological processes. I'll include a chapter about measurement because it and the way that we conduct research has an impact on the knowledge in the rest of the book, as when we talk about mean or average differences between men and women. There are chapters about fatherhood, relationships, emotion, violence, sex, and work, and the next edition will have a chapter on athletics.

Do you have any idea how many men's studies courses or programs there are? Almost nothing. Through my connections to the APA's Society for the Psychological Study of Men and Masculinities and the American Men's Studies Association, there may be as many as 150 offerings of an Introduction to Men's Studies course at maybe 75 to 100 universities across the U.S and Canada in any given academic year. *Australia and Nordic countries too.*

In contrast, almost any university in the U.S. and Canada teaches the Intro to Women's Studies course. As far as I know, there is not a major in Men's Studies anywhere in the U.S. or Canada. The only Master's Degree that I know of is offered through Suny Stony Brook University, hailed as Michael Kimmel's work. I believe there's a university in

Australia that offers both a bachelor's and a master's. *What does Gender Studies include?* When I look at the course listings, they are primarily or sometimes exclusively courses about women. Newer courses focus on transgender issues and some programs include sexual orientation *called Queer Studies.*

Diversity information is mostly woven throughout our text. One of the challenges in talking about men, and certainly in writing a textbook, is that men are not a homogeneous group, so we need to get complicated and nuanced. In order to get beyond broad generalizations, we need to get into the details. As the author of a textbook, I want some of those details and some of those differences embedded throughout the text.

I was amazed at all the color photos in your book Is Masculinity Toxic? That is the prettiest book I will ever write. The book is part of this series called The Big Idea. *What's the conclusion? Is it toxic or not?* Both yes and no. There are folks for whom masculinity works really well and there are folks for whom that works really poorly and a lot of folks in the middle. It depends on who you are and where you stand as to whether or not masculinity is toxic. *You could also say femininity is toxic if you feel you have to get plastic surgery, starve, and wear five-inch heels.* Any role can be overdone in ways that are problematic.

There's a debate about how much of our behavior as men and women is genetic and how much is socially constructed. As developmental psychologists, our knowledge base is very clear that it's "both-and," not "either-or." We can split up the environment into different levels, like Uri Bronfenbrenner's model, the bulls-eye image.[123] He's got four or five different ways that we can think about the environment. The folks who do the physiological work talk about it at the level of DNA, hormones, and neural networks and we can do analyses at each of those levels; again, there are multiple levels.

Skills like learning language and learning to walk are clearly hardwired and still require input from the environment. For example, we know that exposure to multiple languages at a young age, or lack of exposure to any language at a young age, has huge impacts. These are environmental inputs that are required for genetically based, hardwired aspects of human development. It's "both-and." Even these skills that are heavily biologically based, they're still not 100%. Other things that we know that are very much cultural like clothing choices and clothing options, even there some biological elements play a part. The reality is both play a role all the time.

An example of the physiology is the idea that men flood, get more upset in emotional arguments with a partner and so they're more likely to retreat. Psychologist Sue Johnson finds that women reach out and men pull away, which creates a vicious cycle. Is that an example of a physiological sex difference? That is one physiological difference, but we know that not all men are like that. Some men say, "I want to keep working this out" and don't have that flooding experience. And, of course, there are some women who are like, "I need to go be alone."

Training and developmental experience influence what we've learned about how to deal with conflict, as well as how much we've been taught to pay attention to our inner worlds and to verbalize our feelings. At the gross level, there are all sorts of male/female differences. But how that plays out for any given individual's biology in a certain culture is nearly impossible to predict. We know that men are taller than women, on average. But that information doesn't tell me anything about the height of the next person who will walk into my office, nor about whether or not they are happy (or not) about being that height.

Marianne Legato, MD's Why Men Never Remember And Women Never Forget *describes physiological and genetic differences. Do you concur that we have brain differences?* At the level of broad generalizations, there are absolutely differences there. Everybody has estrogen in their system, which plays a role in memory formation. Women certainly talk about when they go through menopause their memory is not as good. On average, after puberty has started, women have much more estrogen than men do, so it follows that women should have better memories than men, but again, there are some women who are low in estrogen and there are some men who are high in estrogen.

As an academic, as someone who went to more years of school than I care to count, a big part of school success is developing your memory and your ability to recall a whole lot of stuff. My memory may be better than it should be based on the fact that I have a Y chromosome because I put in all of this extra training.

What patterns do you see in the presenting issues in your clients? I work exclusively with teen boys and adult men. If you're depressed, anxious, have ADD, have sexual issues, or gender identity issues, I might be the right therapist for you. I work with a lot of guys who have low self-esteem and don't believe in themselves. I do what was called "assertiveness training" in the '90s, but may not be taught in graduate programs anymore. We work on finding ways to express yourself when you are struggling instead of avoiding confrontation.

The folks with ADD may recognize they're in an environment that doesn't fit them and may try to change their environment. One of the conversations I often have with parents and teens who have ADD is whether or not they should expect the kid to go to college. If you're having an argument with your teenager every day about how to do their homework, why would you think college is going to be any different? That is a way to talk about changing the environment that shows up with teens.

A lot of boys get prescribed Ritalin. I think that Ritalin and most psychotropic drugs are over-prescribed. If all we have to do is take a pill once or twice a day, whether that's Ritalin or Prozac or some anti-anxiety medication, nobody has to change the way they behave. The family doesn't have to rethink how it approaches parenting, and schools don't have to change how they approach kids, etc. I don't think that's a good idea, but I think that is often what happens.

One of the things that I do with a lot of kids who have ADD, and their parents, is talk about the disorder at its most fundamental level. It's an inability to control what you're paying attention to, which also means you can't split your attention to multitask. To be successful in school, you have to be able to take notes and still listen to what the teacher is saying, which requires you to split your attention. But for kids with ADD, that is almost impossible. So parents can work with the school to get a note-taker or a way for the kid to get the teacher's notes or other ways to change the environment.

What about anxiety? We know there's an increasing number of teens around the Western world with anxiety and depression, especially girls. Is it because society is more stressful or is it because it's okay to talk about it? I'll go with "all of the above." Life is definitely more stressful now, compared to when you and I grew up before social media and before cell phones. Back in the day, when you or I left school, we didn't have to see any other students. If something happened on a Friday afternoon, I might not know about it until Monday; and the whole city and the whole world would certainly not know.

Teens I work with tell me they're getting friend requests from people they met once at a camp or at a sporting event or whatever. With a lot more eyes on us, it's almost impossible to get those kinds of separations that you and I were able to get that occurred naturally. There's a lot more pressure to look like you have your stuff together. Professionally, I also have that experience; I get queries from all around the globe, a whole different level of awareness.

Kids who "come out" in today's climate don't have the time to figure it out the way folks used to have before social media. There's a lot more pressure to know all of it, and fit the image, very quickly. Plus we have a pandemic, a climate crisis, and political parties for whom compromise and working together to solve big problems is a bad thing, causing more stress. Today's teens are also exposed to that stress, and I think overall have a lot more stress than teens did 20, 30, or 40 years ago.

Professor Jean Twenge emphasizes social media, but I think the main reason teens are anxious is because they have so much pressure to get good grades and engage in activities to get into a good college. These A students with AP classes are also supposed to do sports and paid work, causing a shortage of sleep time, which would make me anxious and depressed. I think that's true for a lot of middle- and upper-middle-class kids, but that's just one group of boys. If we look at other groups, the picture gets more complicated.

Some of the boys I work with have parents who are high school graduates, or maybe not even that; their primary stress is about whether or not they'll get into a four-year school at all, or if they should choose a two-year school. Maybe they're looking at trades, which are only offered at those community colleges.

For the blue-collar boys, their pressures are to make money? Blue-collar isn't exactly a category anymore since most of those jobs have gone overseas; that's one of the downsides of globalization. For these boys, it's a lot more of a struggle to figure out where they might fit in professionally and economically. This is especially true for those kids who've always been good with their hands and are probably not going to suddenly become A students in college. For the last 10 to 20 years about 60% of students start college within 12 months of graduating from high school. There is no economy on earth that needs that many people with bachelor's degrees, but our high schools are set up to send everybody to college. That's a real disservice to kids in general, and more so to boys, because they are more likely to go into those trades, but high schools don't prepare them for that.

Have you had clients who are trans men? I have had trans folks of a wide range of flavors, yes. *What do you find that trans men struggle to change? What I see is they still make assertive statements and don't use questioning inflections.* Yes, changing your speech pattern, inflection, and phrasing is challenging because it's something that we learn at a very young age. Language requires nurture but it's largely hardwired. To try to change those patterns of word choice and patterns of inflection takes a whole lot of effort.

What about walking or sitting? Men tend to stride and sit with their legs apart. All of it is a challenge--learning to move your body differently, roll your hips, change body posture, and how you sit. Pants do not force you to put your legs together while certain skirts and dresses clearly do. It's like learning to drive differently because you have a broken limb. There's a whole set of considerations and skills regarding appearance that girls and women get taught early on. I've tried on a skirt and it doesn't fit the way anything else I've ever worn does. It was loose in ways I'm not used to, didn't have an inseam, and just felt odd. *Kilts and sarongs are international male skirts and fashion designers now are showing men in skirts and dresses.*

Learning to apply makeup is something that a lot of teen girls in America spend a lot of time learning how to do. If you've grown up male, you're not getting those experiences with clothing or practice with makeup or doing your hair. As part of that, a trans man has to get used to the idea that you are always being looked at and evaluated on your appearance with pressure to "pass." As a man, I rarely get dressed in the morning and think about how other people are going to react to what I'm wearing, but I know that's part of the routine for many girls and women. *I didn't realize how often I got checked out by men until I was visibly pregnant and didn't get looked at.*

A young man in the Medium *online newsletter published a post where he said, "Young men are being discarded, they're ashamed to be men and what they need is appreciation." Farrell* calls this the boy crisis.* There is definitely some real merit and resonance to that. I work with a number of teen boys and adult men who talk about ways that the things that they do, and men do in general, are discredited and blown off. Recently, we've had Jeff Bezos, Richard Branson, and Elon Musk getting all sorts of attention for getting into space, indicative of this back and forth about what do guys get attention for or what gets swept under the rug?

I'm co-facilitator of a men's group, including five guys in their 30s and 40s. We talk about things that the guys do that go unnoticed such as provide an income. All of the guys in the group earn more money than their partner or they're on their own. There's not a lot of thanks for making more money; that doesn't really get credited.

Also, guys are often responsible for physical safety, the ones who kill the bugs, the ones that when something goes thump in the middle of the night, it's our job to go find out if that's a bad guy or not. It's certainly not part of the everyday cultural conversation but it is something that we were all trained to do. I can remember being in my 20s and walking my female friends to their car after we had a late night out even though I was pretty scrawny in my 20s and I had no training in any martial art. That generally goes unremarked upon. There's a lot of stuff that teen boys and adult men are expected to do because we're guys and don't really get credited.

Could you say the same thing for women that do arranging, planning, and list-making that they don't get thanked for either? Absolutely. For a lot of younger guys, we are told in many ways that we are primarily valued for our accomplishments like titles or money or some formal status, so a lot of guys are left with the question of "What am I? How would I attract friends and a long-time partner?"

It happens in lots of ways. There are debates about what defines sexism and even whether or not it's possible to be sexist against men, although there are clear times when boys and men are clearly being denigrated because they happen to be male. *Do you think that's a backlash from the women's movement?* As with many things, it's more complicated than that. Sometimes, in order to make a point that creates social change, you have to overstate your case in the simplest form possible. This can set the stage for going too far and some folks have taken issue with Second Wave feminists statements about male power in the '60s and '70s. There are ways in which people have taken that too far and use the fact that the majority of power in the U.S is held by men to justify being mean to boys or excluding boys and men.

Trump probably hasn't helped because he's so obviously misogynistic and crude. Agreed, Trump poured fuel onto the fire and didn't really address the cause of the fire itself. *Hopefully, that fire will burn out some of those cruelties in our system of racism and sexism.* Yes, one of the real challenges at the societal level and individual level is we don't have a good discussion about what does "equal" and "fairness" mean. Does everything need to be 50/50 or can we organize by skills in a way that plays to our strengths? When I do couples therapy, we often end up talking about household responsibilities and chores, including taking care of the kids, and decision making.

We would actually like 50/50 women in Congress and Supreme Court and heads of corporations. If we're talking about Congress, sure, but if we're talking about who our childcare workers are, I don't hear a lot of folks pushing that it should be 50/50. I don't hear a lot of people talking about whether steelworkers and plumbers should be 50/50 either. We don't have a public conversation about where are the places where we're okay with the imbalance and where are the places where we really want it balanced.

I'd like to clarify the debate about the primacy of fathers in the boy crisis because people like Farrell say that's the key, especially divorced fathers who don't have enough time with their kids. Then pro-feminists in the APA Division 51 say they don't want to talk to Farrell, although most would agree that kids do better with both parents involved. Not everybody would agree that kids do better when both parents are involved if one of those parents is a substance abuser and especially gets violent or is an angry drunk. *Right, but that's not related to gender because it could be either parent.* If we're talking about two functional adults who are good parents, nobody's going to argue with that.

However, we have decades of research going back to the '60s and '70s that found kids who grew up with two parents in the house who are arguing all the time do worse than their peers whose parents aren't doing that. *I interviewed kids for* How To Survive Your Parents' Divorce: Kid's Advice To Kids *and that's exactly what they said. If they were in the middle of their parents' arguments, they were glad for the divorce.* What the research tells us is that if you look at kids say two years prior to the parents separating and two years after, on average two years post-separation most kids are doing well again. The extent to which their parents' bad relationship was causing them problems has dramatically decreased. There is, however, a small body of literature looking specifically at dads that finds that boys who grow up without regular access to their fathers on average do worse than their peers.

As a developmental psychologist, I was trained to look at influences that impair children's development. We see even stronger effects for poverty, having been physically or sexually abused, growing up in a violent neighborhood, etc. Arnold Sameroff was a big name doing this work when I was in graduate school in the late '90s. Sameroff said instead of trying to figure out which one of these 15 or so stressors is worse for kids, let's just count them.

Researchers who replicated his work found that most kids are all right if there's one major stressor but somewhere between two and three major stressors is where kids start to go off the rails. A lot of people are now aware of the Adverse Childhood Experiences scale (ACEs), which takes a similar approach. In large studies with a couple hundred or a couple of thousand people, boys not having access to their biological father does not show up as any more or less powerful than any other adverse experience that boys might have.

The other thing I don't hear from a lot of the folks who talk about father absence is advocacy for dads behind bars when 90% of the people behind bars are men. If father absence is that important, why aren't those folks advocating for better sentencing procedures or reduction in charges for those dads to make phone calls that can be ridiculously expensive? Men in prison can be moved by the Bureau of Prisons without warning; where is that advocacy? Where is the advocacy for boys in the foster care system? Are they also talking about fathers whose work requires them to be away for extended periods of time like guys on oil rigs or in the military? I also don't know how they conceive of stepfathers?

Around 70% of American kids will have at least one period of 12 months or longer where they're living with a single parent. Having separated parents is an incredibly common experience. The 2021 "Kids Count" report from the Annie E. Casey Foundation found that approximately one-third of American children live in a single-parent home.[124] If father absence has that dramatic of an impact on boys, then a lot more boys should be having a lot more dramatic problems than what we're seeing. That said, father absence is an easy topic to get people's attention in the same way that we make simplifications like getting to 50/50 in family work.

Do you have kids? I have a daughter who's in sixth grade. *What are you doing differently as a father than your father did? What have you learned from all your work?* I'm in that statistic about divorced parents and I had a stepfather. I choose to not talk about my biological father, but my seven-year-old self might have been upset that my parents separated. My teen self and my adult self have gone back and met my father, including two conversations with him when I was in my mid-20s. Their divorce was probably the best decision for my upbringing and certainly was the best decision for my mother. My father was not a great example and we'll leave it there.

The man I identify as my stepfather, even though he and my mom never got married, was in my life from the age of 10. He was true to his generation, a nice guy, quiet, responsible, and dependable. He served during the Korean conflict and I think it's rather fitting that the only award or medal he received was for good conduct.

What are your principles and goals as you raise your daughter? The goals are that she knows what her strengths and weaknesses are, has good interpersonal skills, and has some sense of how to get what she wants. I hope that she is independent and makes her own decisions and doesn't just follow along with the crowd and knows her own mind. So far, so good.

We've learned that Instagram increases anxiety and depression, especially among girls, so what do you do about limiting access to social media? Fortunately for us, she's not there yet. She has a few folks on YouTube that she watches but doesn't have social media. I'm a big believer, both as a parent and as a therapist, in "dumb phones" or "texting phones" for kids. If adults buy kids phones so we can get in contact with them, that means they only need good texting and voice. My daughter has her own computer and we periodically check her browsing history. We will need to be more conscious than prior generations of parents of asking her about what she's worried about, or her body image, or the pressure to look good on social media. Does it feel like everybody always looks good and nobody's a mess? This is one of the questions that I ask my teen clients and I give to their parents.

It amazed me that Peggy Orenstein in her book on boys and sex reports the average boy gets 10 minutes during his adolescence of talk about sex. I'm pretty sure that was drawn from my research for *Challenging Casanova*. We have a couple of decades of research where we asked high school juniors and seniors or university undergraduates, did you ever have "the talk" and what do you remember about it? Girls are much more likely than boys to say that they had the talk. About 60% of boys say they had the talk for no more than 10 minutes.

The three takeaways for the boys were some version of: don't get a girl pregnant, don't get a sexually-transmitted disease, and don't have sex at all. *My young son told me, "Don't worry, Mom. I'll use two condoms with a rubber band."* However, about 80% of parents say they had the talk with their kids so there's 20% of boys that don't register the talk. Depending on the study, 10% to 20% of the boys have parents who have more extensive conversations with their kids. *That's not many.* No, it's not, and that's part of why I wrote *Dating and Sex: A Guide for the 21ˢᵗ Century Teen Boy.*

There are lots of things that we talk about with our kids whether they want to hear them or not: manners, cleaning up their rooms, maybe what they're going to be as a grown-up, how to manage their money, and who their friends should or shouldn't be. Yet somehow when our kids say they don't want to talk about sex, we honor that, which says a lot about parental discomfort. I'm particularly fond of books by Robbie Harris, Mary Jo Podgorski's the *Nonnie* series, and Debra Haffner.

We also need to talk to boys about romantic relationships because in grades five and six about 20 to 30% will have their first boyfriend or girlfriend, which tends to really just be a title. They don't necessarily sit next to each other at lunch or hold hands, but a parent can talk about what that title means if you have it, or want it, or don't, when other boys say they are somebody's boyfriend. In seventh and eighth grade, dating starts but those tend to be group dates. Again, we can ask our sons what does it mean to be somebody's boyfriend? What are you expected to do? What do you expect your partner to do?

As they move into high school and start having relationships that look more like adult relationships with more one-on-one time, we can extend those conversations. In TV shows or movies we watch with our kids in some we know those characters really well, whether *Harry Potter* or *The Office* or *Parks and Rec*, there's some dating. We can ask our kids, if you had to date somebody from this show, who would you choose to date? Which of these characters would you want to be like? How would you like to present yourself when it comes to dating? That is often an easier place to start talking about dating because we can talk about their strengths and their weaknesses but it's not personal. This idea that there's this one magical conversation, "The Talk " is absurd.

Do you think boys have the same reaction to that boy on Instagram has bigger muscles than me? Absolutely, but we don't hear about it as much. A line of research on male body dissatisfaction since about 1990 focuses on muscularity, pioneered by Don McCreary. It's very clear that a lot of guys are not happy with how muscular or well-defined their bodies are. How physically strong you are is one of the ways that boys rate and rank themselves and each other. The people boys date also pay attention to boys' appearance. Male body image doesn't get mainstream media attention the way that female body image and female eating disorders have gotten attention.

It seems like height is another issue; muscles you can work on, but you can't control how tall you are. Yes, the average height of U.S presidents in the past 100 years is six feet. *The exception was Jimmy Carter at 5'9". Taller candidates are more likely to be elected.* We literally look up to people and that counts. The musician Prince wore lifts and heels since he didn't wish to be the shortest person on the stage. A number of women I know want to date somebody who is tall enough to for the woman to wear high heels. *I've heard that too.*

What's your next book about? I'm floating back and forth between three or four different books to write. One of the books that I'm very interested in writing is about ADD (Attention Deficit Disorder). I'm also thinking about a book for therapists about how to work with men because we know that the vast majority of therapists are women and the vast majority of counseling faculty are female. Therapists express concern about men only coming once or twice and then dropping out of therapy and professional conversation often focuses on why men won't seek help. We rarely talk about ways in which female therapists may not be culturally competent in working with men. *Groups like ManKind Project and EVRYMAN report that men will often say, "My wife took me to a female therapist, but I didn't talk. In a men's group, I feel free to talk because they understand me and aren't judging me."* Yes, absolutely.

I'm also contemplating writing a short book on erectile issues for teens and 20-somethings in good physical health. *How problematic is that?* Viagra and Cialis make a lot of money. Part of the problem is a lot of teen boys and young adult men and even middle-aged men who daily practice having an erection and an orgasm to their screen *...with porn...* sometimes multiple times per day. They don't get nearly as much practice with a live person, so if you've had 300 repetitions in the last six months doing it one way and all of a sudden you've got to do it another way and never had much practice, that may very well create a problem.

I was born on July 31, 1989, and raised in the Netherlands in a small town called Naarden. I was raised in this lovely home next to nature. I have two parents and a brother two years younger. I was 24 when I first moved out. *Leo people tend to assume leadership roles, with a kind of-quiet dignity. Does that describe you*? If you have been with a Leo, then some characteristics overlap, absolutely. *You certainly fit in the leader category.* I do take that role when people are just waiting, and I say, "Guys, let's start," to the point where sometimes I lose the connection with people around me. I get way ahead of myself so quickly in taking charge that I forget whom I'm leading. (*Eric Schneider also discusses this trait.*)

    Let's learn about your education and career path. I learned as I was turning 12 to 14, that I wasn't all that great with languages--or so I was made to believe by the Dutch education system. However, my English was good. *What other languages do you speak besides Dutch and English?* French and some German. When it came to more theoretical topics, I didn't quite get that so I took a more practical approach. At the age of 18, I went into vocational education. I finished the degree in intercultural management last year, which included a lot of different internships.

I'd rather learn on the job and do things. *You're a kinesthetic learner.* From an early age on, my brother, father, and I had a weekly paper run. We religiously saved all that money for four years to go on a big holiday. So, from a very early age, I got this work ethic. I've held many different jobs on the side of my studies, which is reflected in my approach to education.

What's the intercultural part of your master's degree? Although you and I both speak English, there is a lot of difference, which is the intercultural part including the different topologies of anthropology, sociology, and psychology. I focused on intercultural consultancy and training/coaching because that's what I already loved doing at the time.

Denmark traditionally gets placed near the top of the happiest countries in the world because people have social supports and family ties and they value hygge, *cozy domesticity. How are the Dutch similar or different?* When I look around in the Netherlands, the social support system works very well. People like single parents get the support they need. As for health care, we have a subsidy system and it's mandatory that you have health care. It's been taught to me that you may pay a huge amount of taxes but the moment that you fall off the wagon, they're going to pick you up and put you back on again.

Is college free? It's free in the Scandinavian countries of Denmark, Norway, Sweden, and Finland, but not in the Netherlands. We do have a subsidized system for public universities and public education, and tuition is reasonably affordable. The tuition is equal on undergraduate and graduate levels, around 1800 € to 2000 € a year.

When you were growing up, what were the messages to you and your brother about what it is to be a man? My feminine side was not appreciated, the way I was moving, the way I was talking. Still, to this day, when I pick up the phone with customer support and they reply, "Yes, Miss van de Ven," I say, "I'm sorry but I'm Mr. van de Ven." It doesn't bother me as much anymore but in the Dutch language, my voice is a lot softer, a lot gentler, and maybe, therefore, considered more feminine. When I did not fit into certain categories by fellow teenagers, I was pushed and pulled across the spectrum, which was very challenging at the time.

Being a young boy, I had a particularly soft tone of voice. Also certain behaviors, my way of talking, smiling, being kind and nice to people, my gestures and movements were and could be considered more feminine. My passion for dance also falls into another categorical stereotype, that real men don't dance and male dancers are gay. This was a stereotype I too held until I embraced dancing and afterward was made fun of and said to be gay. Being considered gay is something that even after years of hanging out with friends I met during dancing classes and outside interactions, they still kept this assumption even though they danced themselves and I have been in heterosexual relationships.

Before I turned 16, I was a very shy child even though I'm Leo. I have Cancer as my moon, very emotional, shying away from contact with girls and very timid. I wanted to be one of the teachers' best students, "teacher's pet" you'd say. I wasn't all that sporty; I played some tennis and some football but it just didn't catch me. I played video games and watched a lot of movies. What's remarkable about the Netherlands is that it's one of the few countries that doesn't dub any movies or TV shows. I've been exposed to the English language for such a long time and so many different ways of being in a community, reflecting on sitcoms and shows from around the world so you pick up on many things.

One theme in particular from my family is to make sure that you are a gentleman in your behavior, in addressing the elderly, family, and superiors. We have an informal and polite form of "you" just like the French have *tu* and *vous*. Also, how you engage with women is to be polite, be kind.

I started ballroom dancing when I was 16--when I started flourishing as a Leo. Asking a woman to dance was not a problem, as I enjoyed dancing so much that it was common sense. On Saturday evening, we would have a dance night and then ride our bikes home and drop off the girls first to make sure that they got into the door. That's something that was taught to me by my family. I do this still to this day with my grandmas and my aunt, waiting until I see the light going on in their apartments.

Is there scorn about being seen as like a girl as in the US? I do think that's true because up until my 16th birthday, I was shy. I was trying to be a teacher's pet, which made me an easy target and I didn't fit into any single group either. I ate my sandwiches with a few people during lunchtime although I was not in their class. I just managed to get in there because I knew one of the boys at the time.

When I started ballroom dancing, I had a lot more motion going on using my hands, variety in my tone of voice, and crossing my legs and that's when they started viewing me as homosexual to the point where I doubted myself. I have sought to explore this with myself, with people around me. But, having had girlfriends from my 18th year onward, one of the guys that I was dancing with for seven years said to me, "Well Steph, we always thought you were gay." I wondered, "Have you been paying attention to me? I like girls."

In the U.S, high school cliques might be athletes, punks, preppies, people who like different music styles, etc. Did you have those kinds of cliques when you were in secondary school? Yes, the group I hung out with during lunchtime was the more casual group, generally nice people. If I look at my old pictures from secondary school, I can see emos, punks, skaters, jocks, cheerleaders and barbies, and super-study nerds. In my photo, I wore my Eminem T-shirt and a buzz cut. I always make this huge joke about, "Hey guys, can you find me in this photo?" and nobody can find me. I desperately tried to fit in, but no group really accepted me as their own.

Eventually, I got along with the guys in the skater community and the punk emos. They were kind of okay with me, not particularly like "come over," but everyone else was not so great. I met one of my best friends during that time when we were the odd ducklings. I'm very happy he's still there with me in my life, as it really helped to have a comrade in high school.

Author Niobe Way interviewed teenage boys and found they're lonely because they had had close buddies in elementary school but in adolescence, the fear of being

perceived as gay made them back off from close friendships.
Yes, there was definitely no closeness between guys. *But there
was when you were in elementary school?* Yes, to some extent.
I had a few friends and we did hang out quite a lot. As you're
growing up you become more aware of how this could be
perceived by the other person. It's how guys are careful to hug
with claps on the back. God forbid that you put your faces the
same direction, but with my best friend, we can give each other
a close man-hug. It's fine, it's good to see each other because
we've been through so much and we really care for each other.
In that moment, it's the closest affection that we can show.

*In your intercultural work, how do you advise your
clients to be aware of gender norms in various countries?* I've
come down from these strong cultural differences to the point
where I'd like to play into the innocence of the encounter and
learn from it. One thing is to make sure that as a Dutch person
you don't do three kisses as a greeting. And which side do you
begin with? It's different for people in Slovakia as it is for the
Netherlands and can be confusing sometimes. I think for men it
is always safe to reach out with a hand and for women-it's
weird to say this--wait for her to come to you so as not to
blunder. They might not even engage with you in some places
and I've seen where the women didn't even get a greeting from
a man.

*Before we leave the topic of adolescence, an issue
around the Western world is increasing anxiety and
depression, especially among girls. Do you hear Europeans
addressing youth anxiety and mental health issues?* They
definitely are. I've had the pleasure of working with the
National Youth Council (NJR) in the Netherlands. They set up
a new project around mental health awareness and if I look at
my own network, more and more people are jumping on board
this mental health boat. The (NJR) aims to be a platform for the
young generation who want to contribute to society.[125] It
represents and gives voice to young people, youth associations,
and youth foundations. It also facilitates projects based on
important societal topics like mental health and European
politics. For example, the project *Hoofdzaken* (Mindbusiness)
provides a platform for 35 young people to share their
experience in mental health care to make it a bit better for
young people with psychological complaints. They share their

story with healthcare professionals and policymakers and give guest lectures to young students.

Is it because there are more mental health problems for young people in such a stressed world or is it more permissible to talk about mental health? One of my closest friends went through such problems during the time that I left the country to search for myself during my adolescence. There are even jokes about it in the Dutch language, like, "When you act normal, you're crazy enough already." Being "normal" was always repeated to me during my adolescence. *Nordic countries value not standing out from others.*

What do you see in terms of dating practices among people in their 20s? Looking at the Netherlands, I definitely see people getting married and getting kids in our 30s. My brother is 30, married for three years, with a lovely year-old son. His wife is an amazing girl whom I call a very close friend. They were dating for years. Looking at my own friends, there are plenty who haven't gotten married yet. In terms of dating practices, it depends on what kind of a group you belong to.

When we come of age around 20, we're typically in college with a lot of different student associations in the bigger cities, an easy way to meet people. Others meet through dating apps or just see what's happening at night when they go out with friends and you find somebody interesting across the bar. I dare say that it's common practice that sometimes even the woman comes up to the man to engage in a conversation or whatever it is that they're looking for.

What about your work with teams as a trainer, a coach, a facilitator, specializing in intercultural learning and dialogue facilitation? In training, I typically work with young volunteers who are interested in the topic of interculturality or conflict management, learning soft skills and interpersonal skills, as well as leadership and team building. I found an abundance of resources available to design workshops like these. For Intercultural elements, I used to draw upon positivist theories like those of G.J. Hofstede (1980) and Trompenaars & Hampden-Turner (2012). Today I would use disclaimers when using these resources again or look for critical intercultural resources.

My go-to resource for communication and leadership has always been *The Seven Habits of Highly Effective People* by Steven R. Covey. For team building, I drew upon outdoor activities, like rope courses and other sports activities with many handbooks and training manuals available. The Council of Europe also publishes materials on these topics, with a bookstore and online resources.[126] Within the youth sector in Europe, they provide many opportunities for training and tools through the website Salto-Youth.

Do you think it's fair to say that the main social problem in the Netherlands is integrating immigrants like the recent influx of Afghans into Dutch society? Yes, I would say that is a main concern for sure. It has caused a lot of friction in society and in political debates to the point where the immigrant has been ostracized so much they are almost portrayed as the devil, the worst of the worst of the worst. This political discussion has been going on for a very long time, including during my teen years 15 years ago.

If you're working with students in a school with immigrants, what kind of skills would you teach them? Focusing on working together to acknowledge that every person is necessary to deliver something that's bigger than themselves. When somebody brings in a different mindset, a different approach that could challenge the status quo, it can make it even better. There's a synergy that can take place if they dare to listen and learn from each other through experiencing group challenges.

Sometimes talking too much causes too much friction and tension, so I ask them to quiet down. I might put them in a living knot where I cross their hands over to another person so that it becomes a huge knot and they have to get themselves out together. Sometimes I feature a key person who is able to give perspective. Someone who has a different pair of glasses, so to speak, can give you added perspective to get to the solution.

A really fun group exercise in terms of gender that I've done in workshops is the fishbowl. You have men sit in a circle with women around them listening quietly and the men talk to each other as if the women weren't there and then the women do it. Absolutely, I love the fishbowl. It really does bring about very engaging and interesting discussions. *What have you used the fishbowl for other than gender?* Talking about conflict and friction among different layers within an organization. First, we express how they tackle a certain problem at their level of the organization, then ask the next levels to come in along the hierarchical chain. How does that pattern trickle down or up the ladder?

Every progressive group that I've been involved with splinters over who's the purest ideologically like, I'm more feminist than you. Purity implies feeling superior and changes the dynamic of a group. The trainer might give feedback, "I'm noticing that three of you are doing most of the talking. How does the rest of the group feel about that?" When we make life decisions, we ask our friends and our family for their perspectives, why don't we do that at work too?

What do you hear about feminism in European countries that you know about and is there a men's movement? I'm very lucky to say that I've learned a lot more about feminism since the first time it was introduced to me when it was taught to me as anti-male. That was very confusing at the time. The Netherlands is teaching girls to emancipate themselves, to stand up against boys, to push back, and not to always accept and follow what the man is saying. This sometimes didn't always work well because I've been in situations where girls did push back but it felt more aggressive than necessary. But after all these years, I know much better where I can meet men and women on an equal basis.

From feminism, it's become a lot clearer to me about women being considered less than men and women being assaulted and domestic violence. In some places, there really is such an oppressive view about what a woman should do that surprises me. *Even in the Netherlands?* Yes, I find it hard to find examples where a male is speaking on an equal level to a woman. *Disrespecting women is still common?* Yes, in certain ways it still is. There's even the practice of whistling on the streets or chasing after a girl. There's accessibility even to prostitutes, as well the sexualization and objectification of the female body, which is still taking place in the Netherlands. This has a certain influence on the perception of boys and men. *That women can be sex objects.*

What about the men's movement? I've only recently started looking for this because the only thing I picked up about being male was how to be a gentleman. However, what does it mean to be a man? The only thing I can think of is when a man becomes a father, that is the catalyzing moment. There are certain instincts that come up when the baby's there. There are women's associations and groups that talk about issues that women face in everyday life, but I don't know of men's groups.

. I heard an interview of a strong feminist who was interviewing men in the men's rights movements. They discussed issues like masculine toxicity, being the alpha male, physical abuse by their partner, being pressured at work and in other places. I felt like maybe men's groups are a great place for men to go to but I never had the need for it myself, although I'm not always able to engage equally with my partner. I ask myself can I be my own man without having to be the alpha male, without having to confirm being fully masculine with muscles, a beard, and a deep voice and handling certain challenges?

I think partially due to masculine toxicity, expressing your feelings and having emotions is a no-go. A man can be angry, happy, joyful, sad, but more likely he should be angry at the injustice that is costing him one way or another. Men are not expected to show feeling sad or melancholy, feeling the wide spectrum of feeling. Men are beginning to talk about that. Definitely, likely with close friends, because I've known them for years. I know where they're at so I can engage with them. Are there any organizations for men's issues? Yes, some local groups such as Mannen op pad, Mannengroep, and Mannenwerk.

You worked with George Simons in France; what kind of cultural differences have you seen?* Something that keeps popping up on my radar about relationships is that having an affair is something very common in France, or so it is perceived by men and is shown in the cinematography of French culture. *We don't hear about the wife having a lover.* Right, that's not done, not at all. *But the men are having mistresses who are female so maybe some of them are married.* Yes, God forbid that the man actually starts feeling something.

Adultery is one of the trickier subjects that I've come across and it's hard to think about it as a man. What if your partner is committing adultery, what does that do to you? It turns me upside down with rage and with disappointment and feeling left alone. One of my biggest fears is being left alone, so I do everything I possibly can to avoid that feeling of abandonment. At the same time, I don't know how to really express my emotions, not having had that many examples in my environment from men around me, from movies, from TV series, or anything. Going through the few different shades of emotion that men actually are able to show of their feelings, being angry is the way that I deal with that, with not the best results.

Are you in a committed relationship? Yes. *Are you and your partner monogamous?* Yes, we are. We've known each other for six years and I'm very happy to have her in my life. A lot of great things have happened, as well as a lot of rough patches that we've gone through and sort of conquered. There's more work to do, which is why I want to continue looking for better examples of how to engage and communicate equally with my opposites, and with anybody that I'm engaging with, respecting common-sense cultural values, and learning what it means to be my own man.

You mentioned the media. Did you see the Danish TV series Borgen *about a woman Prime Minister?* I know my parents have seen that; I haven't. *It's really interesting in terms of all these issues because she's divorced, she has a new lover and she's judged differently than the men who are politicians. Another interesting series in terms of gender roles is the Danish series* Rita *about a single-mother teacher.*

Is there anything else that you would like us to think about? What's difficult for me is how can you get everybody around the same table for the same topic? For me simply an invitation would work, for some a challenge would work better. Simply start that dialogue and deal with whatever comes your way in that moment, despite resistance, tension, or a rush of emotions to flood you, or whatever defense mechanisms. You get tired out from having to overcome your defenses all the time and show some vulnerability to engage.

This makes me think of is chimpanzee dominance hierarchies described in Dutch author Frans de Waal's book about Chimpanzee Politics, *so similar to human interactions.* Yes, absolutely. We often are influenced by our instinctual brain (*reptilian*) having these instinctual ways of connecting with people around us in hierarchies.

Billy Zheng
Becoming a Man in China and the US

I was born in Shantou, Guangdong Province September 1997. *Virgos tend to be communicative, have kind hearts, be principled; do you feel like that?* I would say so. *You lived in the US?* I lived in Maryland from 2014 to 2020, with my mom and stepdad. I went to high school and attended the University of Maryland. I studied Spanish languages, cultures, and literature because I like languages. I wanted to learn Portuguese but the university only had Spanish as a major.

You're also a photographer but you didn't major in video production? I wasn't interested in it back then and got into the camera stuff early this year. I always edited videos on my phone and used to do GoPro but never worked professionally as a videographer until recently (see starchboy.com). I'm doing client work and projects now but I was very interested in action sports videos because I do sports and I filmed a few dance videos and projects. *I made some dance videos that I put on my YouTube channel and Tik-Tok.*

Are you the firstborn? I'm the only child but I have a half-brother. *Sometimes firstborns have more self-confidence because their parents had more time with them and expect them to achieve.* I don't think so because my parents divorced when I was around eight and I had always been kind of rebellious since I was in middle school and that lasted for a few years. *Did you go back and forth?* Ninety percent of the time was with my mom. *She was a single parent for most of the time when you were growing up?* Yes. *I wonder if that's another kind of influence, besides being the firstborn, not having a traditional male role model around a lot gives you more freedom to express yourself?* Could be.

In what ways did your rebelliousness play out? Normal mischief cases of smoking, drinking, getting into fights, playing video games, and staying out late, from around age 11 to age 15. *You changed because . . .?* Studying. I worked in a computer store after middle school and started to read books through high school and college.

You have a really interesting perspective comparing what you learned about what it is to be masculine and a good man in Southern China and in Maryland. Because I grow my long hair out, in both countries people tend to think I've some feminine in me, and in China, people discourage me. My mom asked me to cut it short for years and is still doing it. My dad is okay with it but most family members have a bias towards men with long hair. *They think long hair means you're a hippie?* That's true and also my earrings and piercings.

What gives you the courage to go against the grain to do those things? I'm doing it how I like and I don't care about how others think. *What do the little Xs on your fingers mean?* They're my 20 tattoos that symbolize my 20 years of consuming animals. Now I'm vegan. *What made you decide no more animal products?* It was from my study abroad in Santiago, Chile where I met a very influential person and we became good friends and he shined a light for me. I did my own research, I watched documentaries, and later studied nutrition in school. I decided that eating plant-based products is a more sustainable, healthy, and kind way of eating. Ever since the 1940s or '50s everything became gradually industrialized and factory farms are very cruel, even for dairy products.

High schools in the US seem to be segregated by cliques. Is there that kind of clique segregation in Chinese high schools and what did you notice in Maryland? In China, from middle school on, people form small groups to hang out with. In Maryland, the first year in high school, I was very introverted because of the language and a whole new environment so I didn't branch out much. From what I observed there were the college-bound or people who don't care about college. In China, school uniforms are worn in public schools but students can compare each other based on the shoes they wear, and also some people are good at sports like running and soccer.

What kind of messages did you get from your stepfather about what it is to be a man? He has always been very supportive of me and my decisions. He would make a comment every now and then but he had pretty good intentions; he's not mean, he's very supportive. *Is he Chinese or American?* He's American from Maine. *How did your mom and he meet?* They met online back in 2011. *Did you feel, "I want to go to the US," or "I don't want to be taken away from my friends and my dad?"* At first, I really rejected the idea and told her she would go alone and I will stay in China. However, after a couple of years, my ideas shifted. When my dad first visited me in Maryland in 2011, I was very happy and I took him to places I liked to visit around the city and restaurants I used to visit.

What was the culture shock when you first came to the U.S? In China, my culture shock is seeing so much activity, people talking, yelling--all kinds of living on the street. In the US it seems like streets are almost empty. Yes, in Maryland we live in the suburbs where the whole neighborhood is mostly empty. My mom said it's boring here because there are no friends and neighbors to interact with. *Yes, I interviewed a couple for my* Happy Marriages *book. She's Chinese and he's American and they had a baby when they were in China and a baby when they moved to Texas. In China, the grandmother, aunties, and neighbors came to help, while they felt so isolated in Texas. Individualism in the States can interfere with having group social support and cohesion.*

Yes, I think individualism is definitely causing some discomfort living in the States and I think families are not as close as families in China. *We don't have the same extended families that live in the same areas and get together all the time because people are so mobile.* In China, people mostly live in the same province, not in different states.

What else was different in Maryland? How badly kids can behave in public school and how impolite kids can be to teachers and how indulgent the public school system can be for misbehaving kids. When I saw those activities and behavior, I thought this can't happen in China because you'd be kicked out as soon as you did it. *I've heard that public schools could have 60 to 90 students with one teacher, so there's no way you can let that kind of freedom of expression occur with 80 middle school students.* Yes, pretty much.

Another difference you must have noted is the US is multicultural, whereas China is pretty much Han? I went to middle school in Shenzhen, a migrant city with people from all over the country from different provinces with different dialects and different family cultures, so it was diverse--not ethnically--but culturally and language-wise. *I've heard that the teacher lectures while the students take notes but there's not a lot of interaction. I definitely saw that pattern in Japan.* There's still some interaction going on but not as much because the class period is short and there are many students.

Do you find the genders are comfortable with each other as friends? Yes, some of my good friends are girls, but in middle school, girls tended to hang out with each other and guys also. I think the whole progression is a little behind the US but genders are less defined. Gender awareness is not as high in China as in the West. Gen Y is more accepting of friendship between different genders than the generation from the '80s or '90s.

There's an interesting phenomenon in the West of young people questioning gender roles. I think the whole LGBTQ phenomenon is not as up to date in China and it's not commonly talked about. People are pretty open--not in the family--but socially.

You were one of the one-child policy generation? Yes, couples who worked for the government would lose their jobs if they had more than one kid. *What's the dynamic of more young men than women?* I wouldn't say this is very noticeable since there's a lot of people in general. My relatives have more boys than girls and up to my generation, they still prefer having a boy than a girl. It's pretty weird. *It puts a lot of pressure on young men to feel, "I've got to have a car and an apartment before a woman will marry me."* Yes, it's expected if a couple is marrying that a guy has a house, car, a stable job, and stable income. *It makes sense because if they're both only children, they're taking care of both sets of grandparents. Do you hear men talking about it's not fair that I have to be the success object to get the sex object?* My social circle is not conventional but I read about the issue in articles and occasional TV shows.

Also, companies advertise they don't want women of childbearing age to apply for a job. Yes, this is very scandalous. I have seen news reports where some companies will demand contracts that an employee shouldn't have kids in the next several years of employment. *They don't want to pay for maternity leave?* Exactly. Men do have a right to a short paternity leave of two weeks.[127] *The government has a new policy to encourage three kids because there are not enough young workers to fuel the economy, but young people say it's too expensive to raise one kid, how can I possibly afford to raise three?* Yes, I see people posting on social media and friends laughing at this policy or criticizing it; it's a big national issue for the next two decades.

The Nordic countries get people to have more children by providing long parental leave, subsidized child care, free education--including university. If the government wants to have more kids they're going to have to make it easier to have kids. They did come up with a package that banned after-school tutoring to facilitate parents' financial concerns. Getting into Chinese public schools is pretty hard with a lot of competition, so in order to send kids to public school, they have to educate them, which is insanely difficult, in order to win the competition to get into the high school. But now, the government discouraged it to make it easier for parents to raise a child. However, the rich kids will still find a way to compete with those who cannot afford private tutors.

What happens to kids who don't test well? Kids who don't test well might be assigned to mediocre schools (mediocre by average testing scores), while others might choose to attend technical, skill-oriented schools meant to prepare them for the workforce rather than for university.

Is it still true that the Gaokao is all-important--the college entrance exam that takes three days. If you don't do well on that you don't get into a good university. It's still a mess. *I've talked to people who took it and you had to memorize what geographical area and what Latin name for this plant, very detailed memorization.* It's a way for schools to sieve out less competent kids but it's not the right way to do it. *It just means that they pick people who can memorize well.* Yes.

If you want to get ahead in China, is it still true that you have to be a member of the Young Pioneers, then the Chinese Communist Party (CCP)? In high school, you're supposed to join a group associated with the CCP, and in college, you're given the opportunity to join as an actual party member, but it's a choice. If you're working in government institutions then definitely you're required to pass the test and study the party ideology.

Another issue is censorship of the media, so how do you get access to news? You use the Virtual Private Network (VPN). It's technically illegal but a lot of people use it and scholars and companies need this so I think it can never be truly illegal. *Do you hear news like what's going on in Hong Kong's movements for democracy?* Yes, the press covers it but mostly negatively. The whole online public discussion leans towards what the party wants.

When you graduated from Maryland, did you debate, should I stay or should I go back to China? Covid kind of messed up my plans so I stayed there the entire summer and in the fall I decided to come back to China. I came back to China in 2015 and in summer of 2018. *Did you see any changes that surprised you when you came back?* From 2015 to 2021, the change is drastic; before people weren't hooked on phones. Now there's Tik-Tok, delivery services, and the convenience that technology offers, and people are more addicted to it. There are always infrastructure changes; the government's always building.

If you had to choose, would you spend the rest of your life in China or in the States? I like both countries for different reasons. China is more humane because I was born here and it's more interesting than living in an American suburb. *Because of the interaction between people?* Yes, there's still local stuff here, farmers who work in the fields unlike the suburban farmers in America who work with huge machines on their huge farms. In the US you get a relatively nicer environment, more freedom of movement and speech. It's complicated, but apparently, I do like China.

What's the media image of what it is to be a good man? From what I observe from my social media posts from friends, one group thinks the Korean and Japanese type of male beauty is the good looking male: cute, smooth-skinned, dancers, singers. *Like K-pop guys?* Yes, and there's the hero type in movies. He's patriotic… *Fights for the motherland?* Yes, that type in propagandist movies.

In the fall of 2021, the Chinese government outlawed youth under 18 spending more than four hours a week on video games the CCP calls "poison" and "spiritual pollution." How can they enforce that rule? I think they monitor by using facial recognition in between games, so if the player is a minor, he or she will be subject to the gameplay regulations. *I read they require using your real name to get a phone number, which is required to access social media.*

The government also started a campaign against "sissy men," celebrities said to be too effeminate or "girly" and "morally flawed." A rule prohibited their appearance on TV and video sites to encourage "patriotic manliness" because "sissies will ruin the nation." "Masculinity education" was included in elementary schools to develop courage and responsibility. But, as in other parts of the world, youth are comfortable with gender fluidity. Young online fans praise male celebrities they call "wife," while they call female idols "brother" or "husband."

I noticed in recent years that Chinese singer/actor idols tend to look more like K-pop stars. I personally don't connect with the hype and don't know girls who are into this. But I do know from reading in group chats that a lot of people dislike the feminization of males in China. Although not using make-up, I have been called "girly" many, many times because of my long hair and ear piercings. I don't care too much what others say about me, but I do wish society could pay less attention to gender identity.

What do you find in terms of the dating scene of people in their 20s? I think people date in person but a lot of the first meetups happen online through apps or social media. *You have a significant other, right?* She is studying in China but we met back in Maryland. *Is she Anglo-American?* She's an African-American. *Did she decide to study in Shanghai because of you?* No, she has wanted to come to China for a long time. She visited three times, she went to Nanjing and other places before doing college in Shanghai.

Does she speak Mandarin fluently? Pretty much, yes. *How do you maintain a long-distance relationship?* It's pretty tough; we ran into a lot of trouble and argued, but last year when she first got here it was fine because it's a total change of lifestyle. We've been visiting each other every four or five weeks since last year but it's pretty tough.

What are you thinking about how to resolve that? I really don't like Shanghai, so our solution is to wait until she finishes college. Then we might stay in China but her family is still in Maryland and we might go visit both ways every year. We don't know yet because it's still three years down the road. *What is she studying in university?* She studies interactive media arts--technology media stuff.

In the far future does it appeal to you to be a father? She really likes kids. I like kids too, but I'm not really thinking about having my own at the moment, but she really wants kids in her twenties. *How would you resolve that?* We both recognize that it's not practical right now because it's a lot of responsibility and money investment and we both are not on the same page yet.

If at some point you have a son, what would you want to make sure that you teach him about what it is to be a good man? From some TED talks and YouTube education content I watched, I think I would make it less gender-defined for the kids. For example, I won't buy them male clothes or soldier toys or watch those violent TV shows or reprimand them for crying or stuff like that. I haven't really sat and thought about this but I should. *Did you hear when you were growing up big boys don't cry?* Exactly, always and even nowadays when I see relatives teach kids this, they still say, "Boys don't cry like a girl." They also say to eat meat to have strength and become a man. *Did you ever hear, "Take good care of your mom?"* I heard this when younger and even in recent years, more in China.

In the US, the feminist movement of the '60s and '70s led to a men's movement. Is there any of that kind of questioning the hazards of men's roles in China? I haven't gotten into discussions with people about this but traditionally in the family, the man is always the one who's working and women are taking care of the kids. From what I see the man is still the one working the hardest and maybe doing business meetings.

What did you notice in Chile about masculine roles? The stereotype is machismo and marianismo where the woman is supposed to be pure like Mary and the man is supposed to be very masculine. I really like Chile's gender culture and Santiago's young generation because I went to study in the university there and their gender identity is even less defined than in the US. A lot of them are defined as hippies and a lot of them smoke marijuana. It's a very nice community among the young generation in Chile; they are definitely against the man working and the woman raising the kids scenario. Their dating culture is even more relaxed and open than in the States, maybe in Latin American countries in general. I wish a lot of other places were like that.

There's more public display of affection; it's more common to show affection in the park, on subways, on the bus, on the street. When they hang out in parks they do activities together like sing together and play music; it's really fun. It's totally different from what my generation does in China, which is comparatively super boring here. Chinese people don't give hugs, but it's super nice when you first meet someone with a little hug and a kiss on the cheek.

The feminist movement in China has been concerned about sexual harassment on the streets and at work and lesbian issues, but they get silenced. Why is the government so afraid of feminist voices? Yes, this is so complicated and annoying. Feminism, the LGBTQ movement, and even the environmental movement or animal rights movement are all silenced. It's very frustrating but I think the logic behind all of this is that the government doesn't like NGOs that have roots in Western countries that might infiltrate Chinese society with Western progressive ideology that might indirectly sabotage the whole regime.

Did the authorities say to you we want to drink tea with you, meaning we're watching you? Yes, I was invited for tea regarding climate change-related stuff. It's the same approach that they use for feminists and animal-rights people. *Mao is famous for advocating equality for women, so it's not the CCP ideology because President Xi says that we want to become a green society. It's just they don't want people to organize in groups?* Yes, the national official policies are all for environmental protection and feminism and gender equality but they fear the possibility of the threat of Western influence. You could see this with the Hong Kong democracy movements because the whole thing was heavily influenced by Western organizations. *They have pretty much silenced it.* With an iron fist and very unrelenting. It's sad.

Because of your activism do the authorities look at your social media or how do they keep track of you? It's not anything perceivable openly. I don't get any threats or calls or anything like that but, for sure, activities are monitored in the background with the data centers and the background tracking stuff online that goes on digitally. There are countless examples online and we have experienced it ourselves. *So how does one be a climate activist or an animal rights activist in the face of that kind of scrutiny?* It's a question that a lot of people want to find out. I would say to be more careful digitally since they have a lot of resources more than what an individual activist can have. Any type of organization to be recognized has to be registered in a government system, which will be even more scrutinized and checked.

If you're fighting a battle, one person can't go out on the battlefield alone; you have to have a strategy and a long-term plan. If it's almost impossible to have a cohesive group, then it's really hard to have any kind of power. One individual is like one little ant that can't change the ant colony. Yes, that's a good analogy. Any type of individual action has more freedom of movement or freedom of action than any organized big-scale movement. We would run into a lot of trouble and we've seen this over and over again. *It seems like one of the main problems in China is still building coal plants, even though China leads in solar. So what can one individual do to stop building a new coal plant?* Nothing, because the corporations have a lot more power.

Your generation has been accused by older Chinese of being hyper-nationalistic, materialistic, and not concerned with social causes. They just want to get their apartment, car, and brand-name clothes. Do you think that's a fair criticism? It's fair to some extent but they're brainwashed by advertising commercials on TV. It's a worldwide phenomenon that people are becoming less likely to think critically. I see my generation as consumeristic, materialistic, wasteful sometimes, and they don't think about the consequences of their actions. The education system is not putting this early on in the kids' thinking. A lot of people who realized it later through their own research, may feel the urge to act but feel helpless or lazy. Not just my generation, as I have seen my mom's and grandpa's generation very heavily influenced by the media.

The media says that happiness is consuming things, buying things--is that the message? There are two facades of the media influence on the public. One is the commercial capitalist, money-driven industries that tell people that happiness is having things. Two is the official traditional part of the equation that says teach people to go back to their roots to recognize the deep cultures and teach people to preserve civilization. *In China, culture means Confucianism, Buddhism, Taoism, respect for the order of things?* Teachings of the ancient philosophers are the valuable part of group propaganda but they're pretty much ignored. The Chinese word for military, power, and force, is made by two characters, "stop wars." Since ancient times, Chinese civilization knew that military force was meant to stop wars. I wish the modern leaders would rediscover its meaning and use the military to protect all humans from true dangers like climate change.

I think the equivalent in the US is leaders say they're Christians but they don't care about the poor or about turning the other cheek. Sure, and here in China they practice Buddhism but not to the actual teachings of the Buddha. *Right, so they go to the temple and make an offering and then go do something lacking compassion.*

Chapter 3: Pro-Feminists

Gary Barker, Ph.D.
Promundo Co-Founder and CEO

I was born in Bakersfield, California on May 24, 1961. *It makes sense as a Gemini that you're a global communicator.* I'll credit my father with helping lead me to this path. My dad was a social worker, which back then was mostly a female profession and still largely is. His caseload included migrant farmworkers, which our family has some experience with as Okies who went to California. The topic touched him and he was a lifelong advocate for providing humane, child-centered services for children who were victims of abuse or neglect. Some of his early casework also included reaching out to men who weren't paying child support. He had a keen sense that men needed to be doing their part to support children--in all ways.

What did you learn growing up in Bakersfield about what it is to be a man? I had the amazing fortune of a father whose profession was in the care field and the care of children. He changed his vocation from a college scholarship football player who thought he wanted to do sports, either as a coach or a professional, when he got injured. Thinking about his own family history, social work called out to him. He also attributed that to seeing his own empowered mom be a community organizer, helping households who needed help. I had a very clear role model of a man who had a football player's neck and build and was also very caring. (*Similar to Michael Messner.**)

After Bakersfield, we moved to Texas, first to Dallas and then Houston. It was a shock to me after living in Bakersfield and then in Southern California with a surfer guy identity and rock music rather than country music. Texas was the land of pickup trucks, guns, boots, cowboy hats, and real bullying if you weren't like that. I was pushed up against the wall as a 13-year-old by two guys who were obviously on the cowboy side of things, who demanded to know, "Are you a hippie or a kicker?" It was pretty obvious with my bell-bottom jeans and longish hair that I was not a kicker (what the boys who considered themselves cowboys called themselves), but to have affirmed that I was a hippie was to invite their fists further into my gut.

I saw early on how different ideas of manhood were formed, how the tribes were identified, and I became aware of how, for many boys, they were serious issues, serious enough to fight over. And even if I looked onto the "cowboys" as a kind of manhood that I didn't identify with, some of them were nice guys, of course, and could cross tribes and have conversations with me, even take me country dancing if I wanted to go, with a huge amount of diversity.

I had a short career with football at 13 and 14 years. I was fast enough to make the school team but not big enough as Texas body sizes go, so I realized this is not the sport that I wanted. I moved on to tennis and theater and creative writing, which didn't match with pickup trucks and cowboy boots. I always felt supported by my dad with no pressure to continue his football legacy.

Another key event in my learning about manhood was in 1978 when I was one of 200 young people who witnessed a school shooting in our high school cafeteria. It was a young man who shot and killed another young man four times at point-blank, saying that the other boy had "stolen" his girlfriend. We all watched in horror. What happened next will always stand out for me: The school sent us outside for about half an hour. Girls were crying but boys were mostly stoic, staring at the ground or asking about how many shots and what kind of gun it was. Then half an hour later we were sent back to class with an announcement saying, "We regret the incident. No other students were harmed. The boy who shot the other is in custody. Now, back to class."

Also, just about every girl I dated in high school had a story of a guy who tried to force sex and told me their strategies for how to stay safe--mostly not about demanding consent, but how do I run away from this guy? All those experiences made me say, "There's something up with manhood. Where does that leave me? I identify as male. I consider myself mostly heterosexual yet this kind of manhood, with so much violence and anger, is not who I think I am."

My first year at university at a large Texas state university, there was a sexual assault case in my dorm. A group of five guys got a woman drunk and had non-consensual sex with her. She didn't bring any charges--this was way back before the push for assault policies on campus and no charges were brought. The big change that my university did was you had to sign in as a guest in the dorms.

It was around this time I was looking for a political space for my activism. I knew about feminism, of course, but I hadn't met any men who called themselves feminists so at the time I didn't yet see that as a space to hang my activism. But I was inspired by lots of others who took on other systems of oppression and violence, including activists who were protesting what the US was doing in Latin America.

Initially, I wanted to move to Latin America to be a journalist covering the ongoing US involvement and US-supported atrocities happening then. I was part of the Watergate generation and saw the power of journalism to achieve change, so I did an undergrad major in investigative journalism. I also saw the power of journalists to promote progressive causes. I led some surveys on gun-control attitudes and abortion rights, and became managing editor for the school newspaper, and wrote some progressive op-eds on the need for gun control. For that, I got threats, letters that said, "If I see you walking out from the newspaper at night, I'll show you where the gun goes." *A young woman started a campaign at a Texas university called "Cocks Not Glocks" where both men and women carried dildos on their backpacks to protest the "campus carry" law permitting concealed guns on campus.* It was probably the University of Texas in Austin. *Right, in 2016.* (My daughter goes there doing her master's.)

Later I did my master's in public policy at Duke looking particularly at Global South issues, particularly women's rights and children's rights in Latin America. I went into the Peace Corps in Honduras coordinating work with street children, including girls who were sexually exploited on the street. That was the start of my work in Latin America.

From there I worked with Advocates for Youth, a reproductive rights and sexual health organization based in Washington, D.C. that works internationally. It was one of the few places at the time where there were discussions about masculinities and sexuality in the context of health and social services. That were about 30 women and me working on the topic, which is pretty standard for many of the gender equality spaces where I've worked over many years. That was a key experience for me to begin asking: What does it mean to be a male ally? Who has the most to complain about in terms of massive harm that masculinities cause? Clearly women and probably gay and trans men. But I believed there was a space for me to be an ally.

Different branches of the men's movement disagree about male privilege, sexism, and patriarchy. Patriarchy, power, and privilege are big, amorphous, and complex concepts, and what they mean for us as individuals is far more than those three clusters. Raewyn Connell did a very thoughtful job of talking about the "patriarchal dividend" and I do support her view that all male-identified individuals have a piece of that dividend. But I also take the view that patriarchy brings different costs and benefits to different men in far different ways.

To speak about patriarchal privilege for a low-income man of color, like those in Rio de Janeiro with whom I did my doctoral research, is far different than, say, me as a white male heterosexual from a middle-class family in the US. Not to mention men like Bill Gates or Elon Musk who have truckloads of privilege. It's complex, to say the least.

Gates went through a divorce last year, which isn't easy. Of course and we have to consider him as a human being beyond his obvious privilege. Of course, many boys grow up believing that we shouldn't and don't know how to express ourselves emotionally in thoughtful deep ways. We get beat up on the school grounds because we didn't act the way hegemonic masculinity defines "normal" behavior, as I know firsthand. Men lose five years of life in the US (men have 76, women 81 years of life expectancy) because of multiple reasons. One year is probably related to biology because the XY chromosome is the worst model in terms of defense against some diseases, including Covid. The other three years of lower life expectancy that men face, on average, are related to lots of intersectional factors, such as: Where do you work? How much do you drink or smoke? How do you eat? Men's higher suicide rates compared to women. Risk-taking, being in the military, being in prison--the risk list that leads to men's shorter life expectancy is long.

Some of those are choices that men made and others are life-directed; for example, if you live in a low-income neighborhood where violence is much higher or if your only pathway to stable income is being in the military. Of course, there's male privilege held by men relative to women and there's a cost to men for what we call hegemonic or harmful versions of masculinities.

I'm tired of the polarizing argument about men either are always more privileged compared to women or the men's rights argument that men are the ones who "suffer" from gender norms. I'm tired of the zero-sum game argument that if you're male, you're privileged, and there's no cost of harmful gender norms and patriarchy for men. We have not achieved full equality for women and girls in the world compared to men, not by a long shot. And hegemonic masculinities bring significant costs to many men's lives. Both are true at the same time. I believe I'm no less a feminist ally by talking about the cost of patriarchy to men, while I also talk about what it means for women and individuals of all gender identities. I can be feminist and I can be on women's side and care about men too. *I agree, that's my position in a nutshell.*

How did you end up in Brazil and co-founding Promundo? I had the opportunity to move back to Latin America in 1991, first to Bogotá, Colombia, where I worked on sexual rights issues with some amazing women's rights and LGBTI activists. Then, a year later, I was invited to coordinate a study with UNICEF in Brazil on girls in situations of sexual exploitation. Another reason that I was attracted to move to Brazil was Paulo Freire's approaches around consciousness-raising and community organizing, which also inspired me to think about how I fit in this unequal world and what is my role in it.[128] How can I be on a journey together with folks who have different levels of oppression in multiple systems of inequality? How could Freire's ideas be applied to engaging men for healthy masculinities? I had the chance to meet Freire at a conference and I was inspired to think about these connections.

I coordinated a study with UNICEF on girls who were sexually exploited on the streets here in Rio De Janeiro and also in Recife. I had the amazing opportunity to work with local street educators to ask, "What does this mean for us trying to think about prevention? How can we look upstream and prevent girls from ending up in these situations?" In both cities, we were pretty clear after a few nights on the street about the trajectory of girls, which was often sexual violence at home combined with poverty and a lack of accountability of public services. I said, "Why are we not talking to the men who are at the bar paying for sex with 15-year-olds? And what about the men in the bar who don't think sexual exploitation is normal and acceptable? Why aren't they saying anything to the men who are sexually exploiting underage girls?"

That line of questioning led me to read more in the field of gender studies. And it led me to think about the tremendous resistance and diversity of men's responses to patriarchy. In particular, it was shortly after that that I read Connell's work pointing out the plurality of masculinities and the complexity of power relations and resistance, as well as acquiescence to patriarchy norms. Her work, to me, is the anchor of our field of practice in masculinities. *Many others agree.*

And what about your personal journey of being an American living in Brazil for many years? At the same time, I moved to Brazil for work, I also met my partner; we've been together for 28 years, and have a binational daughter; we have lived our life together in both countries. She is an amazing activist working in public health rights, both in Brazil and now in Washington, D.C., where we now live. It has been a journey living with her in terms of thinking about my role as an American man in a relationship in a different culture. A lot of my personal and political issues came together back then when I thought both how I wanted to be in my relationship with her and who I was as an American man working in Brazil.

How did all these ideas come together when you started Promundo? When Miguel Fontes and I started Promundo in 1997, I began to connect with gender equality activism in Brazil. We discussed all the topics that hegemonic masculinities tell us not to talk about, the things that a gender equality analysis requires. In contrast, the feminist movement aims to make gender visible, and LGBT+ individuals say we want to make homophobia and transphobia visible. Those of us who are cisgender, heterosexual men, we're basically told, "Don't question the patriarchal system. Don't talk about it. It doesn't get you any points."

They're accused of being whiners. Yes, and we get asked, "Whose side are you on?" It's an uncomfortable space to be in, as a heterosexual man, to hear the conversations that around 30% of men in heterosexual relationships use violence against a female partner. Also, talking about the rate of sexual harassment and the fact that we as men do far less of the hands-on care work. It's very difficult to sit in the room with women's rights allies in those moments. And to tell yourself, I should not be defensive about this or deny this but to ask what's my role here? It's really easy to say well, not me, or to jump immediately to those *other* men, those who use violence, or to suddenly find that the back of the room or your shoes looks much more interesting than having to have a difficult conversation about power, patriarchy, and privilege and see yourself in the system.

We have tried to bring that complexity into our work and to engage men and boys, together with women and girls, to have those challenging conversations. And we saw from the beginning that it's difficult in our field to use inviting language to get men into the room; it's far easier to do the calling-out language than the calling-in language. "Here's what we need from you and here's a language that can help you find that you have a role in this space. We acknowledge that it's going to be really hard to be at the receiving end of anger. Women's anger is real. Although it's not about you, yet the anger looks and may feel like it's directed at you. How do you feel about being ready for that?" By the time you've gone through that list, there may be four men left in the room willing to do gender-equality advocacy. But that's what we have tried to do.

I'm pleased that there's been a lot of advancement in the last years with groups like NOMAS in the US and MenEngage Alliance international (Promundo is a co-founder along with Sonke Gender Justice in South Africa, and I'm a board member). It's a global network of 700+ individuals from 50+ countries and several hundred NGOs working to engage men in feminist allyship. We seek to discover the language of accountability and the language of helping men find their role as feminist allies.

That's been Promundo's question: How do we help men of various identities find what it means to be a feminist ally, as well be an ally for LGBT+ rights? We acknowledge that it's really challenging to do the inward work to think about our own power and privilege. Then there's outward work to be part of the politics. We've had the benefit of learning a lot from the years of political infighting in this space, for good and bad. I think the long, difficult conversation with historical leaders of the women's rights movement in many countries continues to be a necessary conversation.

I see a lot of thoughtful effort from the MenEngage staff, board, and the members on what healthy thoughtful male allyship looks like. Specifically, we have spent a lot of time discussing over the years how to keep work in male allyship centered on gender inequality, on listening to the women who created this field of feminist activism, and finding ways to work together most of the time, while also agreeing that we don't have to agree on everything. We can disagree at times but still find ways to work together. MenEngage in particular has been a necessary global space for dialogue on what it is for us as male allies to be accountable to principles of the global feminist movement and to add our voices to specific global advocacy platforms, while also discussing topics we may never agree on.

How does MenEngage function differently than Promundo or MenCare? Promundo is a research-focused NGO that started first in Brazil and now has independent offices in several countries, including the US (which I head). We do program work, training, research, and advocacy in more than 20 countries engaging men and boys in gender equality and healthy masculinity. MenEngage is a global network made up of more than 700 organizations; they're the pro-feminist male allyship network focused on global advocacy and information exchange. They build the political alliances between those of us who do male-allyship programs and advocacy work and women's rights movements around the world.

MenCare is a campaign focused on engaging men as equitable caregivers and involved fatherhood that is led by Promundo and Sonke Gender Justice in South Africa. As part of the MenCare campaign, Promundo produces "The State of the World's Fathers" reports and we partner across 50 countries in parent training and advocacy related to equitable parental leave and achieving full equality in care work. So MenCare is a Promundo co-led campaign.

I did a series of books on global youth and surveyed over 4,000 young people from 88 countries and found there weren't distinct gender differences. The young men valued being involved with their families and didn't want to devote their lives to work. Our research finds similar trends in that at least a sizeable minority of men nearly everywhere that we have studied agree with women on the need for gender equality. For example, in our multi-country survey, "The International Men and Gender Equality Survey (IMAGES),"[129] a majority of men say they would like to work less (in paid work outside the home) to have more time with their children, and that most men would like to take the full amount of parental leave available in their country and to have even more of it available for them. However, they fear they're going to get looked down on or be seen as less serious and not get promoted.

Families make decisions every day because men's income is higher. A lot of men think they have to look like the tough guy and can't back down from a fight if somebody challenges their honor. That same guy might actually go home and be a really involved thoughtful dad as well as having gotten beaten up at the bar. Many men defy our stereotypes, but most of the time we find a cluster of healthier ideas about manhood goes together. We find a quarter of men, just about anywhere we look, who are pretty much in favor of feminism. Depending on how you define feminism for them, they agree that women are their equals; they accept having a female boss and the like.

A third of them are in the middle and think it's more important that they're the provider due to a lot of identities tied to the provider role. Sometimes they'll accept certain forms of violence and they think women can provoke violence. The third group of men is in the "man box" with harmful views about hegemonic masculinity. In addition to the IMAGES studies, we've done another series of studies focused on young men's views of gender and masculinities, building on Paul Kivel's concept of the man box.[130] The bottom line is that looking across cultural settings, we find that at least a quarter to a third of men are on our side of gender equality and that we need to do a lot more to encourage them to be vocal allies.

What are you doing to get that one-quarter or one-third to take action? We're trying to reach them through workplaces to tell them here are some things you can do to be a vocal ally, saying you believe in equality, so demand parental leave at your workplace, vote for candidates who support parental leave for all caregivers, and believe in subsidized child care. That's the only way we get women equally in the workplace, together with men doing our share. We try to give them political talking points, workplace talking points or action points, and home action points. We're one tiny NGO, so we're trying to leverage with big consumer brands like PNG, Unilever, L'Oreal, all of whom are partners with us in promoting healthy masculinity, as well as engaging with governments to support the policies that make equality and healthy masculinity possible.

You mentioned women's anger, which surfaced during the Second Wave of the women's movement. Robert Bly and the mythopoetic branch of the men's movement, and maybe the APA psychologists, focus on getting in touch with men's grief. That feels like a forced choice. I do think grief is real for many men, and some psychologists refer to it as the normative trauma of growing up male. Men are often forced to cut off parts of our ability to be empathetic, to express emotions, to have deeper relationships and connections to others. I want men to have a heightened awareness of how you were raised in a gendered way. In that heightened awareness, you look at harm that's happened to yourself and the harm that you may have carried out inadvertently or deliberately to others. You look at privilege as well as cost. I think that's a valid approach from the mythopoetic work with men and from those in the field of psychology focused on men's specific realities.

My take on mythopoetic is that I learned a huge amount from it. I worked with a group of men in Brazil when I first moved here to be in touch with ourselves, to take the first step toward being aware of how gender and manhood work in our own lives. I found some of Robert Bly's language around a wound and normative trauma useful. Yet, I found that we could easily get stuck looking at our own belly buttons if we didn't take consciousness from the individual to the political level as well. Men having an awareness about their own gendered upbringing is quite useful. If it stays there, it becomes what therapists can do. (My partner is a therapist and public health person.) I think a lot of men find the inner work emancipating and useful on a journey. Men, I hope your journey takes you to becoming aware of your own ghosts, traumas, and demons but I'm going to push you if you just stay there. We're either going down together or we're going to survive this together. And that means we've got to take the work to the political level.

It seems the biggest branch of the men's movement in the US is apolitical groups EVRYMAN and ManKind Project, The Warrior Weekend Training. I agree. The US is a country that focuses a lot on the self and the individual. That said, I do want men and women to be their best selves. I'm not against men's inner work but it can't stop there. What I'm most frustrated with is how we polarize this debate. There's a lot of very progressive, appropriately politicized pro-feminist men's work that looks on the inner work of such men's groups as almost blasphemous. My argument is, let's see it as part of a journey and part of the toolkit that helps men become allies to get us all to a gender-just world.

On the progressive, political side we can often get into this precious mode of saying it's all structural and systemic. The intersectional feminism that informs our work is about structures, but individuals also need to be on journeys while we're trying to fix the structures. I'd like to break out of it's either A or B thinking and say it's all of the above. Let's each push ourselves on a journey to get better at it, not to be I won't talk to you, and I'll burn your book if you're not political enough or focusing on inner work. It's really complex stuff and let's add women's voices, LGBTI+ voices, and racial justice voices. It becomes even more complicated to try to break out of the "my way is the right way" approach, but we need to find a melding of those approaches.

It seems like pro-feminist men are mostly concerned with violence against women. I think that's been the space where we've listened to women's rights advocates whose first response is to help us stop men's violence, an obvious and necessary emphasis. It touches on the lives of a third of women in the world who have or will experience some violence from a man. At the same time, 40% of men have witnessed violence by their father or another man against their mother while growing up (that's from our IMAGES data).

Given how prevalent men's violence against women is around the world, how much men's violence is the heart of patriarchy, it is absolutely appropriate that those of us who call ourselves feminist allies have listened to women's rights advocates around the world who have said, "We want you in the room as men to work with men to end violence against women as a first step in the process."

So yes, the pro-feminist work, and our work as Promundo, often starts in preventing men's violence against women but we also look beyond that--at consensual sex and healthy sexuality; at promoting healthy masculinities for the benefit of men and women; at achieving equality in care work and promoting men's involvement as fathers and caregivers.

The Icelandic professor I interviewed was on a men's commission that had to pick two issues and picked violence and parental leave. We've got a similar journey--not just parental leave, but fatherhood in general and promoting men's caregiving. So, yes, we agree. As Promundo, our biggest clusters of initiatives at the moment are violence prevention, focusing on preventing men's violence against women, and promoting men's involvement as equitable caregivers.

When I was in Rio, I visited a favela (slum) and saw young men sitting on motorcycles guarding the entrance, and was told they probably won't live past 25. You could see bullet holes in the favela walls. The woman who showed me around had a staph infection on her legs from walking through the narrow crowded alleyways where sewage flows. That's an example of how men suffer from violence too. My Ph.D. dissertation research was in one of the favelas in Rio looking at pathways into different versions of manhood--gang-related versions of manhood vs. those young men who resisted gangs and found other versions of manhood. Being in a gang often goes with a misogynist view of manhood in terms of men's use of power over their female partners.

But the reality of life in favelas in Rio de Janeiro is complex. For all the young men sitting on motorcycles affiliated with gangs, there are 10 times more young men who you don't see who are not interested in that kind of manhood and have other resources and family and life circumstances that allow them to stay out of gangs.

The challenge, of course, is helping all young men in favelas achieve those options. Since around the mid-1980s, favelas in Rio de Janeiro have had a three-way war going on between drug-trafficking groups, the police, and militia groups who are the off-duty police that President Jair Bolsonaro and his sons allegedly have ties to. As a result of this three-way conflict, the rates of mortality from homicides in the favelas are typically far higher than almost any declared conflict in the world over the past three decades, particularly for young men of color. But no Brazilian administration nor the UN, has ever declared them a combat zone.

For some men in Rio's favelas, being in a gang is a source of income, status, protection, and weaponry. The life expectancy for gang-involved young men is late 20s or early 30s, or they are imprisoned. Tragically, the Rio state police are much more inclined to execute young men rather than deal with the challenges of arresting you, booking you, and then putting you on trial in a fair court of law.

But behind the tragedy and the view that favelas are dangerous places, there's tremendous creative force there and a resilience that is astounding. Brazil's most interesting music comes out of favelas, a lot of its cultural stars, football players, musicians, and other artists have come out of favelas in Rio, Sao Paulo, and elsewhere. Some of the most amazing social movements that have an impact in Brazil and beyond have been born in favelas.

Whatever conclusion I ever had about a favela when I started working there I could change it on the same day. It's horrible in terms of inequality and the lack of government services; it's home for millions of people; it's at times hopeless and also full of optimism, and it's full of men who would do anything for their kids and have been involved fathers since the day their child was born. There are violent men in favelas, and there are pacifist men who have taught me about how to control my anger all in these big, complex places.

It's like black neighborhoods in the US. Yes, very much. In terms of histories of slavery, a lack of social policies to address historical inequalities, prison systems that are racist, police who use violence with relative impunity. A white middle class that looks onto such neighborhoods with a view of fear and a constant gaze of racism. And yet if we--as the white middle class--are able to listen, to see the complexity, to allow communities of color to define the terms of engagement and the kind of social justice necessary, we are constantly and often in naïve ways surprised by the resilience and social forces that have allowed such communities to survive in the face of racism and inequality.

President Bolsonaro, before he got Covid, said, "If you wear a mask then you're a fairy." Lula and Dilma were progressive before him; why was this Trump-like man elected? Where do we start with that question? Brazil has a lot of factors that mirror the US political trajectory of the past years, such as the massive proliferation of conservative evangelical churches (about one-third of Brazilians now call themselves evangelicals). About 40% of Brazil's members of Congress have some affiliation with an evangelical church. Not all of those are conservative since there are a few senators and representatives who are progressive or centrist even though they're evangelical, but mostly that is a conservative political movement.

On top of that, you had a middle class angry about the social justice that Presidents Lula da Silva and Dilma supported, namely, the 29 to 30 million people who were lifted out of poverty in Brazil because of social protection policies enacted under Lula and Dilma, particularly cash transfers. Middle-class folks, including some of my family members in Brazil, got angry at the lower-income people who could suddenly buy cars and fly on planes and be in the same shopping centers. There's more traffic on the streets because lower-income Brazilians could buy motorcycles and cars, rather than be stuck in line at the buses.

Unfortunately, the success of those progressive social policies in terms of poverty reduction--which is revolutionary-- got lost in accusations of corruption. *Lulu was accused of corruption in a real estate deal was put in jail*. He was, and he was later declared innocent by the same legal system because the evidence is circumstantial. Almost every reasonable take on that story is was that it was a setup. There is evidence of corruption during Lula's administration--as with every other political party in the past decades and the Worker's Party probably did the most to reduce political corruption in the past decades. But there is no reasonable evidence that Lula profited individually nor that he ordered or covered up that corruption.

But you don't get to defend yourself as a politician saying we're less corrupt than all the other 49 political parties. And now we have Steve Bannon and the likes giving Bolsonaro and his family advice on how to run their campaigns, emphasizing that a hate- and anger-based campaign runs better than a hope and justice theme, following the Trump playbook.

To go back to Promundo, why did you found it in 1997? My colleague Miguel Fontes worked in HIV as a public health researcher, while I came out of the gender lens. In Brazil at the time, we had a great confluence of women's rights activists who advocated that we needed men and NGOs dedicated to engaging men. Miguel and I made the case to partner organizations and funders concerned about the high rates of men's violence against women in Brazil and that we needed to build an evidence base of what worked to engage men for change. We should go beyond simply talking about the need to engage men, to designing theory-based and evidence-based programs and policies. Some thoughtful program officers and foundations, and some UN partners, and others joined us in working on the issue of men's violence against women with this lens of building an evidence base.

We started our NGO the same year as two other NGOs in Brazil who were doing work on the same problem, a group called Instituto Papaya (Daddy Institute) in Recife, and a group in Sao Paulo called ECOS that worked on sexuality, gender equality, and communication. We backed each other up, did research and advocacy together, and designed approaches together. Our brave funders said, "If any women's rights organizations get upset with us, we'll tell them why and tell you to go work with them." There was also a confluence of some individuals in the LGBTI + field who supported our work. It was also an exciting time of Brazil stepping out with its new constitution in 1988 and a flourishing of civil society groups coming out after the military dictatorship and then straight into popular elections.

How did Promundo grow into a global organization? We were doing a lot of exchanges from the beginning with groups in Latin America, particularly Mexico and Nicaragua because they had been doing activism and research on men and masculinities before we were. We started designing our first evidence-based approaches, our Program H (H for *homens*, men in Portuguese, and *hombres*, men in Spanish, in English called Manhood 2.0). It's a training curriculum for working with young men on promoting healthy masculinities and engaging as allies for gender equality and violence prevention.

We partnered with three NGOs in Brazil and one in Mexico to pre-test it elsewhere in Latin America, and also in English in the Caribbean. Our funders told us there's not much work that's been happening with boys and men that's gone through deliberate research to build a theory of change. There's not a big impact instrument used to evaluate and to refine a model and then train people to take it to scale. We went in with that thinking there really wasn't much programmatic work with men and boys with that lens, at least in the Global South and in Latin America.

We put out the materials and the results in Spanish, Portuguese, and English. We had engagement from the World Health Organization, International Planned Parenthood

Federation, the UN Population Fund, and other UN agencies that were interested in learning more about this research on evidence-based approaches to engaging men for gender equality. In a fairly short amount of time, groups were saying, "We would love for you to adapt this to India, to the Balkans, and are you interested in adapting this in Tanzania and in South Africa?" In the meantime, we were trying to coordinate lots of challenging work in Brazil with all those political backdrops that I described before. In terms of funding, we felt that we had staff who were good at making the cultural connections between work that we developed here in Brazil to other Global South settings.

Along the way, it made sense to have an office in the US (given our funding base in the US) as well as to do advocacy with the World Bank, the UN, and the US government, and to coordinate the international work. That, in turn, led to a conversation with colleagues in Portugal where we have a partnership with the University of Coimbra and now we have an office in Spain to work together to influence EU funding and policies.

And also along the way, we were invited to partner in several conflict settings where our experience from work in Brazil's favelas was relevant. We partnered with a group of therapists in the Democratic Republic of Congo based on research we had done there on masculinities and conflict.[131] That partnership led to opening a partner office there. Our approach has been autonomy for every organization in our cooperative arrangement. Each of the Promundo-affiliated NGOs is independent; none of us are the headquarters. We work together fully voluntarily, without any dues. We share ideas and partner when it makes sense. We had an allergic reaction to the centralized headquarters model of organizations that too often become bureaucratic and led or dominated by the global North organization. We wanted to avoid that.

What works to involve boys and men? My simplistic way to organize youth, and I guess adults, is to provide pizza and a band. What have you found works to get young men involved? Sometimes, we do all that: To get them in the door we offer pizza, gift certificates, and cool t-shirts. What's important after that is a group education model inspired by Paulo Freire's consciousness-raising, which is what good feminists organizing in the '70s and '80s did. We discuss, "Let's look at how gender puts women in second-class position, and how that plays out both in the political spaces and the social world we exist in and how it plays out in our personal lives." We learned everything we do from the best of feminist activism, and from Freire's community organizing approaches, to learn how to help young men and adult men become aware of how masculinities work for us, bringing privilege at some moments and bringing us costs at other moments. Once we've got the light bulb going off in men's heads, the next conversation is: What do we do? What is our responsibility as citizens who believe in a better world? What do we need to do from doing our half of the care work at home to voting for a feminist candidate for political office to what can I do in my workplace to make it a safe place for all individuals at the workplace?

After awareness-raising, we try to turn it into action in key institutions. How do we turn it into larger-scale action? How do we get these approaches built into Ministries of Health and Education, and Gender Equality Ministries, and big employers, and national after-school programs, and national youth sports programs? Political activism needs to go with that goal. We keep doing lots of training with individual men and design new methodologies and carry out evaluations of them. Probably a third of our work is training and about half of our work is research. How do we evaluate our work? How do we stay tuned to rapid changes and men's views and practices? The rest of our work centers on advocacy and campaign work, particularly about fatherhood, including our Global MenCare campaign and our Global Boyhood Initiative.

Interviews for my 50:50 Marriage *and* 50:50 Parenting *indicated what most appealed to men to do their share was an appeal to logic and fairness, like "Is it fair that you have more leisure time?"* We follow that approach as well. What we do is probably a one-two approach: We'll soften you with empathy (discussing fairness) and then we'll come at you with facts, or we start with facts and then come at you with empathy. We appeal to men's connection to others, like their children and their fathers, which is a lot of men in the world. I'm okay with men finding the benefits to them for being pro-feminist and living gender equality. I'm absolutely fine with men coming to feminist salvation through their connections with women and girls in their lives. It's about your daughter being safe but you care about every girl being safe? If you care, here's what you have to do.

We share our research data that make the case from research on the cost of harmful masculinity in the U.S economy every year.[132] Our Man Box study found that more young men are in the "man box," meaning if they hold restrictive harmful ideas about manhood, they're more likely to harass somebody, to have considered suicide, and to have other harmful health outcomes. So we use that data along with empathy and the immediate self-interest information. We include information about the harm that happens to women and female-identified individuals and to individuals of other sexual orientation and gender identities, and the harm to cisgender heterosexual men as well. We help men see their self-interest is in healthier masculinities while also making the moral and ethical case for why women and girls deserve gender equality.

Studies show that men who do more family work have more sex. Or better sex. Our evidence also suggests that when men show a cumulative true commitment to equality at home, that leads to the aggregate better sex lives. I'm fine saying that. *If I'm resentful because I'm doing all the work and you're sitting on the couch, then I'm not going to want to have sex with you.* If you think you are the man who gets to make all the decisions and you're violent or aggressive verbally or in other ways, your partner is less likely to want to be intimate with you. Yes, the intimacy is better, including the sex that comes from a relationship of equals.

We've had men give testimonies like, "I came from a background where when I came home she had to have sex with me," who evolved their thinking to say, "I now see that was violence and we've talked about it. I want a different relationship that is better for her and is also better for me." There is a redemptive journey that men can genuinely make that includes better intimate lives.

In terms of specific programs, what are you doing around fatherhood? Our anchor for this work is a global journey to get men to do our share of the unpaid care work by doing a lot of advocacy and research on where we are in terms of men's time use compared to women. What are the policies that make a difference, such as analyzing parental leave policies across the world? We've done research with our Nordic partners on the barriers even in the most progressive countries in the world. What are the barriers in some of the most progressive workplaces to men taking leave?

We use that information as our advocacy platform, coming up with recommendations that we need to start early with boys because the division of labor in the home starts really early. It's not just women doing three times the hands-on care work and housework that men do, it's girls as well. *Which means they don't have as much time at school.* Precisely.

We're trying to look as well at how social protection (poverty alleviation) policies work that typically make cash transfers to women, to mothers, for lots of good reasons, whether in the US welfare system--as fragile as it is--to countries that have much more universal ones. We provide a lot of policy recommendations to involve men in that suite of recommendations to governments. We also designed a program tool called Program P (P for *paternidade* or fatherhood in Portuguese and Spanish, called Fatherhood 2.0 in English). That's our gender-transformative fatherhood training module, so far implemented in about 15 countries.

We're working with Ministries of Health in a couple of countries to take it to scale to every expectant couple. We are doing a bit of a reverse affirmative action and calling it Fatherhood Training Material so that men will come. If you call it parent training, women come and just a few men. We've done a massive impact evaluation with that approach and we're working to roll it out. Impact evaluation results in Rwanda and elsewhere have found a reduction in men's use of violence against women and increased participation by men in multiple care activities, compared to men in the control group who did not participate in the training.[133]

We're also working with media content makers in Hollywood to try to tell better stories of men's caregiving. We hope it provides some input for other countries as well, when too often our children are watching TV shows that portray dads as bumbling. We include single dads and new family arrangements. There's still a lot of default to the nuclear heterosexual family, which is not the modal form of families in most of the world. We are also trying to show the diversity of men's caregiving as grandfathers, uncles, brothers, cousins, stepdads, and unrelated father figures such as a priest or coach. We show men caregiving in broader ways, not just changing diapers.

How do you contact those media influencers? We're working very closely with the Geena Davis Institute on Gender in Media. We're now doing our third study with them. They help bring influencers, we do the research, and we bring that research to content creators.

Thinking about young men around the world (except in Sub-Saharan Africa), more women are in college and youth face increasing rates of anxiety and depression. A lot of scholarship, and a lot of research, is coming out about those topics. A 200+ page report from UNESCO is looking at the data on boys in school from primary through to university. In 100+ countries in the world, boys fare worse in terms of school drop-out and academic outcomes overall. Obviously, there are still big gaps in girls' education compared to boys in parts of Sub-Saharan Africa and South Asia, but in much of the world, boys are doing worse in school. The major conclusion is that we can't talk about that gap without talking about poverty.

It's mostly middle-class students who go to university and at the secondary-school level, it's an issue of low-income boys dropping out. Why don't boys see incentives to finish school? Do they find certain kinds of employment that don't require finishing school? Do they feel pressure from their family to drop out to work full-time even if it's a job that ruins their body in a matter of ten years? What are the learning styles that mean some boys from some backgrounds don't find easy to sit still and school is seen as uncool? The UNESCO document and lots of researchers say it's all the above.

We also need to look at how gender plays out in school for girls in specific ways, particularly in certain parts of the world where the gap between girls and boys is quite big and where girls begin childbearing at young ages. We need a more complex gender conversation about education in terms of boys; again we need to find a way to have this conversation without polarizing it.

Why is it only 40% of men in US universities when the economic argument may not fit? That's a question researchers are still struggling with. I don't think we yet have a good answer on why a university education is not attractive to middle-income boys when it is so clearly associated with better economic and life incomes than not having it. *Some men's rights advocates say that US universities are hostile places for men, where you have to go to rape training, etc.* There are definitely colleges like Smith where cisgender men aren't welcome, but that's such a small experience of men in universities in the US! I think we need to look at the experiences of young women on campus that continue to show so much nonconsensual sex. When young men get to campus, they are not doing poorly in terms of who gets what salary after graduation. Our conversation about consent needs to find ways to call men in, not just call them out. I would not buy into an argument that somehow feminism has made college campuses impossible for men. I think the better conversation is: How can we promote healthier masculinities on college campuses in the US for the good of all of us?

What about the mental health are you finding globally? What we're seeing is a lot more hidden mental health problems with young men and adult men. The main norm that gets in the way is that men are not supposed to ask for help. That starts with boys being told don't cry, or to play through the pain, or tough it up, to not show that you are vulnerable and need help. That carries over to when you get lost on the road and need directions or feel anxious. Women's suicide attempts, for example, are more frequent than men, seen as a cry for help, while many men don't even think you can ask for help.

Depression in men often gets masked as anger, and sometimes turns into men's violence against women, so we've got a lot of challenges about how to make men's mental health visible. The biggest issue is how to enable men to seek help and to be more self-aware when they are facing mental health needs, in other words how to destigmatize help-seeking for men. Our surveys with young men and adults typically show higher rates of loneliness than women do. Women will ask for help and report having closer friendships.

We did one of our studies in the US on adult and young men's experiences with online gaming where many men reported that it was the place they felt they could most find friends and just be themselves.[134] They're playing games that mostly have to do with killing somebody else, but at the same time, that's the space where you feel you can be yourself and find camaraderie. I don't think games cause violence but they can encourage aggression. What are we doing wrong that gaming feels the safest space to be yourself for young men? All that is the cauldron of what's up with men's mental health, with harmful effects for men and women.

I think the challenge is that we've got to take the gas out of the men's rights approach, to say this is not about men as victims. This is about affirming that we're all victims of harmful ideas of masculinity and it plays out in women's lives in specific ways, and it lays out men's life in specific ways and I'm tired of counting who suffers more. Men's mental health brings problems for women in that they pick up the pieces when men kill themselves, die early, or can't function. We live connected lives and we need to pay attention to men's mental health for all our sakes. In other words, let's look at how gender affects all of us and be allies for men's and women's mental health. *It seems like common sense that we don't have a women's side of the planet and a men's side of the planet.* We love to make it into identity politics, so we forget it's relational. I saw a sticker on a UK subway some years back that said: "Men are from Earth. Women are from Earth. Deal with it." That's it really: We're relational. We're in it together. We have no other planet to seek refuge from our gender wars.

Do you think that it's more true of the U.S. that there's fear of being seen as not masculine enough? Is it more relaxed in Brazil where you don't have to prove you're masculine? I think it's hard to make a country comparison like that. Harmful ideas of manhood are alive and well here too, and in much of the world, and there is lots of research in Western Europe (supposedly more gender-equitable) that shows the same (*as Stephan van de Ven reports from the Netherlands*). More than half of young men in many countries say they think feminism has gone too far--that's from research in Denmark and the UK.

There may be more organized and active anti-feminist men's groups in the US than in other places; that, I think we can affirm. *Like the InCels?* Yes, especially in the US, we do everything bigger, even our polarization. So I do think, based on researchers we follow, that there is a larger, more organized presence of anti-feminist groups in the US. UK journalist Laura Bates in her book *Men Who Hate Women* does a great job documenting this and I'm proud to say she is a board member of Promundo-US.

Overall, are you optimistic or pessimistic? Did you think gender equality would progress faster? Did you anticipate Trump, Bolsonaro, Putin, Xi, and other autocrats? I don't know if we didn't see it or we didn't want to believe that anti-democracy rulers could rise in so many places. But in terms of Promundo, we have seen some of this coming. We were getting right-wing pushback on our educational materials, such as Program H developed in Brazil that Bolsonaro called "The Gay Kit." Some right-wing mayors in Brazil pushed back against us, as did some evangelical preachers. We didn't anticipate that the backlash would be so articulate and so unified and so powerful.

On the other hand, I have a 24-year-old daughter and from hanging out with her friends and our research, I see reasons for optimism. Her generation is fully on board with a feminist agenda and believes men need to be part of that, and call us to think of gender in non-binary ways. So, the bottom line for me is that I trust my daughter and all the young women on this planet who say, "Hell no, we're not going backward when it comes to women's rights." I would bet on the force of young women and young men allies that we're going to win, but probably after I'm in another dimension.

That's why I don't worry as much as some people about the Trump cult because I think that young people are progressive, and as they get older and have more power they will support democracy. The issue is whether their votes are going to count. *If they're not gerrymandered away.* Yes, I think the progressive side wins if our votes are adequately counted. A rights-based, equity-focused platform wins the most votes in the US and Brazil--if our votes are counted and elections are fair.

Anything else that you would like to add? I like the angle that you're taking, including the diversity of voices, because the work itself doesn't exhaust me--it is the polarization that exhausts me including those within our space who pitch A versus side B. We need to get beyond the zero-sum view of gender. Let's end the polarized infighting--that's what I'm trying to devote my energy to. Gender equality is good for all of us and the planet, period.

I was born in Salinas, California, in June 1952 to parents who had just moved there a couple years earlier. My father had been in the Navy during World War II and was a student and a football player at UC Berkeley before that. My mother was from Chicago and the two of them met during the war and got married. He got a teaching job at Salinas High School as the P.E. coach and basketball and football coach. They raised their family there with two older sisters and me. *Cancer people can be a little moody, intuitive, does that apply to you?* I never put too much stock in the astrological signs, but I don't think I'm particularly moody for sure. I'm fairly level, maybe to a fault.

Does your book King of the Wild Suburb: A Memoir of Father, Sons, and Guns, *refer to you personally?* Yes, it was a memoir about my relationship with my father and grandfather.

My grandfather was a working-class guy who fought in World War I and then moved from Michigan out to Berkeley and Oakland with my grandmother after the war. He was a hunter and he raised my father as a hunter, who retained that as a way of bonding with his father. They initiated me into hunting when I was a little kid. The title refers to Davy Crockett, "King of the Wild Frontier."

As I was initiated into that kind of hunting culture with men, it became a really important way for me to connect with my father and grandfather. I also played sports with my father as well, playing high school basketball for him as my coach. The memoir was a path to think about my socialization into a mid-20th century version of masculinity that eventually I came to be critical of. I also think it probably served me pretty well in terms of the kind of layers of privilege that I was raised with.

Did having two older sisters provide a glimpse of the world of young women and dating and their dramas? I really looked up to both of my sisters. My father was in the Naval Reserve, gone one weekend out every month, and then during the summers, he would go off for several weeks to trainings. I was with my mother and my sisters a lot when my father wasn't around so that domestic world of my sisters and my mom became very important to me on a deep emotional level.

As I started taking college classes, I realized that my sisters had been raised in this post-war mentality that most girls go to college to find a husband, while I was told you're going to go to college because you have to be able to take care of a family. From the get-go, my sisters and I were given an uneven message, which I realized as I started to think about gender a bit when I was at Chico State.

I realized that my sisters were dealt an unfair deal and both of them came to see it that way. Although we were a very sports-oriented family, there was nothing for girls in high school pre-Title IX. Terry had pretty high status for being a cheerleader in 1965, but my other sister Linda had no outlets to express that. In retrospect, she resented that and felt sad about it and I felt sad for her. As a 35-year-old, she finally got involved in a community softball league and loved it so much.

My mother expressed disappointment as well when she was in her 60s and 70s, telling me, "Wow, I wish I had the opportunity that a lot of the girls today have." She worked during World War II in the USO, dancing on tables having a pretty good time. When she married my father, the expectation for white middle-class women was to not work outside the home. She was home alone a lot with me and my sisters and was unhappy about that. Later in life, she told me how limiting it was and that she resented it. I learned a lot from my sisters and my mom about the limits placed on women and the sort of responsibilities that men have to help make a different kind of world.

Why did you decide to study sociology at Chico State and UC Berkeley? I went to a community college thinking I was going to be a great basketball player, but I ended up sitting on the bench and watching everyone else play. I transferred to Chico State majoring in biology and imagined I'd be a high school teacher like my dad, but I took a couple more sociology classes and caught fire with it. In the 1970s women's groups were challenging sexism and I was stunned by this. I continued in Chico for an MA where I was much more intellectually engaged and met really cool people. I had identified myself as a Marxist by then. When I finished my master's and then went to UCB for the Ph.D., I had become more interested in feminism.

What parts of what you learned from your father and grandfather were you critical about and what parts did you retain in your identity as a man? A sense of integrity and a sense of responsibility for other people around me, for your family. My father was one of those coaches who was concerned first and foremost with what kind of boys and men he was helping to shape, what kind of citizens he was helping to shape, so winning came second. Unfortunately, that has gotten flipped with a lot of organized sports in recent decades.

I learned the ways in which he was a very successful man locally. He'd been a military veteran, he was a highly respected high school coach, had played football in college as a good football player, with all those markers of masculine success as a successful family breadwinner who was very respected in the community. When he died, there was a headline in the local Salinas newspaper that read, "Mr. Basketball dies." I was drawn to all of that kind of masculine status and public adulation that comes with being a successful man but, on the other hand, my dad died in his mid-50s from colon cancer.

Masculinity killed my father as much as cancer did because he had been raised with this idea that you ignore pain; you give up your body for the team, country, and your family. He ignored the symptoms, always very proud that he didn't use any of his sick leave. He would go in feeling terrible, his back hurting, or sick, but he would never stay home because he had this ethic of giving up his own health for other people around him and ignoring his pain--men don't whine. He hit me with that a bit when I was a little kid; don't be a cry baby if you hurt yourself playing sports; spit on it and go play. By the time my father finally did go to the doctor, his cancer was very advanced. We know that with colon cancer, if it can be detected early, there's a high success rate in treating it and you live a long life.

Those lessons men learned from the Navy, sports, and culture in general in the middle of the 20th century, led him to think that he should not be a whiner, a complainer, or look for help. A lot of men don't seek help for health problems and don't take care of themselves; it's linked to the quest for success, masculine adulation, and status in the community. So, as a sociologist, I take the feminist critique of men's power and privilege in the world very seriously. Historically, men have institutional power and privilege. It gets baked into us as little boys that you're supposed to strive to be at the top of the pyramid, and privileges are out there if you work for them. You'll be adored by other people for it and get material benefit from it as well.

The costs we pay for hammering ourselves into narrow definitions of masculinity end up harming us. You can see it in health data like men's life expectancy is shorter than women with heart problems, cancer, high suicide rates, and the ways men suffer from hidden depression that's undiagnosed. All of these things are the other side of the coin of men's power and privilege. To me, those two things are analytically inseparable. The promise of privilege that the culture teaches boys and men to strive for psychologically limits our relationships and compromises our health.

Some men who identify as feminist seem to think if you acknowledge that men suffer in any way you're denying the real *oppression of women.* Most of the men I know who define themselves as feminists or pro-feminist don't make that distinction. They do focus on the ways in which narrow definitions of masculinity are limiting and hurtful to men. I've written about men's movements over the past 30 or 40 years and there's a historical movement-based dynamic at work here. Back in the '70s some of the early men's liberationists were psychologists like Joseph Pleck and Robert Brannon and then Farrell* (who's not a psychologist but was part of that first wave of men's liberationists). They were reacting to the critique coming from feminist women about men's power and privilege.

There's clearly a tension between identifying the fact that men have power and privilege because of the history and structures of patriarchy and that men are hurt because of it too. Some of the tensions within organizations for men like NOMAS that developed in the '70s to early '90s ended up blowing apart partly along that fissure. It also had to do with race and sexuality, but there was that fissure between the costs and privileges of masculinity. Some men in those organizations emphasized the costs of masculinity. Herb Goldberg and Warren Farrell went that way, along with leaders of men's rights organizations.

Other men, like John Stoltenberg,* who were more oriented towards radical feminism, emphasized the injustice of men's power and privileges. It's like being a white person and saying, "Racism hurts me too." Yes, racism dehumanizes white people, but it's not like it hurts us in the ways that it does the people in racially subordinated groups. So, a lot of feminist men were saying that we really need to focus on the harm that men and masculinity do to others: sexual assault, rape, and sexual harassment of women in workplaces. We should focus on those problems and not whine about our feelings, which resulted in a schism.

I've always thought it would be really productive to hold on to the connection, but not go in the men's rights direction, which too easily devolves into an anti-feminist and sometimes very misogynist anti-woman discourse and action.

. Also, I'd not want to go in a pro-feminist direction that ignores men's psychological and emotional needs because that could devolve into self-flagellation that's not appealing to most boys and men. We need to explain to males what you're going to gain from taking seriously the feminist critique of patriarchy and men's power and privilege. We gain a much broader humanity, possibly better health, and better relationships with children, women, and male friends or male lovers. There's so much to gain from broadening and deepening your humanity.

The other important aspect, which came out much more in the '80s and '90s, is black, poor, working-class, Latino, immigrant, and queer men don't usually have direct access to male privilege. And if you're thinking about the costs of masculinity like low-life expectancy, it's men in those social groups who are paying more of those costs of masculinity. The early death and victimhood from violence is mostly not men from my social groups who are paying those costs of masculinity as much, so when you start looking at class and race, it complicates the picture a lot.

When I talked to Daniel Ellenberg, president of the APA Men's Division, he said some psychologists don't want to talk to authors like Farrell about the importance of fathers.* Those schisms between different groups run pretty deep and have been going on for many decades. I've spoken with some of the APA group a number of years ago and there's quite a range within that group in terms of their perspectives on fathers and men's rights and feminism.

Some recent trends are scarier than what I was criticizing in the '90s, like the Incels' online misogynist groups. They have a sense of entitlement to women's bodies and get really angry if women aren't willing to have sex with them. However, there's a range within the big umbrella of a men's rights movement. There are, in fact, some men under that umbrella who, frankly, I think are probably not worth talking to. I think there's a way to dialogue the gap between a feminist orientation and a father's rights orientation--it's bridgeable with ways to find common ground. I think what a lot of pro-feminist men feel, and I identify with them, is that the primary commitment we have is to progressive social movements, especially feminism and racial justice movements.

Explain more about the schism relating to the importance of fathers, with men like Farrell and Fred Hayward* emphasizing the importance of fathers. Andrew Smiler* told me studies show the harm to kids is numerous traumas, whether the father was in the picture or not. However,* *studies show that kids do better with two parents.* Not necessarily: If it's a two-parent family where there's violence and conflict, kids are better off with a loving single-parent, so we can't just simply say two parents are always better. Years ago, the sociologist Constance Ahrons wrote *The Good Divorce,* showing that parents of children who have maintained good communication and primary commitments to the kids can be way better for the kids than if the parents stayed together in conflict. *In my book* How to Survive Your Parents Divorce, *kids said if the parents were in conflict they were relieved that they got a divorce.*

Do you label yourself as a feminist? That's evolved. When I was cutting my teeth on this sort of work in the late '70s and early '80s, there was a lot of hand wringing about do men call ourselves allies or pro-feminists? A lot of men thought that we shouldn't call ourselves feminists because it was an identity attached to having the experience of being oppressed as a woman. When I got my job at USC in the late '80s, I was struggling with that and was calling myself a pro-feminist. I was hired in the program for The Study of Women and Men in Society, the one straight guy who was hired into this program made up mostly of women who were senior to me. They had fought for feminism and Women's Studies to get a foothold in academic disciplines.

Carol Jacklin was the co-author, with Eleanor Maccoby, of the famous book, *The Psychology of Sex Differences.* She told me, "Michael, I want you to call yourself a feminist," so from then on I have called myself a feminist. She said it's really important for men to feel comfortable calling themselves feminists and be ready to explain to people what that means to you. She felt like it was waffling to call yourself a pro-feminist or a feminist ally. To me being a feminist means trying to absorb that feminist critique of men's power and privilege and ways men benefit from being born male. It also means that you are committed to acting to bring about equality in the world along lines of gender and other intersecting lines. I think among most younger people it's not an issue anymore as I find a lot more young men on college campuses who are very comfortable calling themselves feminists and most young women want them to as well.

What about your research interests and book titles and what you emphasize in your men's studies courses? I have loved being a teacher, a mentor with wonderful graduate students, and a researcher for years. Many of my books and articles over the years have focused on gender and sports, and on men and feminism. A few years ago, I decided to focus my research on groups of people who are working to bring about progressive change. The first project in that effort was a book, co-authored with two then-grad students Max Greenberg and Tal Peretz (both wonderful feminist young men), titled *Some Men: Feminist Allies in the Movement to End Violence Against Women.*

Next, I turned to a topic that has fascinated me for years; military veterans who become peace activists. The first book in this project, *Guys Like Me: Five Wars, Five Veterans for Peace* (2019) focuses on the trauma of war and the ways that men veterans often suffer in "manly silence," but some find their voices, become active in healing themselves and working for peace and justice.

The second book in this project, *Unconventional Combat: Intersectional Action in the Veterans' Peace Movement* illuminates the experience of younger "post-9/11" veterans--mostly women, people of color, and queer-identified--who bring their intersectional knowledge of race, gender, and sexual oppression to their work as peace and justice activists. All of these people--feminist anti-violence activists and veterans for peace--inspire me.

John Stoltenberg
Masculinity's Alpha Code

I was born in Minneapolis, Minnesota, June 1944. My father's ancestry was Norwegian and my mother's was German. *That Congressional committee that wants Anglo-Saxon heritage preserved would like you very much.* I wrote a book called *Refusing to Be a Man* and I should probably follow it up with a book called *Refusing to Be White.*

Do you identify with Gemini characteristics of having lots of projects and being interested in communication, with multiple sides of your personality or not? Yes, my life partner Andrea Dworkin was into astrology, although few people know this. So I had my horoscope done and I'm probably as Gemini as can be. *What was Andrea's sign?* Libra. *You're both air signs so that makes it easier.* I went to college in Minnesota and I did graduate work in New York City.

You've written about how it was difficult to be a boy and that you felt different from other guys. I had an experience that was more widely shared than I knew at the time when I thought I was the only one. I was unathletic and fat. I didn't realize until junior high school that I probably wasn't heterosexual, and then it became clear that I wasn't. *Your present marriage is to a man, after two marriages to women, so you're able to express that orientation.* I had a number of defects that I thought of as deficiencies, and I thought that I wasn't a real enough boy. I was teased and bullied. I don't think I got it as bad as some kids today, but I got it enough to make me feel very ashamed. I basically threw myself into achievements to rescue myself from this sense of unworthiness as not being enough of a real boy.

Later in my life when I started writing about these subjects, I realized, wow, just about anybody who was raised to be a real boy or a real man has a story like I had, with expectations to be more masculine than I could be.

You wrote that the male role is negative in that it involves being dominant, putting other groups down to feel superior, looking down on women, and even hating women. Do you still think that's true? There's a man whose identity is dependent on putting down somebody else; he can't be who he thinks he should be without making somebody else lesser. There is a classic paradigm that we see when male people bond to do that together over and against a third party. They pick a person to put down on the basis of ableism or race or gender expression--this tactic runs the gamut. It's a way of jointly proving they're men by putting down someone else, and it's a way of staying safe from one another.

I wrote a piece called "Why Human Oppression Happens" where I trace oppression to the core belief that if you're not a real man, you're less than nobody. Many male-assigned-at-birth people are raised and traumatized to believe they have to occupy that identity norm: Be a real man by treating someone else as lesser. There are many stories of the traumatization into real boyhood and real manhood, expectations that people bury because it's humiliating to think about when you were weak and the victim. *This makes me think of fraternity initiations.* It's much better to remember myself as the triumphant one.

Some male-bodied people do escape that, but they don't escape the culture that makes that identity necessary and sustains it. In that piece about oppression, I trace it back to this idea of "a real man." I tried to find a language that was not used for other things so I talked about the "alpha code." This belief is programmed into you; it doesn't come with your hardware, it has to be ingrained in you through trauma. The idea of manhood that is very problematic is that abandonment of selfhood in pursuit of the identity "real man."

There's another way of talking about men as courageous, supportive, and protective--all things that all humans are capable of but a lot of people call that manhood. When I use the word "manhood," I'm referring to the alpha code-driven manifestation of it--an identity that requires a lifelong quest to be a real man. It's ceaseless. You have to keep repeating acts of dominance in order to sustain your belief that you are a real man by making yourself credible in the eyes of other people. My work has been to articulate how manhood is a social construction and not an anatomical attribute; it is about acts and ethics. It's an identity achieved through a particular ethics of domination and superiority that can go all the way to murder or rape. *It seems to me that Trump is the epitome of that negative masculinity and he is very popular with millions of people.* He's exactly it.

Do you think that in a way it's healing in that Trump brings it to the surface and demonstrates this alpha male behavior is disgusting or do you think he perpetuates it? He fuels it in the way he found a way to make public the connection between white supremacy and male supremacy. The dominant behaviors necessary to maintain the alpha code idea of manhood transfer very easily to racial superiority and white supremacy, because ethically they're joined at the hip. What Trump achieved was to make that connection transparent.

He did a lot of damage, but he put it all out there: misogyny and race hate together epitomize the alpha code in action. Maybe in 20 to 50 years the country will look back at his presidency as the epitome of the worst alpha code behavior at the highest level of governance, by the most powerful person in the world, and learn not to let that happen anymore.

Do you think that Biden's emphasis on compassion is in some ways an antidote? Yes, and so is Kamala Harris, the way they are in sync about emotion and empathy is very restorative in modeling human empathy. A very interesting story about

Biden was during a debate for the Democratic Presidential nomination, Harris confronted him for his opposition to busing. It was a public takedown. Later, when Biden picked her to be his VP nominee, I realized here is a man who doesn't bear a grudge, who is not on a high horse or on some vendetta about a woman who humiliated him in public. Instead, he said we're going to make a good team. In that moment, he let go of the dominant model of manhood--the stuff he was trained into that says you're never supposed to be a loser.

The majority of white women voted for Trump in both 2016 and 2020. When you hear some of those women being interviewed they say, "I love him." Are they trained to think an alpha male is sexy? I'm always reluctant to do the same public analysis on women that I do on men since I don't have the knowledge base. Andrea Dworkin wrote a book called *Right-Wing Women* (1983) where she lays it all out. In a nutshell, she explains that women understand how dangerous male supremacy is in the world and they make a deal to be loyal to one man's misogyny because it's less risky than being out there in the field, subject to a pack of men's misogyny. That's a very loose paraphrase and I urge anyone who wants to follow up on this to read that book. She was really prophetic in that she decoded what Trump's female support is about.

Do you think boys today have any less pressure to be alpha males? One of the most interesting breakthroughs happening right now is that gender normativity is blurring and dissolving before our eyes. An extraordinarily high number of young people are identifying as nonbinary, gender nonconforming, questioning, and so on, and this trend looks exponential. The '60s, despite the so-called sexual revolution, were very gendered, very sexist; but something is afoot in the world making it possible for someone to not be trapped in a gendered expectation and to be able to see a way out of it.

I wrote another piece called "We All Need a Gender Off-Ramp." The metaphor is that hegemonic gender is like a superhighway where people are looking for an off-ramp for themselves. The off-ramps don't always go to the same place, but more and more people want to go someplace else, and young people are showing the way in droves. It's too soon to know where this is going, but I sense in my gut that this is a good thing. I can see supportive cultures growing up around kids who didn't feel they fit in, but social media is making all of these isolated niche experiences a shared language for them, and that's pretty good. There are more options, there are more visible and tribal options, which is really quite extraordinary.

I didn't have a personal conversation with another gay person until I was in college. I was completely alone in it, whereas now gay people can marry--which my husband Joe and I did as soon as it became legal. If I were to say something people should pay more attention to, it's that your escape from gender needs to be more about your ethics and not so much about your aesthetics. Fashion feels like a departure from gender expectations and gives you a feedback loop of "I'm not trying to be a real man if I dye my hair blue or green," but the theme of my work is in the ethical domain. That's where you will escape the gender hierarchy, the gender hegemony, the gender templates.

You can be a six-foot-six burly football player and be the kindest person anybody knows and it has nothing to do with your genetics, with your time spent in the gym, time spent shopping for clothes, or making up. Now, how we read each other is, we see--there goes somebody who's nonbinary or there goes somebody who's transitioning. We're reading all the aesthetic signals but not necessarily reading the ethical information until we get to know the person. Everybody gets our aesthetics first but when it comes down to it--interpersonally and relationally--it's not about the green hair or the bicep; it's about fairness, equity, respect, and empathy.

I have a grandson who's ten and what I see among his friends is they don't see one sex is better than the other, which is encouraging. That's an important trend; I don't know how widespread it is, but I know that it is happening. A lot of kids have been raised in educational systems and in families with non-gender-specific toys, games, and activities like we've watched a generation of girls playing soccer. In my generation, girls didn't do that. That athleticism completely changed the physicality of female people in space in and in life.

There are some good things happening about breaking down gender barriers and eroding the archetypal information, part of male-supremacist culture for eons, about what you have to do to be a man. All those rules are crumbling and that's good. But in a parallel universe, the alt-right wagons are circling with rigorous reaffirmation of gender hierarchy. *That always happens, you make advances and there's backlash, as explained in Susan Faludi's* Backlash.

I wrote two books about Women's Culture. *Among those creative women, there's what I call a woman-is-wonderful school, viewing women as in tune with nature, they have cycles like the earth, they give birth like the earth. In my recent book* Climate Girls Saving Our World, *many of the young women climate activists said the same thing. I wonder if that's a danger of saying men's alpha role is dangerous so therefore women are somehow better?* This is a complicated subject and again I'm going to cite Andrea on it because she wrote an extraordinary piece called "Biological Superiority: The World's Most Dangerous and Deadly Idea." She was speaking to an audience where the women-is-wonderful idea was translated into a separatism and women-are-better-than-men school of thought.

Cultures that affirm marginalized and dominated peoples are important. I would never say there should not be a culture of support and affirmation for anyone who's on the receiving end of dominance and superiority. So on a personal level, it's a salvation but is it a political solution? I would go so far as to say that the political solutions needed have to be much more focused on the dominance and decoding it and disempowering it. That was one of the reasons Andrea and Catharine MacKinnon understood they had to take on pornography as a system of harm and empower people harmed by it to fight back. They identified the centrality of pornography in creating the world in which women are raped and brutalized in their homes. In that sense, they were quite prescient.

I don't think anybody raising a kid who worries about how much access they have to online sadism would disagree that there's a cultural force there. It's hard to imagine violent pornography being stoppable at this point, but no amount of viewing "woman is good" will shield against it. *In porn, they show women liking being raped or grabbed or assaulted-- turned on by it, is that part of the genre?* Yes, the smile on her face is forced.

Niche markets for pornography exist where she has to be seen suffering for it to be gratifying. *It makes a lot of money so it's really a thriving business, which is sad.* The internet has made niches more monetizable. When pornography was VHS or print magazines, if three people were into something, there wasn't a video or magazine for them, but now they can find each other on the web and create a cult around a particular degrading practice.

Violent practices are spreading; choking, for instance, was not a thing decades ago, but it is now, taught and learned through pornography. *The woman gets choked almost to death?* Yes, until orgasm. *For the man?* Yes, and ostensibly for her too. It's almost gone mainstream now. There's an Oscar-nominated film that has a choking scene in it--*Promising Young Woman.* My point is that pornography is a precursor and a driver of behaviors that are part of this ethic of degrade, dominate, and dismiss.

As a radical feminist, do you believe that gender roles are socially constructed? You and Andrea say that they're myths but what about the role of hormones? It seems testosterone and estrogen have an impact on our behavior. I don't deny that we have physicality and we come with various extents of this and that. Let's say, for example, testosterone is a precursor of a certain energy, athleticism, strength, and exuberance, what do you do with that? That's where it becomes an ethical question. Does that energy turn into aggression or does it turn into an inclination for a physical challenge that could be exhausting but good and nobody gets hurt?

I did a sexual assault prevention media campaign with the theme line "My strength is not for hurting." Let's say embodied strength is something that comes with the plumbing in male-bodied people, what's it for? Let's position strength as a good thing; no one's going to say you've got to toss your strength, but how do you use it? I developed an entire media campaign centered on consent that was picked up by the Department of Defense and changed it to "My strength is for defending." Its tagline was "Preventing sexual assault is part of my duty." It was locating sexual assault prevention in the sense of duty that military people are trained to abide by and it was very well received.

I interviewed a transman for my Happy Marriages *book who said that the main thing that changed for him after taking testosterone was his visual turn-ons. Before he'd see a beautiful body and appreciate it but with testosterone, there was more of a visceral reaction to breasts and so on. It doesn't seem accurate to say all gender roles are socially constructed or myths if some of them are influenced by estrogen or testosterone.* No, I was saying that gender identity of a real man is problematic because the only way you get to that is with an ethic of derogation, degradation, and dominance because the alternative is being a nonentity. If you're traumatized into the belief that's who you've got to be, the alternative is annihilation.

I've read that in male prisons the organizational system is gangs with hierarchies and in women's prisons they form family groups. I've found a lot of these sex differentiation theories and studies are a way of staying comfortable in a binary world, while a lot of people want to escape that. The scientific world has been built on maintaining gender polarity and with it the implicit approval for male supremacy. It's important to remember that in a world where gender identity is so fraught for those who are into this alpha code, the world that is constructed to keep them dominant is a very dangerous place. So much oppression is required societally to keep those identities sacrosanct.

Albert Kinsey observed that we all are on a spectrum in terms of our sexual orientation. I think our sense of our gender is like a point on a color wheel where you might feel a little more blue one day or a little more red one day. In fact, gender awareness of oneself can migrate over life as for some people it changes over a lifetime. Sometimes it's dramatic in people who transition, but we're all gender fluid more than we like to remember.

How has your sense of yourself changed? Now, I don't ever think about whether I'm presenting enough as a man in contrast to some male-bodied people who like to talk at the bottom of their vocal range all the time until their vocal cords get so rough they give out. They're terrified of their upper register. I'm using that as a model of what it means to be in constant panic about whether you're presenting as male enough. A lot of folks are uncomfortable with not following all the coding that confirms our delusion that we're a bipolar species.

The big turning point of my own salvation from gender panic came for me when I read Andrea's book *Woman Hating* explaining that man and woman are social constructions that don't really exist. I felt freedom from the cookie-cutter I was trying to fit into. I found it was possible to be who I am without constantly thinking about "am I male enough?" I stopped walking around feeling like an imposter.

You and Andrea married and lived together for 31 years, how did you do the roommate roles and keep from falling back into traditional roles? There were things that were her job and mine and ours. We both had been married before, she to a man who abused her. She's written a lot about that. She had it really rough for several years. We both knew the worst traits that came out in ourselves in being in a marriage. I look back with horror on my first marriage in terms of the things I did to be the husband. I remember to my shame putting a sticky note on the refrigerator that said, "clean me."

What keeps recurring to me is how the worst traits came out from me trying to be a proper husband. I've learned from my first two marriages and in my current marriage to the kindest man I know. Andrea was in recoil from the masochism of being the obedient wife, and in my first marriage, I hadn't thought in terms of an equilibrium of equality, equity, and empathy because we were both in the same game, just playing the two different parts of it.

Andrea and I began having a conversation that never wanted to end. We first met having a conversation; we knew each other from the same circle. *You both left a poetry reading because it was sexist and talked outside.* At the time she had been assigned to write a story for a publication about a man who was in prison for killing police and had also beaten women. She was in a lot of conflict because she needed the money. Everybody was telling her to do the story but when we started talking I understood why she wouldn't want to. I was probably the first person to affirm that, which began our conversation. She came to know me better than I know myself.

How was your relationship influenced by both of you identifying as queer? Mostly the absence of heterosexuality in our lives in any way. She did almost none of the things that women do to present themselves to the world as feminine, like she wore one earring, that's it--but so did I. *Were you free to have same-sex relationships outside of the marriage so your commitment was to be best friends, people who loved each other, married, but you could have other kinds of relationships?* I'm going to speak for myself and not for her but yes. The understanding was no lies, no secrets. The unfaithfulness was not in the sex with somebody else; the unfaithfulness would be the deceit.

How does one keep from being bored or lose interest over 31 years with the same person? In our situation, there was a lot of stuff from the outside that came into our lives and needed dealing with, like somebody wrote something or there was an assault or an attack. So much came into our lives about the politics outside--through her work primarily--so there was stuff to talk about that we both were alarmed or distressed about. She's written very vividly about a very dark time after her rape in Paris in 1999. She had just finished writing *Scapegoat: The Jews, Israel, and Women's Liberation.* It took her nine years and was massively researched.

She needed a holiday, so she went to Paris and stayed in a nice hotel where she was drug-raped. She called me right after, and I said get the first plane home. She wrote about the ordeal in an essay called "My Suicide" that she kept on her computer without showing anyone. I discovered it after she died, a literary suicide note. I read it and had to put it away, I couldn't bear it. Years later I looked at it again and saw potential in it to bring the words to other people in the form of a theater piece called *Aftermath.* (A Montreal production was online in April and May 2021.)

What neither of us understood at the time was how a rape impacts the relationship. Nobody knows to talk about that. It's something I've not even wrapped my head around, but there was a year or so that was very, very hard. The aftermath of the rape was traumatic for her, it lasted a long time. The last years of her life had joy again, but there was a while when she was in very bad shape and I didn't fully know how to be there for her.

In hindsight what would you say to do if your partner is raped? It was very complicated by the fact that it was a drug rape and she kept searching her memory for it, as all the evidence was circumstantial. But she, who knew a lot about sexual violence, didn't know anything about drug rape. It took her a while to talk to a rape counselor friend who told her these are the symptoms, these are the things that drug rape survivors go through. There are patterns of symptoms, but neither of us knew it; we were both ignorant.

When you had conflict situations or disagreements, did you have ways to work it out that other people could learn from? We did work it out sometimes sooner than later or later than sooner. The loss of her was huge, but I'm very grateful that the last couple of years were very good years despite her many health problems. It was a very happy life again, coming through a really dark time. We had a lot to work on about the move to D.C. because I got a job here and we were like a good team figuring it out, as it was a massive job.

Let's talk about your books to see how your thinking has progressed. The first one was Refusing to Be a Man. Broadly speaking, it's a philosophical grounding for what became the ethical approach that I started working on in the sequel called *The End of Manhood,* which is more practical, more like a self-help book. The two books are in a conversation with each other. As my thinking has moved beyond that, it's taken gender diversity into account much more and how that plays out in many people's lives. I've also become outspoken as a radical feminist who is trans-inclusive rather than trans-exclusive--which is a huge schism in radical feminism.

What's an example in The End of Manhood *of a how-to?* I talk about lovemaking in a way that doesn't mean asserting oneself as "the man there," which is different from being somebody who's full of ardor and erotic passion. When you're erotically with somebody and you're feeling their feelings as well as your own, it's a different zone of eroticism. This doesn't mean it has to be any less passionate or orgasmic.

Andrea wrote a book called *Intercourse* with eight chapters and in each chapter, she takes on a dimension of intercourse. She has a chapter called "Communion"--where two people meet as if as one--not one person does something to the other. I have a chapter about that kind of lovemaking as an example of what it would mean to love justice more than manhood. Basically, that's the maxim of the book: "The core of one's being must love justice more than manhood." And by manhood there, I mean that paradigm of dominance. If you love justice more, if you want to embody it and love justice more, you really do have to leave off your loyalty to that kind of manhood; you just have to let it go.

My book *What Makes Pornography "Sexy"?* started with a workshop that I created called "The Pose Workshop" in the era of *Playboy* and *Penthouse.* I would show pictures from the magazines and have men replicate the women's poses and have the other men in the circle watch. I don't think the workshop translates to internet porn very well, but in those days it was a really mind-changing moment about recognizing what her subordination meant physically--to inhabit it, to mimic it, to mirror it--to appear as "sexy." At a certain point, I said I can't do this anymore, I'm just going to write a book about how someone else can do it. *I'm thinking of Jean Kilbourne's slideshows of advertisements with a lot of women doing oral sex things with lipstick tubes and such, so I can imagine.*

Is your master's degree from Union Theological Seminary the foundation for your emphasis on a moral approach to thinking about gender? I was a philosophy major in college with an emphasis on English, too, and I did a lot of theater. I was pretty captivated by Soren Kierkegaard. It was a Lutheran college, and I got to seminary because I had a fellowship that would take me there. I didn't plan to go to seminary and I was never going to be ordained but I got this fellowship that would take me for a trial year and I stayed.

It was an interesting fit because I found the philosophy of religion really interesting and I got involved in theater with a theological spin. I was a playwright then. But to get to the core of your question, the relationship between the ethics of acts and how it informs my understanding of gender is very deeply related to my love of theater, which I still think of as the art form most conducive to expressing issues of ethics in interpersonal relations. *Like the ancient Greek theater.* Yes, they started it. I studied systematic ethics in seminary. I got a brain loaded up with a lot of stuff about ethics from a religious point of view, and I just took it secular. The most influential book that I ever read was *Honest to God* by the Anglican Bishop John A.T. Robinson. He posited that God is not out there but God is between us; just between you and me right now could be God. That was a mind-blowing breakthrough for me and I still think that's the truth. *It's like quantum physics, the connection between everything.* Yes.

What about your 2013 fiction utopian novel Gonerz? It's about a dystopian future but it's about a utopian group of kids--four characters who are 12 going on 13. They live together in a quarantined space to be pure breeders because a malignant virus has taken over the world and people are dying in droves. So the government sets up breeding farms. *Like the Nazis did.* And they select four kids--two are called "wombers" and two are called "spermers." The novel is told by one of the four in this housing unit and it's their story--their adventures and their loves. I feel it's the best thing I've ever written; it kind of counts as a young adult novel but it's probably way too sexually explicit for that. I conceived it during the AIDS crisis. I can remember exactly the moment it came to me; Andrea and I were in a coffee shop around the corner and I took a napkin and started writing a few things--the genesis of this idea of kids surviving a cataclysmic crisis.

Margaret Atwood's genetically modified characters in her novel Oryx and Crake *also explore the social construction of gender.* The four kids invent themselves as they go along and they're all polyamorous. They don't think of themselves as male or female and each of them is lovers with two others, so there's always one of the four they're not lovers with. Picture a quadrant and each has pretty deep love relationships, sexual relationships, with two others in the quadrant. They're very loyal to each other in their community, their home, their family. They make up stuff from old TV shows that are being beamed to them. So it's beyond gender in the ethical sense; it isn't absent gender in the anatomical sense.

Do you have a next book brewing? Yes, I've been trying to put together a collection of *Refusing to Be a Man Two*, because I've done a lot of short pieces and I'm cobbling them together.

You said that we need a revolution in terms of capitalism and gender. Do you see any revolutionary signs of change? I just read *White Feminism* by Koa Beck. She's very illuminating on the subject of how a faux feminism has been adopted by capitalism and made into a marketing tool that doesn't change anything. That's still rolling around in my mind: the extent to which a liberal feminist individualism, a buying into self-pornographization, has become monetizable. It's distressing. *I think of Jane Cunningham and Philippa Roberts' 2021 book,* Brandsplaining: Why Marketing is Still Sexist and How to Fix It. Capitalism has cashed in on what looks like feminism but has left intact everything about sexual assault, pornography, the traumatization that goes into inculcating manhood into penised people--that's all untouched.

A similar case can be made for the way capitalism has appropriated diversity and done a Benetton ads look on everything without making any structural changes. *The media view of women can and should do everything, look great, have a big career, make baby food. That pressure may be part of the reason that girls around the world report more anxiety and depression.* Yes, it's terrible on kids.

Do you think that girls are more likely to be labeled depressed and anxious because boys aren't given permission to say, "I feel sad?" Boys get social permission to vent their feelings in anger and violence in a way that girls don't. There's a reason our serial killers are mostly cis white men. *And school shooters.* Girls punish themselves, boys have ways to punish others. It's the same sickness that they're trying to escape but it's gendered.

How does one break out of these gender stereotypes? Actions matter, interactions matter. Pay attention to how you are behaving in relationship to other people, your talking and listening, your actions, what you do in front of your kids, not just what you say. Be aware of the ethics in your actions. That is the common language that we have to learn how to speak to reach into each other's lives without hurting and with love.

Jesus said that 2,000 years ago and he never made any distinctions based on gender. He didn't buy into the culture's despisal of prostituted women. *He healed a woman with an issue of blood, talked about theology with women when you weren't supposed to, and they were first with him at the crucifixion and resurrection.* They just didn't get to write any of the gospels…*or revise them years later. The Gospel of Mary is one of the apocryphal gospels.* That is the core of his ethics. *The Golden Rule is in all religions.* Yes, it should be more present in our daily lives. *Especially among people who profess to be religious.*

Jack Straton, Ph.D.
Former Co-Chair of
National Organization of Men Against Sexism

I was born in 1955 in Colorado and then moved to Oregon when I was three and grew up in Eugene. *I'm interested in your astrological sign.* I'm a Leo with Leo rising and five planets in Leo but I was the shyest kid you could find. I was so shy I wouldn't even ask my best friend for a glass of water, so it's a very interesting combination, isn't it?

Now you're a professor in front of groups all the time. What happened to make the shift? A key piece of it was I started doing anti-rape activism in 1985 and found myself stepping forward when the TV cameras were turned on, rather than backward. Something about wanting to make change and knowing that this connection was important drew me out of my shell considerably. Of course, by that time I'd also been a professional drummer for a number of years, so I guess in one sense sitting there playing dirty blues is as profoundly exposing yourself as you possibly can do.

There's been a long path out of my shell, including playing music professionally and understanding that I had been telling myself a story about who I was that was incomplete. Although the shy person is still in there, it's nothing like the whole story anymore. *It seems to me, the key is to focus is on getting the message across rather than yourself.* Yes, that was a key piece of it for sure.

What did you learn growing up about what it was to be a man? Young men that I interviewed for the book said they learned around middle school "don't be like a girl." It makes me sad to realize that is still the message, which has been the core of growing up into being a man. One of the things I understood in the late '80s was that if I was going to be working against sexism, so much of men's behavior is rooted in all of that bullying we experienced around not being "like a girl," which is what "being gay" was for us in our ignorance. If we are going to stop sexism, we also needed to deal with heterosexism and homophobia.

I grew up with a very interesting role model in that my father was one of the kindest human beings on the planet, very sweet, very nice, interested in the life of the mind. He really enjoyed life and his children. I had an incredibly deep relationship with him. Though he's now gone from the planet, I'm always pulling out phrases that I heard him say.

My Thanksgiving and Christmas were always fun when I would bring guests home because when we'd walk in the front door, my father would walk out of the kitchen with an apron on and greet my friend. Then we'd go into the back room and my mom would be watching football on TV. This wasn't because he was drawn to being a cook but because my mother had undiagnosed hypoglycemia and was wiped out all the time and somebody needed to cook for the family. The narrow box that most men see as a picture of how they're going to be a man was not there for me since I saw a much broader spectrum of what it is to be a man.

Nevertheless, I certainly picked up on a lot of the masculine traits you might imagine. I was really good at tackle football in seventh and eighth grade when I literally destroyed my knees because if there were five people in-between me and the ball, that wouldn't matter; I would go get the ball. I find it incredibly amusing that there are these parts of me that never disappeared but so much of my current persona is around compassion, caring, and love. I'm curious if my knees weren't bad would I go back to playing tackle football and be that same aggressive person?

How many siblings do you have? I'm the youngest of four, two brothers and one sister. *What did you learn from them?* I have one brother, Peter, who's a year and a half older than me and he and I were pretty good friends, although we struggled fighting over who got the couch and so on. We were mostly on good terms, occasionally punching each other out as siblings will. My oldest brother, David, and I were not as close, though he taught me how to play football and go mountain climbing. He and I now are great friends so it's all come full circle.

Who were you in high school? I went to high school with kids who I had gone to second grade with and I was a musician, so there was a group of people who were my old friends and musician buddies, with some crossover with the first group. I seemed to have been blessed with a mind that works pretty well so I was in the advanced mathematics section and made some friends in that group. That was the hippie era and I had hair down to my waist by the time I was in 10th grade. I had a lot of role models to tap into for how to make it through this really awkward period of high school.

When I went into 10th grade, it was really one of the major turning points in this shyness bit because I decided at that point that I was done with playing that role. Instead of being the shy kid, I decided I was going to be the life of the party kid. I pulled it off because I had this whole new group of friends who didn't know me. Interestingly, my second-grade friends didn't know how to deal with me in this new role.

After that nine months, I realized that my old "shy-kid" story was no more real than this new "party-kid" story about myself that I was putting on. Then I thought, "What I am going to do now--pick a story a year?" I realized that I was going to put my innermost core on the outside of my skin and be the most authentic person I could be. It's been a very successful way to be a human being in the world, a gendered male human being in the world, finding my authentic source and voice and being that person with everyone. Unpacking that source was a process for six or eight years, and I gradually found comfort in who I was coming to be.

I stopped drinking alcohol when I turned 21 because it wasn't fun anymore. *No longer a rebellion.* I have the same hypoglycemia that my mother did so the alcohol was going to kick in all of those systems since virtually every alcoholic drink is sweetened in some way. At that point, I became like my grandfather, a teetotaler who was the first radio evangelist in the nation in 1923,[135] John Roach Straton in New York City. He was referred to as the "fundamentalist pope" by Stanley Walker in H.L. Mencken's magazine *The American Mercury*.[136] Even though I was playing "demon jazz" in nightclubs, I was still a teetotaler, so I don't know whether he was rolling over in his grave or clapping.

Did you major in physics as an undergrad? No, here's the interesting sequence. Out of high school, I went directly to the University of Oregon in the same city I'd grown up in. I found that I could only take a photography class if I majored in photography, so I did. My brother Peter would take various classes and I always did everything he did. He took a computer programming class so I took a computer program class. He took a physics class and I took a physics class.

I was thinking how the hell am I going to survive this physics class? It's pretty intense stuff, and so during Fall term, I signed up for karate, thinking that would be something really different to do right after my general physics class. That was fine until we got to the part where you're learning how to punch your fist through somebody's chest and rip their heart out and I thought maybe this is not my cup of tea.

The next term I took Kundalini Yoga and the first day he had us lifting our legs up and down for 20 minutes and after that I was more stoned than I had ever been in my life. I thought, "This is really great, I mean I could go talk to a cop right now," with no fear of being busted for being stoned. So I continued doing it. I got my degree in photography but did not want to be a wedding photographer since I thought that would kill my joy in photography. I wondered, "So what do I do now?" I ended up playing music professionally for about three years in a jazz band. Bill Sabol was the piano player and Steve Mosher was on bass. We would be out on the road and Bill did

Zen meditation and I was doing my "kinda loony yoga," as I call it. Each of us looked like we were having fun, so we taught each other.

We would get up and do a half-hour of yoga and then go out and find breakfast in the afternoon, which is always a struggle, then go walk through the sunshine for a while and go back to the motel and take a nap. We'd get up at 4:30 pm and do a half-hour yoga, half-hour meditation, half-hour yoga, half-hour meditation, and a half-hour yoga. Believe me, any acid trip you could imagine pales in comparison with the buildup from doing that day after day after day. We would go down to the club and play music for four hours, which was another form of meditation, and then we would sit on the motel rooftop and talk about the nature of reality until four in the morning and go to bed. I can't imagine having a life that was more blessed than that. It brought in $600 a month to live on, but my rent was $185 so I could make it work.

That went on for three years and then Bill had the temerity to decide to move across the country with his wife rather than staying and playing music with me. I was heartbroken; it was incredible that all of this energy that I put into this creative enterprise was out the window. I kicked around for a few years and did some landscape maintenance for a year with the bass player Steve until I decided to go back to school. Since Bill and I had talked about cosmology on the hotel rooftops, I thought, "Hell, I'll go learn the language of cosmology." I got a Master's and then a Ph.D., doing research not in cosmology but in quantum theory. My life of the mind now is doing quantum scattering theory, as joyful an enterprise as anything I've ever done. I continue to do photography and music, plus the creativity in mathematics. Creativity percolates through all that I do on a professional level and on a heartfelt level.

In your physics classes, are the majority of students male? I teach mostly astronomy as my physics course and a freshman inquiry course, which is a whole other department at the university, both with more women than men. Physics majors are still only 20% women, also at the Master's and Ph.D. levels. In terms of faculty nationally, it's about 14% women, though they are a quarter of new hires. There's something about the way that we are being with each other, and with students, that's not working for keeping women in the pipeline. *It seems that women go into fields like biology, physiology, and medicine that are clearly life-affirming.* We really need to work on this and we've been saying this for 20 years now; we're making some progress but it's not good enough.

How did you get interested in diversity issues, gender issues, violence intervention? One of the turning points in my life was in 1984-85 when I was getting my Ph.D. After a couple of rapes at the University of Oregon, the Women's Resource Center put a note in the school newspaper saying, "Any man interested in forming a men against rape group, phone us and we'll get it going." I phoned and then I waited and waited. After two months, I went into the Center and a woman handed me a list of men who'd phoned in. I realized it was my job to follow up with all these people, so I organized the first meeting. A couple of men thought we should form a service to escort women safely across campus, while the other four of us thought maybe there's something more fundamental that we needed to do, but we had no idea what it was.

I talked to the Rape Crisis Network in town, the activist feminist women who were working on ending sexual assault and domestic violence. They were very skeptical of yet another group of men wanting to do something because they had experience with men who wanted a great deal of praise for very little work. However, they were willing to give us a chance, and ultimately under their tutelage, we learned how to do presentations in classrooms.

What we learned early on is that we think about the rapist as some stranger in a bush or alleyway, but the vast majority of rapes are committed by men known to the women. So if "normal men" are raping women, then normal men can talk to normal men about it and try to make sure that that behavior stops. It became very clear that there was a great deal that men of good heart can do in trying to stop this literal war against women.

The group in Eugene grew from 4 to 21, down to 12 up to 18, and down to one and a half when I left. I moved to Washington DC and started Men Against Rape there. This group has survived to the present day under a couple of name changes. Currently, it's Men Can Stop Rape and they do magnificent work. (Lesson: I didn't have to do that work, and I should not get credit for it, but simply providing a spark allowed other men to pick up the baton and carry on what already existed.)

It sounds like educating other men is the key. Yes, we need to go to kids and talk with them about respecting girls and women, finding common cause. James Baldwin said, "In order to oppress someone you have to dis-identify with that person," so learning how to identify with women is a key piece.

The respect needs to carry over into acknowledging boundaries and not brutalizing women. It seems like that last step is a no-brainer, but apparently, there are plenty of men who feel like they're entitled to physically and psychologically abuse women. And they're also taught that women are the "appropriate targets" for whatever violent inclination is bubbling up in them at the moment. (They don't beat up cops, so they are certainly in control of their responses.) So yes, education and education and education may well do the trick, but it's a long-term prospect.

In advice books to women about how to attract a man, a theme is men need a conquest so don't be too easy. The woman's job is to make him feel like he is the conqueror. There's this very interesting film called *Amandla! A Revolution in Four-Part Harmony* about the role music played in the revolution in South Africa. In the film, you see this woman standing on the corner, a black woman with a black child, and this bus comes along labeled "Whites Only." When she doesn't get on the bus, her child looks up at her and says, "Why Mama?" Abdullah Ibrahim talks about how "the whites made the laws but the blacks had to enforce them," and I think the same happens in our society around gender.

There's a belief that a good woman doesn't say yes even if she means yes, so it's the man's job to get past that "no," which she really doesn't mean. Yes, and so the instruction to the boys and men is: push and push and push. If you have some integrity, when you hear a "no," you actually stop. Wouldn't it be better to explore the joys of the human body in concert with your partner and find what is enjoyable and fun and work towards consent, where someone is inviting you to a beautiful experience? *It's said that rape isn't about sex, it's about power and control.* Yes, it's complicated because men are taught that sex is tied up with power and control, although it needn't be that way.

An interesting study done in 1981 by Peggy Reeves Sanday was based on her thinking that if there's something natural about the way men are in society, we should go to the most naturalistic societal settings possible to see what the root of human behavior ought to be for male sexuality and male behavior. [137] She found that out of 95 tribal societies around the world, 47 were rape-free and only 18 rape-prone, and the others somewhere in between.

Of course, we live in a rape-prone society which indicates there's something about our culture that is way off. Even though we are going to do the work of individual men educating individual boys, we have to rethink the culture itself, the huge force behind the education of individuals. Racism and sexism and other "isms" are systems the way communism, socialism, and capitalism are systems, world views, and methods to reinforce power. We live under sexism, a system in which power is the fundamental thing. That power moves should come out as expressed in sexuality should not be a surprise to anyone. We are living in a worldview in which power is key.

The male culture has crafted this civilization we work within, but it's often the women who have to enforce the rules. So the stories that you hear from advice columnists around what women are supposed to do in order to attract a man are all folded up into this culture. My advice to young women is, "Be authentic, be yourself, and someone is going to be drawn to you and you may be drawn to that person." Look for people who are authentic in their lives. What you'll find is what a deep connection is and all of this should start with friendship.

Sexual attraction is fabulous but choosing a partner based on the heat level is not as wise as truly choosing it based on how much you like this person, how much fun they are to be around. Do you find yourself becoming a better person when you're around that person?" *An example of women enforcing the patriarchal rules is female genital mutilation, it's their mothers and grandmothers that cut their genitalia.* Yes.

What about child custody? That's another issue of yours. Yes, while I was living in DC, I got wind of The National Organization for Men Against Sexism (NOMAS). I was drawn to that and took a road trip up to New Haven, Connecticut, where I attended my first conference. I was in some ways the sole driving force behind the two Men Against Rape groups that I had formed and then worked within, so it was an amazing experience to walk into a room filled with other men fired up to do something, like John Stoltenberg,* John Cohen, and Jim Hanneken. It energized me to sit in a room with 26 other men and some women who were fired up to do something about ending men's violence.

How did you get from that first meeting with NOMAS into custody issues? About two years after that, the Ending Men's Violence task group got a message from Stoltenberg saying, "I have an inch-high stack of articles on child custody. This is a huge part of the backlash against the women's movement and we need to get on this. Is anybody willing to take up this burden?" I thought, "God, no, I've got too much going on in my life." Then I thought, "Who else is going to do this?" So I said, "Yes, please mail me the packet."

I got a fabulous education on the ways in which men who abuse women will use the court systems to continue that abuse, to get access to their wives and children (whom they also may abuse). I wrote up a summary of that stack of legal briefs and academic papers. Ultimately NOMAS decided to form a new child custody task group, which I chaired. I spent a number of years writing on behalf of women who were facing overwhelming odds against retaining custody of their children because their abusive husband was a lawyer or the ways in which courts have been biased against women.

Protective mothers of children get labeled as "unfriendly parents" because they don't want the abuser to have access to their children. They get custody taken away from them and the abuser gets the children. Court systems have been set up to privilege manipulative, verbally and physically abusive men to either get custody or use the threat of a custody challenge to pressure their former wives and partners into lower child-support payments.

This has been a long struggle. I was somewhat effective at creating ideas but not very effective at actually helping women. In 2008, Barry Goldstein came onto the team and the work that he's done has far outstripped anything that I started to do. He has taken up most of the work on this issue for NOMAS and written a number of books on the subject.[138] A few legislatures are starting to look at his Safe Child Act.[139]

Kansas and Missouri have joint legal and physical custody as a preferred mode. Is this becoming more common? There are a number of ways in which joint custody percolates through the various states. There are many ways in which you can have, if not a presumption of joint custody, if one parent asks for it and the other does not--knowing that he is abusive--then the parent who asks for it "should get sole custody of the child." So there are various ways in which the idea of "the best interest of the child" being "joint custody" comes into play. This is a very general overview since most of my activist attention has switched to looking at racism and figuring out how to move us out of the 20th century on that front.

Men's rights activists like Fred Hayward maintain that the courts have been biased against the father.* If you actually look at the cases, you'll find that's nonsense. A series of state gender-bias task forces found that gender bias is pervasive and it "permeates the decision making, operations, and environment of state court systems."[140] "The studies indicated that while gender bias sometimes affects men, its impact is overwhelmingly and disproportionately against women."[141]

If you look at the entire spread of custody arrangements, what you find is that it's more likely for mothers to be granted custody than fathers because mothers have been the primary custodians of the children: the one who takes the kids to soccer, buys their clothes, feeds them, knows their doctor, and so on. So, after a divorce, it makes a lot of sense for the person who has been the primary caretaker to continue in that role. During "the marriage the parties after all set up the caretaker arrangement together, and would hardly have done this while thinking that the actual primary caretaker was less fit than the other parent."[142] Since women are much more often the primary caretakers, mothers *should* get custody since children's well-being after divorce strongly depends upon the quality of their relationship with their primary caretaker, as has been well documented over the years.[143]

Whenever custody is contested, however, we see that from the 1960s to the 1990s, sole custody awards to fathers increased from 36.7% to 45% and awards to mothers decreased from 50% to 44% (with a few third-party and split awards).[144]

This rough parity alone is enough to refute Hayward's claim. But it actually masks a deep, underlying bias against mothers that shows up in courts whenever a mother alleges that the father has abused her or the children. An analysis of over 2000 court opinions by Meier *et al.* found that more than 1 in 4 women who alleged abuse actually lost custody as a result of that claim. For those cases in which the courts found the claim creditable, mothers still lost custody 14% of the time when they were the target of the abuse and 19% of the time when the child was found to be physically abused.[145]

Lawyers for fathers often introduce the pseudo-scientific theory of "parental alienation," as a counter allegation that the abuse claims are simply an illegitimate method to alienate the child from the father. Whenever they did so, one in two mothers lost custody as a result of that abuse claim and alienation counterclaim. When the court credited that alienation counterclaim, 73% of women lost custody. When the court credited both claims, still 43% of mothers lost custody.[146]

The final indignity to which courts subject mothers is the insertion of official personnel--Guardians *ad Litem* (GALs) and court-appointed "neutral" evaluators--who are not generally trained to recognize abuse, especially child abuse, or the risks stemming from such abuse. This significantly lowers mothers' chances for custody. That there is no corresponding loss to fathers when they allege abuse by the mother, shows a clear systemic bias against mothers. [147] Given all of this, the outlook for battered women and protective mothers is actually pretty dire.

Warren Farrell's point is that the boy crisis, as he calls it, is caused by a lack of male role models that teach traits that men can best teach boys and he thinks that the court system is partly to blame for that. He says he cites hundreds of studies showing that the biological dad positively affects the children's development in more than 50 developmental areas. I think it's very useful to see both men and women in action in their lives as adults.

When I do presentations on gender issues, I always have a woman as my co-presenter so that the people can see us interacting with each other and respecting each other. In some ways, the actual words that tumble out of my mouth are much less important than the way I treat my co-presenter. I think the same applies when you're looking at relationships: A child growing up and seeing a respectful pair of adults, in this case, male and female, working together for the child's benefit, even if sometimes they piss off the child by taking away some privilege. That message is really key.

However, seeing a pair of adults in which one is manipulating and controlling and abusing the other, is not great role modeling for either girls or boys. Certainly, children who are living with a single mother may yearn for that other role model and very often will find it in a teacher or a minister or a coach or some older male friend. We need to make sure that those role models are available, but early evidence that children living with their mothers seemed to do better if they had ongoing contact with their fathers has been contradicted by two larger studies based on more representative samples.[148]

Indeed, another study by Zill found that the well-being of children following divorce is not related to father-child contact. [149] Of course, whenever the father rather than the mother is the primary caregiver for the children, there would likely be severe consequences to terminating the relationship.[150]

When you realize that so many relationships have an abusive element to them,[151] it shouldn't be surprising that children's wellbeing increases when a family is relieved of the ongoing tension and storm clouds of violence on the horizon. Being relieved of that tension is a benefit to children. There are lots of opportunities when the child is a late teenager and into the 20s and 30s to form a different relationship with each parent and there's a great deal of growth that can happen.

We all continue to grow and there are lots of opportunities for men to realize that they want to have a relationship that is a real one with their children. If the children are interested, they can actually make a go of trying again later in life when he has decided that the controlling behavior is not working for him.

There's a lovely phrase Booker T. Washington used in 1909 in the context of racism: "One man cannot hold another man down in the ditch without remaining down in the ditch with him."[152] We can translate that into the gender context: In order to hold a woman in a ditch, you have to stay in the ditch with her. My advice to men is, "Why are you staying in the ditch? Go and play on the meadows and have a much fuller life than in the ditch holding women down."

When you were co-chair of NOMAS, what were your priorities? In 1990, John Cohen and I decided that we wanted to try our hand at running this organization made up of four distinct groups: Ending Men's Violence activists, Gay Rights activists, Men's Studies scholars, and men who were interested in Enhancing Men's Lives. When we got around a council table with four different groups of people to try to work out common causes, it was a great education in communication and facilitation that I have used for the rest of my life. We found there really are ways to find a commonality across divergent points of view and move forward together. You don't have to have everybody agreeing on every point to have an organization that works.

I was in the NOMAS men and women's task group, which were the best meetings. They'd start with an emotional check-in and follow an agenda with time certain so people didn't talk and talk like in other meetings. They ended with an evaluation and summary statement. Men and Masculinity (M&M) conferences were fun as well as dealing with issues. My life in those conferences was waking up in the morning, having a pre-conference meeting around sexual assault issues and then going to workshops, having a lunch conference around domestic violence issues, then going to more workshops, and having a pre-dinner conference around child custody issues. Being able to go and dance with other men and with the women who were there, and shake it all loose was fabulous. So, it was a really different sort of conference than tie-wearing conferences.

I took my young son to the M&M in Seattle where men roughhoused with him and he was on Shepard Bliss's back piggybacking around the room.* Yes, the process was central. There were process guidelines always in evidence, so if something wasn't clicking, someone would say, "I think we need to talk about this underlying issue here." After that was resolved, you'd come back to the content level, and figure that out, and then move on to the next issue. At the end of each meeting, there would be time set aside for process, to talk about how things went, what your feelings were as you end up this intensive process. This made the meetings actually something you would want to go to rather than something you would dread. *Yes, I felt that too.*

I was at the Hartford M&M where we had a debate because they didn't want "masculinists" to speak. I see that kind of competition as to who is the purest ideologically in most liberal groups I've been involved with. In that particular conference, there were some men attending who were pretty badly disrespecting the women in attendance, like saying, "You don't belong here." This caused essentially a revolution within the Ending Men's Violence wing saying, "We can't have women who come to this conference being verbally abused by men who come to the conference." *I had no sense of that at Hartford.* That was a moment when the organization really needed to look at are we creating a place that's safe for women?

I absolutely love having conversations with people who are politically different from me because there's so much that I learn and it's a joy to try to communicate across what seems like fissures sometimes. However, provocateurs and rude people should not be invited to a conference that is supposed to be building and nurturing and joining together. I can understand your desire to want to have these conversations and I think they're absolutely key for us to have in the present political climate. I think that we all need to have more conversations that are difficult ones. And yet if I'm putting together a workshop around bringing black and white people together, Chicanos together, Native Americans, and so on, I'm not going to invite the Proud Boys in. However, I would love to sit down and have a conversation with a member of the Proud Boys on a park bench somewhere and see if we can come to some sort of meeting of minds.

In your diversity training, what do you teach? When I came to Portland State in 1994, they had this new program called Freshman Inquiry, a year-long interdisciplinary course to take the place of the more common general education sequence of one science, one social science, and one literature course. Our job was to teach communication skills, critical thinking skills, diversity skills, ethics, and social responsibility. It was clear to me that Portland prided itself on being this liberal bastion, but just scratch the surface and there are all sorts of issues around race that need attending to. I have a dear friend who came here from London and said she never thought of herself as a black woman until she moved to Portland.

I focused very intensively on race as the central discussion of the diversity conversations I had with my students. A group called Uniting To Understand Racism formed to have community dialogues, so I started attending those and then facilitating them. One group did not want to stop meeting after our six weeks and that group has continued for 20 years. We continue to have these incredible conversations centered on race, but because we know each other so well we can bring in gender, not as a way to flee the conversation but as a way to deepen it. We can talk about sexual orientation, we can talk about class. I can't imagine going through life not having a group I can talk to on such a deep level. It fills me up with incredible friendships and deep learning about myself as well as learning about other people through conversation.

We have a check-in where people talk about what their life was like the last month and often out of that a topic will emerge. There are not that many venues where a Chicano can talk about being profiled on the train and have a bunch of Anglos sit around and say, "God, that was really shitty, I'm really sorry that happened to you." Most often there's denial, minimization, and false universalization to try to get away from these sorts of topics.[153] Actually being heard is really good for the person who's dealing with racism, and helps the rest of us understand our roles in this society and that we are not "the good ones" sitting around talking about "the bad ones."

As Phyllis Frank says, we're all taught the same choreography and the fact that we're noticing that we're dancing it, at times, is eye-opening and liberating to actually take a look at what the dance steps are. We understand that it's not so much an individual thing that we need therapy for when we need to understand the systems behind a lot of what's making people of color's lives miserable, and women's lives miserable, and so on.

Like poor neighborhoods have poor schools so you don't go to college? Yes. The People's Institute for Survival and Beyond does this magnificent training on institutional racism.[154] They point out the fact that virtually every institution in this country that was not formed under the period of slavery was formed under the era of Jim Crow. If we find that institutions are slow to change, we have to realize that they are built on this incredible substructure of oppression that's been going on for 400 years.

Therefore, it's important to understand how the systems come into play and understand our roles in these systems. For instance, if I'm someone with a little prejudice around race, that I may or may not be aware of, as I sit within an institution like the university, those prejudices may come out in a subconscious way as I'm writing letters of recommendation for students or hiring new faculty. If I'm unaware that's a possibility, the chances are that the power of the institution I work in can magnify my individual prejudice by a great deal.

Being a mathematician, the equation that pops to mind is that oppression is institutional power times prejudice, (literally, oppression=institutional power x prejudice) so whatever bit of prejudice you have gets multiplied by the institutional power. In some ways, I'm a more dangerous person than Billy Bob Smith, with whom I share a phenotype, out in rural Idaho in a white nationalist community, because he may not be connected to institutions at all. He might be viciously anti-black but the chances of him harming an African-American person in this society are less than the chances I would if I'm not conscious of my prejudice. And even if I am conscious, sometimes it seeps out in very strange ways. We all need to analyze our roles in institutions and work on our unconscious bias so that we're acting more humane and just.

Do you think that the impact of Trump was healthy in the long run because he exposed all the racism, classism, sexism, and misogyny? He gave people a voice that has been pretty vicious. I would imagine that there are many paths to hearing the voices of people who don't feel like they're being heard by the more liberal end of the political spectrum that would have resulted in a much more positive alternative universe than the one we find ourselves in.

Looking at the men's movement today, it seems the biggest branch is the small men's groups like the ManKind Project or EVRYMAN. There's also the Christian Men's Movement, the Promise Keepers with an enormous number of men coming together to look at masculinity--maybe not in ways that I would agree with for the most part. We're talking about hundreds of thousands of men. The Mythopoetic Men's Movement is men who want to get together and talk about their absent fathers and meet in the woods and dance and bang on drums--maybe tens of thousands rather than hundreds of thousands.

Then there's the activist men's movement with about a thousand or maybe hundreds of men who were doing work to end men's violence, heterosexism, and racism through the lens of anti-sexist work. *That would be NOMAS, Division 51 of APA, and Men's Studies groups?* Yes, men's studies scholars--many not affiliated with NOMAS--are seriously examining gender issues in a way that I very much approve of. The ending men's violence cohort is strong and dedicated, doing what we can to transform the planet. Getting out and working in your community and educating young men about the ways you've been harmed by your gender socialization--there are lots of roads open for people.

One of my criticisms of the Mythopoetic Movement is, what's next? You've talked to men for a number of years now and you've enjoyed being in their company, is there something you can do with this reservoir of joy that you've filled up? The parallel criticism of the ending men's violence movement is that it has been a lot of striding out with no firm center to your being, trying to go here and there without a central focus in your life. I think the two movements actually are incredibly complementary and should do more bonding together to try to figure out how do the most activist men find a better center and how do those most interested in centering find more activism?

What I see with young people is they're not really concerned so much about gender, they're gender-fluid or they're non-binary. What do you see in your students? It seems like instead of isolated couples of one boy and one girl going out on a date, it's often groups of boys and girls going out together and I think that's wonderful. Relationships built on friendship are so foundational to everything else we get in life. But even with gender fluidity, and people feeling free to express themselves in this society, there is still a great deal of sexual assault and domestic violence happening. So the changes in roles are great, but not sufficient.

We're living in a literal war on women. Can you imagine if Presbyterians beat up 25% of Methodists, and another 25% experienced an attempted assault, the newspapers would be all over this religious war? Yet when we talk about 25% of women having been raped by the time they're in college and another 25% surviving an attempted rape, the response is "That's normal," or we don't even want to talk about that. We really need to reframe the problem, call it a war, and figure out how we stop it.

What do you think is the main avenue to stop the war? Education is a piece of it, having systems in the police and the courts that do not disadvantage women is a piece of it. Having more women in the political sphere is a piece of it, so that young men look up to people in power and see women and not have to feel strange about that. Having more women in the professions, in sciences, as doctors; all of that is important.

We're absolutely moving forward but I'm going to be long dead and buried before we're close to having a society in which women are treated equally and not bludgeoned. That's pretty saddening but it's not unexpected given how we've come out of a culture for hundreds or thousands of years in which women were considered barely better than cows or chattel. Great strides have been made, but still, with that culture, that legacy, that long ball and chain we're dragging along as we try to run up out of the ditch into the meadows, it's going to be plenty of work.

One thing that women have going for them is they're 60% of the university students in the US and are more likely to graduate. What do you think is happening to those young men? I really grieve for the young men who are lost in society, who don't see a path to the self that they want to be. So men who are slightly older need to have conversations with them about their lack of self-worth, which is tied to some of the acting out that happens. We don't need to slap young men down because they're part of this horrific war against women. We need to build them up and make them understand that they're incredible, beautiful, creative individuals who have every promise coming forward into life. They need to find their center and express it in everything they do and move forward hand-in-hand with the women and the girls in their lives.

There was this one girl I knew when I was five years old and we did glitter painting together and whatnot. Then in second to fourth grade, all of a sudden the girls were something you had to avoid because they were these strange creatures. Then in seventh grade, you're put face to face with them and you're supposed to kiss one of these *things*. Can you imagine what's going through a boy's mind with a sequence like that? I think things have gotten somewhat better, but this is not so outrageous that you can't imagine it happening today.

We are coming to understand that gender is not such a fixed deal, whatever particular attraction we happen to have to particular people. Recognizing that for some people, the body doesn't fit one's identity is important. All of this fluidity is a good thing. I think those of us who are confirmed cisgender folks can *also* marvel at how beautiful it is that we feel *good* in our gender roles, while perhaps coming to understand how our being-ness may be separate from that gender.

As I've learned from gay and lesbian folks how to have friendships across gender lines and how to be free of some of the boxes I was put in, I'm also learning from transgender folks to understand that who I am and who-I-am-as-gendered are not the same thing. Learning how to be a beautiful human *creature* on this planet is central to all we do. Here we are living in this land of people who were much better stewards of it, and maybe more sensitive to those who have variations in how they are in the world. We need to learn from them on this as well.

There are plenty of the original peoples who are still in our communities who we can learn from, and maybe that's a step I haven't taken and some others need to do. We can learn from the elders in the First Nations, Native American, American Indian communities, "What are some of the things about gender that you can teach us?" *Like accepting there are Two Spirits and some people in a third gender category.* That's right.

I read Medium, *an online newsletter mostly written by young people, and am seeing a lot of young men saying, "All I hear is toxic masculinity. I'm made to feel guilty for being male."* Guilt is not a useful response for anyone. My friend Tess Wiseheart spells it out as an acronym of "Going Under Into A Lifetime Of Timidity" (GUILT) or you can change the last letter to "Tyranny" for some men. Some men feel so bad about sexism that we pull into our shells and expect women to take care of us because we're feeling so emotionally overwrought. And of course, that's not good for the women, either, because they have other things to do in their lives. Rather, the men need to set the guilt aside as useless and get out and do something to make the world a better place.

There is no need for us to be bemoaning the world in front of us; we just have to work. With work, we can transform the current world into the one that we want. Or we can bemoan the world that we have and feel guilty or put upon, but that's not a path out of the ditch, by any means. We need to figure out ways to get ourselves out, and the women in our lives out, of this situation that we find ourselves in that was not of our making.

There is no reason that I should feel guilty about any sexism I picked up on in my life because I never asked for any of it. I have to take a fire hose and stick it in one ear periodically to try to hose my cranium out to get rid of the crap that's hanging from the roof of my cranium that I picked up as a child, on the bus, from the news media, from ministers, and teachers. It's coming in all the time so we need to be hosing our crania out periodically.

We also need to look inward and find our true, beautiful, loving core and know that's where we need to be and that's *how* we need to be for those around us. If you are that, everything else is superfluous. It doesn't matter what other people think about you if you know yourself to be the solid human being that you are. It does not matter what they're saying about you or about people who look like you, which has no meaning when you know who you are. You are the precious individual self you were meant to be.

If you're trying to be some other individual out there, like the one you see on TV, or the one you see on the basketball court, or whatever--and that's not you--you're just going to be miserable trying to be "that one." Try to be the one that you are, and your life will be rich. *I'm thinking of women who spend money on plastic surgeries so they'll fit some image and how painful that must be.* I was talking to the women in my classes about how women paint their faces so that men will love them for exactly who they are. Is that not only bizarre but saddening?

Professor Ingólfur Vilhjálmur Gíslason
Gender Equality in Iceland

I was born in Reykjavik, the capital of Iceland, November 1956, a single child. *I think of Scorpio people as intense, with deep feelings, passionate, sometimes challenged to bring the feelings to the surface. Does any of that apply to you?* I'm usually pretty calm, I don't think so.

What messages did you get growing up in Iceland about what it was to be a good man? Young men I've interviewed in the US said they got a lot of messages about don't be like a girl. I don't remember such messages. What I mainly remember is being told to be a good provider to take good care of my future family and you don't hit a girl. I remember crying and I don't remember anyone saying that I shouldn't. *How many children do you have?* I have two daughters and one son and five grandchildren.

What did you notice in terms of gender in your child-rearing? There was no conscious decision on raising them differently. My son is the youngest, so I was better experienced and he had two elder sisters who assisted in bringing him up. He tried to play football [*soccer*] and didn't like it, so he was not pushed in that direction. He tried fencing and practiced that for a number of years. All three were involved in music. He is the one who stuck with it the longest and has a band going on a European tour. My girls have been more academically inclined, one is a sociologist and the other a behaviorist. We've always tried to emphasize independence, doing what you really feel like doing.

What surprised me about raising my son is that I didn't give him guns, but he and his friends would take sticks and mimic shootings and I don't see girls doing that. Yes, my wife is very much against guns and we never bought guns for our children, but our son certainly found sticks and some other things to use as a gun. I don't think my daughters did that. I think he more or less went along with the other guys, but he also played with dolls, perhaps because he had older sisters. I don't recall him being teased because of his dolls, similar to my grandsons who also carry dolls around and that doesn't seem to be a problem. However, I don't think I would have played with dolls.

Why did you decide to go through the arduous chore of getting a Ph.D. in Sweden? I have always been interested in social issues and was never in any doubt that I wanted to research social issues and wanted to make a difference. Back then, I was mainly interested in class, so I wrote my thesis on the origins and organization of the first Icelandic capitalists. Gender played no role there, they were almost all males and I wasn't all that interested in gender issues at that time.

I moved back to Iceland in 1990 and was out of work for a couple of years but then I got work at the Center for Gender Equality, a government agency that had recently appointed a men's committee. They handpicked five men who were entrusted with the task of trying to get more men to participate in the discussions on gender equality. They had a lot of ideas and were very committed. I was made a secretary for this committee, which was a changing factor in my life. I got interested in gender and particularly the situation of men.

I started reading articles and books; back then it was in no way an impossible task to read everything that had been written about men and masculinity. I think there was just one journal on masculinity and not all that many books. Now, I think we have 10 or 11 journals, loads of books, and masculinity courses in all major universities. *I list 14 journals in the resource list.* The field exploded in just a few years.

Originally, this committee was appointed just for two years, so they decided that in order to make a difference, they would focus on a few issues. Firstly they would take on men's violence against women. They reasoned that as long as women as a group think that they have a reason to fear men as a group, there can be no gender equality, so men had to face that issue. They focused on awareness-raising and initiating psychological treatment for violent men, which took several years to accomplish. Secondly, they focused on parental leave.

The basic structure for that law suggested by the committee was adopted in 2000 when a revolutionary new law was adopted, so they made a huge difference. It was very rewarding to be working for them. Generally, we were well received, particularly among young women. Many of them said, "Finally, we have the men on board!"

How much paid time off do the mother and the father get in 2021? Parental leave is now 12 months long and each parent has six months. It's non-transferable except for six weeks. Extension of the leave to 12 months was adopted in 2021 but the really revolutionary change occurred in 2000 when the leave was extended from six to nine months and divided so that there were three for fathers, three for mothers, and three months they could share. In addition, economic compensation was raised from a flat rate benefit to 80% of salary. Around 90% of fathers make use of their rights and they take the time that only they can use.

Does the employer help pay for leave time off? All those who pay wages in Iceland pay an insurance levy that is used for a number of purposes and one of them is the parental leave. *The employer doesn't pay directly to the employee?* No, that would be a terrible system and would increase the discrimination that young women already face in the labor market. Particularly new firms would hesitate to hire young women.

The US Congress is not able to legislate paid parental leave although they don't complain about huge military spending ($770 billion in 2022). I think the US is one of the very few countries in the world that doesn't have paid parental leave. We have seen many positive effects of the system of parental leave that we adopted in 2000, one is that when the father makes use of the leave, divorce is rarer than among couples where the father has not used his part of the leave.

We've also seen huge changes in the division of care for the children, as parents now share much more equally than before 2000. This is found not only during the time when parents are on leave but for at least three years after the child is born--the period we've studied. Fathers gain confidence that they can do this as well as the mothers. *That's a big influence, as I found in my* 50/50 Marriage *and* Parenting *books.*

We have done surveys among first-time parents and prior to 2000 care was divided equally in about 40% of families by the time the children were three years old. We are now up to 75%, which is a huge difference. *That's so different from the US!* We ask first-time parents to keep a diary on how they divide care per week. After a year, the great majority of children in Iceland enter kindergartens that are heavily subsidized.

Back to the other theme of the men's committee, what did you find worked to reduce male violence? Some men's rights people in the US say, "Women often initiate it so you can't just say it's a problem of male violence." Reading international studies, it's certainly not only men who are violent towards women. However, the more serious the violence gets, the more repetitive it is, the higher the proportion is of men as perpetrators. We should acknowledge that women can be violent in domestic relationships as well as men because for one thing, we know that that is the case. Secondly, if we portray it as only men being violent, then we are back to some kind of essentialism and that women are generally better, which I don't think is good for gender equality, and of course, it's plainly wrong.

The committee initiated an awareness-raising week-long campaign and got all the major newspapers and TV stations engaged. We published a small pamphlet called "Violence," distributed it into all schools, and encouraged teachers to use it as a teaching tool to talk about violence with the kids. We had this concrete goal of getting psychological treatment for violent men and managed to do that.

Unfortunately, this is the one area where Iceland seems to have made little progress since violence seems to be on a similar level as it has been for decades. Even though some statistics indicate improvement, we just don't know enough about the development. It probably got worse during the Covid 19 close-down, but this is of course difficult to measure in that what we call violence today wouldn't have been called violence 50 years ago and so on. Both here, and what I've seen in other Nordic countries, the level of domestic violence seems to be very similar to what it has been for decades but, again, this is an understudied phenomenon.

Is it overly simplistic to say that perpetrators were victims themselves growing up or saw a parent be violent, so it's a learned behavior? International studies seem to indicate that around 30% of violent men came from a violent household and are repeating, while there are men who came from very peaceful and happy homes who become violent.

Do you find any correlations with alcohol, drug use, and frustration in terms of your job success? We've only had two studies on violence in Iceland and they didn't show any relationship with work or poverty. Alcohol and drug use certainly plays a role, but in what way? It can be used as an excuse, but it certainly is a factor as seen in street brawling and street violence; when people are drunk, they're just more stupid. Unfortunately, only one of those studies asked both men and women about their experience, both as victims and perpetrators.

Around 4% of men said that they had been physically abused by their wives, but 8% of women said that they have been violent towards their men. This discrepancy calls for explanations. Perhaps it's so humiliating for a man to be beaten by a woman that they won't admit to it. Another explanation, which I'm more fond of, is that the men never really felt threatened by the violence of their wives; perhaps she threw an ashtray at him and he regarded it as just a childish act. Perhaps women are more ready to call something violence because they are more afraid of it.

Is there a helpline? Yes, Icelandic police have radically changed their routines regarding domestic violence and abuse. They bring help; for example, if there's a child in the household, a person comes from the Child Protection Agency. They phone a couple of days later to talk to the couple and distribute the leaflets for treatment for the violent men and inform the woman about the women's shelter and take her to the shelter if that is what she wants. They've been getting much better at this, perhaps because we have had a woman as head of police for a few years. *In the States, the police used to think domestic violence is a personal, private issue.* We are way past that.

Around the world, except in sub-Saharan Africa, there are more women in college and graduating from college. Is Iceland more equal since you're more egalitarian? No, it's very similar: The graduates from the University of Iceland are between 65% and 70% women. This is seen as a problem and we've had a couple of conferences to discuss what can be done. Generally, women are outperforming men and boys in all areas of education. They have always out-performed boys in reading skills but now this also applies to mathematics and similar fields.

Boys are much more likely to drop out of schools: We don't really know why. Most of them seem to be doing fine in life without a long education. Perhaps they don't see the point of a long education. Another explanation is that the general feminization of the whole educational system is an issue here as the overwhelming majority of teachers from kindergarten until university are women but I'm not convinced that is the major explanation. We know in traditionally masculine countries such as Great Britain, in at least some areas, boys refused to learn to read because they regarded that as sissy and something that only women do, but I doubt very much that is an issue here.

Some point to the lack of positive identity in terms of being male, so boys don't feel encouraged to study. Yes, it's quite possible. I had that discussion with one of my colleagues some years ago who has five boys. She canceled her subscription to a feminist magazine because boys and men were being portrayed there as only bad and she didn't want her boys to grow up with the impression that their gender made them bad. Of course, girls spend more time with their families than boys do, and perhaps they are more encouraged to seek education. It's a complicated problem but I don't think it's because we've given girls any unfair advantages. It's more that we've removed obstacles in their way and therefore they are performing as they have always been capable of. Perhaps we need to work more on boys; I don't know, but at least they don't seem all that unhappy.

Perhaps males do a cost analysis of is it worth it? Here students graduate with around $40,000 in debt. There are no fees in the University of Iceland but if you're not working, you have to take out study loans, so our students also graduate with heavy burdens. Boys not seeking higher education is much more of a problem in areas outside the capital where I see men without any education beyond the basics doing very well, like fishermen or even manual laborers.

It's much more equal in the capital area, which means that probably there is an economic motivation in a combination of gender and class. The only educated people those boys see are women teachers, or if they are lucky enough to have a doctor in the village, more often than not it's a female. So perhaps it's role models and an economic situation.

Nordic countries, including Iceland, are among the most committed to gender-role equality and also among the happiest, partly because citizens have access to affordable education, childcare, eldercare, medical care, and housing. Why are the Nordic countries so committed to equality and why are they happy? The two are closely connected as it's immensely important if people are to be happy that you don't have to be constantly worrying about your health or taking care of your family members.

Politics has a lot to do with it, the legacy of the domination of the Social Democrats in all the Nordic countries. Iceland has been the exception since we've never had a really large Social Democratic Party, but we wanted to be as good as the other Nordic countries. The party that was dominant in Iceland in the 20th century, the Independence Party, is a centre-right party but in order to become a dominating party, it had to secure a lot of the working-class votes. This meant that they adopted many welfare ideas from the Nordic countries, perhaps giving them an Icelandic twist but still made sure that we had the welfare system. So politics is the main explaining factor.

The Nordic countries have for decades had close cooperation and it is a source of embarrassment if someone is a laggard in any area. This was used by both women's groups and the unions when they pushed for changes in our parental leave in the 1990s. But that leads to the question of why the Nordic countries as a whole do rather well in this area; I think that the political domination of social democracy is a major factor. Social democratic parties have pressed for individual independence and a liberation from the shackles of the market so that regardless of the market situation of people, they should be guaranteed a dignified life. This helped pave the way for women into the labour market and heavily subsidized daycare and healthcare.

Secondly, religion has not played any major role in Icelandic politics. We have never had a party pushing for "Christian values" or advocating that the man should be the head of household or similar mumbo jumbo. At least in Iceland religion plays a very small part in what that we do, say, or think. A few times people have tried to form a Christian party but they've never succeeded in gaining any seats in parliament. Except for special occasions when people are being buried or marrying, or something similar, they don't much care about the church or what God has to say about anything.

Thirdly, we've had strong movements pushing for gender equality. Why they have been strong is another question but perhaps (and this is very much speculating) Icelandic women have been more independent than women in many other countries. The seasonal character of the Icelandic fishing economy meant that women often had to take care of everything connected to the family and household for weeks or months, so it was difficult to advocate that they were incapable of this or that or in any way inferior to men.

What people say is the small homogeneous population made everyone feel like I want to support you because we're in this together. Many men were away as fishermen so women were responsible for the farm, so that both genders were important economically. That's probably one of the explanations, but during the '50s and '60s, we had very similar gender roles to other Western countries when the housewife and provider were seen as the best of all worlds. It wasn't until the end of the '60s, that wonderfully revolutionary time, that we began to see any changes.

Catholicism was almost uprooted completely in the Nordic countries, but the Norwegians have a fairly strong Christian party that has opposed steps towards gender equality, particularly within the family. We also had fairly strong women's movements. Icelandic women have traditionally been forced to be the heads of the households, both because of the seasonal character of the economy, and also because we lost a lot of young men who drowned at sea. There were a lot of young widows, which is part of the explanation.

What's the impact of gender equality on men? I think they are fine with all of this. They have obviously gained from gender equality, both by not having to shoulder alone the task of being the "provider" and, in the last two or three decades, having real opportunities to do what they have said that they wanted to do--spend more time with their families and their children. They have grasped that opportunity.

I and two colleagues have conducted a number of studies on the use of parental leave and the effects on family life and found that around 40% of parents who had their first child three years before the changed law in 2000 reported that care was divided equally between them by the time the child was three years old. For parents who had their first child in 2014, that figure was 80%. Simultaneously, men have reduced their working hours.

Of course, there are examples of resistance, but nothing of any importance, no movement or political party. Resistance mainly takes the form of small groups belittling women in social media and that can, of course, be very difficult for individual women but again, these groups have no social force. Opinion polls show strong support for gender equality. It is too often forgotten that when Vigdís Finnbogadóttir decided to run for president in 1980, she had urging from fishermen, mainly males. Opinion polls prior to that election showed very similar support for her among men and women. She ended up being the first democratically elected female president in the world. She was very popular during her 16 years as president and in all probability meant a lot for the younger generations as a role model.

What's striking to me when comparing North America and the Nordic countries is that we train to compete to be number one. In contrast, in the Nordic countries to stand out is seen as inappropriate. A friend of mine taught physical education in a Swedish high school and posted news that one of his students got an award for an athletic event. The administration told him take it down. A young Swede told me the pressure is still on to conform. Stephan said in the Netherlands "being 'normal' was always repeated to me during my adolescence."*

I was in Sweden studying social support for families. I stayed in an apartment building called Haslby family hotel, where they had communal childcare and dinners. I was told that even houses are not supposed to stand out in their color palette or whatever, so, we don't stand out as individuals or in our architecture. It's certainly not the case in Iceland. You will see that houses in the same neighborhood are all sizes and shapes and painted in different colors.

I conducted my Ph.D. studies in Lund in Sweden and saw the tendency that your friend talked about. They even have a word for it "Jantelagen." Wikipedia defines it, "The Law of Jante characterizes not doing things out of the ordinary, or being personally ambitious as unworthy and inappropriate." However, in my opinion, this is not a major characteristic and Sweden gives prizes for the best Ph.D. thesis and so on, so they do promote excellence. However, they emphasize the participation of all who want to participate and in children's sport, for example, the emphasis is on play rather than outperforming others. I don't think you will find this tendency here in Iceland, perhaps because the Social Democratic party in Iceland was never in a similar dominant position as in the other Nordic countries.

In Iceland, children up to teenage years are encouraged to play, to participate, and to cooperate. I live next to a fairly large football center where every summer teams of young children gather for a week of football. It's not the goal for one team to win the most and everyone gets a medal in the end. The idea is that children learn by playing and if we introduce competition, then we take the play element away. That doesn't mean that we never compete or that we never encourage excellence. That's done later on in life but it's many a boy's dream to play football for the Icelandic national team. I recently read an interview with a ten-year-old girl in the newspaper who also had a dream to play for the Icelandic national football team.

After the ages of 12 to 14, it's more of a competitive environment, at least in sport. We've had some debates about whether we should grade children and we still haven't quite settled that debate. At least for young children they don't get a grade, they're told what they've done right and what they've done wrong, but they don't get A's and B's. *How old are they when they start getting grades?* Around 12. I don't know about the effects of video games but we certainly have major social actors pushing for more competition at a younger and younger age. The worst of the lot are the sport clubs (mainly football). I doubt that anyone has done more to destroy free games among children, something that I think can seriously undermine democracy.

Some Nordic countries have had alcohol problems, partly because of the long dark winters. I've also been told by Swedes that drinking is the one time when you can be emotionally expressive. Is alcohol an issue in Iceland? Yes, but more with the older generation. We had a strange ban on beer in Iceland up to 1984, so what we drank was mainly strong liquor like vodka and Icelandic Black Death, and of course, people got very drunk and lost their inhibitions.

I've interviewed a number of policemen on a project and one of the things that we discussed was that they often encounter very difficult situations like abused children. They said that what has been slowly changing is how this is dealt with internally. Now, they don't leave the police building before discussing difficult situations they have encountered. Prior to that, you just went home and said nothing until you got drunk. It reminded me very much of the young men in Germany who were talking about their fathers participating in the war. The fathers never talked about it unless they were drunk and then they cried and cried a lot, but that has changed.

Today, people drink beer or they drink light wine. Finland was the prime example of this Nordic drinking, the fairly strong silent Finnish men who never showed any emotion except after drinking two or three bottles of vodka and sitting in a sauna. We are not that emotional at least officially.

Around the world, we see Japanese men after work going to the bars and drinking together or Brits and Aussie mates in pubs. Is male bonding supported by alcohol? Generally, in the 20th century, it was not seen as fitting for men to show their emotions, at least not if they were sad or anything like that. This reminds me of the reminisces of one man from the first years of the 20th century, who lost three children and he stated in the book that even though he was sad, he didn't think that anyone had seen that in him. He managed to suppress his emotions and the same went for his wife; their goal was that nobody would see they were sad about their loss. It's rather strange, but perhaps because the struggle for life was so hard and so intense, you couldn't break down.

The military doesn't want men to be sensitive and cry; patriarchy doesn't want men who are sensitive because then they wouldn't do hard work away from home for so many hours. The whole system is set up so that men don't get in touch with their sensitivity. Is that a fair statement? Yes, but it's rapidly changing. In Iceland, more and more men come out and talk about difficult experiences that they've had in their youth, like sexual abuse, being raped. Some of them say, "I'm talking about this because I have children. I want them to understand me and that they should not be afraid to talk about their feelings about good and bad experiences." I really think this is changing, perhaps more rapidly in Iceland than in other countries. We of course don't have any army, one of the lucky things about being an Icelander.

Before we leave politics, I was following the Pirate Party that started in Sweden and came to Iceland in 2012, led by Birgitta Jónsdóttir, because they tried to be very egalitarian in how they made decisions. She ended up quitting the party because she felt like their values weren't being applied. They're still around and did fairly well in our recent election. There are so many difficulties in applying that idea and, as you said, Birgitta thought they were not doing what they were preaching, so she left for a while.

In a utopia, you continue to discuss until you have all reached an agreement. *Consensus.* Yes, but that means that you have to have the time to engage in those discussions. Single women with three children don't have that time, so voting is for them a necessity for their voices to be heard. Complete consensus is a very difficult principle to apply and I don't think they have succeeded, but they certainly were a fresh wind in Icelandic politics.

You mentioned that now there are many men's studies journals internationally. Which one is on the top of your list as the most interesting? I would take *Men and Masculinities* and *NORMA. In the US, often men's studies academics are pro-feminist.* I think the great majority of the journals are feminist, perhaps with more emphasis on gender equality in general. They've published articles on important men's issues such as paternity leave and men as the victims of violence from other men and from women, and on structural violence such as being forced to be in an army.

A professor told me a woman was scheduled to speak in a Canadian university to talk about men's issues but, due to protests, she wasn't allowed to speak. Just focusing on how women are harmed by men doesn't get to the way men are harmed by traditional gender roles. I don't think we can talk about women's or men's issues without taking the situation of the other gender into account because it's always related. We have a Nordic Society for Studies on Men and Masculinity and we're around 50/50 men and women and we've never seen that as a problem. I can easily join in feminist discussions both here and in conferences and can talk about men or women without a problem.

What's the current status of Men's Studies in Iceland? Of course, we are very few, only around 370,000 people, so there's not much specialization. I teach a course on masculinities every other year, mainly attended by women. That's typical but I think that most of my colleagues in social sciences talk about gender issues and the situation of both men and women when they lecture on their subjects. Gender is obviously one of the main social issues in every society. It's fully accepted that gender is a major factor in all social life, but regarding Men's Studies, I doubt there are any other courses than the one I'm teaching. We've seen more and more studies on important areas of men's lives, from how important singing is in their lives to fatherhood and men in female-dominated work. *What textbooks do you use?* Most often I've used a book called *Masculinities* by Raewyn Connell, an Australian; she is the guru in Europe or at least in the Nordic countries. I have also used *Men And Masculinities* by Chris Haywood and Máirtín Mac an Ghaill and the same title by Stephen Whitehead.

What topics really engage the students? Violence, sex, and sexuality engage them, and fatherhood--those are the main issues. *What I hear sometimes from young women is, there are no good men out there. Do you hear that kind of criticism from your women students?* No. I usually begin the course by asking them what they connect with the word "masculinities." They're shy, of course, but in the end, I get some suggestions and they're usually positive things: Strength. *protective, supportive.* A colleague in Great Britain who taught a similar course said that his students usually bring up something negative like alcoholism, violence, and abuse, but my students don't. *That's the beauty of living in such an egalitarian country.*

The general agreement in the Nordic countries is that gender equality is something worthwhile and we should use the means of the state to achieve it. *You wrote an article titled "Gender Changes: From rigid roles to negotiations."* I was trying to argue that almost everything about gender was up for negotiations now. When an Icelandic man and woman decide to live together, it has not been decided beforehand if the man is going to work and the woman is going to be at home, if it's going to be 50/50 or 70/30 or whatever. They discuss it and they negotiate and nothing is pre-given. I've interviewed couples who sit down on a Sunday afternoon and plan the next week to decide who is going to do what and some of them write it down and put it on the refrigerator. They don't seem to be stuck in any pre-given roles.

In the Western world, a new phenomenon for young people is gender fluidity. Are Icelandic teens doing the same kind of exploration? Yes, but I don't think many of them do, but it is fully accepted. We've been working on eliminating gender from laws. For example, the law on gender equality never mentions men or women.

You're having more refugees from Islamic countries, so how is that going? They're not all that many yet and we've not seen any major problems so far but, of course, we have Islamophobia in Iceland too. There were some protests a few years ago when they got building permission for a mosque, but very few attended the protest. They threw a pig's head on the site where the mosque was supposed to stand and it was so silly that most people left.

A real issue in the Western world is growing teen anxiety and depression, especially for girls. Is that a problem there or not because there's so much social support? Studies indicate that this is growing, particularly among young women. Mainly it seems to be a body issue that they're not happy with their body; we are talking about 14, 15, 16-year-old girls. *Social media aggravates the problem.* Yes, it does and it's very difficult to see what we can do about it. It's not something that affects the majority, probably about 10% to 12%.

I asked my students if they feel any pressure to be a certain way because they are women or dress in a certain way, they say that they don't. I have a master's student from southern Europe and asked her if she intended to return and she said, "No, I'm never going back to because here in Iceland and in the Nordic countries, I can go out in the evening and I can paint myself or not. I can be in a dress or jeans and nobody gives a shit. In my home country, I would be frowned upon, other people would point at me and criticize me for the way I looked." I thought this was in a way a wonderful tribute to the situation in Iceland. Most of my students wear jeans, but some wear skirts or dresses. The women and men are much more confident and once I had a male student come in a skirt, but I knew he was very special.

With all this equality, is there no need for a woman's movement? There are feminist groups, most certainly, but they are very different from what they were before. They mainly take up one issue and use social media to get the message across. They are often fierce and they have made a difference and stirred things up. They mainly focus today on violence and sexual violence, as well as the representation of women in mass media.

Do they use the #MeToo concept? Yes, that was a big movement in Iceland. Just a few weeks ago, they managed to get out three members of the Icelandic national football team who were accused of sexual violence, while the issue was investigated. This caused a heavy debate and it led to having the first woman as the president of the Icelandic Football

Association so that she could clean up after the men. *That happens a lot in corporations, called the savior effect.*

In the U.S, I would say the largest men's groups are ones like the ManKind Project where they have weekend warrior trainings with ongoing groups to support men in their emotional development. Are there groups like that there? No, the only men's group we have is the one that focuses on child custody after divorce. They're men who think that they don't have access to their children or not as much access as they want to, that the system is not supportive of them, and that their rights are being violated. Often they're right, as there's no question that we have a very slow-working system in this area in Iceland. It's generally acknowledged that we need to interfere more quickly so that if men have the right to be with their children after divorce, they are to be helped to use that right.

When I was working at the Center for Gender Equality, twice people came to the office and cried. One was a woman who had recently found out that her co-worker was paid much more than her and said, "I have read about this but I never thought that I would experience it" and then she cried. The other was a father who was completely losing touch with his son because the mother was moving with the child to another country where he wouldn't get the help he needs for his hearing problem. There was nothing that I could do in this case and the mother probably left with the child.

Is there anything else that you'd like people to know? The main point is that Icelandic men feel fine. I think most of them feel that they have gained by the steps we've taken towards gender equality; it's better for all of us that women are as free as they are. In reality, men and women who support gender equality have every reason to work together and we are slowly moving in the right direction.

Chapter 4: Father Absence is a Key Issue

Gordon Clay
Changing Gender Norms

I was born in Kansas City, Missouri on March 8, 1940. *Are you a sensitive sometimes indecisive Pisces?* Not indecisive but very susceptible, suggestible. Sometimes I get off track when somebody distorts my belief system.

I was raised in a lower upper-class racist family. I would have become a typical middle-class man if my mother hadn't died of leukemia when I was only one and a half years old. My parents had a magical relationship and I would never have been in the men's movement if she had lived. My stepmother was an evangelical and abused me physically and sexually and my step-grandmother was also physically abusive.

My father divorced my stepmother when I was 16, but that abuse damaged me for life.

I took workshops like Re-Evaluation Counseling, Holotropic Breath Work, and Rolfing to get the abuse out of my body. As the Rolfer was working on me, my legs, arms, and head began to flail while my shoulders to hips were still. My next session, the same thing occurred, and he asked me if I had ever been tied down. When I talked with my sister about this, she turned her head as if she was laying down in her crib and remembers me being tied to a short-legged chair. All I remember is the chair but my body remembers being tied down. Those evangelicals truly believed "spare the rod and spoil the child."

I stopped crying when I was eight, while I was getting whipped with a razor strap for something my stepmother falsely told my dad that I did. I remember him saying, "This is going to hurt me more than it is you," and I thought "I'll show you that you can't get me," and sucked it up. I didn't cry again until I was in my 40's during a workshop with Clarisa Pincola Estes and Michael Meade at Mills College in Oakland.

My father worked all the time and never talked much so I spent most of the first 16 years of my life in my room. I think that's why I feel so comfortable with the isolation the pandemic has brought us. I realize that I prefer to be a loner and call myself a "himit," a male hermit.

What about your education and career path? I have a BS in marketing with an English minor. I attended Baker, a Methodist University that was 80% Greek, 50% men, and 50% women, with a lot of partying. Most of the women were there to get their MRS degree, as portrayed in the 2003 movie *Mona Lisa Smile* about Wellesley College women students in 1953. I see that as the major shift in how girls are now raised, a total change in the last 60 years away from the focus on being an educated housewife.

I met my wife, Barbara, in my senior year in college. She too was going for her MRS degree although I didn't realize it at the time. I never believed in monogamy but in "love the one you're with" and ended up getting her pregnant. I did what was expected of me and we married in 1965. After graduation, we moved to Chicago where I started in the advertising business with a lot of travel, late nights, and, yes, a lot of partying. Over a 35-year career, I went from Account Executive to Account Director, to VP, Account Supervisor, and for the last 13 years, I had my own sales promotion agency in the San Francisco Bay Area.

You've been involved with the men's movement for over 45 years. Why? I was never faithful in my marriage. I had a friend, also named Gordon, who wrote a monthly article about his sports car racing for a local racing magazine I edited. I knew he would occasionally have lunch and play tennis with my wife, but I never suspected anything was going on. One day I drove by his house to pick up his article and there was her Mercedes. Once again I had been betrayed.

I became very suicidal and called my physician. He talked me down and then ask me to promise him that I wouldn't do anything until we talked again. I agreed and a couple of hours later he was at my front door with a therapist.

In Kansas, you're allowed to get a divorce immediately if one party is likely to harm themselves, and that was me. Barbara had wanted out of the motherhood role from day one and wanted me to have custody because if she had custody, it would have ended her relationship with Gordon. Our 62-year-old judge had never given a child to the father, much less a girl child. Barbara was on the stand when the judge said he granted custody to her, but she refused. In frustration, the judge adjourned the hearing until the next day to decide whether to put our daughter in a foster home or with me.

That was the defining moment when I started my involvement with the men's movement. That night I took my daughter to get passport photos and the next morning, before court, I applied for passports. I was not going to live in a country that made those kinds of decisions. The upshot was that he did grant me full custody and we all lived happily ever after.

I went to my boss about more flexible hours to come into work after I got my daughter off to school and be home when she got out. This was in 1974 before the film *Kramer vs Kramer* where Dustin Hoffman's character got custody of his son. My boss agreed. My daughter Natalie worried about me getting enough sleep and seemed to be taking over the household duties and playing less with her friends. I talked with my therapist about the fact that it was almost like she was becoming my wife. While she didn't like it, I got her in a therapy program to clear that up.

Having custody got me into working with men in Kansas City about fathering because all of the input that I got from women about raising a daughter didn't compute, like playing on the jungle gym at the park and letting her take chances and playing in mixed leagues. Because of the different way men seemed to raise children, I started a men's group called "The Fathers' Network" to talk about mixed messages, such as Dr. Spock saying at the time that the only real value for the father was to provide the income for the family.

Two years later, in 1976, Natalie, my girlfriend, and I moved to San Francisco. My daughter felt free to talk to me about everything, like getting her period and planning to become sexually active. In Marin County, there would be five girls in my house every night when I got home and part of the reason was that I was willing to talk about anything.

I found out about the California Men's Gathering and went to the fourth where I found out about NOMAS (National Organization of Men Against Sexism), at that time called the National Organization for Changing Men. I went to the sixth NOMAS conference where you and I were on the women and men task group.

Two men who were instrumental in the early men's movement were authors Herb Goldberg and Warren Farrell; did they influence your thinking?* Not really at the time. Although I had had a difficult time getting custody, even with my former wife's enthusiastic encouragement, I held a more egalitarian view of the world where everyone has an equal right to education, is paid according to their skill level and desire, and women have reproductive freedom. I ended up a few years later as co-chair for NOMAS, the largest pro-feminist organization in the country to this day. I had requested and was given permission by the Council to invite several leaders in the Men's Rights (Equalists) movement, like Jack Kammer,* Fred Hayward* and Tom Williamson, to the 1988 conference. Held in Seattle, it was titled "Our Fathers, Our Children, Ourselves." *I was there with my son.*

All I was doing was suggesting let's talk, let's communicate back and forth, as we did with Michael Kimmel and Robert Bly. They came and all hell broke loose because

Bob Brannan, and a woman whose name I don't remember, played good-old patriarchal backdoor politics and tried to get me thrown out. NOMAS, at that time, was very angry with anyone who talked about men's rights or father's issues. However, there were enough cool heads on the Council that I remained as co-chair for the rest of my two-year term. However, I began to see that the practice of feminism didn't really seem to be about equality for all, especially people of color.

One of the pleasing things is that I got Charlie Kreiner involved with NOMAS. He was the leader of men's work in the Re-Evaluation Counseling (RC) community that formed groups all over the world with men working on their issues. His RC theory about power and patriarchy is if anybody is dis-empowered, everybody is dis-empowered. They actually allowed him to run for the NOMAS Council seat and he was on it until his death in 2007. Kreiner woke NOMAS up. He introduced a lot of the theories about how we don't shame men, we don't push against them. We work with them to see the wider perspectives and I think that worked for a while.

Why was NOMAS uncomfortable with fathers' rights issues? That's the poison in some areas of feminism in that there weren't any men's or fathers' issues that were important enough for NOMAS to deal with. I looked at the NOMAS website recently and it still doesn't feel like there's space for positive masculinity. If they look at any adult behavior in task groups, it's invariably the negative behavior of men they discuss. Moshe Rozdzial is the co-chair of NOMAS (*a therapist in Denver who I interviewed)* and we remain friends and I really honor the work he is trying to do within that organization. I think Barry Shapiro is still involved with NOMAS and he's got a wider perspective but people like Bob Brannan and John Stoltenberg* have no perspective except that patriarchy is awful and everything is men's fault.

NOMAS had a children's task group, but it was only looking at the damage that men do to children, although according to the annual Child Maltreatment Report From the States to the National Child Abuse and Neglect Data System from the U. S. Department of Health and Human Services[155], five out of the six maltreatment issues are perpetrated by women--53% to 46%. Child Protective Services seldom considers this except in extreme cases. The only category where men led is sexual abuse:-60/40 and the majority of those men were not the fathers of the children but the mother's boyfriend.

Suzanne Steinmetz wrote about domestic violence in *Behind Closed Doors: Violence in the American Family* after 10 years of research and wrote another book 10 years later. After the first book, she got death threats because it was seen as an unacceptable message to come from the feminist side of the issue. Michael P. Johnson wrote a similar book of note titled *A Typology of Domestic Violence: Intimate Terrorism, Violent Resistance, and Situational Couple Violence.*

In a child development book, *The Continuum Concept,* researcher Jean Liedloff found no male violence in the indigenous culture she was studying. She returned several years after her book was published to find things had changed. The father of one of the families was called to the state capital as the ambassador for their tribe and the son learned violence from that urban environment and basically caused a cultural change in the tribe after the family returned home. This indicates that the message that men are born violent is wrong; it's not testosterone, it's the training to be tough, don't seek help, don't be a victim. Today, so many parents are detached from their kids, because they spend so much time working and their children are emerged in internet activities, many averaging more than eight hours a day.

Are you a feminist? Not when it ignores the hazards of the male role and the training the culture and fathers AND mothers have done to establish those ways of being a man in their sons. True gender equality is when both women and men have a voice and that looks very unlikely in this fifth wave of feminism. The radicalization of the women's movement is harmful, such as the increase of women bashing women for staying home, bashing Michelle Obama for wearing heels, and bashing men for toxic masculinity, mansplaining, and just being men. It's no wonder that in 1970, 7% of Americans ages 25-50 were single and working-class, and poor Americans were just as likely to enter marriage as more affluent Americans. But in 2018 the percent of single people has risen to 33% for high-income individuals and 42% for lower income.

What a boy has to look forward to is a culture that ignores him and in many cases, directly works against his best interests. The US selective service, paternity leave, infant genital mutilation, lack of parental rights once the child is conceived, paternity fraud, boys falling behind in education, child custody and support, alimony, lack of resources for male victims of domestic violence and their children, workplace and war deaths, suicide, sentencing disparity, life expectancy, false rape allegations, criminal court bias, homelessness, veteran's issues, and a high level of misandry doesn't paint a very rosy picture for marriage and its potential, and likely, negative aftermath.

I have yet to see a culture that doesn't, at some level, assign specific roles to men and other roles to women. I long to see an "-ism" that is intent on creating a world where all jobs and duties are open to everyone based on their skill to perform the job, including all high-risk jobs which generally pay more because of the high risk of death on the job.

In the early '80s, I staffed weekend "Rites of Passages" for teenage boys. One of the fathers knew I had a daughter, as I did, and wondered why I didn't create a Rite of Passage for Fathers and Daughters. I realized the opportunity, not to replace a mother's initiation of her daughter in the ways of womanhood, but an opportunity for fathers, especially divorced fathers, to invite their daughters into the man's world through initiation. Realizing that many of the wounds the daughter receives from his father are much different than those the son receives, I revamped "The Male Experience" and began running both workshops on both coasts for 25 years.

I also taught a workshop on "The Male Experience" at Harbin Hot Springs in Northern California, where George Simons* participated. I was trained by Michael Harner on shamanism and took Gay Luce's nine-month Nine Gates Mystery School.[156] In all of this work, I began to learn from the stories attendees told about how wounded they all are. I read in Jungian therapist Linda Schiersen Leonard's *The Wounded Woman: Healing the Father-Daughter Relationship* about six kinds of fathers, each with their own way of wounding their daughters, even the perfect father. Generally what's considered the perfect father is a man who doesn't show a full range of emotions. The daughter then falls in love with a man like that.

In 1985 I created a four-day, three-night residential retreat called "Healing the Father Wound® " for men only and another for women only and facilitated them on both coasts for 25 years. It's about getting down to the deep stuff, exposing it, and digging it out. It helps to stop keeping it a secret, the stuff that you have never told a therapist, or a secret you don't dare tell your significant other--something you're ashamed of in your life that's still drawing you down. If you don't reveal it, you can't heal it. That year I facilitated three weekends in California and two in New York.

I also developed a six-day retreat for six women and six men called "Clearing the Air between Women and Men" that I co-facilitated for 19 years, on both coasts. The main goal was to release the repressed anger towards the other sex that often turns into passive-aggressive behaviors. I developed a process called Tantrum Yoga® which is a safe, non-hitting way to release anger. It took us three days to get rage out in a safe way. I included six women and six men who made a commitment to never be in a romantic relationship with someone in the workshop, similar to the process used in Re-evaluation Counseling. From there it was easy to get to a place of OHNSI (Open-Hearted Non-Sexual Intimacy). Since all feelings are just our personal algorithms, it allows us to go in and adjust them to create healthier expressions and behaviors.

In 1990, I took a weekend called the New Warrior Training Adventure where I found my life mission to ending men's isolation as my goal. In 1996 I expanded a quarterly resource magazine called *Menstuff,* which I had started years before, into a very healthy website. [157]-I continue to post new material, men's events--including at least 15 regional men's gatherings--and new columns every month.

I've worked on improving relationships between men and women, like the NOMAS Women and Men's Task group that you and I were in. A founder of the ManKind Project, Bill Krauth, and his wife Zoe Alowan from Ashland, do tribal work with men and women. This approach is antithetical to Justin Sterling's workshops on "Men, Sex, and Power," headquartered in Oakland. They taught women, in my opinion, to be subservient to men and that they're "100% responsible" for the relationship. [*They're now called "The Women's Weekend" and "The Men's Weekend" for "strong, masculine men."*] The one good thing that did come out of Sterling's work is that the men were encouraged to form groups to do improvement projects for their local communities.

I think if women ran the world it would be much the way it is now. Prime Minister of England Margaret Thatcher colluded with President Reagan to damage our whole world economy around power and control. We're still going to go to war to fight each other. There is no androgynous society where the women and men have equal power, equal opportunity. and equal responsibility. Even in matriarchal societies like the Navajo, women and men still have specific roles and you don't cross those lines. *Kurdish Rojava in Northern Syria is committed to equal representation and women serve in the military; that's the society that I know of that's trying the hardest to have equality.* Israeli women have been in the military in combat roles forever and in a lot of Latin American countries, the women fight alongside men (*FARC guerillas in Colombia included women*). Women and men should be allowed to do any of it.

What other men's groups and organizations are active now? I have information on my website, Menstuff.org, which gets about three million hits a month. It lists hundreds of men's groups and organizations, though I haven't been able to keep it current during the pandemic.

I have a section where I've broken down the major men's movements into six groups: Pro-Feminist, Men's Rights, Mythopoetic (the Robert Bly section with a lot of the therapists), Re-Evaluation Counseling, Men's Recovery, and Promise Keepers. Ed Barton built a huge men's studies collection in the Michigan State library. I think the American Men's Studies broke away from NOMAS to form a more egalitarian way of addressing men's studies. Daniel Ellenberg,* a psychologist in my men's group, organized a Zoom conference from Rutgers University called "Creating Connection and Community through Courageous Conversations." The goal was for the APA to better understand diverse perspectives on the lives of men and boys.

The Promise Keepers are emerging again; they had a big convention in an NFL stadium in 2021. The women's movement attacked them because their religion preaches that women are subservient to men, but their religion and the women believe it too. The Promise Keepers encouraged men to make seven promises to their family. I've talked to a number of wives over the years who were so thankful that their husbands went to Promise Keepers, making them better men and fathers. I feel positive about that aspect of Promise Keepers.

My view is that about 10 years ago, men started moving away from doing personal work and started doing relational work like Harville Hendricks and other relationship trainers. In my opinion, you can't clean up your relationship before you work on your own stuff first and then come back to the relationship work as your better self.

Many of those groups have gone to sleep except the New Warrior Training Adventure known as the ManKind Project. It was started in 1985 in Wisconsin by three men. To date, there are over 60,000 men who have done that work through over 200 weekend trainings a year in 22 countries. I went through the training in 1990 and know that I've got indigenous Swahili and Maori brothers and brothers inside Folsom Prison [see the documentary *The Work*[158]] that have done the deep work to get in touch with who they really are at their core, not how they've been trained to have power over people.

What's the purpose of the Warrior training? Part of the theory is being initiated as a man and it feels a lot like getting in touch with your inner child through different processes. It's challenging and incredibly powerful and most of the men come away with a mission. They're often seen by their family and community as different men who have matured and been initiated as a man, rather than through the military experience or getting somebody pregnant. They set up an eight-week course for the men after they take the Warrior training to integrate the training into their lives. Some I-groups go on for years. They talk about how they are or aren't achieving their mission and what can other I-Group members do to support them with their process.

Some men are doing their own self-improvement work like New Warriors, similar to what women did in CR groups during the Second Wave of the women's movement. But many women haven't been doing any personal work for years and are often not prepared to deal with men who are coming out of the

ManKind Project who are much more in touch with their feelings.

Some women have a particularly hard time dealing with those men who have gotten in touch with a tremendous level of grief that they have held at bay their whole lives. Sadly, the shock for some women is so great that they tell their boyfriend or husband to man up and get over it. Messages that many men can readily identify with coming from their fathers, coaches, buddies, and even girlfriends. It's getting safer for men, though, as famous athletes are allowing tears and others are willing to be fined for missing a game to be at the birth of their children.

What do you hear about young men doing the work? A lot of Millennials are doing it. And Elders are initiating young men. I have a good friend in the Bay Area, who is working with a group of Chicanos doing a training called "Boys to Men" that's been around for probably 15 or 20 years, initiating young boys to become healthy men. (*Also see Jerry Tello**).

The feminist and pro-feminist movements have had a hard time getting people of color involved for years. When I took the ManKind Project training, it included a number of gay and BIOPIC men. As long as fifteen years ago, we were initiating trans men. I staffed one of those trainings near Sacramento to ensure the safety of all and to see if it triggered any of the staff's homophobia. I referred to David Steinberg's work and books on healthy sexuality.

What kind of ceremony or ritual creates the initiation? It's secretive. You never took "Clearing the Air Between Women and Men," but the purpose of that kind of work is to trigger openings and vulnerabilities in the subconscious that have been hidden all of their lives. If people knew what the outcome is or how it's done, the experiential aspect is lost, as is the impact.

It's like an initiation done in some tribal communities where the boys going through it don't have a clue of what it's all about. It's like the walkabout in Australia; they just know that they've got to go out in the wilderness for a month and survive. If they did know, it's like the mind becomes your worst enemy because it basically likes you the way you are. It knows what you'll do and how you'll react. The mind is a trickster. In a sweat lodge, it says you have to have cool air or you're doing intense breath-work and it tells you to slow down. You run a 26-mile marathon and during that run, almost everyone hits a wall. That's basically the subconscious mind asking you not to change. Like Tony Robbin's walking on red hot coals and Balinese men trance dancing on red hot coals, many cultures I have experienced use trance to divert the mind so the real transformational work can happen. Our youth were actually going to raves and using ecstasy and other drugs to reach this same state, though they weren't really aware of what was happening. That's what experiential processes do to break through the mind's resistance.

Many indigenous peoples use Peyote and Ayahuasca. My sister was a Lakota pipe carrier and worked with a Peruvian medicine man and brought him up to Portland every year to do ayahuasca journeys and Masa rituals. My belief is that a lot of change happens in other realms than the conscious mind; it needs to circumvent the mind so that real, permanent change can happen.

Why do you think teenagers are increasingly anxious and depressed and have a lot of mental health issues? Cell phones have destroyed children's knowledge, thinking, decision-making and desire. They average six to eight hours a day on social media and that was before the pandemic. They're on Twitter, TikTok, and Instagram where they get trained not to think, or communicate verbally. Therapists have told me it's very difficult to work with young people these days. They have been disconnected from their parents over the last 15 years, and attachment goes out the window. They often spend much of their time in their room on their computer. They can't communicate like you and I are communicating because they have learned to receive a text, think about an answer, send it, and wait for a response.

I don't think our education system is keeping up. Generation Alpha toddlers can find the programs they want to watch on a Think Pad without needing parental assistance. Youth are saddled with the reality that over half of the jobs currently provided by humans will either be eliminated or done by robots by 2030. Those who learn how to solve problems, and I credit Common Core for this, will have the advantage because it is unlikely many jobs in this millennium will be permanent and workers will continually have to reinvent themselves to keep up. I wouldn't be surprised if the medical profession isn't primarily staffed by robotic surgeons and staff, eliminating the years a human needs to train and the incredible debt they have to incur to become a doctor. AI is going to advance very quickly.

There's an incredible book written by Jean Twenge called *iGen: Why Today's Super-connected Kids are Growing Up Less Rebellious, More Tolerant, Less Happy, and Completely Unprepared for Adulthood.* The kids are not thinking, they'll go to Google to get the answers and not have to figure it out. Kids can't concentrate in class.

You've been in a men's group for over 45 years. What are current issues men talk about in your group? My group of seven are all therapists except me, including Daniel Ellenberg.* It started with Shepherd Bliss* back in the day when he offered salons in his house, a catalyst for us to get together. We would go to the California Men's Gathering together and put on workshops and rituals. Right now, we meet quarterly talking about what's going on in our lives and the difficulties of aging. We seldom talk about relationships except around health. We sometimes discuss possible alternative scenarios dealing with a difficult client situation and always end up sharing a great meal together.

Anything else you'd to add in terms of men's changing roles? I think men are getting soft in a good way, like, we're seeing football players tearing up and not getting put down for it. NFL and NBA players are saying "I'm going to feel what I feel." We still have this incredibly masculine culture of big boys don't cry, but I think we're seeing more fathers telling their sons that it's okay to cry. We need cultural change on how boys are taught to be men. More men are getting in touch with their responsibility to raise a son and a daughter in conscious terms. My hope is that after the hate created during the Trump Era, people will take the pendulum the other way and really get back into conscious communication and caring about each other. I see a future giving us the opportunity as men and women to become familiar with our true emotions and feelings and access them more readily. This will help men deal with many life issues that currently create an environment where too many men become suicidal.

The fact is that boys and men currently die by suicide at three to four times the rate of women[159], and it's not because they use lethal means. They use lethal means because they have been trained that they should be able to handle anything, not show weakness and, by all means, don't be a victim or ask for help, which translates into their serious intent to die when something that is extremely painful happens.

This scenario has been under-researched for decades, leaving a reliance on information in the ER from the very few boys and men who fail on their first attempt. I contend that these are two very different groups of men, and prevention and intervention techniques need to be developed to address ways to reduce the level of serious intent.

Universal mental health promotion and suicide prevention campaigns often do not meet the needs of men in relation to language, content, or cultural acknowledgment. Men's health needs and barriers are unique and should be addressed to effectively reach men and boys and educate the public to encourage a shift in the way we train our boys on what it is to be a man. After all, boys will be what we teach them to be.

We all experience life's ups and downs such as relationship breakdowns, financial difficulty, or losing a job. These moments can really change us and sadly, leave most men feeling they don't have anyone they can confide in. Therefore, in 2016 I started a communication plan in Curry County, Oregon and in Del Norte County, California, to change cultural norms as to what it is to be a man, similar to what women started doing back in the '60s. This plan is designed to empower men to get involved in their own mental health and support the mental health of other men. It is important to be sensitive to the psychological traits of men of all ages with messages appropriate to their needs.

The first stage of this program began in July 2016, eventually establishing partnerships with over 160 retail businesses in Curry and Del Norte counties to place a counter card, often near check out, that holds crisis wallet cards. We targeted auto parts stores, gun shops, dispensaries, law enforcement lobbies, libraries and book stores, tattoo parlors, liquor stores, thrift stores, outdoor stores, schools, health care offices, and restaurants.

In order to make for better, safer, healthier work environments, the next stage is to start with male-dominant professions and industries that have high suicide rates such as law enforcement, forestry, fishing, and construction. and train employees to notice how fellow colleagues are doing and make it standard protocol to check in with each other when they see signs that something is going on by Trusting their Gut. Starting the conversation, asking "Are you okay?" And, "It's okay to say 'I'm not okay.'"

These are the initial steps to take to address the immediate needs to reduce our growing suicide rate. The longer-term process is to start with educators, the health care industry, and particularly pediatricians, to change the culture in teaching our boys what it is to be a real man. I'm reminded of a definition that Star Hawk wrote in her book, *The Spiral Dance*,

> *"If man had been created in Spirit's image,*
> *He would be free to be wild without being cruel,*
> *Angry without being violent,*
> *Sexual without being coercive,*
> *Spiritual without being unsexed*
> *And able to truly love."*

I was born in New York City in December 1943. I'm a Sagittarius; my wife is an astrologer so I know I'm right on the cusp. *Do you feel like someone who has deep questions and is adventurous and likes to travel?* Yes, in my professional work I moved from being the CEO to being the VHS (Visionary, Healer, Scholar in residence), so I have a lot of that. My rising sign and moon are in Libra. *So justice and balance are very important to you?* Indeed.

   You wrote that you felt vulnerable and weak as a boy, like a lot of boys. I was both weak and also strong. When I was five years old, my father became depressed and had a "nervous breakdown." He couldn't make a living to support the family and went to a mental hospital after taking an overdose of pills. I lost my father, and my mother had to go out to work, so I was kind of on my own. I felt vulnerable as my tight-knit family came apart so I had to develop a lot of skills for taking care of myself and others, starting with visiting my father in the mental hospital with my uncle because my mother couldn't handle that. I became very independent and somewhat worldly but I had a deep hole in the soul where my father's energy would have been. *Do you have siblings?* No siblings, it's just me.

Did this lead you to be a therapist? I grew up wondering if I would go crazy or break down and not be able to support my family. I thought I would go up to medical school and become a psychiatrist and somehow help people like my father and others. I went to UC Santa Barbara and got my bachelor's degree and then went to medical school at UC San Francisco. I saw that medicine was restrictive and very much a mostly all-white boys club. Given my background with parents who were very radical at times, it didn't work for me and I felt there was more to healing than the restrictive biological model, so I dropped out of medical school. I had to see a psychiatrist to leave because the view was that you must be crazy to give up a four-year, full-tuition scholarship.

I went into social work, which seemed to be a broader field and something I was drawn to, and got an MSW. I went into numerous fields like treatment programs for addicts, private counseling, organizing communities, and then went back to school. That was 10 years ago when I got a Ph.D. in International Health because I really wanted to do more in-depth study on different ways in which men and women experienced depression.

When Covid hit, I gave lectures all over the world on some of the information about infectious diseases that most people didn't know. The work that I have been doing in recent years is combining all these different levels of science and the individual, small group, family, and societal issues and putting them together in programs that can hopefully help men, women, children, and the world in which we are all a part.

I'm hearing from men that the core of the men's issues is the lack of involved fathers, which is even more difficult with divorce. Yes, it's certainly true in my life and after working with men and their families for 52 years, I see it as a common pattern both for men and women with fathers who were absent physically or emotionally through death or divorce. Often this is multi-generational and these patterns influence our health, our relationships with our love mates, and how we present ourselves to the world.

You've concluded we have basic biological differences; your chromosomes are XY and mine are XX and that really does influence us. I'm trying to get a handle on what mothers can't teach boys. Having been raised by a mother, there's a lot mothers can teach but they can't teach what it means to be a man. Robert Bly, a colleague and friend over the years, said poetically, "Males at any age need to be in the company of other men in order to hear the sound that male cells sing." With tens of trillions of cells in the human body, scientists say that every one of them is sex-specific with XX or XY pairs of chromosomes in each cell. They influence how our bodies function and on an energetic level the male vibration is different from a female vibration.

I'm reading that brain differences are very minimal but you quote researchers who found the female brain tends to be more emphatic and the male brain tends to be more interested in systems and structures. A professor of neuroscience, Lissy Elliott reported, "I recently completed a painstaking analysis of 30 years of research on human brain sex differences, and what I found with the help of excellent collaborators is that virtually none of these claims has proven reliable."

I used to hear that because women have more corpus callosum connection between the left and right brain, they're more holistic, but Elliott says, no, that's only because women's brains are a little bit smaller. She says the idea of a male and a female brain is a "zombie concept." Women say, "I don't want to emphasize the differences because they've traditionally been used against women. We're told women are too soft and gentle, so they can't be brain surgeons and business executives," although obviously, that's not true. However, in trying to create a level playing field, in some ways we have denied both the biological, psychological, social, and spiritual gender differences.

Simond Baron-Cohen, Ph.D., Professor of Psychology and Psychiatry at Cambridge University, is the author of *The Essential Difference: The Truth About the Male & Female*

Brain. He found that women as a group tend to be more empathic, while men tend to be more oriented towards systems and patterns. However, I score way high on empathy. *It gets even more interesting because there are some men with XYY and others who are born with undifferentiated genitalia. So we're a complex species.* Absolutely. *In terms of the spatial orientation, I read that female humans and rats tend to navigate by landmarks while men tend to navigate by vectors, more geometric.*

Sharon Moalem, M.D., Ph.D., the male author of *The Better Half: On the Genetic Superiority of Women,* explained, "Here are some facts: Women live longer than men. They have stronger immune systems. They're better at fighting cancer and surviving famine, and even see the world in a wider variety of colors. They are simply better than men at every stage of life." Dr. Moalem's research indicates that the difference is based in genetics, with females having two X chromosomes, while males only have one.

John Gottman and Sue Johnson have done scientific work about couple relationships. Both report men are less likely to bring up marital problems than women because they have a higher arousal rate and get more flooded and withdraw because of the way their body reacts to stress. I think Gottman describes it well. He did some of the early research and it fits what I've seen clinically that men often don't talk about a feeling because they're overwhelmed and they don't have words for it. They clamp it down, overwhelmed by feelings.

Men actually have more reactive brains as shown when researchers hook men and women up to a sensor and then a researcher walks by them and bumps into them. Men have a higher arousal rate, they get more triggered by it, and it takes them longer physiologically to recover. This shows why we've misunderstood them. *Do you think that it evolved because of 98% of human history that we were hunters and gatherers and it paid off for hunters to react quickly?* Yes, if you don't understand the way males and females evolved in the two million years we were hunter-gatherers, you don't understand the differences that still are part of our brains. *Women shopping is like gathering and football is like hunting for the ball.*

Let's say a wife is angry because her husband is sitting on the couch, yelling at the football game, while she's got the baby, cooking, and answering the phone. What would be an effective way of getting him to help? Start with being aware of her own overwhelm and what helps her calm down before she tries to engage him. Second, realize that because of the way men's brains operate maybe he's so focused on the game because it simulates the hunt with the Lions, the Tigers, the Cougars. He may be so totally focused that he doesn't hear or doesn't listen well enough. Rather than yelling, "What the hell are you doing?" she could say, "I know you're really engaged with the game but can you stop for a minute because I really need your help now," in a calm voice. Usually, when guys are approached that way they'll go, "Okay, just let me finish this one play and I'll be right with you."

My clinical experience is that I observe a lot of differences between men and women, as well as a lot of things that are the same. There's a whole body of work that I've been involved with for years on evolutionary biology and psychology that looks at male-female differences. We know from epigenetics that actual genetic makers are either turned on or off, based on psychological, social-relational, environmental influences, so it's a complex subject.

Professor Marianne J. Legato, M.D., is a woman doctor, surgeon, and cardiac specialist who founded The Foundation for Gender-Specific Medicine in 2006. She realized that women have different symptoms of heart attack than men. She draws from research from all over the world that indicates the sexes are really different, as Riane Eisler believes as well. I've worked with her over the years at her Center for Partnership Systems. Eisler recognizes that the problem isn't gender differences, but the domination society that we have been living in for many thousands of years.

In our ancient partnership roots... *As egalitarian hunters and gatherer bands*...which is 99% of human history, differences were celebrated living in partnerships. Domination is a harmful way of looking at the world, damaging to the earth and our inner worlds. Patriarchal dominance created a lot of the violence and created an unsustainable world. *And endangers our environment.*

Men's studies writers emphasize that gender is socially constructed and fluid and teenagers who identify as nonbinary think biology has nothing to do with gender. In a dominator society, binary is part of the deal. Egalitarian societies, whether Native Americans or indigenous cultures around the world, recognize that males and females are different in many ways and there are variations in sexuality. *It's like the concept of* berdache *about Plains Indian males, and other indigenous cultures, that there's a third gender.* Exactly.

How are the songs the XY cells sing different from the XX songs? Scientists found that the way proteins are created are different in a XX environment, more protective of life so women live longer. We know that at every age, from babies on up, males die sooner, while some of that is the way we relate in our environment, but some of it turns out to be biological. Another example is Ambien, a very common sleeping medication, but the way females metabolize is different.[160] Males metabolize it more quickly so they don't get the same benefits. There are probably these kinds of differences in any medication but they haven't tested for it. When they do, they find biological differences in the way the brain metabolizes drugs. It's simpler to study the biological changes of men because their hormonal ups and downs are not as prevalent. However, my books, *Male Menopause* and *Surviving Male Menopause: A Guide for Women and Men* show that in fact, there is a male change of life that has similarities to what women experience,

What can men do about it? The first thing is to recognize that, like women, men have biological rhythms and changes like hot flashes, and at midlife, testosterone drops in men, and men have estrogen, like women have testosterone. First, recognize there are hormonal changes; second, measure them. Third, see if they are outside the normal range and if you have symptoms. I've written books on treatment programs including change of diet, exercise, and other ways of balancing, other than taking supplements.

You mentioned that there is a harmful American male diet. I think of Donald Trump's hamburgers and Cokes. That's the summary of the male American diet, MAD. There are a lot of overweight men. We live in an obese world, while others starve, and a lot of it has to do with eating too much animal products, too much fat, too much beef injected with hormones. My mother thought that since I didn't have a father in the home I needed to get manly. Back in the '50s when I was growing up, I had meat three times a day because it was quick to make. For breakfast I had a hamburger, for lunch, I had chops, and for dinner, I had steak, so I thought that's how men were supposed to eat. I got fat until I learned that eating vegetables was healthier and actually felt better for me.[161] *It's better for the planet. It's amazing how much methane cows release.* Yes, not to mention what we do to the land in order to produce what the cows eat. *Cutting down the rain forest, our planetary lungs.*

Another important difference I'm increasingly seeing is men and women communicate differently when they're talking to the same gender. When I hear my wife on the phone talking to one of her girlfriends, it feels like she goes all over the place and I'm like, get to the point. When I talk to my friend Lenny on the phone, it's like, "Hey, you want to play ball today?" "Yes, I'm going to beat you. What time?"

I was impatient with my wife, saying, "Come on, tell me what you want at the store," until I saw the differences. In his well-researched book, *Duels and Duets: Why Men and Women Talk So Differently,* Linguistic Professor John L. Locke, says, "Men and women talk differently. Men duel while women duet." Men compete with each other, one up one down, while women are generally more engaged in relationships. I'm exaggerating, but we need to recognize that we're talking different languages. *Linguist Deborah Tannen talks about how girls tell each other secrets and boys exchange information and establish dominance hierarchies.* Exactly.

When you're in your men's group, you're talking for hours and you're not just talking about I'm going to beat you on the court. I'm probably more of the female-type brain than anybody in the group, so I talk more, I organize, I'm more concerned about the relationships. But, if women eavesdropped on us they would be surprised at the depth and the breadth. *Did you feel odd at first in the men's group talking about feelings and relationships in depth?* Yes, I remember I went to a conference that broke up into same-sex groups. I thought if there's ever going to be a place where I'll find guys who want to talk more relationally, this would be it, but even in that kind of feminist environment they wanted to talk about football and what women were hot, and I was disappointed.

It's gotten better over the years as men are getting obviously more relational, and women are getting more patterned and organizational. Women have learned to work in both worlds a lot quicker and more easily than men. Men still have a long ways to go before you have as many healthy integrated men as women.

Young men still don't want to be seen as gay or sissy, or do you think that's changed? It's changed but there's a lot more stigma if guys are accused by other guys of being feminine. *In* The Crisis of Connection, *Niobe Way reported that in adolescence boys are lonely because the kind of deep friendships they had as little boys erode because they don't want to be seen as gay.* Yes, as you get into adolescence we close off affectionate friendships, which leads to depression. We remember from our childhood when we had best buddies and hugged each other.

We feel in order to be male, in order to attract women, in order to be successful, we have to repress that side so men grow up feeling cut off, feeling lonely, and that's one of the main sources of depression for men. It happens even more as we get older and the friends we had die off. I think that's part of why the suicide rate goes up significantly in men as they get older while it goes down for women.

You outlined the five stages of a relationship and found the hardest one is Stage Three when disillusionment sets in. What did you learn from your three marriages that helped you identify those stages? My first two marriages were like a lot of people's in that I thought there were two stages. You look for that perfect partner, you fall in love in Stage One. In Stage Two you build a life together and plan to live happily ever after. In my first marriage, I had children and after ten years it didn't work out. I thought I picked the wrong person so I picked somebody else who I thought was right and got another divorce.

We know about disillusionment where people fall apart. You're not who I thought you were and maybe I picked the wrong person. In fact, disillusionment is a good stage of a good marriage, a way in which the illusions that we project on our partner come down. Our childhood wounding creates a faulty love map because we're recreating a lot of the problems we had in our families that we never resolved.

If you're a family therapist teaching other people how to have a good relationship, it's more embarrassing when your relationship falls apart. I thought, before I do it again, I better learn some things so I did some therapy, some healing myself to gain more in-depth understanding, and was able to identify the five stages. I fell in love for the third time but this time I had a better sense of how to work with my current wife; we're now married for 41 years.

In Stage Three we have an opportunity to heal the old wounds and get a better sense of how to relate to a real partner. *If I'm feeling you irritate me, I'm not attracted to you anymore, the chemistry's gone, how do you get past that?* It's not easy because it's like the opposite of manic where you feel so good, while in the disillusionment phase you feel so bad you want to get away. In my book *The Enlightened Marriage: The 5 Transformative Stages of Relationships and Why the Best is Still to Come*, I explain that a lot of the projections have to do with the families we grew up in and the traumas we experienced. The good news is if you stay with it, you go deeper, you get through Stage Three.

Do you think we can deal with Stage Three by ourselves or do you think we usually need a therapist to help? It depends on how wounded you are and how communicative you've been able to be. People have told me my book helps to have a guide, so in a way, I'm giving my therapy through the book and I have classes that people can take. *Harville Hendrix's book,* How to Get the Love You Want, *helps with getting out of Stage Three. Which other ones do you like?* I agree and John Gottman and Sue Johnson's books are excellent. There are, fortunately, a number of really good supports and resources out there.

In Stage Four we get to real lasting love where we've gotten past most of the illusions and healed a lot of wounds from the past. We're no longer projecting our unmet needs on the other person. We have a partnership based on equality and are able to get Stage Five, which I didn't know existed when I started. It's about finding our calling as a couple and finding our unique offerings in the world. I think couples have our unique calling to bring our unique passions to something we're creating together.

In our case, we have five children together and 17 grandchildren. Beyond that, my wife and I have a shared vision of what we can bring to the world where couples live in full harmony, where families are really healthy. What might that create in terms of a better government, better education, better policing, and better ways the genders and ethnic groups can relate. That's the potential and one of the things we teach at MenAlive.

How is your wife involved in that outreach? One of the reasons she thinks we have a good 41-year marriage is I have been in a men's group for 42 years. My most recent book is called *12 Rules for Good Men,* which was inspired by my wife. She said with all the conflicts going on in the world, and between males and females and the #MeToo movement, and to get past the abusive sexual ways in which many men have been with women, she saw males need guidance healing and getting past the armory that a dominating society imposes on men.

She challenged me to write this book about what does it mean to be a good man? The first rule is to join a men's group. It's really part of what men need to do for healing in the way that Robert Bly talks about, hearing the sound that male cells sing. My wife and I are also in mixed groups, including a village circle we've been meeting with for 17 years where men and women come together to do our joint healing. That is part of what our journey is together and hopefully what we bring to the world in our various books and offerings.

What are other specific ways to raise good men besides making sure they have contact with supportive men? Another core aspect is healing our anger and ambivalence towards women. We learn a distorted view of women because of not having supportive fathers and because women themselves grew up in families that were disordered. My mother grew up in a family where she lost her father when she was young and was fearful from the time that I was born that I would die. When you're raised by a very fearful mother, you grow up with pain and hurt, and anger. Being able to deal with feeling cut off from the larger society is another part of the healing, healing our relationship to the planet.

It seems pivotal that we are angry with our mothers. Is that because they're the dominant parents yet they can't satisfy all our needs or is it because they're safe and we can dump our frustrations on them? There are a hundred reasons for being abused and feeling angry because of that. All of us come out of the body of a female. If we're going to be males, at some level we recognize that we're different from the body of the person we came out of. The joke is we spend all our life trying to separate from woman's energy, then we spend a lifetime trying to get back by trying to have sex with women or get back into the womb and men are afraid of that. As discussed by Karen Horney, Nancy Chodorow, and Dorothy Dinnerstein.

Part of males' anger towards women is our ambivalence that we both long to bond with them, be held and nurtured, and the fear of losing ourselves in the power of a woman's body or energy. The healing has to happen on multiple levels: psychological, social, spiritual, and in a relational way.

Increasing numbers of teens in the Western world, especially girls, are presenting with anxiety and depression. What have you observed about how boys express anxiety and depression? Traditionally, studies indicated that females experience anxiety and depression at higher rates than males, but clinically and in my personal experience, I saw a lot of men, including myself, who were depressed and anxious. The way you assess mental problems is not with objective clinical blood tests, so if you're asking the wrong questions, you're going to be biased. A lot of the kinds of symptoms that women were talking about were often different than the way men experience depression, and so were the scales that showed that men were less depressed than women.

What my research showed is if you look at things like irritability, anger, and alcohol use, which are more symptomatic of the way men experience depression, then the imbalance decreases. I developed a questionnaire called "The Diamond Male Depression Scale" with 50-some questions. We know that the suicide rate for males is much higher than it is for females.

You wrote that you went through a stage of being an attachment junkie, as well as experiencing erectile dysfunction and ADD. How did you get out of all that? It was a long journey and I'm still getting out of it. It started with my wife and me going to a treatment center for one of our sons who had a drug problem and as part of the family recovery day, they gave the parents a simple depression test because they had found that many families with addicted kids had depression in their families. My wife scored high on being depressed, while I scored low, so my wife got some treatment and got better.

She said to me, "You know, Jed, I think you've got some depression, too," but I denied it. Finally, to quiet her down, I went to a doctor and did an evaluation; he said I have bipolar disorder, but I didn't believe it and I wanted another opinion. She looked me in the eyes and said, "I'll give you another opinion. You have some problems, you need to get some help." To quiet my wife down, I went to a much better therapist, a woman who spent much more time with me and said essentially exactly the same thing the other guy did.

I took medications for some time, changed my diet, and worked on my relationship over a period of about eight or nine years in treatment, and got better to a point where I didn't need the medications anymore. I kept doing counseling, our relationship got better, and the depression lifted. I still keep track of my own mood and my ups and downs. It wasn't easy to get me to a therapist, as you can tell. I think that's true for many men, so a lot of what I do in my clinical work is to help women understand how to get through to men who are in denial.

Regarding your experience with the men's movement, what different branches are most influential? I've been involved in all of the aspects of the men's movement over the years from the feminist men's movement, the men's rights, mythopoetic, and recovery group. I don't think that any of the movements really capture the full energy of what men are doing and the big changes that are going on in men's work. I call it "men's work" rather than the men's movement because none of them are as vital as the women's movement and because I think men as a group tend to do engagement in a different way than women.

There are groups like the ManKind Project, which is worldwide, vital, and growing. My own program at MenAlive.com has been going more than 50 years, since my son, Jemal, was born on November 21, 1969. There's a huge vitality that's going on in men's work but it doesn't hit the news. A lot of the work is building the bridge between what men and women are doing, which has been my work over the years. Let's find what unites us rather than what separates us.

Where do you see young men gravitating? They're in all kinds of groups, like mensgroup.org which is doing men's groups. I have connections with organizations all over the world that are doing really vital things in men's work. There are hundreds of them as I share on my website, and as well as Gordon Clay's Menstuff.org website.

How can someone participate in MenAlive? It's multiple programs and if people come to the website menalive.com they'll see articles on ten different areas of health, the 16 books I have written, and programs including *The Five Stages of Love, Healing the Family Father Wound,* and *Saving Your Relationship From the Irritable Male Syndrome.* I have programs that help with hormonal change and other changes we go through as we get older, programs for leaders in the world, and a training program for men and women who recognize that humans are out of balance with the community of life on Earth. I look forward to hearing from people who would like to learn more about our work at MenAlive.

Warren Farrell, Ph.D.
The Boy Crisis Resides Where Dads Do Not Reside

My family lived in New York City (NYC) and New Jersey until my dad got a job managing a Dutch company when we moved to The Hague, which radically broadened my worldview when I was 14. A year later, we moved back to New Jersey, where I attended Montclair State University for my BA prior to going to UCLA for my master's degree in 1966. After UCLA, I got married to a woman who was offered a job with IBM in NYC, so I did my doctorate at NYU. When the feminist movement surfaced in 1969, I changed my doctoral dissertation to focus on feminist issues, which catalyzed more than a decade of feminist activism. When my wife and I parted ways in about 1978, I returned to the California I had discovered at UCLA.

What led to you writing your dissertation about the women's movement? When I was teaching political science at

Rutgers University in 1969, the women's movement surfaced. As I shared with my class its long-term implications, my students told me, "Warren, when you speak about the women's movement you have fire in your belly--if you see such potential, why don't you change your dissertation to that?"

I knew they were right. So, I approached my dissertation committee. They said the women's movement was just a fad and wasn't worthy of my study. I pushed back, saying I don't agree; I think that the women's movement is the beginning of an evolutionary shift in gender roles. Until now both sexes have been dominated by the need to survive. To survive, most societies developed rigid roles: women, raise children; men, raise money. No one had rights; everyone had obligations. However, once people in developed nations are not dominated by survival, I believe there will be permission for both sexes to be freer from the rigid roles of their past to seek more flexible roles for their future. This is no fad. The women's movement is just the first stage of a gender liberation movement.

They were intrigued, but didn't buy it, saying some version of, "Don't men have the power, and wouldn't they be the first ones to take advantage of any privilege emanating from this so-called 'evolutionary shift'?" My response was, "No, men are designed to protect women. We know women will fall in love with the 'officer and the gentleman,' not the 'private and the pacifist' so we're willing to die in the hope that if we do manage to live, we will be called a 'hero' and everyone's respect will lead to our being accepted by a beautiful woman for love, sex, and raising a family. It will be a long time before men really make that same evolutionary shift because we receive respect, and therefore love and sex, by never complaining about ourselves."

Maybe because I had just been appointed assistant to the president of NYU, they were a bit more "flexible" than they might otherwise have been. They sort of shrugged their shoulders, rolled their eyes, and agreed I could change my dissertation topic to the politics of the women's movement. That got me involved with the National Organization for Women (NOW) chapter in NYC.

At one point NOW debated kicking men out because they felt men were too often giving women unwanted advice, and NOW felt their "consciousness-raising" (CR) groups allowed women to "open up" more when they were only among women. The kick-men-out debate was resolved with a decision that changed my life: The two sides made a deal that if they could get me to form men's groups that would benefit the men and give the women an all-female safe space, they would keep men involved in NOW. I agreed to the challenge. I can't say I knew what I was doing, but it turned out that the guys were as pleased as the women.

The positive result led to my being asked if I would run for NOW's Board of Directors in NYC, which I did. My election led to publicity in myriad media outlets: from features and op-eds in *The New York Times* to multi-page features in *People* and *Parade* magazines, to all the morning shows and seven appearances on *Donahue* (the '70's version of Oprah).

As I spoke around the country, I formed men's and women's groups at each venue, including one that John Lennon joined, which led him to putting his solo career on hold to raise his son Sean full-time. I have started more than 300 men's groups, including the one I am part of today that includes John Gray (*Mars/Venus*) and John Mackey (founder of Whole Foods).

With the men's groups, once confidentiality was guaranteed and I stopped trying to impose my feminist ideology on the men, the men slowly began to open their hearts. One man after the other who had become a dad talked about a career he had forfeited--whether as an artist, musician, writer, actor, or elementary school teacher--to take a job that was much less fulfilling that paid more. They talked sadly about the hours their "dad job" consumed or the travel it required; about how they felt caught in what I came to call "the father's catch-22": being expected to love their family by being away from it.

I could see that the dads were not experiencing high pay as "power" or "male privilege." They could feel that the stress they were experiencing might lead them to die earlier. In brief, I came to feel that we guys were learning to define "power" as feeling obligated to earn money that our family would spend as we died earlier. I slowly realized that instead of experiencing high pay as privilege, they were experiencing the road to high pay as a toll road. Even John Lennon, with all his money and fame, told me that if he hadn't joined one of the men's groups I formed, he would never have had the courage to renegotiate all the contracts that would otherwise have prevented him from having the time to raise Sean full time for four to five years. During my third year on NYC NOW's Board, my wife became a White House Fellow. We moved to Washington D.C. where I became "the wife of a Fellow" and taught at American University and Georgetown.

How did you narrow your dissertation topic? I did an extensive study of how a broad section of men's attitudes changed based on a variety of reading material I gave the men, and how other men's behaviors change when they were in the men's groups I created. *What did you find changed their behavior?* At the beginning, they were very protective of women in that they didn't want to live in a world where women were held back. But most of the men quickly "got it" that women earning money put less pressure on them to feel the need to kowtow to their bosses and do jobs that they didn't like because they paid more. It became apparent to me that the more fulfilling the work, the less it pays because the more fulfilling the work the more people want to do it, therefore the greater the supply in relation to the demand, thus the lower the pay.

Your mother died when your brother Wayne was only 11, so your father became the primary parent until he remarried. How did that shape your attitude towards parenting? When my mom died, I was already married to my former wife, Ursie, but I knew that my father was actively involved and saw my father become a different person. When I was growing up, my dad focused on teaching me responsibility and accountability. I rarely had a vacation day, was expected to work during school breaks in the post office or as a caddy, or delivering papers and milk, and so on. There was no such thing as an excuse.

When my mom died, my dad wanted to be a friend to my brother, which created problems. My brother was much more rebellious than I and took more risks. He became a very good skier but was killed by an avalanche when he was at the University of Utah. Since this followed the death of my biological mom by just a few years, the combination was pretty devastating.

To look at your career path, you were a professor and then you've managed to make your living as a writer and a speaker, which is unusual. Yes, and it's a little amusing too. My only full-time teaching was one year each at Brooklyn College and Rutgers University. All my other appointments were part-time, or adjunct appointments, such as at the School of Medicine at the University of California, San Diego. All the publicity I mentioned led to my being the leading male spokesperson for women's issues in the world, which led to many speaking engagements that paid substantially. That subsidized my writing, which led to more publicity, which led to more speaking!

Also, both my former and present wife are excellent earners--I never had to worry about either of them financially. This allowed me the freedom to express compassion for boys, men, and fathers, even as that compassion led to the evaporation of both my feminist support and about 90% of my income--perhaps a loss of eight to ten million dollars over the course of my life (still in progress!)

You coined the term "Lace Curtain" because after you became a gender liberation spokesperson, you didn't have the same kind of calls to appear on Oprah and so on. Yes, I had been on Oprah three times. The next time they asked me on, I explained to the producer that while I mostly agreed with what feminists were doing, I also felt that there were boys', men's, and fathers' issues that needed to be integrated into the gender transition. I could feel the energy of the producer at the Oprah show freeze and she quickly said, "Thank you very much Doc, it was really nice talking with you," and I never heard from the Oprah show again. The pattern was the same at all the morning shows, at CNN, and so on.

Similarly, *The New York Times* published almost all my op-eds until I started integrating compassion for boys and men--then I experienced rejection after rejection after rejection. As for speaking engagements, I went from more than 50 a year at colleges and universities down to somewhere between zero and one per year. With Woke Culture and Cancel Culture, this reaction from the mainstream media and from colleges and universities has magnified considerably.

When I say this, people often look puzzled as to why this is so. Almost all the people in the mainstream media who deal with gender issues have either majored in Gender Studies or taken multiple gender studies courses in college. They tell me, "Warren, 90% of the top corporate leaders and politicians are still men. Isn't it obvious to you that we live in a world dominated by a patriarchy, in which men make the rules to benefit men at the expense of women? And look at the gender pay gap--it still persists."

I do validate that this must create a feeling of powerlessness for many women, but when I add any of the challenges boys, men and fathers also face, they almost invariably think, first, "He must be anti-woman," and second, "If men really want anything to change, they can change it--they have all the power." *The zero-sum game problem.*

Sometimes a parent whose son is experiencing the challenges I discuss in *The Boy Crisis* eventually opens her or his heart and ultimately thanks me profusely. However, when they present to their producers or editors the possibility of doing a show on the boy crisis, for example, the suspicion of their colleagues is palpable--"Has she turned?" "Is she naïve, being influenced by Warren Farrell?" They encounter the Lace Curtain.

If it isn't the producers above them, it might be a copywriter below them. For example, the *AARP Magazine* asked me to write an article on men's issues. They liked it so much they asked me to write another version for their younger readers, to be published simultaneously. As both articles were about to go to press, a low-level feminist copywriter protested so vociferously that *AARP Magazine* ran scared and pulled both articles just prior to publication.

This is not just happening to me, but to virtually every man worldwide who writes sympathetically about men. *Like Jack Kammer.** To such a degree, one example after the other fills an entire chapter in *Women Can't Hear What Men Don't Say.* Perhaps I should have titled it, *Women Can't Hear What Men **Do** Say*! I see this every day. Today, for example, I looked at my issue of *TIME* magazine featuring the 100 "World's Most Influential People." Twelve editors made those choices--all women. [*54 of the influential people are women, about representative of their numbers.*]

It seems obvious that everyone benefits if we have flexibility and androgynous options available to all of us. What is the media afraid of? We live in an era of cognitive dissonance. A husband who becomes a dad may quit his low-paying job that he loves to take a higher paying job that he doesn't like to support their newborn, yet the woman may still believe that because men-in-general move up the corporate ladder faster than women, that men have male power or privilege. She doesn't see that the gender pay gap is significantly affected by precisely the decision he made to take a higher-paying job that he liked less once the child was born.

That dad is unlikely to confront that cognitive dissonance because being a man means "manning up," which means not complaining. Men feel that if they complain they will be less respected and therefore less loved. Women often marry men who, when she complains, he tries to protect her, and fix the area of complaint. Therefore, complaining is dysfunctional for men, but often functional for women and so the cognitive dissonance is not challenged.

In Woke Culture and Cancel Culture, that cognitive dissonance permeates virtually every college in the social sciences. A cab driver in Santa Cruz told me he had spent 70 hours a week driving a cab so his daughter would be the first person in their family to go to college. He was so happy when she did, and it made him feel like his sacrifices were worthwhile. Then his daughter came home on her first break and explained to him how he had male privilege and was part of an oppressor group. He told me, "My heart was broken, and I felt like all the efforts I had made to have her go to college had turned against me." He also stopped voting for Democrats because he felt the party was sort of supporting all that feminist stuff that was making him the enemy.

Is it accurate to say that capitalism causes the hierarchical system that keeps men and women in these stereotyped roles? Absolutely not. Capitalism creates wealth, and wealth frees people from being dependent on survival, which allows us freedom from the rigid roles that imprison both sexes. Hierarchical systems are common to socialism, capitalism, tribalism, monarchies, the military, dictatorships, and both large and small informal groups (what Roberto Michels called "The Iron Rule of Oligarchy").

Hierarchical systems use either what I call social bribes (*e.g.,* being called "hero" or "CEO" or "General" or "His Majesty" or "Queen Elizabeth") and/or financial bribes to create incentives--or bribes--for people to sacrifice a part of their lives to create a company, run for office, or die at war. The purpose of those incentives, or bribes, is for the culture to get people to compete to fulfill one of its needs (e.g., food) or desires (e.g., iPhones). My Ph.D. in political science is showing!

Formal hierarchies are much more associated with men because men are more likely to create measurable systems of accountability and responsibility, and to assign tangible social bribes ("you've been promoted to. . . General, or Executive Vice President'") when goals are achieved. This makes the men more respected by other men and considered more "marriage material" by women. In the Boy Scouts, it's merit badges; in football, it's becoming winning quarterback, and so on.

Women have developed much more intangible types of hierarchies, such as developing a positive reputation among friends, communicated by a friend or family member telling her, "You're such a good mom," or by being rewarded or punished by gossip in the community.

You developed a formula that in developed countries we have more freedom economically to divorce, which leads to absent fathers and the boy crisis. The root of divorce is a lack of communication skills and an inability to express your criticisms in a constructive way. You identify the father's gift is to teach self-discipline, how to set boundaries, and how to take risks in a constructive way. Dads push kids in different ways than moms do, and kids need both. We know that babies light up when their dads come in the room because the dads play with them and they are soothed by their moms.

Yes, almost all of the 53 largest developed nations have various degrees of capitalism, which allows people to have more freedom from survival needs, including the freedom to divorce; to have children without being married, or to become gay or trans or celibate. That's the good news.

The bad news is that this often leads to children not having fathers around to teach them the boundary enforcement and postponed gratification that leads them to be successful. This negatively affects both girls and boys, but in part, because girls at least have same-sex role models and boys with single moms don't, this has been the primary force developing the boy crisis. As I document in *The Boy Crisis*, "the boy crisis resides where dads do not reside."

The children who do best are the ones that have two parents with the communication skills to develop "checks-and-balance parenting" where the mother and father listen to the value of the other parent's different approaches, and together come to a win-win solution, usually balancing safety and risk. Ideally, they communicate well enough so that their children can see them working through their differences, so they'll know how to do that as well.

The state of Kentucky is a leader in terms of custody arrangements. Are you finding there's a movement towards recognizing the need for dads to be involved after divorce? A little bit of progress is being made with two states recently making equal shared parenting the default position: Kentucky and Arkansas. Unless custody is defined as equal physical custody as well as legal custody, it's not equal. "Joint legal custody" means only that the dad (usually) can have input into the medical problems or school decisions, while joint physical custody means approximately an equal amount of time with both father and mother.

In doing the research for *The Boy Crisis*, I discovered that children do better in more than 50 developmental areas when they have equal shared-parenting after divorce. These and similar findings are slowly being recognized in courts, despite enormous resistance from the American Bar Association and many feminist groups who have extended "my body, my choice," to "my child, my choice," not wanting women to be deprived of the choice of how to parent after divorce.

Ideally, though, if you want your children to have a life that is close to what it would be in an intact family, there is a need for what I call the "Four Must Do's" of divorce. First, is equal shared parenting--the children having about an equal amount of time with mom and dad. Second, is proximity with the parents living within about 20 minutes drive time from each other so that children don't have to forfeit activities like soccer practice or the birthday of their best friend.

Third, is not bad-mouthing. Fourth, is the parents' communication needs to be consistent and frequent, not just when an emergency erupts. Each of these facilitates father involvement as well as maximizing the benefits to the children of having both parents work in harmony with them even if they are divorced. In *The Boy Crisis,* I explain how to communicate about these differences so your partner can best hear them.

In my book, How to Survive Your Parents' Divorce: Kids Advice to Kids, *the kids said the most difficult part was being in the middle of fighting.* Absolutely, one of the biggest forms of child abuse is bad-mouthing the other parent. Let's say the boy looks in the mirror and sees his father's body language and nose and eyes, but has been told his father is a narcissist, irresponsible, and a liar. He can't talk to his dad about it because his dad will get furious at mom, which will only increase the instability that he's already experiencing. He can't talk to his mom about it for the same reason, so he feels he must keep it to himself even as he's fearing that he might actually have a biological propensity to be a narcissist, irresponsible, or a liar.

In Women Can't Hear What Men Don't Say, *you write that dads don't speak up about these issues.* Correct. Missing the value of dads is not moms' fault, because moms can't hear what dads don't say. And it's not dads' fault, because dads can't hear what no one says as neither parenting magazines nor books explain the value of dad-style parenting. For example, why roughhousing the way dads tend to do it usually leads to children having more empathy. It sounds counter-intuitive, and have you ever heard a dad say that to a mom? Is the science there to prove that's true? Yes, but no dad knows that it is true.

Roughhousing leads to a greater ability of the children to make distinctions between what is aggressive and what is assertive. It also teaches the children to postpone gratification by not pushing their sister or brother aside to win the wrestling match, if they want to continue the roughhousing. Dads tend to be less tolerant of excuses; instead of repeating themselves like moms tend to do, they just say, "OK, no more roughhousing tonight." *That was one of my father's main ways of relating to my brother and me. We would each pull on a leg to try to topple him.*

Postponed gratification is the single biggest predictor of success or failure, especially succeeding in social skills like knowing that difference between aggressiveness and assertiveness. This is what leads to children having friends and the discipline to be a basketball player or an actor or a musician or gymnast or whatever. That discipline is crucial.

Most moms are very good at identifying a child's gifts, good at encouraging the kids, good at telling the children to include their sister or brother, but when the child doesn't follow through, moms just tend to repeat their admonition, until they finally get fed up and "lose it." Then they feel guilty, and compensate by bending over backward to do something nice, so the children don't really feel the consequence.

Roughhousing also leads to girls understanding that males can have physical contact without it translating into sex. We know the value of roughhousing even from studies of rats by J. Panksepp in *Affective Neuroscience*. He found that rats have very sophisticated systems of roughhousing with their offspring. The young rats that engage in roughhousing live longer, are healthier, and seem to be emotionally connected in ways that let them succeed in the rat community.

Dad-deprivation is not just a problem among children of divorce. Overall, in the US, 42% of births occur to mothers who are not married; the percentage jumps to 53% among births to women under 30. Even if the unmarried mom is living with a man, those arrangements last only an average of three years. After the parents separate, the children typically see their dad much less, if at all.

Most judges, both male and female, agree with equal shared parenting. However, if the mother uses the word fear--like "I'm afraid of his anger"--the judge worries that if she or he ignores that and is wrong just one time, that could be the end of his or her career. The result is that I feel the basic rule of thumb in family law is, "The mom has the right to the children; the dad has to fight for the children." I've done expert witness work for more than 100 fathers who wanted equal involvement with their children but were prevented from having it. The average father who contacts me has already spent about $75,000 before he calls, which means he may spend between $150,000 to $200,00 just to provide his children with an equally involved dad. Obviously, few men can afford that.

The research shows that children benefit more from a dad's time than a dad's dime. Richard Warshak (author of *Divorce Poison*) interviewed 110 psychologists and researchers. Although it is hard to get three academics to agree on anything, all 110 of them agreed that their research showed that the closer to 50:50 that the children have with the parents, the better the children did, while the children who had less than 30% of time with their dad had significant problems. This was published in a journal of the American Psychological Association, as the *Consensus Report*. [*See Andrew Smiler* and Daniel Ellenberg* for psychologists' views of the effect of father absence.*]

As seen in our TEDx talks, my view of the boy crisis is more often and better received than talks on both crises by pro-feminists Michael Kimmel and Michael Flood, as evidenced in the likes and dislikes of viewers (30 times as many views in about the same time period at 1.5 million). I have a ratio of 27 likes to 1 dislike, while Kimmel's has more dislikes than likes.

We've limited boys to a narrow range of expression. Do you see any changes? There's more flexibility now for boys than there was when I was growing up, but the closer the boy gets to puberty, the more he comes to realize that straight girls don't fall in love with crying boys; and straight boys don't respect crying boys--so if you're straight, hold it in.

This is not so true for boys raised by single moms. Most single moms are very empathetic and protective, leading to many of their sons being very sensitive. However, this often leads to a son who is more self-centered than empathetic. Empathy does not beget empathy. We definitely see more sensitivity among the boys raised by mothers, more permission to be feminine, discouragement from playing with guns, and so on. However, these boys are usually not more well-rounded in terms of taking risks and being able to tough it out.

A lack of boundary enforcement tends to lead them to be more manipulative and coercive. Without postponed gratification, they are more likely to be "failures to launch," which triggers depression, withdrawal, video game addiction, and addiction to alcohol, drugs, and porn. Dad-deprived boys are much more likely to drop out of high school, and more than 20% of boys who are high school dropouts are unemployed in their 20s.

Becoming a functional, happy man usually involves both parents helping the boy experiment with discovering his "unique self" (as Marc Gafni puts it); and enforcing boundaries so that the boy develops the discipline to not just dream, but to achieve his dreams.

You also say in The Boy Crisis *that boys raised by single mothers are more likely to have ADHD.* The extensive research of Mogens Christoffersen found that when young children live with only their moms, 30% have ADHD; when they live only with their dads, 15% have ADHD.[162] This is despite the fact that infants with developmental problems are about 15 times more likely to be parented primarily by the dad than the mom.

Since US kids grow up watching more TV than they spend time in school, what are the current media messages to boys about what it means to be a man today? Almost all the media either shows men as heroes for rescuing women; or women as their own heroes who don't need men; or men as jerks; men as incompetent dads. On the Lifetime channel, a man who is good-looking and seemingly trustworthy, ends up seducing a woman who falls victim to the awful human being he turns out to be. In video games, boys learn to identify with males who can defeat any enemy or overcome any obstacle.

But what's more important than the media is real-life for young men today. Here's an example: I was being filmed for a documentary about the boy crisis. As we took a break, I saw a young boy walk by and, as he looked with curiosity at the cameras, I asked him if we could interview him about his experience in school. He cautiously agreed. He was in the ninth grade at an all-boys school in San Francisco.

I asked him what he learns about boys versus girls in school. He said, "We learn that the girls have been oppressed by boys who have male privilege, especially white-male privilege." I asked, "Who teaches you this?" His answer was "Everybody." I asked, "Do you believe this yourself?" "No, I see it in a more complex way. I think there are certain ways I have privilege and certain ways I don't," but he wouldn't talk about this. I asked, "Have you ever heard that the 'future is female?'" He responded, "Of course, all the time; and I hear about white male privilege all the time, including from my friends at the public school."

If your son is learning in ninth grade that the future is female, do you feel that inspires him about his future? Whether in the media or in real life, when the women's movement was starting, we certainly heard that women were victims, but we also heard Helen Reddy sing, "I am woman: I am strong." Today we more often hear, "I am woman: I've been wronged." I am happy the media has allowed us to hear women's version of #MeToo. I am sad, though, that #MeTo is a monologue that teaches us that women are victims and men are insensitive sexual harassers, date rapists, rapists, and oppressors.

In the process of starting some 300 men's groups and listening to hundreds of couples in my couples' communication courses, I have learned that men have their own parallel set of feelings. No one has given the sex that becomes successful by repressing feelings, the permission to finally express feelings.

We say that it is part of toxic masculinity that men keep their feelings bottled up until either a volcano erupts, or they act out (*e.g.,* becoming an alcoholic), but then when men do share their experience of being denied custody, being falsely accused, or being treated like a wallet, they are accused of being a misogynist. Millions of men feel damned if they do express feelings, and damned if they don't.

Whenever I've gone to colleges where I've been asked to intervene on a date rape or sexual harassment accusation, I insist on speaking to both the male and female separately and then bringing them together to facilitate their ability to hear each other. I haven't had a single case where the guy and the woman haven't ended up saying, "I never realized she/he saw it that way, but yes, I did ignore her 'no;'" or "Yes, I did give him flirtatious, inviting eye contact shortly after I said 'no.' I did it because I didn't want him to feel bad after I rejected him, but now I can see how he must have experienced it as a mixed message."

You gave the example of Denmark doing a good job of teaching kids to communicate from preschool on up. I'm thinking of New York a program called "Oh boy babies" with a book about them. The older boys got to take care of the babies and they loved it. Yes, I spent some time in Denmark where they're teaching communication skills in very early years. *In the Danish TV series about a teacher named* Rita *(2012-2020) her teen son joking said with his brother, "You don't think I'm man enough to go camping,"* so even there, masculinity can be *uncertain.* Nothing can better prepare a boy than early education, not only to develop emotional intelligence and caring skills but to get the message that society needs him to have those skills--in marriage or as a dad. When a man knows he's needed and sees that you appreciate his contribution, he's much more likely to become constructive, stop drinking, and come back into the family.

A list of foolish TV fathers includes Archie Bunker, Homer Simpson, Al Bundy, and Peter Griffin. An article also listed good dads: Eric Taylor, Danny Tanner, Joel Graham, and Jay Pratchett. I haven't seen any of those shows; do you think they are, in fact, positive models? I haven't seen any of those shows either. It is interesting that when we hear the names Archie Bunker, Al Bundy, and Homer Simpson, we know immediately who they are, but when we hear the last four shows, we're not familiar with even one of them!

Around the world, more women are graduating from university, except in sub-Saharan Africa, and going on to graduate school which is a pipeline for professional leadership positions. Academics used to say that school favors boys, that teachers interact with and encourage boys more, but there was a shift. As we saw with my dialogue with the ninth-grade boy, teachers and students are focused on "the future is female" and "male privilege" rather than "the future is the students who work hard and intelligently."

When I grew up, most boys were filled with fun and games and fooling around and not so good at school until sometime between 10th and 11th grade. That's when a boy would experience the perfect storm of congruent messages: girls aren't going to be interested in you unless you're successful; mom and dad will be disappointed in you unless you go to college--and the better the college, the prouder they'll be; and your peers are beginning to respect boys who are successful rather than jokers. The conclusion: you'd better damn well get your act together!

Nowadays, that is not the case anymore since the culture has shifted: it's all about "you go, girl." Boys feel that if they succeed it will be dismissed as "male privilege" or if they fail, it's because they are losers. They're still expected to be the ones to risk sexual rejection by initiating (girls have the option, but not the expectation), but if they initiate too quickly, they're a sexual harasser; if they initiate too slowly, they're a wimp. And of course, different girls will feel differently about what is too quick and what is too slow; and many girls will feel differently after a few drinks.

The biggest shift, though, has been the shift from the intact family to the Era of Dad-Deprivation. Dad-style usually means filled with unconditional love, but with conditional approval; building bonds by rough-housing, teasing, encouraging a testing of his limits, and the entering into unchartered territory--from exploring in nature to exploring intellectually, and holding his son accountable via the enforcing of the boundaries he sets.

The boys who are dad-deprived have a much harder time discovering a sense of purpose at school, with most schools cutting back on vocational education. Even as the Centers for Disease Control finds that after a minimum amount of studying, every 5-10 minute interval of being physical (*e.g.,* recess) allows both boys and girls to do better academically, recess is being cut back. This especially applies to boys, who have an enormous need to be physically active before they can concentrate.

And even when recess is intact, what used to be considered playful--boys teasing each other--is now at risk of being considered bullying. These and many other factors lead to boys now being only half as likely to become a graduate of a four-year college. [*Males are 40% of the undergrads and have a 59% graduation rate while women have a 65% rate in the US.*[163]] The men who don't graduate are rarely of much interest to college-educated women.

It's disturbing to me that the rates of teen anxiety and depression have gone way up, especially for girls. Social media seems to have a more powerful impact on girls than it does on boys, but girls are also much more likely to be able to share their feelings and fears with other girlfriends. They are more likely to report their depression and attempt suicide, whereas boys are more likely to repress their depression and actually commit suicide. I analyze this difference in-depth and create solutions for it in *The Boy Crisis.*

Boys suffer more from breaking up from a long-term relationship than girls do. One reason is that when a boy feels rejected, he doesn't feel comfortable talking it out in-depth with other boys, and when he does, the other boys give him minimal empathy before they start challenging him ("How are you responsible?") or changing the topic ("Why don't we watch the playoffs?"). This is one reason the boy often becomes more emotionally dependent on girls and feels so isolated and lonely after a breakup. Girls have a much better instinct about what people need when they're in grief mode--they need first to be heard, agreed with, and given time to repeat and rehash what's bothering them.

Boys are much less likely to have such an emotional support system; they are more likely to commit suicide when they feel that nobody loves them, that nobody needs them, and there's no hope of that changing. That's only three of the 63 red flags of depression or suicide that I offer as an inventory in *The Boy Crisis*. I feel this inventory should be given to every boy and girl in school--especially in schools with large numbers of middle and upper-middle-class students, whose parents often set expectations that make those boys who are a "failure to launch" feel depressed and ashamed of themselves. The inventory can alert the school's psychologist as to who needs her or his help.

What do you think is going on with kids who are questioning their gender, trans, non-binary--rethinking gender? It's wonderful that we have a world in which there's permission to rethink gender. I also think that every virtue taken to its extreme can become a vice, and if that virtue becomes a fad it can become very dangerous if changes that can't be reversed are made in order to be part of the fad.

What trends are you seeing currently in the men's movement? We don't hear about a men's movement because almost all animals, including humans, have evolved with the female selecting the Alpha male for sex. Males become Alpha by being the most capable at protecting women. If a male complains, he's not an Alpha male. In brief, women fall in love with Alpha males, not whining males. Lois Lane ignored Clark Kent until she discovered he was Superman! A men's movement feels like men complaining. When males complain, it feels to most women like fingernails scraping on a chalkboard and it feels pitiful to most men.

The ManKind Project is an outgrowth of the mythopoetic portion of the men's movement and has been very helpful to hundreds of thousands of men. But it keeps its therapeutic benefits to itself. There's no complaining that the culture can hear so it's accepted, and gets virtually no coverage in the media, and therefore in the public consciousness.

Then there are the men's rights activists, or MRAs, featured in a documentary called *The Red Pill,* by Cassie Jaye, a feminist filmmaker. She started out expecting to condemn the MRAs but ended up having her listening skills trump her ideology. She did a superb job of documenting the concrete men's issues both the MRAs and I, in *The Myth of Male Power,* articulate in a way any audience can hear.

The part of the men's movement most often singled out by the media, and condemned as misogynists, are MGTOWs (Men Going Their Own Way) and InCels (Involuntary Celibates). These men for the most part wish to be involved with women (the InCels' celibacy is involuntary), but feel like if they put their penis in a woman's body, they put their life in her hands. For example, if she becomes pregnant, she can abort, or sue for support. It is not women *per se* that he fears, but the system--especially the courts that he fears are highly likely to deprive him of any child he and she may create.

The most progress is being made by the groups advocating for equal shared parenting after divorce since 85% of Americans feel children do better when they have both parents. People like me say there are some 20 to 40 issues faced by boys and men that need to be dealt with for the benefit of both sexes--the issues I articulate in *The Myth of Male Power* and in *The Boy Crisis*. We need to understand why our sons are falling so far behind our daughters in more than 50 different developmental areas. It's not good for our daughters because they want functional boys who'll become functional fathers and functional men. Women don't fall in love with losers.

I consider myself a gender liberation advocate, but at this point in history, I feel that gender liberation has succeeded a lot more with women than with men. We don't need a women's movement demonizing men, nor a men's movement demonizing women. We need a gender liberation movement freeing both sexes from the rigid roles of the past toward more flexible roles for our future.

Do you have another book in the offing? I'm updating *The Myth of Male Power* and will most likely call it *The Paradox of Male Power.* I've been teaching couples' communication courses around the country for the past 30 years. The course is called *Role Mate to Soul Mate: The Art and Discipline of Love.* It teaches couples how to handle personal criticism both without becoming defensive--even feeling defensive inside of themselves. I've put that course on Zoom as well, which I plan to distribute to poor communities so that parents will not have to pay for a therapist to learn how to handle personal criticism without becoming defensive. This will allow them to model non-defensive communication to their children.[164]

Mark Sherman, Ph.D.
Advocate for Boys and Young Men

Since you're a songwriter as well as a professor, let's start with you singing a song, [heard on the YouTube video of our interview.] I wrote a lot of songs in the 1970s and many were humorous. I was a college teacher for 25 years so this song is about not liking giving grades, although I loved teaching. Some students who got a poor grade would try to explain and bargain with you, so I joked about this in the song, with lines like "Please professor give me a B.'…I really love psychology, I want to make it my profession. I want to save the world at only a hundred bucks a session." A wonderful young director named Allyson Ferrara made a YouTube video with the song. Google search "Please Professor official music video."

How many times did you get those requests to raise a grade? It wasn't super-frequent because I was a pretty reasonable and fair grader. It bothered me, though, because young people often had real problems in their lives and I knew they were struggling, and yet their grades had to be based on objective data. Humor has always helped me to get through everything.

Where and when were you born? December 1942 in Brooklyn, New York. *Sagittarians ask deep questions, are adventurous, and free thinkers. Does any of that apply to you?* Not physically. I've never been particularly courageous when it comes to things like rock climbing, but I was adventurous in terms of being on the wild side for a little while, since, after all, I'm a child of the '60s and '70s. As far as free-thinking, absolutely. I'm a strong believer not only in people's thinking outside the box; I'm very much a believer in openness to all kinds of ideas.

Why did you decide to study psychology? I really liked science and math in school and the Russians had launched their Sputnik satellite in 1957, so there was a lot of pressure on boys to do science. When I went to college at the University of Pennsylvania, I became a pre-med not so much because I wanted to be a doctor, but because my dad was a doctor. He never directly said to me I want you to go to medical school, but it was very obvious that he did.

I was a math major and I loved applied math, but this was pure math and I met my match by my junior year and decided I can't do this. Fortunately, Penn had a major called natural sciences. The only course I was missing for this major, as a senior, was psychology. I had started college before I even turned 17, so I was still pretty young. As a senior, I took the general psych course in a big lecture room with a great teacher named Henry Gleitman. I thought, "Wow, I really like this stuff." I was doing well in it pretty easily, so I felt maybe I should go into this. Overall, I did very well in my senior year, with my grades way up from the previous two years when I had been at the bottom of my grades U-curve (no F's, but a D and at least one C). So there's a message to students who may struggle, to stay with it, especially for guys, who don't mature as fast on the average as women.

I wanted to go to graduate school and applied to Clark University where I got in with a stipend, so I thought, I'll apply to some top places, including Harvard. To my amazement, in the summer I got a postcard from Harvard saying, "Are you coming?" although I hadn't gotten the original acceptance letter. I had a job that summer working in a psychology lab where I asked a graduate student for his advice. He said, "Are you kidding? B.F. Skinner's at Harvard!" So I went there partly because my brother was already an undergraduate there.

Why did they select you if you had such an uneven GPA? I did very well in my senior year and I probably got really good recommendations. Also, I had high scores on the Graduate Record Exam. So there I was, 20 years old, with only seven other students in the experimental psych program at Harvard. I realized I met my match, but challenges are great for us; we do ourselves a disservice if we don't take them on.

What experimental work did you do? By the third year of grad school, I had finished most of my coursework, had taken my comprehensive exams, and became interested in psycholinguistics or psychology of language. That's what I did my thesis on--how we comprehend sentences. I taught a course when I was a professor called Psychology of Language.

How did that lead to your interest in gender? As a heterosexual guy, I was curious about women's lives, and about the way they talked. (*You had one brother and no sister.*) But I believe a lot of what we do is based on chance, to be honest with you--sometimes even big decisions. I was at SUNY New Paltz in 1976 talking to a friend in the Psych Department, where I taught psychology of language, experimental psych, statistics, general psych, and a course called behavior modification. (I had taken a course with B.F. Skinner my first year in grad school.)

We were talking about someone who had given a talk to our department, agreeing that his research was kind of silly. My colleague said, "Suppose we proposed the thesis that what happens after you have sex is more important than the orgasm itself?" We both kind of laughed because that seemed ridiculous. But then we thought, "Wait a minute, has anyone really studied what happens after people have sex?" The word "afterplay" was barely used back then, but we figured that might be a good title, although we had no idea we'd be doing a full book on it. In our pilot study, we discovered that though men weren't particularly aware that what happened afterward was important (some of them went to sleep, and although that's kind of a stereotype, it turned out to be common). Women felt how they were treated in bed afterward was very important, so we wrote a book proposal.

My colleague, who was more adventurous than I was, got on the phone with the agent for Shere Hite, the author of the best-selling *The Hite Report,* and by early 1978 we sent in a book proposal. The agent particularly liked the title, and she liked the proposal, too, and soon got us a publisher, Stein and Day. We had a rush deadline, but we did the research with anonymous questionnaires and interviews. *Afterplay: A Key to Intimacy* came out a year later in 1979.

Who were your subjects? Ordinarily, they're college students. We sent anonymous questionnaires to friends of ours in different parts of the country to give them to people to mail back. It wasn't just college students; we had a decent age range. Our sample was largely heterosexual, at a time when people weren't coming out as readily. It sold pretty well; the paperback came out two years later, and there were lots of articles about the book in magazines over many years.

What did the book say besides the obvious that women want to cuddle and pillow talk? It wasn't so obvious then, at least for men. I hate to say it, but men were kind of clueless. I don't want to put my gender down, because I'm very pro-male. But I think that men weren't aware, so getting up and leaving right afterward was something they might do but women didn't. Also, women didn't want to be interrogated about orgasms. *Shere Hite found that a lot of women faked it and 70% of women need direct clitoral stimulation and don't have an orgasm from vaginal penetration.* Absolutely, but we found that women didn't like it when a man said, "How was it for you?"

The period directly after intercourse can be a very tender period, like a bubble. If you say the wrong thing, you burst the bubble. We found some men were afraid of intimacy, especially if it's a new relationship. The quality of afterplay correlated highly with how good the relationship was. We believed that improving afterplay could improve the relationship. Certainly, there was nothing to lose by improving what you did after sex.

What did you find in terms of gender differences? For many women what happened afterward was just as important as an orgasm and not all women had them. I almost felt like we were gender anthropologists in this different world, a good experience. Women particularly didn't like when the guy jumped up out of bed and didn't like a comparison with other partners, even if favorable.

You also did research on same-sex conversations, which predated Deborah Tannen's work by about six years. It took me a couple of decades to begin to get over that. After *Afterplay*, I had lunch with a young woman graduate student in our department. During our conversation, I realized I had no idea what women's conversations are like because when I was growing up I hung out only with boys. So I thought, hey, there's a research project: What are same-gender conversations like?

I got together with a colleague in the Communications Department, Adelaide Haas, who had done research on boys talking to boys and girls talking to girls, so she was an ideal person to work with. We designed research questionnaires and interviews. We learned a lot and realized that male and female uses of language (content and function) could cause problems for couples.

In the early 1980s, I wrote to *Psychology Today*, and an editor said they were very interested in this, and could I write something quickly? Our article, published in June 1984, was called "Man to Man, Woman to Woman" and it got quite a bit of attention, including in *TIME Magazine*, which was very exciting. One of the main findings was that men were into problem-solving. If a man had a problem and mentioned it to another man, the other guy said, "Here's what you do," sometimes even if the man didn't ask. Women were more likely to empathize. I started listening to women's public conversations in restaurants, for example, and reading women's magazines. And I concluded that when a woman hears "Here's what you do" from a man, she might feel that he doesn't think she's capable.

I realized that when my wife came home from work and talked about how her boss was treating her, ordinarily I'd say, "Why don't you do this or that?" I learned to ask, "What specifically is she's doing that's bothering you?" and "I guess that makes you feel such-and-such." This made a noticeable difference.

We couldn't find a publisher, and then years later I saw Deborah Tannen's book *You Just Don't Understand*. I had actually used that phrase in a book proposal to agents. Her book became a huge best-seller. Tannen never cited us, although we had published in regular academic journals and *Psychology Today*. *I know what you mean because my book* 50-50 Marriage *was one of the first books about egalitarian marriages but I'd see books years later claiming to be the first book about equal marriage.* Money has never been my goal in life; we do fine, but recognition, even fame, would be nice.

Tannen said when girls talk to each other, they tell secrets and when boys talk to each other they're establishing dominance hierarchies and instruction. Did you find that too? We didn't much talk about dominance hierarchies or secrets, but it was a question of advice vs. empathy, which is similar to what you're saying. *To update, what have you seen in your five grandsons when you hear them talking?* Unfortunately, they don't live near us, but I bet you'd still find that boys until the middle teenage years are mostly hanging out with other boys. I had to sort of learn how to talk to girls, like a whole new experience for me.

When I grew up, boys had cooties, and we were pretty separate in our play. It was unusual to have a best friend of the opposite sex but that's really changed. I'm still not sure about boys and girls mixing so much. But generational changes have been rapid, such as gay people having much more freedom to come out of the closet. I agree about comfort with diversity among young people. That's a real positive.

You said you respected B.F. Skinner but he's associated with putting his baby in a Skinner box, and really strict behavior modification techniques. That's not exactly correct. It wasn't a Skinner box, but a crib size chamber. In the last six months, I spoke with one of his daughters, who's now in her 80s (Skinner died at 86 in 1990). He believed that in a chamber you could keep the temperature adjusted so the baby could just be in a diaper, and thus be comfortable. But that was it. I believe both his daughters have turned out fine, so I think he was misjudged.

In a small seminar with Skinner, I was in a bit over my head because I was new to psychology and just 20 years old. He was a little odd, as geniuses often are, but it became evident to me that he was really something--even at Harvard, he stood out. He stressed the importance of positive reinforcement, which is so vital, and trying to avoid using punishment if you can. He recommended "time-outs," which are now routinely used. I used his ideas with our own children. For example, we would ignore tantrums and were very quick to reinforce good stuff and it worked well. In child-rearing, teaching self-control works well too, so he made a major contribution.

When I started using behavioral methods to study, I did way better. I told students that when you prepare for exams, the most important thing you can do is "recitation" where a friend quizzes you, or you quiz yourself, on possible questions. When I had my comprehensive exams, I gave myself sample questions and would spend a half an hour writing the answer and I did well. When you actively do something, it sticks with you. *Right, as a student at UC Berkeley, I didn't have to think about many essay tests because I'd already outlined answers and quizzed myself with index cards.*

What got you involved in the men's movement? Doing an academic study of the linguistics of gender is much different than activism. I wouldn't necessarily say I'm in the "men's movement," since that term doesn't sound so positive to many people. It seems to have a lot of mixed messages, and some see it as at least somewhat misogynist. I'm all for men, and especially for boys and young men, who are my major concern, but I have always been very supportive of women. In fact, years ago I would probably have been labeled a feminist. I was highly supportive of women's studies at my college, which started one of the first programs in the early '70s. My department was all men when I got there in 1970, and I was one of the first guys who said we've got to hire a woman. Eventually, women made up half the department!

I have three sons, and in the early 1990s, when the youngest was about 11, I began to notice that girls were definitely doing better than boys in school; and yet books were coming out, like David and Myra Sacker's *Failing at Fairness: How America's Schools Cheat Girls.* He gave a keynote speech at a conference on gender equity around 1994 that I attended. I had data right in front of me about how boys were not doing so great, but all he talked about was how girls weren't being called on in class often enough and weren't being noticed. I commented, "I understand, but the data indicate that it's the boys who are really struggling." He derided me in front of an audience of about a hundred people, but nobody said anything in support of me.

As I looked back, it reminded me of a famous study by Solomon Asch, where the subjects listened to false perceptions from others going against what they saw with their own eyes. And in spite of the fact that boys are struggling today as much as ever, the culture is *still* focused on how we can make things better for girls and women.

Around the world, except in sub-Saharan Africa, more women graduate from university and go to grad school. In fact, women outnumber men in the US colleges by a considerable margin, a trend that started in the early 1980s. I think all the attention still went to women, such as "Take Our Daughters to Work Day," which began in 1993.[165] I wondered aloud, What about the boys? Several years later it did become "Take Our Daughters and Sons to Work."

Young women are still a big minority in STEM fields. Yes, but interestingly, in Sweden, which is about the most gender open place you can find, the disparity is even greater. Overall, women seem to be more interested in relationship and people topics. *Yes, they go into biology and life sciences.* Things are definitely changing, but education is a depressing place for boys, where they struggle a lot, particularly boys of color. One of the problems for boys is reading and writing, language skills, which are crucially important. *Observers said for decades that primary school favored girls because they had better fine muscle motor coordination and they could sit still longer, while boys were more often kinesthetic learners who need action.*

Kelley King wrote *Writing the Playbook: A Practitioner's Guide to Creating a Boy-Friendly School,* and Michael Gurian wrote *Saving Our Sons: A New Path for Raising Healthy* and *Resilient Boys,* and *The Minds of Boys:*

Saving Our Sons From Falling Behind in School and Life (with the late Kathy Stevens). Gurian believes in gender differences in learning, and feels that classrooms and schools are not great environments for boys, which is controversial; but he cares deeply about girls, too--he has two daughters. Recess at many schools has been curtailed to a significant degree although activity is probably even more vital for boys.

I have a big exercise ball for my 10-year-old grandson so he can wiggle around when he's doing homework. What the boys his age like is the Percy Jackson series of novels about Greek gods, all about magical power. Okay, but when kids write stuff that is adventurous and perhaps a little violent, as I did when I was a boy, it can be an alarm bell now because of school shootings.

You're working to get the White House to study the status of boys as they do for girls. Warren Farrell* organized a group of us to lobby for a White House Council on Boys and Men because when Obama became President in 2009, he only created a White House Council for Girls and Women. *He did start a group for young men after he was in office.* He launched My Brother's Keeper in 2014--to address opportunity gaps faced by young men of color. Shortly after his inauguration, President Biden issued an Executive Order establishing a Gender Policy Council, but nothing in this order says a word about boys and men.

What about violence and being incarcerated? And what are other men's issues? I've written quite a bit in *Psychology Today* about violence. Yes, men commit it more often than women, but they're far more often the victims of it and they're most of the prisoners. Also, the suicide rate for young males is way higher than for young women. Addiction and fatal overdoses are higher among boys and men. On almost every problem, you find more boys and men, which needs attention. To have a Gender Policy Council that doesn't even mention these issues is a glaring omission.

Is testosterone the reason men are more violent or are they socially conditioned by violence in the media, including video games? If it's nurture, are there other countries where boys don't have these kinds of problems? I think it's a combination of both nature and nurture and if there are other countries where boys aren't having these problems, I'm not aware of them. Looking at statistics and watching my two pairs of grandsons fighting with each other the way brothers often do, I definitely see it, in spite of parental attempts to curtail it. We took care of one of those pairs of brothers for a couple of nights. I hate to yell at kids, but I found myself yelling, "You guys have got to stop!" *I had a younger brother and we fought.* There you go, so it's not strictly gender.

Studies of primates like our chimp cousins report that young males do more rough and tumble play, and human fathers do more roughhousing. Yes, Warren Farrell* has definitely talked about paternal roughhousing. Girls have changed since when I was a kid, so they're pretty adventurous now but I think boys and young men are still more adventurous, more likely to take real risks. I wasn't a super risk-taker, even as a young guy, but I remember, as an 18-year-old, racing a pick-up truck on the Long Island expressway when it was under construction.

Also, studies show female primates may be just as aggressive but more indirect, like the boy will punch someone and the girl will say, "Teacher, punish him." The word that teen girls use about their interaction is "drama" about relationships. Yes, one of the findings in the work I did years ago on male-female communication, was that the girls would talk more about family than the guys. Also, the girls would talk more about other girls than the boys would talk about other boys.

Regarding men's organizations, which do you look to currently? The groups I associate with are concerned with the well-being of boys and men. Aside from the coalition to establish a White House Council on Boys and Men, another group is the Global Initiative for Boys and Men; Sean Kullman is very involved with that. I'm on an advisory group with The Boys Initiative where the Executive Director is Vermelle Greene. There's also a division in the American Psychological Association I've had involvement with called The Society for the Psychological Study of Men and Masculinities. They publish a journal and are quite pro-feminist--an interesting group. The men's rights groups make some good contributions but sometimes do border on misogyny.

An interesting film, *The Red Pill,* was directed by feminist Cassie Jaye, who started out wanting to do a hit job on the men's rights groups and talked to them. She also spoke with Farrell, who knows all these groups. She found they're making some really important points about child custody, where they definitely want to be involved as fathers.

Another point is that women do commit acts of domestic violence against male partners with great frequency. I know several men who have been victimized by women, and other pro-men groups say we can't ignore this. The groups differ a lot in how they speak about women, sometimes in a way that I'm not comfortable with, although they have some little true nuggets. The left goes to extremes sometimes too. I don't like their term "toxic masculinity," which is too often used as a general term.

You wrote an article called, "The Third Gender," about men in academia. My observation is many of them monologue and take turns talking in meetings where it's about being heard and having publications to make up for not being popular in high school. That was a humorous piece. I remember meeting my middle son's soon-to-be father-in-law, a big guy about three or four inches taller than me, a "real man" so to speak, and I felt like this little kid, and I'm respectable. That's what I was getting at by "the third gender." If you're making fun of yourself, you're not going to alienate other people so I enjoyed that.

Do you agree that a lot of academic men were not the popular people in high school? I think that's probably true unless they had other things going for them. As soon as I started playing guitar as I was finishing up college, girls seemed a lot more interested. Had I been doing that in high school, those years might have been very different for me. I don't think the academic stuff turned girls on when we were in high school. My father used to say to me, because he knew I was not happy about this, "Hang in there Mark, they'll come around," but it took a while. The girls were interested in the big guys, the jocks, tall, good-looking. I was skinny, not super-handsome, and not very tall, so I didn't feel so good about myself. But that changed as we all got into our 20s, and the girls became women who were interested in men's brainpower, sense of humor, etc.

Are you pessimistic or optimistic when you think about the possibility of real gender equality? Things have changed dramatically since I was young, such as women outnumbering men in law school (when I was finishing up my Ph.D. in 1969, more than 90% of law school students were men). Yet, I think women legitimately still feel they haven't arrived yet. On the other hand, boys and young men are not doing as well as girls and young women in schools, at all levels. I'm cautiously optimistic because otherwise, I wouldn't keep doing this work.

Jonathan Haidt and Greg Lukianoff, who wrote *The Coddling of the American Mind*, say we've got to be open-minded. Cassie Jaye, who makes the same point in a wonderful TEDx presentation, says in her film, "The truth is in the middle," but the middle doesn't excite people the way the extremes do. *President Biden seems to be in the middle.* Yes, I think that's true. I like him a lot, but I wish he'd pay some attention to the problems facing boys and men.

Why did Trump get 70 million votes? Why do people love him? I think not-well-educated young white guys, who are not the elite, feel that Democrats have forgotten them. They feel disenfranchised, they feel like nobody cares about them, but Trump made them feel he cared. When Hillary Clinton was running in 2016, Farrell and I talked to people involved with her campaign who were pretty high up, and asked, "Can Hillary say our boys are struggling too, and we have to pay some attention to them"? But she didn't say a word about boys and Biden isn't doing it either.

Anything else you want to add? I would like to see our country, the government, the media, and the academy recognize that males, especially younger males are suffering, and we have to start paying attention to them. As Farrell often points out, "We're all in the same boat." If boys or men are suffering and not doing well, that's going to hurt the people who love them as well, and ultimately it's going to hurt the whole country.

Chapter 5: Differences Between Feminism and Equalism

Fred Hayward
Founder of Men's Rights, Inc.

I was born in the Bronx in 1946. I'm a Cancer moon child. *Do you feel like a homebody who's sensitive?* I love being at home and I love traveling. I've been around the world and my son lives in Italy. I've been to Europe over a dozen times. *Where's the most exotic place you've been?* My last trip was to Antarctica with my son, who wanted to go there as a graduation present. So, highlights of my life are swimming with manatees, dolphins, stingrays, and sharks and now I have walked with penguins.

What about your educational and career path highlights? I majored in math at Brandeis University and, then around junior year, I decided I wanted to become a diplomat. My father worked for the United Nations and I always did a lot of traveling and was very interested in diplomacy. So after I got my degree in math, I went to a small graduate school in international relations called the Fletcher School of Law and Diplomacy. I received a couple of masters there and then had one of the briefest diplomatic careers in American history. I was at the American embassy in Bangkok and it turned out that I was nowhere nearly as diplomatic as I had thought I was. It was the Americans that I had trouble with; I got along great with the Thai people and other foreign diplomats.

After that, I taught public school math. I got more and more interested in men's issues and went to a national conference on Men and Masculinity in 1976, which at the time was the only thing called a men's movement. I talked with supposedly the top people about men's issues and some of my observations and theories. I kept hearing things like, "I never thought of that before." I thought, "You're the top people in this field and you never thought about the draft and low male life-expectancy?"

That was the first time I met Warren Farrell who, at the time, was a feminist icon hero. It seemed like he hadn't thought about these issues either, but he's the kind of person that's so open to things, an amazing person. He told me, "What you have to say is valuable; you should consider speaking out. Figure out what you're good at and enjoy and just do it. That's your career. Have faith it will work out." So, I quit teaching in order to work in the men's rights movement--except there wasn't one--so I had to try to create a movement.

What I didn't know at the time was 400 miles to the south of me, near Baltimore, there was another guy who wanted to create the same kind of movement and had formed Free Men. Richard Haddad, unfortunately, passed away in 2019 so I'm the surviving founder. We found out about each other and became lifelong friends. My Men's Rights, Inc. was more activist, with projects, while Free Men was more of a membership group. Since they were a little different, I then founded a Free Men chapter in Boston, where I was living at the time. I was president of the local chapter of Free Men at the same time that I was directing Men's Rights, Inc., which I incorporated in 1977.

I've always called myself an equalist rather than a masculist because I felt that masculism would only be the flip-side to feminism and, therefore, just as bad. In other words, if I would wrongly start theorizing that women had all the power and I would generate anger by men towards women, the way feminism was generating anger and resentment towards men. I called it Men's Rights, Inc. because the abbreviation for men's rights could be MR, a satire on "Ms."

I saw feminism as a knee-jerk reaction of "whatever men have, it's better than what we have, so that's what we should want." Therefore, if men only have one title, then we demand one title. However, a real equalist movement would say, look, here's an obvious gender issue: women have two titles while men only have one. But instead of the knee-jerk response of giving women one title, let's talk about why there are titles and what is best for people.

Because part of our male role is to initiate relationships, it's actually quite helpful for men in a social context to know whether a woman is married or not. When you meet "Mrs. So-and-so," you know she's not available. But in a professional context, like for a job, it's not only not relevant whether she's married, but it should be equally irrelevant whether she's a woman or not. So, the last thing a real equalist movement would do is create a brand new title to differentiate between men and women. "MR" was a satire on "Ms." and their shortsighted feminist practice of thinking everything that men have is better than everything that women have. *The Swedes have a gender-neutral pronoun* (hen) *instead of him or her.*

The men's rights movement is associated with fathers' rights after divorce and custody issues. Was that the focus of MR Inc.? No, the issue that I was personally dealing with in the late '60s and early '70s was the draft. My female peers were saying "You could do anything you want as a man," when actually, my four options were to leave my country, publicly declare I'm gay, go to jail, or join the army and kill people and maybe get killed. These were very narrow and unpleasant options for me at the same time that they were looking at me and enviously complaining that I could do anything while only women were limited.

What did you do about the draft? I became a diplomat, which gave me a deferment, and I was in Southeast Asia during the Vietnam War, watching my colleagues screwing up. My job was to lie in order to represent my country the way I was supposed to be representing it. Once I ended that career, I lost my deferment and was then expected to risk my life for the very policy that I didn't even want to lie about, let alone kill or die for. So, I started teaching math because math and shop teachers were deferred at the time.

When I decided to form this movement, the father's rights movement had predated me but they weren't looking at the big picture. They didn't see the connection among all of these issues, such as the way the male draft is based on society's view that male life is more expendable. If you're more expendable than women, that implies that your family doesn't need you as much as women, so then your children don't need you and you lose custody. As a teacher, I saw boys dealing with a lot of issues and saw so many problems that were all interconnected.

How has your movement evolved over the decades and what have you achieved? MR Inc. lost its tax-exempt status and doesn't exist anymore, but I introduced really important innovations. One of them was to change the way we should view the male-female dynamic. Feminism mistakenly looks at men and women as basically, opposites--as competitors. So, if women don't have power, men do have power; if women are innocent, men are guilty; if women have disadvantages, men have advantages; and if you help men, you're hurting women because men already have it too good. *The Zero-sum game.*

But, that's a fundamental misunderstanding of the male-female relationship, because we're not competitors--we're interdependent. This changes everything! It means if women have a problem, it creates a corresponding problem for men and if you don't help men with that problem, then women can never get equality. One example of this is the earnings gap between men and women. Contrary to feminist assumptions, men's higher earnings are not an advantage. We're interdependent in relationships, so we both consume at the same level. In fact, women consume at a higher level than men.

So, by me making more money, I get locked into a sex role of providing. If society is saying that it makes financial sense for me, the father, to work because I can earn more money, I miss out on the incredible experience of parenting.

Raising my son was the most rewarding experience of my life. But after a divorce, men have to support two households and have even less time with their children. So higher earnings aren't an advantage for men. As a men's rights advocate, I want women to earn more money because that's in *my* interest. Conversely, women should want men to have joint custody because that is in their interest.

Karen De Crow, who was the president of the National Organization for Women in the '70s, said, "Women can never compete as equals in the job market as long as they have that extra burden of child care, so we need men to need to share it." After she heard me speaking, she said I was "music to her ears." She and I shared frustration that, although men's advocates support equal pay for women, feminist organizations vigorously oppose joint custody. She joked, "Opposing it?!? Hell, we should be jamming it down their throats." Instead of generating anger and resentment towards the other sex, looking at men and women as interdependent would generate empathy and concern and a desire to help. That would be a big improvement.

Another contribution was pointing out that, for every species to survive, they have to have food and protection, and have children and socialize them. Those are equally vital jobs for a species' survival. That is why in traditional sex roles, men dominated in the productive sphere--government and economics--while women dominated in the reproductive sphere. It wasn't a male conspiracy; providing and protecting were simply male jobs. This is how species survive. Other species divide sex roles, too. It's not like there was some evil patriarchal conspiracy where men went around to all the other species and trained male ducks and male antelope how to oppress female ducks and female antelope.

I give feminism credit for getting us to rethink this division of labor. But, just as feminists were looking at the male sphere of production and saying we want equal access to Equal Employment Opportunity, the men's movement is looking at the reproductive sphere and saying we want equal access to power there, which includes joint custody.

It's more than just joint custody. For example, women enjoy a variety of reproductive choices that men don't have. In a lawsuit where Karen DeCrow was a guy's attorney, she was defending him against a paternity suit where the woman tricked him into fathering a child. To the court's satisfaction, witnesses proved that she tricked him, yet she still won over 90% of his pension in child support. The same people, feminists included, who lecture men like him, "If you didn't want to be a parent, you shouldn't have had sex," bristle at the idea of anyone saying those same words to a woman. But, that's what pro-choice is all about. I thought those were two really important innovations that I spoke out about.

For every woman's issue, there's an equivalent men's issue, but feminism insisted on being the only voice, so they defined issues in terms of women. Like, men have access to careers, so men don't have an issue, and men don't get pregnant, so men don't have a reproductive issue. While men don't have a big issue with Equal Employment Opportunity per se, we do have a very big issue with access to the way women exercise power, earn rewards, and attain fulfillment. That's what joint custody is all about.

From a male point of view, this means we need to share being a provider and a protector and initiating relationships with women, while women need to share the power of parenting with men. Although society has taken affirmative action to facilitate the flow of women to the workplace, it takes affirmative opposition to the men who are trying to raise their children by putting obstacles in their way.

You addressed social issues like Ladies Nights at bars and campus violence. We shouldn't underestimate the importance of women shouldering their share of the burdens and risks of initiating relationships. That's why I drew attention to Ladies Nights in Boston because taking initiative in relationships is a very formative role for men. For men to understand the way women perceive harassment and for women to understand why men end up drinking more, listening less, objectifying women, and all the other behaviors that women resent, we need to fully share the role and the risk of initiation. It's the only way men and women can together create more healthy ways of starting relationships.

I guess I had a knack for media and *The Boston Globe* had a big write-up headlined "The Man Who Banned Ladies Nights." *Ladies Night means women get free drinks at bars?* Yes, which means men are not only paying for the drinks of women they are meeting but indirectly paying for the drinks of women they never even get to talk to. I went to the Massachusetts Commission Against Discrimination and said, "Suppose there's an inner-city bar that wanted to attract more affluent white suburbanites and offered White Wednesdays with free drinks for white people, how would you feel about that?" It clicked and they immediately outlawed Ladies Nights.

I started getting contacted by reporters and I redirected the dialogue to talk about the male role of initiating relationships and how damaging it is. Then I started getting on talk shows. They often would take an antagonistic approach and think that I was going to be funny and stupid but at the end, they often said, "This is really interesting! Do you want to come back?" A producer at one radio station offered me my own show on the spot. He said, "This is fascinating, how many hours can you do this?" I said I could keep going because there is always more to talk about.

I also challenged auto insurance, because young men have to pay higher premiums. I pointed out that their statistics don't account for miles driven. I established that men are doing the bulk of driving, so of course, we are in the most accidents. I next focused on life insurance and redirected media interest to a conversation on men's lower life expectancies. Can you imagine the hue and cry if women died younger than men and we didn't even talk about it, let alone do something about it? Anyway, to insurers, since men die earlier, they collect before the average woman collects so it made financial sense for them to charge men higher premiums. But the Supreme Court had just ruled it's illegal to use sex-based actuarial tables for pension plans, even though by the same reasoning, it made financial sense to charge women more in pension plans. After all, women live longer and take more money out of the fund.

I kept getting on more and more talk shows talking about gender issues. *I read that Oprah asked you to leave her show.* Yes, I got kicked off. Again they assumed this guy's going to be an idiot, so we'll make fun of him. They didn't really do their research and assumed I'm a sexist because I criticize feminism. Oprah said something to the effect of, "We all know men don't really have any serious issues, but our next guest wants to talk about them anyway. Please welcome Fred Hayward."

I wasn't in the mood for that, so I said, "Blacks are eight times as likely to be incarcerated as the rest of the population. Why do you think that is?" Then her assumption was that I was attacking blacks, and I'm not just a sexist but also a racist. She gave the typical explanation: that blacks have more serious social and economic problems, there's legal discrimination, etc. I said, "Well, men are 24 times as likely to be incarcerated as the rest of the population! So by your logic, doesn't that mean we do have something serious to talk about today?" They cut to a commercial and the producer said to me, "I'm sorry, you have to leave. This is not going the way we planned." It was live television and I left in shock but I was on two more times after that and we got along better.

You did a television show in Sacramento for two years. What were the themes? We talked about domestic violence because the scientific research has been consistent for 45 years that women initiate domestic violence as often as men. We had shows on circumcision, on black men, and men's health issues. I had a stripper on and we talked about sexual power. I had a champion boxer on and we talked about violence in boxing. I interviewed a judge on child support enforcement; we did stuff on the women's and the men's rights movements, parent alienation syndrome, custody mediation, and sexual harassment.

What men's organizations do you look to today? I see a lot more female involvement, like with the father's rights movement because they're second wives or grandmothers who can't see their children. These women are blowing me away, like the Honey Badgers, founded in Canada. And there's the 2016 film *The Red Pill*.[166] A feminist documentary filmmaker, Cassie Jaye, decided to do an exposé of the Men's Rights Movement as a backlash to women's equality and whiners because men are privileged. I was the second person she interviewed and we talked for an entire day. She kept saying, "I can't help feeling there's something wrong with what you're saying, but it's all logical."

She spent a couple of years interviewing men like Warren Farrell and realized that we're not angry losers; we're intelligent people in loving relationships who are totally supportive of equality for women. It's really feminism that's doing a disservice to society by squelching discussion and trying to intimidate people from speaking.

Jaye has the integrity that very few people have--to admit she was wrong, knowing that she was going to lose her funding and her friends if she changed the direction of the film. But she did it anyway. It reminded me of Farrell when he went from feminist to equalist. He knew he would lose a lot of friends and his well-paying speeches. Cassie's film was the most streamed video at the time on YouTube, but Netflix wouldn't show it due to feminist pressure. *Warren calls this the Lace Curtain.* Cassie documents in her movie how feminists are trying to censor and squelch discussion of men's issues, and then it happened with her movie, too.

This makes me think of when you and I were at a National Organization of Men Against Sexism, NOMAS, conference in Hartford and there was a big furor because I said, "Let Fred speak." NOMAS needs local people to organize the annual conference, so when I was living in Boston, I was invited to be on a panel discussion called "Dialogue within the Men's Movement" at the 1981 conference in Boston. But the national powers in the organization like Bob Brennan, Michael Kimmel, and John Stoltenberg* threatened to scuttle the whole conference. *Because of you?* Yes, so I was dis-invited.

Warren was on that panel, a good feminist at the time; he didn't know me, but he put an empty chair on the stage and said that to dis-invite the person that we wanted to dialogue with is ridiculous. When I found out what he had done, I reached out to him and we've been dear friends ever since. In 1987, the people in Hartford organized that year's conference and invited me, too. When the national powers found out, they created a kind of loyalty oath. If you were to speak, you had to be "pro-feminist, male-positive, and gay-affirmative."

I said, "My dictionary says feminism is the advocacy for women of the same political, social, and economic rights enjoyed by men. Find anything in any of my speeches or writings where I'm against that or against gay rights. I certainly shouldn't have to prove I'm male-positive because that's probably what bothers you. I think you're the ones who would have more trouble satisfying your three requirements because of the male positive part, but I won't raise an issue with that." So, they reluctantly allowed me to come and I was warmly received.

I did a couple of workshops and the participants really liked me. Those people at the top were saying, "Oh my God! We were calling him a Nazi before, but he's actually the devil the way he's conning these people into liking him." I was never invited back again, and they deleted "male-positive" from the qualities someone must have to speak at an organization purporting to be the premier enlightened men's group in the nation. It's almost funny if you think about that.

What are the different branches active today? There are some who want to go back to traditional sex roles, like Promise Keepers. There are some people who define themselves as MGTOW, Men Going Their Own Way, who have pretty much sworn off relationships with women. There are Incels, which stands for involuntary celibacy. But the bulk of people just want equalism, fair treatment for men and women.

There's an annual International Conference on Men's Issues. It's heartwarming to think 45 years ago I had this vision and now there are thousands of people who are grateful to me for what I did and are carrying the torch. I have so much respect for them and it's very uplifting for me. The 2019 conference in Chicago was organized by the Honey Badgers women's group, and in 2020 the conference was held in Australia. In 2021, it was going to be in London, organized by a political party, but was held online.

They're equalists. Some of them are more traditional. Personally, I never really liked traditional sex roles but at least they were in balance. Feminism has knocked out the balance that maintains us as a species. They've eliminated negative stereotypes for women while doubling the negative ones for men. So, you always have to show the woman as more intelligent and show her winning in competitions. *There are still so many ads with women as sex objects, so you can't say they've knocked out stereotypes of women.*

No, I said they've eliminated NEGATIVE stereotypes about women. There is nothing inherently bad about being considered a sex object. What is damaging is to be considered only a sex object. And women won the battle to be more than sex objects a long time ago. To be honest, there's a huge upside to being a sexy object of beauty, which is why women spend billions of dollars every year to look sexy.

For men, it is just as damaging to never be considered a sex object, to have your body only be appreciated if it is wrapped in a Porsche. Or maybe for having muscles that can work hard and protect a woman. For men, I believe it's a step forward to show women appreciating our bodies. What has long been unhealthy for both of us is teaching boys and girls that they are unworthy if they fail to meet unrealistic standards.

In general, if someone is being hurt, emotionally or physically, it's men who are the recipients of that. *Or they're shown as bumbling like Homer Simpson.* Right! And if a man and a woman are in a marriage or are parenting, if one of them is more competent, it's going to be the woman. Advertisers know that if they show women the way they portray men, women will complain.

To switch to access to education, around the world more women graduate from university than men do. [167] *Why?* A chart (aei.org) shows undergraduates are 77 men for every 100 women. For every 100 women who earn an associate's degree, there are 63 men. [168] In AP honor courses in foreign languages, 100 are women and 64 are men. In graduate school, there are 73 men for every 100 women. On the other end, men are more likely than women to be homeless, diagnosed with communication disorders and learning disabilities, be suspended from school, abuse drugs and alcohol, die of opioid overdose, and die of homicide, yet violence is presented as only a woman's issue.

Why are women ahead in terms of education and professional training? Because we've been paying attention to it and working on it. Feminists say men already have it too good; we can't waste resources on them. As long as there are any areas where they're below men, the sole focus has to be on women.

I felt when I was starting this movement that we're creating a social time-bomb. Our society can't survive if we don't pay attention to this problem and I think we're seeing this now. I'm very pessimistic about what's going on and I have to tell you I don't love the Democratic Party or the Republicans. If they were really concerned about what happens to children when they're separated from parents at the border, they would support joint custody instead of applauding a system that tears millions of children from their fathers without caring what it does to them. Because one of the Democrats' special interests is feminists, I think things are going to get much worse for boys and for men.

If you were in charge, what would you do to encourage boys to go to college? First, start Commissions on the Status of Men, the way we have them for women, and a White House Council for Boys and Men, the way we have one for women. In school, boys get discriminated against, they get discouraged. One of the big things now is sexual harassment: President Obama put out a letter threatening loss of federal funding unless reforms were implemented to deal with sexual assault on campuses, but the reforms denied men due process. Betsy DeVos, Trump's Secretary of Education, introduced due process for someone who's accused but President Biden plans to undo that. Many boys get kicked out of school but the media doesn't cover what's really happening to boys.

Speaking of boys, let's talk about your son, Jack, who's now an adult. You said that you were tricked into being a dad? My girlfriend was trying to get me to have a child with her but I said, "Not until you deal with your anger problem because you have a terrible temper and I don't want our child to be a weapon. You need counseling." She proofread an article I wrote about that man Karen DeCrow defended--the man who was tricked into fathering a child--and my girlfriend told her friend that she was going to trick me also. Her friend later confessed to me, but it was too late. So, she had the child and told me, "Don't forget I've read all your articles and seen your talk shows. Unless you're in a relationship with me, you can forget you have a child because I know all the things a woman can do and I'll do them."

Everything that I was raising awareness about for the previous 17 years was rolled up into one disaster for me to live through. One of the problems was she chose for him the one name I had objected to because it brought back a very painful childhood memory. I said to the legislature, "I'm Jewish. I lost half my family to the holocaust. Are you telling me that if she named our child Adolf Hitler there would be nothing I could do about it?" So, they actually amended the law, and the judge was all set to change his name but his mom told my son, "If you change your name I'll never be able to rest happily in heaven." My son at the age of five or six had shown more wisdom than the court and came up with his own name, Jack, but his mother prevailed. I still call him Jack, though.

What kind of custody arrangement did you have? Initially, I couldn't see him at all but then I gradually got more and more time. The mediator said that since I had missed out on the first three months of our son's life, it would be too traumatic for him if I suddenly started parenting him. Instead, I should take a full year of "incremental build-ups" before I could be an equal parent. And he denied there was anything "sexist" about forcing me to pay a female caregiver who had also missed out on our son's first three months and didn't love him the way I did.

I finally convinced the court to override the mediator and, by the time he was eight months old, I had more of his waking time than his mom because she was at work. That was the way it was until school and then we ended up with pretty much equal time. *Was that because she agreed to it or did the court mandate it?* She never voluntarily let me have one second of time with him that the court didn't mandate. And even when I had more time with him and more of the expenses while she had the greater income, I still had to pay her child support.

Did she do parental alienation like bad-mouthing you or was she good about not doing that to him? Oh no, she was terrible. I saw her pick him up once, look him right in the eye and say, "Daddy is a very bad man." If there were other kids around, she would sometimes warn them right in front of our son that I was dangerous and they should stay away from me. My son would come to me and say things like, "Mommy said God's on her side," or "Mommy said children don't need fathers," and I'd have to try to answer all that.

After 14 years, my body finally gave out. I got sicker and sicker and realized it's the stress and the only way to survive is to give up custody. It was a two-year process of getting sicker, realizing why, and going through the legal formality of giving up custody.

My girlfriend at the time had three grown children, and I had a really good relationship with them. During that two-year process, they started reproducing, so on the day I lost joint custody, I had four little grandchildren to adore me. I don't know where I stand on religion but it was really like God saying, "You did everything you could for your son, and he's off on a good path now, and here's your reward."

I barely saw my son for about eight years after that. Maybe once a year, I would run into him and we'd always have a good time. He'd always say let's get together but his mom would figure out a way to get him angry with me again and it would never happen. After eight years, he was in college and my girlfriend and I bought a house. He had always maintained a good relationship with her and, being an architect major, told her he wanted to see her house. She warned, "Your dad will probably be there," but he said okay. We had a great time and we invited him back for dinner that same night and we've been close ever since. We talk every day even though he lives in Italy.

During the fourth year of his architecture program at Cal Poly, he went to Florence, Italy to study architecture and realized he loves Italy, he doesn't love architecture, and his real passion is cars. So he got his degree in architecture and then applied to design school in Milan to study car design. He's been in Italy ever since. *Did Jack ever come to grips with what his mom did?* I would have to say no, he doesn't really want to know those details. I think he's afraid that it would damage his relationship with her. He still loves her a lot.

What are you hearing now in terms of young men's issues? More and more men are confronting inequality as a serious issue rather than quietly taking it like a man. They see discrimination against them--violence, divorce, custody, and the way women treat them. *I've heard young men's resentment of affirmative action; they feel like women get favored in access to jobs, etc.* I published some articles using a female pen name because of the Pink Curtain. *Or Lace Curtain.* A couple of times I sent articles to some publications and they would be rejected so then I would send the same article back a little bit later under a woman's name and they would buy it and print it.

One of those articles was on affirmative action. The brunt of the article was that raising children is a legitimate occupation and important work. There is a well-documented pattern of discrimination against men in this occupation. Are you willing to take affirmative action to increase the number of men getting custody? Are you willing to tell judges they have a target of awarding custody to men 50% of the time? If your answer is "No," but you still claim to support affirmative action, then you're a hypocrite.

What I hear from young men globally is they don't want to give their life to making money and they want access to their family life. Yes, that's a big thing that I hear. I see that young fathers are much more hands-on with their kids and they are enjoying it.

You said you're pessimistic about moving towards equality in gender roles? I'm a pessimist because we already undermined so much of our society and I don't know if we can rebuild in time. I'm worried about the Democrats' media and social media, movements in academia that get rid of professors if they dare to be conservative, and plans to pack the court. We've screwed up the voting system and people don't have confidence in it anymore. The news media have become advocates instead of journalists. I fear we're heading towards a one-party state which I wouldn't want for either party. I'm pessimistic about the way people are so easily being manipulated. When half a country demonizes the other half, it never ends well.

What do you think is the legacy of Trump in terms of views of masculinity and femininity? What I most loved about him was that he didn't stand for political correctness. I think he's a bully, insensitive, vindictive, barely articulate, a jerk, and more, but there are some positive things. To me, that was a big one. He was willing to stand up and say, I don't care what I'm supposed to say, this is how I feel.

So it's okay to say I can grab women's genitals if I want to because I'm famous? It's not okay to do it but in a context where you're joking around with people or just trying to impress them, people say things that aren't true. I believe strongly in freedom of humor. And, I think the cancel culture is terrible. I worked with a guy whose 40-year career was ended in one day because of one Tweet: "All lives matter. Every one of them." That sentiment is the basic thrust of every respectable religion, but noisy, intimidating people say it's really a code for white supremacy, even though the last thing a white supremacist would believe is that all lives matter.

The majority of people feel like they can't say what's really on their minds, and that's no way for a democracy to survive. I think the majority of people believe political correctness is BS.

There's Men's Studies in academic programs, Men's Studies journals. What are they focusing on? I think the first men's studies program was at Tufts University around 1979 when I taught a course because I wanted to start this movement and there was a lot of research that had to be done. I knew I couldn't do it myself so I thought I'd teach a course and assign it. I got a lot of good stuff out of it. But, a lot of the men's studies programs are really run by feminists and they don't teach the kind of analysis that an equalist society needs.

I was born at a very early age in Baltimore, Maryland. *What month and sign are you?* I'm not a big believer in astrology, but I'm the prototypical Gemini, born June 1951. Do you believe in it? *I think it's symbolic, although I don't know how a constellation affects a behavior pattern, but I think it's a map for our life lessons.* I understand and appreciate your interest in mysticism and things that we don't even have a clue about, the real truth of our understanding of the universe. We're still a very primitive species just sort of waking up. *Well, 95% of the universe is dark energy and dark matter, which we don't understand. Most of our DNA is called junk DNA. Quantum mechanics is weird and spooky according to the physicists who*

discovered it, as discussed in my trilogy about visionary scientists.

What about your education and career path? My parents worked together; he was a doctor and she was a nurse. Once in a while she had to work and couldn't pick me up, so when kindergarten was over, the best way for me to get home was to ride the bus. I went to a Catholic parochial school for elementary school in downtown Baltimore. I went to Baltimore Polytechnic Institute for high school, sort of a math, science, and engineering school, which at the time was only for boys. It's now very gender-integrated and the girls are doing really well. When I went to college, I thought I wanted to be in journalism but as I ended up majoring in Political Science.

I went to Georgetown Law School for a year until I decided I hated it. I took a year off and went to Arizona and taught seventh- and eighth-grade math, science, and social studies in a little parochial school. When the priest wanted me to teach religion, I said, "Father, I really can't because I'm kind of a fourth-degree agnostic." He said, "That's all right, don't worry about it." I was only 10 years older than the students at the time and that was great fun. I went back to law school to see if I liked it any better and it turned out I liked it worse.

The reason I thought I might want to go back was I worked for the Arizona Civil Liberties Union to investigate the Flagstaff Municipal Court, which had some very questionable constitutional and due-process practices. I investigated them and wrote a report, sort of a spy on the court, which was fun so I thought maybe I do like this law stuff and went back to school at Georgetown. One of the courses I took was environmental law, but it was about how to get around environmental laws and I thought I don't really want to do this. I've been sort of like a tumbleweed across the desert ever since. I don't really have a career in anything to speak of.

You have a social work degree and you've worked as a social worker and in correctional institutions working with men. A year working in a jail, a year in parole and probation, a year at the National Fatherhood Initiative, but I didn't go to social work school until 2005 when I was 54. Most of my paid income has been through either PR, marketing, advertising, or IT. I don't really have a career in the sense of continually or progressively increasing responsibilities.

A very consistent theme is your feeling that men have not gotten a fair shake. What led to your interest in men's roles? An early memory was something that I used to hear as a kid. You're very well aware of the harm it does to little girls if they hear, "Gee, you're really good at math for a girl." What's the message to her? "You're a weirdo, what's wrong with you?" What I remembered hearing as a little boy was, "Wow! You're really good with babies for a boy." I remembered thinking, "What's up with that?"

My first conscious awareness as an adult was when I was on a co-ed softball team in the early 1980s. After our games we'd go out dancing and partying, maybe having some dinner or maybe not too much dinner because that would ruin your appetite for beer. Two weeks in a row, I was talking to female teammates who were telling me about their boyfriends, going on and on with their tales of woe. They ended their stories by saying, "So he's a real jerk, don't you think?" I said, "Maybe he's a jerk, but from his point of view, from what you're telling me, the way it looks to him might be such and such." They both said, "Oh my God! I never thought of that." That's when it occurred to me that the male point of view is not very well understood or well-articulated.

I said to my girlfriend, who was also on the team, that I wanted to do something like start a magazine. She suggested that magazine printing is expensive, as is postage, so why not try a radio show? So I did a weekly radio show from 1983 to 1989 at a student-run station at Towson University. The show had various names, mostly "In a Man's Shoes." It did pretty well and it was a lot of fun so I tried to get some commercial stations to take it on, but the sales staff said, "We can't do this show, nobody will buy ads on it." Their concern was that the advertisers would be afraid it would make women mad.

The current evolution of your radio show is two podcasts called "Men Are Talking" and "Good Will Toward Men," the same title as the book you interviewed me for.[169] I started podcasting--as both a host and a guest--in 2021 because since 1983, the Lace Curtain directly or indirectly has been making it difficult or impossible for me to reach audiences with ideas and information about male gender issues. I'd say podcasting is probably the most robust medium available today. A person with a passion and a message can get into podcasting with less than $200 worth of equipment and a Zoom account.

What are some of the topics you've explored on the podcasts? The gay movement as an ally of the larger men's movement and vice versa, your relationship with yourself, men's needs, the men's movement, and counter-feminism.

On your website, you describe yourself as "the counter-feminist social worker" and say, "The most sexist idea of all is that only one sex is harmed by sexism." Along with being a podcast host, I am also interested in being a podcast guest. I made up this whole idea of a counter-feminist to distinguish from anti-feminism, which says it's all a bunch of malarkey, women have it easy. A counter-feminist listens to women talking about feminist perspectives and problems women have and then says, yes, and let's talk about the rest of the story, the ways that what's going on with men is connected to what's going on with women. Let's talk about solving these problems because we're not going to solve the problems if we don't have a way of approaching balance. A counter feminist says "Yes, AND. . . ."

Are the main issues that men die earlier, commit suicide more, don't get proper health care, and boys don't graduate from university as much as girls? The most influential book to me as I was undertaking this radio show was Psychology Professor Herb Goldberg's *The Hazards of Being Male*. The second most influential person to me was Fred Hayward.* He's brilliant and I learned a lot from him.

The goal the three of us have in common is to make sure that boys and men have as many options for happiness and fulfillment, a fully human life, as women and girls do. In this day and age, we've done a lot of work to make sure that women and girls have full options but I see some situations in which men and boys do not yet have that benefit. A boy touches another boy and he's got to say, "no homo!" Boys think about what they want to study in college…well, petroleum engineering looks pretty lucrative, right? And then of course there's the divorce issues and the whole cultural problem that in some ways, women are valued more than men.

Women's feelings are more likely to get empathetic responses than men's. Tom Golden is the one who first put this awareness in my head. Imagine a woman sitting alone in a restaurant crying...should I go over and see if she's okay? Imagine a man sitting alone in a restaurant crying, it's not the same feeling. We are still a pretty primitive species and it hasn't been that long since, for our survival, we found that women were maybe a little better than men at some things and men were maybe a little bit better than women at other things, so we specialized to give us the best chance of not being eaten alive and for our babies to survive. *We were hunters and gatherers for most of human history.* Yes, protectors and nurturers. We had to specialize when we were primitive when the world could easily put us into extinction but we still cling to these vestiges.

Suppose a little boy back on the Serengeti grasslands was sitting around the campfire and it came his time to go out and take a spear out on the perimeter to keep the lions away, but he cried and said, "I want to stay here at the campfire with my little brother and sister and my mom and I don't want to go out there," what happened to him? What happened to him was a really strong dose of what still happens to the boys today who express any interest in being around the campfire, relationships, belonging, safety, comfort, expressiveness, warmth, affection, and those feelings that we all need.

Because of the primitive necessities, they were out there--maybe 12 of them--covering a three-acre campsite; they're alone, all spread out. Bravery is what became valued in men, especially the men who really enjoyed the challenge, so we're still pretty primitive. Just as women have said over the past 50 to 70 years that we don't want to be stuck around the campfire, there are a lot of men saying we would like to get some access to that campfire. Men haven't been able to get back in as much as women have been able to get out.

As Karl Marx said, agriculture, settling down, and having private property are what caused the sex roles to really divert. Yes, I've heard that agriculture was a huge paradigm shift for us, but what did that change? The man was still the one who had the muscles so, in the interest of efficiency, he's going to be the one out there pulling the plow. *In Africa, it's women who carry the burdens and do the heavy work.* I keep hearing what the women in Africa do and I keep wondering what do the men in Africa do? Why don't we talk about that? It might be because they are down in the freaking diamond mines, which is just another form of being out on the perimeter, taking care of external business. *See Felix Mbewe* for his description of what men do in rural areas in Zambia and that women do more work.*

What kind of personal experience do you have with the double standard of male access to the good life? Being in the men's movement, I learned probably the most important thing the movement has done for me is to get me to the point where I can trust my feelings, not to think that you're always wrong if you want some changes. This has really helped me live a happier life because before whenever I was in a relationship with a woman and it wasn't going well, I was completely vulnerable to shaming and feeling I was wrong.

Now I realize I'm somewhat right and somewhat wrong and she's somewhat right and somewhat wrong and we've got to work it out. Learning to trust my feelings got me to the point where I could say to a woman with whom I was in conflict, "You can't tell me how I should and shouldn't feel, I'm telling you how I feel. Don't tell me I'm wrong, don't try to shame me, don't try to shut me up, don't try to turn it around and make it all about you." I don't go for that anymore, I don't take that bait. I say, "I understand you've got some skin in this game too but so do I, now can we talk about it?" and that has helped a lot.

In your marriage, what have been the issues where you've had to work through this kind of dialogue? We've only been married seven years: I didn't get married till I was 60. I think my wife might say that one of the reasons we have a happy marriage (I'm her third husband) is because I know how to fight well, which means fighting fair, not being afraid, not saying stupid stuff because I'm panicked, not saying hurtful things because I'm hurt and angry.

What has helped me when I'm in conflict with a woman is to say I would like to have some ground rules. Number 1, let's hold hands while we talk because it discharges the negative energy like a lightning rod. She can feel that I mean her no harm. The second rule that I found works is we take turns--flip a coin--so whoever is talking gets to talk until they have said everything they want to say while the other person has to just listen. That doesn't mean they believe a single freaking syllable of what you're saying. There's no need for you to interrupt and jump in and cut the other person off because it doesn't mean you agree with the word of it. And then the other person gets to talk with the same rules.

My wife and I had a couple of those when we were new but we haven't had one in a long time. I think my wife really appreciates that she can trust me. I'm fair and when we have a disagreement it's easy for her to own her part of it and it's easy for me to own my part of it. It doesn't mean you're a bad person, it just means you've got some stuff going on.

In the men's movement, it seems like a major focus is on fathers' access to their kids after divorce. What are you seeing in terms of any movement in terms of shared joint and physical custody? I was the Executive Director of the National Congress for Men (NCM), which started as a generalist men's organization. One of the interesting things about Hayward* and me is that he sort of got mad at me when I was director since NCM was in the middle of an identity crisis about whether it was a generalist organization or a fathers' rights organization-- most people participating in NCM were divorced fathers. I remember getting some advice from Farrell* who said, "An organization is going to be what it wants to be and it looks like NCM wants to be a father's organization, so that's probably the way you want to go." That sort of hurt Fred's feelings because he was in on the creation of NCM as a generalist men's organization.

Yes, I'm very concerned about father's issues because fatherhood is the central issue for men whether they're fathers or not, very much like career opportunity is central for women whether they want to be a CEO or not. It's about being recognized for having those skills, abilities, talents, and capabilities so that women can do math, make tough decisions, and all of those things that we doubted women could do as business people. Dispelling those doubts is good for women in a bazillion ways, not the least of which is it's good for them to uplift what they believe about themselves.

Fatherhood is central for men because father's issues are based around the negative stereotypes of men being cold, unkind, uncaring, selfish, mean, impatient, and all that stuff which in some people's minds justifies treating fathers badly. *I would add deviant, there's a suspicion of men around little kids.* Yes, some male school teachers leave the profession because they're afraid of the suspicion and don't want to be accused.   The larger issue wrapped around fatherhood is the idea of options for men to have full emotionally, connected, expressive human lives. If you've got a kid, what's more human than wanting to love your kid, be with your kid, help your kid, teach your kid, and have the kid grow up happy and strong and loving?

Are there advances in terms of states' presumption for joint custody? The National Parents Organization, which is all about shared parenting, does not think that we're doing so well on making it the norm. Their website (sharedparenting.org), includes a map showing a state shared-parenting report card. The only state they give an 'A' to is Kentucky.

Three main constituencies stand in the way of shared parenting--one is divorce lawyers. The more they can make divorce look like a kill or be killed enterprise, the more they can offer protection to their client against these horrible people over here. They're a protection racket. The other option is mediation and in two to six sessions it's done and maybe you need some tune-up sessions in a couple of years. Today we still have a lot of women whose primary identity is as mother and to have some man say that he can be just as good a parent as you can be--no way. There is what some of us call an industry around the idea of male violence against women.

The other constituency that often shows up in state legislatures when they're considering a joint custody bill, along with the lawyers, is the domestic violence advocacy crowd who are also making a lot of money. Some of those executive directors of those shelters are pulling down 100k to 200k salaries. They tell legislators that you can't have "forced joint custody" because it endangers women and children.

Gloria Steinem said in 1995, "Over the past 25 years, women have done a good job of convincing the world that women can do what men can do. Our challenge over the next 25 years is to convince the world and ourselves, that men can do what women can do." She added, "So far I don't think we believe it ourselves." It makes sense because for a man to be able to accept that a woman can use a monkey wrench is an easier pill to swallow than for a woman to accept that a man can be as deeply loving and nurturing as she can be.

Many women seem to believe they create life mystically, like just some magical power, when in fact it's the union of the sperm and the egg that creates the life. The zygote sends out its own placenta and finds a place to attach to the uterus to draw sustenance. It's understandable why there's resistance to fathers, but we have to overcome it if we're going to really have fairness and equality between the sexes. If men don't have fairness and equality at home, women aren't going to have fairness and equality in the workplace. Lots of men are working at jobs they don't find satisfying.

As a little boy, I remember thinking I could not imagine anything sadder than to be a man who has to go out all day and be away from his wife and children and then come home tired. My father was an old-time family doctor so I saw that big-time because the hours that man put in were phenomenal. He made house calls until he was way past his prime and came home tired and grumpy. I thought, "Wow! I don't want to live like that."

When he died, all of my four brothers and sisters were at the funeral home, and patient after patient came to pay their respects to old Dr. Kammer. They would tell stories about how warm, kind, caring, and loving he was and my siblings were looking at each other wondering, who are they talking about? When he came home he didn't have anything left. He was basically a stranger in his own house and I did not want that.

What other organizations do you see that are active doing the work besides the men's rights and fathers' rights groups? I've dabbled in every aspect of the men's movement I could touch. On one extreme you have the NOMAS, a very pro-feminist organization. On another extreme, the anti-feminists point to scripture that talks about how men are supposed to have dominion over women. Probably there's a 4chan about them or a subreddit on Reddit.

Regarding the mythopoetic guys, I did sort of a cousin, the New Warriors training weekend. Years and years after my father died, they helped me have my first cry about his death. They can be pretty powerful in a lot of ways. But, for me, to not talk about all of these cultural, societal, and political ways in which things could be made better for men is wimping out. Often you'll hear these men who are all about doing the work and getting in touch with their feelings and really owning their stuff and you say to them, "Have you ever looked into what percentage of the men who come to your meetings and at check-in say they're feeling lousy and terrible and depressed? How many of them are saying that because they're divorced and are having problems seeing their kids?"

You might find out that not being able to see their kids is one of the reasons for a lot of the problems you're seeing including alcoholism, depression, suicide attempts, not doing well at work, and unsuccessful relationships. Maybe one way to help men with all of those problems is to get to the core of the problem? What if several hundred of you guys walked around the halls of the state legislature and said to the legislators, "We know you don't hear this a lot but you really need to do something about joint custody because a lot of problems are caused by the fact that a lot of men are bereft of their children."

In Good Will Toward Men, *your first book, women talk candidly about the balance of power between the sexes. Your second book is* If Men Have All the Power, How Come Women Make the Rules? *The third one is for young men,* Heroes of the Blue Sky Rebellion: How You and Other Young Men Can Claim All the Happiness in the World. *Like Farrell, you feel like there's been a Lace Curtain in terms of getting the word out about your books.* Nicholas Davidson wrote a wonderful examination of the difficulty that people of my ilk, *The Failure of Feminism,* and basically anybody who disagrees with the feminist analysis of the world have a really hard time in the publishing industry.

You and I had a great interview in my first book of interviews with 22 women, most of whom identified as feminists. We talked about the advantages women have and the disadvantages men face. As we were wrapping up the book, my editor sent me a note saying, "I'm getting incredibly excited about this book" but he was fired right before the book was published.

I have a long treatise about what the Lace Curtain did to my book. Some of it was internal to the publisher, some of it was in newspapers, etc. St. Martin's Press basically tanked the book although we had great opportunities to sell the book, such as the manager of the Barnes and Noble flagship college bookstore at Trinity College in Hartford read the book and loved it. He offered to let all of his bookstore manager colleagues throughout the whole Barnes and Noble network know about this book. He even wrote a sample letter to them about the book. We offered this to St. Martin's Press to help sell the book, but they completely ignored it.

I was hurt, sad, depressed, frustrated, and since I'm a man what did I identify as my feelings? Anger, although having been in the men's movement for quite a while, I knew that anger is often a secondary emotion. I saw this huge machine that sort of squashed me. So after a couple of years of feeling that way, I wrote the second book: wry, witty, pithy, and acerbic.

I found an agent for it in New York, Nancy Love. I asked her what's your normal percentage and she said, "15%." I told her I want you to take 20% because this is going to be a hard book to sell and I want you to have extra motivation to sell it. She said, "No, no, I can sell this book," but she couldn't sell it. The executive vice president of Warner Books wrote, "While there's much truth at the heart of this, I didn't particularly like the one-liner approach, and the contempt this book would inspire among the women in-house would be immense. I'll let one of my male competitors be the one who gets pummeled." By doing that, he proved the whole premise of the book. Here's the supposedly powerful male editor and who's making the rules? He's afraid of what the women are going to say.

We make a mistake when we look at the patriarchy at the top and don't look down. That has been my most popular book, sad to say because it's not nearly as good a book as *Good Will Toward Men*. It's not nearly as healing and progressive a book but it's my most popular book. The book for boys is my foray into trying to talk to the little boy that I was back in the day when I was seeing all the stuff going on and wondering, "What the heck is going on here?" Of course that sold virtually nothing because I didn't even bother finding an agent for that, I just published it myself.

The main message of *Heroes of the Blue Sky Rebellion* is you're going to feel a lot of insecurities as a boy growing up, a lot of people are going to tell you you're wrong, you're not a man, you're a wimp, but just trust your feelings. Remember that the game is not the years between 13 and 23, but the years between 23 and 93. Right now you're going through a tough time but maintain your integrity, be who you are, and then when you get into orbit you'll have a happier life.

It starts out with a fable about an island with two tribes on it, one representing girls and women and one representing boys and men. The story is about boys and girls initially keeping to their sides of the island but the girls and women's tribe eventually demanded the right to come to the men's and boys' side of the island. Things became a little crowded for the men and boys there. They were fishing people while the girls and women were agrarian. Some of them started saying, "Why can't we go over to the other side of the island where there's rain and lushness? Don't tell anybody but I'd like to grow plants and flowers too."

The elders from the men's side of the island came rushing over the mountain and said, "You boys get home right this minute. We didn't come over to this side of the island and look at us. We turned out just fine." The boys said, "Didn't you always tell us about the power of the big blue sky? Look there's big blue sky out there too, and look at the sunrise and the pinkness of that sunrise added to the blue only makes it more beautiful. We're not giving that up, so it's a new day," and that's what "the blue sky rebellion" was.

Why do you think it is that around the world more women are graduating from university, but more women express anxiety and depression? When we talk about diagnoses of depression, we've really got to be careful of our criteria. There is pretty good indication that our diagnostic criteria miss a lot of depression in boys because often male depression manifests in ways very different from female depression. [*See Jed Diamond.**] Boys and men will often manifest their depression through acting out, not withdrawing, by being angry. In lots of ways that are more difficult to measure, women are thriving in ways and in numbers that men and boys are not as seen in suicide statistics and in drug and alcohol addiction statistics.

We've had a constant 50-year pep rally for women and girls, "You go girl, you can be anything you want to be. Girls rule, girls are great." Sometimes you even see posters *and t-shirts* that say, "Women are perfect." What do we hear about boys and men? "Boy, don't go there!" They don't want to be criticized for being male chauvinist pigs or some kind of microaggression. I think boys at some very deep fundamental level think, "The future is female; I guess I'll play video games, to hell with it." That's what I think is the fundamental problem and it's very sad.

You've mentioned female supremacy, toxic femininity, and female shadow; please define. The ways in which men were raised to believe they were superior to women was one of the first messages from feminism. As a counter-feminist, I say now let's talk about the many ways in which women believe they're superior. I don't think there's any question that female supremacy is a problem in some very important domains, such as parenting. The incessant, imbalanced scrutiny and criticism of men--of which the "toxic masculinity" harangue is a central element--is dispiriting and depressing to men. (See my video on toxic femininity.[170])

Shadow is a Jungian concept, the idea that people will displace and deny those aspects of themselves they don't want to acknowledge. If you're raised to believe that, as a girl or a woman, your identity and your wonderfulness is built around being kind, caring, loving, compassionate, and empathetic, you get involved in a movement of women who are like, "We're going to go kick butt and take names." *Like the #MeToo movement?* Those people get into a power trip about how strong their movement is and how much they can do to those men who used to make them feel bad. Rather than being able to internalize and incorporate a nice amount of that good fighting spirit, they deny it and project it, claiming that they're not doing anything unjust to men--that's the shadow.

What are they doing that's unjust? It's pretty clear that some women are doing some pretty mean things to men on an individual level like falsely accusing them of child sexual abuse so they can get custody of the kids; that's very shadowy. We've talked about the male shadow for a long time but it's hard to talk about the female shadow when the brand image of females is angelic, mother, sweetness, and light. *There's also the witch and bitch in the dual view of women in Western history, along with the Blessed Virgin.* If you say the word bitch these days, you get slammed. Words like misogyny get very quickly applied to anybody who dares to bring up that other part of the duality. What happens when it goes underground? It becomes shadowy, right? *Yes.*

Do you think that Donald Trump as the epitome of negative male shadow was healing, to bring it to the surface so it can be examined? No, I don't think he brought anything healthy to the surface. I understand that he really motivated a lot of women to think if this joker, if this horrible man can become President, we're in a world of trouble and we'd better keep working. However, more white women voted for him than Hillary Clinton in 2016 (*and more for Trump than Biden in 2020*). One of the biggest put-downs in male culture is you're a loser and that was quite a common epithet he would throw at people, particularly men, an ugly perversion of traditional male ideas of power.

Why do you think he got elected? Because a lot of what people believe has been driven underground. To tell people who wish that there was a better immigration system that they're wrong and deplorable, even though it affects their livelihood, wasn't wise. The idea of political correctness, probably more than anything, fed into the appeal of Donald Trump. He said what people were thinking but didn't dare say. So what's the cure for that? Let people get it off their chests, have a discussion with them. Some of what they say might be helpful, but we don't do that.

We have these polarized points of view, the Democrats as the Mommy Party and the Republicans as the Daddy Party. They ought to have a happy marriage where they hold hands when they argue and get into the committees and work it out. We have horribly dysfunctional marriages in our institutions because the Republicans don't want to acknowledge the value and legitimacy of the liberal principle, the Democrats don't want to acknowledge and value the legitimacy of the conservative principle. We have to figure out how to optimize the combination.

I'm interested in models, examples that we can duplicate. When you look around the world are there any countries that are doing better than we are in terms of equality for men and women? I can think of some countries that are really good at equality for women but I don't see them as working for equality for men, only for women. Sweden is often held as a paragon of women's advances. *Yes, and they always couch it in terms of advantages for men and women, such as taking parental leave. When I was in Stockholm, I saw a poster of a big wrestler taking parental leave, for example.*

I do see some interesting things coming out of Great Britain. There are some people in parliament who are saying they need to pay attention to what's going on with men and have established a joint special committee to look at men and boys. Australia has some really interesting and helpful initiatives for helping men talk about what's really going on in their lives.

Anything else that you'd like people to think about in terms of how to give boys and men a fair shake? Some of the best advocates for boys' issues are MOB's, "Mothers of Boys," who might look at the statistics on high school graduation rates, suspension rates, discipline rates, who is taking AP courses, and what percentage of boys and girls are going to colleges. If they find a discrepancy, they can go to the administration and ask, "What are you doing about this? What can we do about this?" I think that's one of the places where the rubber meets the road and that might be a good place to activate some energy.

Chapter 6: Men's Groups and Community

Shepherd Bliss, Ph.D.
Author, Activist for Cooperative Masculinity

I was born in September 1944 in California. *I think of Virgo people as being kind, communicative, sensitive. Does that apply to you?* It depends on my mood and what's happening in the world. I have very little patience, such as with American war-making--that's a priority for me. I was in the army for 13 years and my family gave our name to Fort Bliss in Texas. I was the fourth generation in the military. *You ended up in the ministry with a divinity degree. What path led you in that direction?* I was at the University of Chicago, where I got my doctorate, and then my postdoc at Harvard.

What was there about your growing up years that led you to Harvard and a Ph.D.? I spent a lot of time studying and hanging out with the right people. I like books. I've contributed to 24 books and edited a lot of books in my life and I still do as much of that as I can though, as you age, your mind changes.

You also co-edited The Men's Studies Review *and hosted the* "Changing Men" *radio show.*

Do you have brothers and sisters? Yes, I'm the oldest of five, three boys and two girls. I had a wonderful mother, but my father was problematic, he was a military guy so he was kind of rough with the boys--not with the girls. He was a classically absent father, away at work. One of my brothers became a Marine.

The big thing in my childhood was living with my uncle and aunt because when my mother had cancer we all got farmed out when I was 14. I chose my Uncle Dale and Auntie Alva, who were Iowa farmers. That's why I became a farmer while I kept teaching here and there, but was no longer doing full-time teaching. *Where did you grow up the 14 years before you were in Iowa?* In the military, you move about every three years. *Where were you as an undergrad?* The University of Kansas.

Do you think that your military background led you to go in the other way to peace and being an ordained minister? I appreciated the discipline in the military; I believe in the defense of our country so I'm not an extremist. There's a time when you need to defend your loved ones and your values. I became a mixture because the University of Chicago Divinity School taught me a lot about kindness and caring for people and I still have some of those things I learned in the military in my gut. *Does that mean that you're a Christian?* I'm an ordained Methodist minister but I'm not just a Christian.

How did you get interested in men's roles? Noticing how my father treated my sisters with a lot of kindness but not the boys. He trained us to be warriors but asked for forgiveness before he died. He apologized for his behavior toward me. Economically and politically, men have control, but in our personal lives, we're expected to suppress our feelings and expected to go off to wars in front of cannon fire.

How did you get from Kansas to Chicago to Boston to Berkeley and now farming in Sonoma County? I'm a very public person but I'm also a very introverted kind of contradiction sometimes. It gets me in trouble in certain situations.

You were married to a Japanese-American woman; what was that relationship like? We lived in Berkeley together and then we ended up spending part of our time on the farm where I am now. I called her about two or three years ago just to have a friendship but she didn't respond. Then a couple of months ago, she called me and said she's still living in her family home. Her parents were in the concentration camps for no reason other than they were Japanese-Americans. When we got married, we made an agreement not to have children, but then when she got to around age 40, she asked, "Can we renegotiate that contract?" I wasn't ready to renegotiate the contract so she left. Then she decided she only wanted a child with me so she never had a child. It was my fault, but she's back in my life now and I'll see her.

How did you get involved with the men's movement and the mythopoetic Robert Bly branch? A woman that I was involved with in Boston, who I was very excited about, invited me to go out of town with her. We went to a conference where the keynote speaker was Martin Luther King, Jr. soon before he was assassinated. That changed my whole life due to his beauty and his capacity to speak and his impact on people. I was still serving churches then, trying to learn how to do that, and he really helped me a lot.

I thought I could do a lot of good because I had so much military experience, which back then was almost totally male. I'm glad now that there are more women in the military now because they bring a lot. It was very clear to me and to all my four siblings that my mother was the strong one, not my father. When I was hired at Radcliffe College, I formed a men's group where men could do what they need to do, tell stories, which was very influential to me. *Was that after you heard Martin Luther King, Jr. speak?* Yes, he inspired me. This is contradictory, but I'm an extreme introvert, I live alone, and I spend a lot of time writing and watching non-violent DVDs. *You have an organic boysenberry farm?* Yes, that's the main thing I've done for 30 years; organic boysenberries apparently aren't available anywhere else.

What brought you to California? I lived in Berkeley, the home of some of the earliest pro-feminist gatherings, with founders like writer Joseph Pleck. I taught psychology in a seminary and at John F. Kennedy University. The men's groups I was in were supportive and always pro-feminist. I saw so many men getting in groups that I couldn't be a part of because they were anti-female. I coined the phrase "toxic masculinity" and I support "cooperative masculinity," which is nature-based.

I've been involved with many different kinds of men's groups and conferences. Poet Robert Bly used to do a lot of them, a very dynamic speaker. There are pockets around the country where men's groups are still pretty strong in areas, like in California. I'm definitely not into men's rights, I'm not into that extreme, but we just ignored them. I was active in the National Organization for Changing Men (NOMAS) and California Men's Gatherings, as well as the mythopoetic movement. The groups have met in the Mendocino woods since 1982, telling stories, dancing, listening to men like Robert Bly and James Hillman.

Is the thrust of your writing that men need to get in touch with their inner masculine, deep self? It includes don't oppress women. *Does the need for male bonding in the wilderness doing rituals, poetry, singing, chanting, and dancing come from our lack of initiation ceremony for young men?* For me, it's about male bonding, like when I was in the military and in seminary. Being with men can be healing and ours is a time for revisioning masculinity. This is a connection to what men have done forever, developing male friendships and contact with father figures. Robert Bly is interested in the "deep masculine," to connect with feelings. He said, "Grief rather than anger is the doorway to a man's feelings."

There are other countries where the men are much more cooperative and I have visited some of those countries, including Chile. One of the places where I was, and wish I'd stayed longer, was Cuba. It's very clear to me that the American empire is over.

In the mythopoetic approach, do you identify with the archetype of the trickster, the fool? Not exclusively, it's just one of the archetypes. *What are other ones that you identify with?* Love of the masculine, love of the feminine, love of children, love of parents, love of elders, have gotten to be very important for me.

In 1995, you said that your priority was gender reconciliation. How much progress have we made towards gender reconciliation by 2021? Women have taken the leadership and raised a lot of legitimate concerns and questions. We're finally beginning to have women in key places like Vice President Harris and more members of Congress. I think a lot of the negative male stuff toward women comes from a feeling of inferiority. *Neo-Freudian Karen Horney thought that history revolves around womb envy because early people didn't understand that men played a part in the conception of a baby.*

How have the themes that men are talking about in the men's group changed over the years? One of the big ones is fatherhood. I made a conscious decision not to have children because I didn't have enough confidence in my skills to be a father. A lot of us talk about family and politics. *Do you think there is more gender reconciliation now?* Yes, but we still need a lot more. We have just three women on the Supreme Court and very few in the military but all the studies show that the women who joined the military are good military officers.

You've talked about male modes of intimacy that are not face-to-face like women's, rather more side-by-side in action. I find that men have deep friendships and deep feelings and men can open up but in a different way than women and that's what's confusing. Women have sort of dominated in the field of feelings but there's what Robert Bly calls the "male mode of feeling." It sits down around grief, a sense of loss, and a kind of understanding that I think is special to men. Female intimacy is face-to-face, the talking, the making love. The male mode of intimacy is more side-by-side, running together, playing racquetball, the long-term projects.

I often found that there was a verbal disparity between men and women; I can't keep up with their verbal exchange. I always thought there's something wrong with me, but men have been out in the woods all these years, hunting and providing. There's something very honorable about man's silence at times. I'm not talking about withholding; I'm talking about containment, the kind of boundaries that men have. There's a dignity and strength to that. I like a man who can communicate with a gesture, who can communicate with his eyes.

When I lived in Berkeley, a lot of the men were very pro-feminist and very active. Some were gay, some were bisexual. *Male intimacy means we play basketball or we build a deck together rather than talk about our feelings?* Yes, I think the statistics show that women do talk a lot more every day than men. I tried to do some mixed male and female groups but they're difficult. I haven't found any groups here that did succeed. I think a lot of gender reconciliation is up to men taking more initiative and being willing to listen and being in men's and women's groups together.

You also write about the male body and the male feeling that I'm inadequate if I don't have six-pack abs. I think a lot of men judge other men by their height although it's actually healthier to be shorter.

Why are some of the biggest men's organizations conservative Promise Keepers and the Oath Keepers? I think it's fear of feminine strength since we all had mothers and we tended to go to them for help and knowledge. I think a lot of men have fear of women and their power. *Does that mean that if men were more involved parents, if we allowed them not to work so many hours, that some of that fear and resentment of women would change?* Yes, change comes slowly but there are other countries where the women are more valued. *Are you thinking of the Nordic countries?* Yes.

If you were going to give a talk to a group of young men, what would you advise them? I would embrace the importance of circular organizing. Say you have 10 people in a group, you all go around and share. I think men aren't really bred to be competitive but they are encouraged to be that way and to be in charge, although we all know that in most families the women are really in charge. *How did that play out in your marriage since you were so conscious of female strength and not being the dominant one?* Arlene is very strong. I think it's very important to welcome men crying. It's so natural and all the studies about crying say how redemptive it is. If you let enough tears go then you can get to another place. Also, listen, listen, listen--don't interrupt.

What do you think is the legacy of Trump's version of masculinity because 70 million Americans voted for him? Trump initiated the end of America but sometimes things have to get worse before they can get better.

Randy Crutcher, Ed.D.
Author of *The Passion Principle* and Men's Group Leader

Crutcher's remarks on our 1987 video:

I'm an activist in the men's movement. Ever since I was a young boy, I've experienced the tension between how I was expected to perform and who I really was, how I felt inside, and how I presented myself to others. It wasn't until the last few years that I discovered most men experience that tension and pressure to be a man according to a described role. For me, the role has provided some benefits and some privileges-- sometimes to the disadvantage of the women in my life.

In addition, it has made me compete with other men, which too often leads to distrust and uneasy relationships. Fortunately, there's always been a part of me that has rejected this male role as I seek to meet my own needs as a complete and total human being learning to live intimately with the women, men, and children in my life.

His 2021 Update

I was born in Los Angeles, California in 1953 of white working-class parents who were each the first generation in their families, (one the first to become college-educated. They became educators

As a Gemini, do you feel like a multiple personality, many interests kind of person? I know there are many parts of me, but I'd not characterize my makeup as multiple personalities. I would say that the old saw, "variety is the spice of life," does apply as I look over the course of my life. The consistent pattern is that I did follow in my parent's footsteps to some extent with becoming an educator and involved in the helping professions. I have a passion for learning and understanding the larger systems, social and ecological, that shape our lives, experiences, and outlooks.

As you grew up, what were the messages that you got about being a man? I had a very intimate relationship with my father. As the first son, I got a lot of attention and did a lot with my father. I worked alongside him and played with him. He was a physical education teacher so he taught me a lot about how to use my body. He was a very body-positive bodybuilder. I didn't know until later how fortunate I was to even have a present father, let alone a teacher, mentor, father who continued in a way to be that teacher-mentor. He passed away this year at age 96 years. He was much smaller in stature than I, a scrappy little street kid in Depression Era Los Angeles with a single mom and a sister. He had to build himself up, to defend himself in an era when definitions of masculinity inevitably meant you were going to have to defend yourself physically if you were working-class, and he was.

His anger was just under the surface, part of a defensiveness and a machismo, balanced with being very sentimental, very emotional. He was not afraid to cry, especially when we buried our first family dog. I got the message it was okay for men to cry, although lots of forms of healthy emotional discharge are discouraged for men and narrowed down to the expression of anger, often to hide fear, hurt, and vulnerability. If we feel fear, it generally comes out as an expression of anger and often gets projected into physical fights. The making of bullies, who are often the most fearful and vulnerable (and abused themselves), stems from the negative and toxic messages about masculinity.

Do you think that's changed for Generation Z? Yes, we have different parenting models. I mentioned my dad was kind of unique in some ways. When I worked with men in my own generation, I discovered that their fathers were oftentimes either physically and emotionally absent, if not outright abusive. I taught a Sociology course at Humboldt State University called "The Changing Family" in the '90s when we looked at models of parenting and fatherhood, especially in Nordic countries with paid leave for both parents.

Though we've not adopted the same incentives or structural supports, the number of men who have chosen to be stay-at-home fathers has increased in the US despite very little structural support or messaging that it is an honorable choice. Given that, I'm actually very impressed with what's happened with fathering models and positive parenting, though the lion's share of parenting and home-making duties still sits on women's shoulders, no matter that they may be 50/50 or even primary breadwinners.

What do you see among boys? A boy's experience and growth as a full human are reflective of his immediate male role models. In the absence of that modeling, other influences can take over, for better or worse for that boy. I help a bit with a project in Kenya where Emmanuel Baya started Magarini Children's Centre for 300 orphans, boys and girls. He is their role model and father figure who comes from the heart, not the head. He's brilliant and resourceful beyond imagining but he always comes from the heart and models that for all the children in his care, teaching them how to get along peacefully and become self-sufficient.

I have boys in my extended family who are diagnosed with the now-familiar ADHD, and boys, in general, are perceived as hyper-active. Research shows boys, in general, are on a different development path, usually behind girls in social-emotional development. I believe these so-called "diagnoses," are more a reflection of industrial-era thinking that the individual must conform to a factory-school environment, literally confined to four walls for much of the instructional period. It's not how boys were taught and learned for most of our species' history.

To really deal with what we call "adjustment problems," we need to adjust our institutions and create safer and richer learning environments that are active and interactive in new but probably ancient ways. I have friends and colleagues who've been doing that for decades, including Healthy Play As a Solution. They can effectively create a very different school culture and experience for both students and staff. But these kinds of programs need to go big scale mainstream to have the greatest impact for the new generations of boys.

There's a debate in the men's movement between long-time men's rights leaders like Warren Farrell who says the boy crisis is caused by not having a role model of a nurturing father, while pro-feminists disagree.* I'm not sure it's that polarized around parental influence. If you spoke with someone like Michael Kimmel, a notable academician, author, and pioneer in the Pro-Feminist Men's Movement, (co-author of a book on the history of pro-feminist men with Tom Mossmiller), I don't think he would deny the importance of a father in the life of a boy. He is one himself. His body of work is focused on the inequitable distribution of power and resources among the genders.

Some father's rights men fault mothers who keep the dads from seeing the kids after divorce. It does rankle pro-feminist men to hear any man who lays the blame for his struggles at women's feet. If there's even a hint that women are the source of the problem, they would argue that's really not looking at the larger system of inequality that was primarily created by men. The slogan "the personal is political" came out of the feminist movement and it means that nothing you do in your own private sphere is independent of the influence of the larger social and political systems in which families and marriages exist. And yes, men are hurt by that system, but not by women as a social group.

What led you to do the men's work that you've done for so long? In my experience with my own father, I was kind of confused because he was both macho and sensitive. School then took over as the major socializer in an era when it wasn't okay to be a sissy, to be gay. It still isn't! There was a huge threat and I always felt even when I was young, this is just stupid, why are we being separated this way?

In high school, I was kind of in the middle between the nerd camp and the jock camp. I went to school in a somewhat remote rural community where academic success was not admired among the boys. I stood out as a curve breaker for grades because I was really interested in everything, studied, and took the tests, but I wasn't really identified as a nerd because I was also on athletic teams. I saw tremendous bullying and I was once bullied myself but I didn't fight. I let the stupid taunts roll past even as I questioned my courage and confidence to stand up and punch this guy in the face. I knew that would be a stupid thing to do--that was a tough internal conflict. And as the principal's kid, I was aware of other consequences to getting in a public fight.

Fast forward to young adulthood, I was given an opportunity to join a men's group when I started graduate school in psychology. The group included Vietnam vets, guys just a few years older but seemingly from a different world. I was fascinated by listening to their experiences. I had a low draft number but if the draft had not ended just before it was called, I likely would have gone to Vietnam. That group felt safe enough for me to share what was painful and hard during my boyhood and adolescence, a topic that was no longer forbidden in the safety and agreements set forth by the leader. That was wonderfully freeing and liberating. The leader of the group, Paul, said, "We're writing a grant to start a men's program but we realize we can't finish, we're moving and thought you'd be great for this work. Do you want to take this over and finish the grant?" I thought, "Wow, this came out of the blue!"

A woman and I finished writing and submitting a state family planning grant. We were awarded $100,000 over the course of three years to educate men about reproductive health and birth control and their role in unplanned pregnancy, with the goal of reducing unplanned pregnancies. At the time, they were at a higher rate and cost the state money in services. We expanded it into a Men's Health & Wellness Center where you could walk in and get counseling as a man for whatever crisis or struggle you were going through. We initiated several kinds of men's education programs and support groups targeting the

US Coast Guard, Army ROTC, the State Conservation Corps, college students, and the community at large.

Our work always boiled down to how men feel about and navigate their relationships, not just the technical aspects of reproductive health like how to prevent unintended pregnancy and disease. We explored how they were relating to the people they are most intimate with, along with taking precautions or not. Right away I reached out to network with other men in California and eventually men across the whole country, not just in the area of human sexuality and health, but eventually domestic violence. A couple of years into running the men's center, women who were running a shelter came to me and said, "We can work with these women forever but they're like lemmings jumping off a cliff and the men in their lives are at the top of the cliff. Could you work with the men?"

That was really intimidating at first. How would I do that? Are these guys killers? I had to get in touch with my own tendencies to be aggressive or overbearing in my relationships and eventually came to the realization that I was on the same continuum with these guys. They just got more physical beyond verbal abuse and really did some serious damage to the ones they said they loved. At that time partner abuse was not clearly against the law and police were dealing with it in a very different fashion than today. One of my men's groups developed a group program focused on alternatives to violence that eventually included a police academy training component.

I worked with a woman who worked at Boalt Law School at UC Berkeley who was trying to make domestic violence a crime with real consequences and pushing to have police and law enforcement deal with it in a very different way, not a conflict mediation approach, which led to people and officers getting hurt. Nancy Lemon proposed that when you were arrested, you were told that you'd committed a crime and the consequences would be going to jail, or in some cases going into a diversion program if there was one. There were not many in those days, only individual therapy which was often ineffective in stopping the violence.

We ended up starting a county diversion program working with deputy district attorneys. Fortunately, attitudes and policies were beginning to change and more programs were in progress or getting launched. I continued to network and resource share with men in the domestic violence and male batterer intervention groups movement of the 1980s.

What did you find are the keys to ending violent behavior? We developed quite a rigorous protocol in our intake. If we discovered there was a problem with alcohol or drug abuse, they couldn't be in the program without also attending to that at the same time. They would need to do individual counseling, or commit to a drug program intervention because if your cerebral cortex is not operating and the central nervous system is knocked out, no amount of cognitive behavioral therapy is going to stick. The prefrontal cortex is easily overridden by the mid-brain.

We began to use psychodrama to put the man in the woman's place so he could experience what it was like to be under threat. That also put a spotlight on what he was thinking at the moment he was about to hit or become abusive, slowing the whole thing down like a slow-motion action film each step of the way, in the hopes that this level of awareness and understanding could give the man more self-control and self-discipline. Anger management alone is not sufficient.

All of that was presented within the framework of pro-feminism, which is not only do women not deserve this, but you're demeaning yourself as well as the woman. In this society, the bulk of domestic violence/partner abuse is male to female, a result of structural inequities. We'd educate about the programming the men received that we called male role expectations and socialization, aspects of which are referred to as "toxic masculinity" today, a term I don't care for though I understand its genesis.

What was the success rate? I wrote a master's thesis on the effectiveness of group treatment based on researching several programs at the time, the late '80s. We found the programs that were simply anger management were ineffectual because they were only technique-based. They didn't get at the root of a man's thinking, his cognitive structure, along with impulse control. We asked the man if we could have permission to speak with his partner on a very limited basis. We asked her four yes or no questions with no elaboration: "Has your partner been physically violent in the last month? Has your partner been verbally violent? Do you feel free to share about this? Have you seen any change?" We emphasized they need not respond unless they wished to.

At a certain point, men weren't able to be in the program unless they would agree to this because we felt that was real accountability. We'd come back to the group and say your partner said you've been physically violent; do you want to talk about that? You made an agreement you broke, so what about that? At the time there weren't that many programs doing that. We drew that from a model program, the Marin Abused Women's Shelter Men's Program. We had some of the men complete our Men's Alternatives to Violence program who were dentists, student body presidents, and others who became facilitators in the program. That certainly seemed a measure of success!

Did you find that abusers often were abused or had abuser fathers? Yes, they may have been directly physically abused, but not uniformly so. The larger percentage had witnessed their father or male figure in the family abusing their mother. So observation alone could make it okay in that man's mind to later abuse his adult partner.

You've been in men's groups for decades. What's been the impact on your development and have you seen changes in what men are talking about in the groups? I have pretty consistently participated in men's groups since my 20s, with some breaks. For the last 10 years, I've been in a local men's group that has been wonderful. The ages run from 48 to 68. We love that our youngest member has gone through the throes with a step-kid and his own kid, going through all this parenting stuff, and then there's a man my age who is retired.

We have a life-span variety of rich life experiences to share about. We talk about men's physical, psychological, and emotional health and our relationships. Also, our guys tend to talk about their struggles with work and work-life balance and then the challenges around how to transition from a successful career to the next step--developmental issues I would call them.

Do we still train men to be success objects and women to be sex objects? Yes, if you look at the media, they still use sex to sell, which is all about objectifying women's bodies. If the advertising industry can get in a little trigger around people's self-image, they will use that as leverage to sell things.

If anything, it's been magnified by technology and a zillion outlets.

As for success objects, I find it interesting to look at the more recent impact of Covid--many people are re-examining what the heck they're doing and why. I've been working in a training field for the last 10 years where we help people leave the corporate world and live a more balanced life by getting clear about and following their true passions and sense of purpose, for both men and women. They may have felt constricted to follow in the old nine to five which became the 24/7 when the internet made it possible to work all the time. Being a "success object" continued for men but really took off for women in the last 30 years moving more into management and governance, leadership levels across the sectors. I'm encouraged by the re-examination of work, even though "essential workers," often don't have the luxury of stopping to examine much of anything beyond daily survival.

If someone asks you, "I'm in this high-level corporate job that's killing me but I have to pay my mortgage and my kids' college tuition," what can you do for him? I provide him (or her) with a self-exploration tool I've used for over a decade called "The Passion Test."[171] It helps them get razor-sharp clarity about the top five most important things in life and how they feel about them. The goal is to bring the head and heart together, which is also the work of leaving restricted masculinity (or masculine-defined levels of achievement) and evolving towards full humanity. That tool helps them determine what lights them up so they can recover their energy their inspiration and their authentic motivation. It gets them in touch with the DNA of their own happiness and possible fulfillment. The tool has been remarkable in my own life to keep me on track to do what I love.

Wallace Stevens was a poet who worked as a banker and then wrote beautiful poetry and led the rest of his life outside of those hours. I think the biggest restriction on men and women becoming their full selves and living full lives is the way we've structured work. Everybody could be working four hours a day and getting everything necessary done but there's still this dominant Protestant work ethic that has us believing our identity is tied up in our productivity and work. A universal basic income is considered freeloading, but it makes more sense now than ever with increased automation replacing human work. Or there might be certain aspects in a person's job that can be changed to be more aligned with what he's passionate about. For any particular man, he may need to move laterally in a company, up, or even down, or leave; these are options that he can better consider when he's gotten in touch with his heart and what really moves him.

Can you give an example of a case study who stepped down from a high-earning job and found another way to earn money? Leaving a job--if that's the only alternative--can mean different things for different people. There may be a step down in income, but it could also mean there is an opportunity to make as much or more income than what the company dictated. Or it may mean that people do a variety of things. I train people to facilitate the Passion Test process and they can immediately go out and do workshops and work with people one-on-one and keep 100% of the money they ask for this service helping others to get clear and take steps to a fuller life.

I facilitate an internet group with a man from Afghanistan, a Swiss man who lives in Kauai, a Norwegian man who lives in Tokyo, and men in every time zone in the U.S. All of these men have developed their dream businesses and had to shift due to changing social and economic conditions. The Norwegian man is importing fish from Norway to Japan. My Colombian friend had a successful eco-tourism business until Covid closed that down. Now his job is working with tennis associations around the world because his stepson became a tennis pro and brought him into a whole new realm. He gave his son a Passion Test. His son had so much pressure to go to college but he decided that he was going to go into pro-tennis and later was able to go back to college. The father not only encouraged his son to be true to himself, he modeled it!

What are your top five passions? Quality time with family and friends, time in nature, writing for pleasure and profit to positively influence the world, staying fit and healthy, and connection to my spiritual self.

The Passion Test was developed by Chris and Janet Atwood and described in the bestselling book *The Passion Test: The Effortless Path to Discovering Your Life Purpose.* I've worked with these authors and trainers over the last decade and during that time, a clinical psychologist who'd developed his own passion discovery classes came to me and said, "Look at my manuscript and see if you want to do something with it."

I reorganized the book, inserting my own work and experience with The Passion Test as a coach and facilitator. My co-author Bruce Hutchison has worked in prisons and assisted living centers. Our book is called *The Passion Principle: How to live YOUR Most Passionate Life* with the emphasis on *Your* because my agenda is to help remove the chains of our institutional conditioning, along with getting clear about what really drives you and how to overcome obstacles, most of them mental. It helps get you down to the nitty-gritty of creating an action plan such that tomorrow you're going to do something to step further in the direction of living your most passionate life, one you're in charge of. It's also designed for use by professional helpers working with clients.

Does that book have anything to do with your dog and cat cards? A friend of mine worked for the State of Colorado educating communities, schools, and students about our rivers and how you can be a steward of your own local waterway's health and abundance. We went cross-country skiing one day with pet dogs who were jumping and flying through the snow with great abandon. We wondered, "What would they say about their experience right now if they could speak English?" Bingo, we came up with this idea of creating a deck of cards that would use people's love of their pets to share messages about how to live a better human life. Many people never open a self-help book, so how do you get the messages across about positive psychology and developing your intuition, inner guidance, and inner wisdom? We landed on our own love and their love of dog and cat companions.

In the guidebooks to each deck, there's a 400-word entry for each of 60+ themes to provide a stimulus to insight and suggestions on how to deal with that human issue or energy. It could be jealousy, anger, or other shadow aspects of human existence, as well as contentment, fulfillment, and joy. On the back of every card of the Divine Dog Wisdom Card is a picture of a dog looking at the moon in wonder. We're inspired to help foster a sense of wonder about self-discovery and the world.

Let's pull a card right now to answer, "What would be the most useful step to take to encourage young men to reach their full potential?" Gayle, you picked the **Excellence** card. The guidebook says, "You're being called to strive for your personal best and some endeavor you're passionate about or that's deeply important to you." It never fails to amaze me that when the intent is strong, the perfect card emerges. We need to redefine success and excellence as we help and support each boy, teen, and man learn how to define that for himself. It takes a village of conscious men to provide that support.

As a boy, I always felt I had to prove myself by someone else's standard and that's why I finally landed with passion discovery as the key to not just individual transformation, but societal transformation. If we can release people from restricted standards outside of themselves and fortify their internal locus of control based on their own life spark, their own life design, we'll have leaders who are better able to overcome oppression and change systems for the betterment of all.

There's a Passion Test for kids and teens to help youth engage with what really interests and excites them about learning, which can make a profound difference in individual young lives and, by extension, society. It helps 9 to 13-year-olds get clear about the top two passions in their life by helping them vividly visualize what it would look like if they were living those passions fully. They draw pictures, make vision boards, and engage in hands-on, interactive activities. The program facilitates positive peer-group support for these youth and also integrates elements of the Healthy Play program mentioned earlier.

My wife, Dr. Karin Lubin, a former elementary school teacher and principal, is a program trainer for parents, teachers, counselors, and administrators in how to implement after experiencing the activities firsthand. I've seen young boys, who experienced the Passion Test for kids and teens grow up into amazing young adults in the last 10 years, especially when they received family and school support to use it as an ongoing tool for self-exploration and empowerment.

Do you agree there is a boy crisis? The theme I'm hearing is that we're ignoring boys. I'd definitely agree that in general, our society is ignoring boys and their inner lives while continuing to pressure them to conform and achieve. The most recent research I've seen proposes that because boys mature more slowly, they are not as prepared to jump into a college environment at age 18 as girls are. We really have to focus on the environment as much or more than the individual.

I got fed up with higher education because I didn't feel like it was helping students achieve their full potential and I left. I started working with the California Conservation Corps, young adults between 18 and 21, half of whom had not graduated from high school. They came from the inner city or rural areas of the state. They had to learn to work together to do valuable work and acquire valuable skills. They were able to complete a high school diploma through the John Muir Charter School, created by a close colleague of mine. Many went on to college and careers in conservation.

I saw these young men who were not initially college-bound become very skilled and powerful, not just in the use of a chainsaw, but in how to interact with men and women of all colors on their crews, which became their families. The old saying is it takes many villages, many crews, many tribes to accomplish the job of helping an individual reach his or her potential.

My philosophy of education is that it needs to be on-demand and adapted to real-life learning experiences. I started graduate school at the beginning of my career in education, but it took me 10 years to finish my master's and another 10 years before I found and could commit to a doctoral program that fit with my values around transformational education. To me, degrees only make sense if they support lifelong learning, rather than for the sake of mere ladder climbing. Our institutions of higher learning are not consistently set up to develop the whole human being.

Has Trump been harmful because he made "toxic masculinity" seem cool to his followers? Donald J. Trump is a hurt little boy who was never truly fostered or cared for regarding his social-emotional development. His father was an enabler, not a nurturer. Though they've done so, it does not take Harvard-based clinicians to diagnose that most of his behavior is a defense mechanism to protect his weakness and vulnerability, not unlike most bullies. His bully persona, bravado, and insistence on his own personal reality based on unfulfilled needs is one that's been used by others to gain power and control where they too felt they did not have any-- primarily white males, but also women.

Trump is symbolically fantastic at bringing out the shadow so we can grapple as a society with what has often been hidden like a shameful secret, that in the land of the free and brave, not all are free, and many are systematically oppressed. I worked so hard as a college Psychology and Sociology instructor to get people to look at their own unconscious biases and internalized oppression so we could deal with it, root it out, and begin recovery. The historic hurt and pain are on the street and in our faces by an order of magnitude now and have kicked social movements into high gear. There's no longer room for apathy. My biggest grief and regret until more recently was the apathy that I saw everywhere. So, perhaps it had to be someone like Trump to break the spell, while simultaneously casting one based on historic biases, hostilities, and social fragmentation and isolation. It's a very confusing time because people seem to be falling asleep and waking up at the same time.

The Republican governors who outlaw mask and vaccination mandates and social distancing, how is that helping us understand our oneness? For too long people have been in their silos thinking that lots of people think like they do. It was a wake-up call to realize there are lots of people who don't think like I do and we're going to have to deal with that. It's really tough right now when people are dying as a result of this polarized situation we face. This strong hyper-individualism within our society began early in our history as a nation but was inflamed by Ronald Reagan's anti-government rhetoric supported by many of the ultra-wealthy.

This is where the US really started to split apart with emerging extremist ideologies driving wedges and decaying bi-partisanship to the point where today the so-called Republican ideology has absolutely nothing to do with early Republicanism with its tenets around anti-slavery and government assistance to those in need. Dwight D. Eisenhower, the WWII general, a Republican President would probably be labeled a "socialist" by those who've recently taken over the Republican Party. It's the current dog-whistle that extremists are using to frighten people into their camp. It probably won't work as Millennials simply don't respond to that kind of red-baiting as the Cold War generations did.

With no agenda but obstructionism and protection of the ultra-wealthy, it will be interesting to see where things land for these self-identified Republicans making the federal government their foe and bogeyman for their supporters/voters. Heather Cox Richardson, an American political historian, and many others have pointed out that the majority of Americans actually agree on a wide spectrum of environmental, economic, and social issues, so we have to be careful when we talk about polarization and unity.

Back to masculinity though, the redefinition of masculinity to claim more aspects of our emotional selves and learn pro-social means of communication leads us to create more cooperative groups that have a chance to withstand these natural selection/survival of the fittest pressures and to thrive. Cooperation will win in the long haul. It's why we're still here as a species. As Martin Luther King said, "The arc of the moral universe is long, but it bends towards justice." Along the way, it's anything but pretty.

I place relationships at the core of what I'm about so the men's work is the air I breathe. As novelist Tom Robbins said in 1972, "The world situation is desperate…as usual." Arguably it's more desperate than ever but what do you do? You get clear about your passions, you find a place where you can make a difference and you stick it out. Leadership guru Meg Wheatley says it for me, "We need to create islands of sanity, and ask, 'Who do we want to be?'"

You're making an equation that for humans to survive we need to cooperate; in order to cooperate we need to enable men to be fully in touch with their feelings, therefore the men's movement is a key part of our survival. I love the work you and I did years ago based on the partnership society that Riane Eisler wrote about in *The Chalice and the Blade*, which included a workbook and manual we were interested in when you and I were in the NOMAS' Men and Women's Task Group. For my money, the greatest place to invest our time and attention are partnerships between men and women, creating cooperative relations in the home and the boardroom. That's how we move from a dominator to a partnership society; Eisler's language is still fresh for me.

We have a lot of spokespeople, some identified as "thought leaders," who say wonderful things but what are the quality of their relationships? We need to be teachers who follow our own teachings with integrity, which is not an endpoint; it's a constant striving to get better at it. I found earlier on in the men's movement that a lot of people who were espousing certain values were not expressing them in their relationships with each other. (*Jerry Tello* agrees.*) That's a big source of conflict, the inability of men to meet across ideological lines to engage with each other on a respectful personal level when some of the worst human behaviors have been on the main stage in the last few years. We need to make agreements about how we communicate, interact, and make decisions such that everyone can save face and be willing to engage.

As an organizational development consultant, I've helped people explore their own values and motivations before I bring them together. Among other questions, I would ask, "Who are you in conflict with?" I might find individuals in both groups who were not so iron-clad in their ideology that they could not enter any neutral ground. We simply can't expect everyone to join the party, but we need to keep inviting while creating safe and respectful containers for those encounters. In his book, *The Third Alternative*, Stephen M. Covey provides multitudes of examples where people in different groups came up with solutions together that were better than either group could do on their own. He found it required a higher level of personal emotional-social maturity to achieve this.

As an example, I was working in a conflict situation with people who wanted to ride motorcycles and ATVs on public land where some of us were trying to restore the damage done by its impact while creating an area close to homes and towns that would be an exclusively non-motorized trail system in the Central Sierra Nevada mountains of California. I didn't realize how heated that issue had become on the national level (akin to the sense of entitlement around owning and using military-grade weapons) when I entered the fray, but there were enough people in a healthy dialogue to work out a local compromise that gained national attention. We set aside acreage for motorcycles and for non-motorcycles, pedestrians, equestrians, and mountain bikers.

The point is you have to look for people who are willing to engage and let the others go. What I learned in conflict management is you can't resolve a conflict in which people are unwilling to take into account other people's points of view and needs. Work with the people who are flexible enough and can shift and change because there are plenty of them. There's no war between people ultimately, but rather a war between belief systems.

Do you agree that the peer-group support group for men is the biggest branch of the men's movement today? Gordon Clay* made the observation that the various groups with differing viewpoints are moving towards harmony and cooperation. That sort of thing won't get much media attention since the more conflictive and violent the issue, the more attention it will get from the sensationalist media. The Battle of the Sexes seems to be a popular commercial trope that just won't die. It also does nothing for a society's maturation. It's tough to assess what the "biggest branch" of a rather nebulous men's movement is.

Anecdotally, over time, I've known men in local support groups that began with an announcement through churches along a very large spectrum of religious beliefs. The idea of "fellowship," is long-enduring, with a sense of isolation for many men being addressed by these church-based support groups.

The ManKind Project *[see Boysen Hodgson*]* is a 40-year-old-plus organization that has a large reach in the US and outside. I went through the weekend training that's constructed as a men's rite of passage with an emphasis on discovering one's purpose. Men are offered ongoing groups after the weekend called Integration Groups that help them incorporate what they learned over the intensive weekend. Many men go on to staff and serve other men on these weekends.

Only a few like me get fired up about being part of a larger organization (though I am not currently) but there is a need to identify with something larger than oneself and to belong. Many men (and women) identify with a group like a sports team or band. I'm not big on sports but there have been organizations that I'm pretty passionate about and identify with, so I understand this human need and the many forms it can take. What is truly different in men's support groups is that the emphasis is on gaining support for growing up, becoming a man that is healthy in every way, from relationships to life work and fulfillment on all levels.

What are the other branches? Gordon pointed out that we need to look at how many men get together in Alcoholics Anonymous and other 12-step groups as another kind of portal for men getting in touch with themselves and what's really important in their lives. They find out, "If I open up, they won't shame or kill me, wow!" The AA model has provided a place for tens of thousands of men, though it's not seen or documented as a "men's movement."

Does Re-Evaluation Counseling (RC) also fit in the support group category? This organization was founded by Harvey Jackins and is currently led by his son Tim Jackins. With little media attention, (Harvey's decision), it has provided people with some of the deepest insights and understanding of oppression and internalized oppression that you see represented in other work and organizations that do get media attention. This way of viewing human beings and how we heal has been very instructive for me personally. *Also for me and my brother.*

I led RC men's groups as a structure for moving through the distress that reduces one's ability to think clearly about one's life and relationships and then to be able to act from a rational perspective. The RC process of discharge is one that helps to release the trapped or stuck tension and emotion, a natural process that gets interrupted by hurt, trauma, and systemic oppression. I appreciated the many agreements about safety that allow people to feel safe in exposing their feelings and moving through them rather than stuffing them, which many now know leads to mental and physical disease.

The structure for an RC session is you pair up and take turns being counselor and client. The counselor mostly listens but may offer suggestions that help release past hurtful and charged experiences in the form of tears, shaking, crying, yawning, or talking non-repetitively. Gradually over time and session work, when "the material," that arises no longer produces discharge, the client is considered to have "re-emerged," from the hurt of the experience such that the memory is neutral with no charge to it. (*Emotional Freedom Technique has similar outcomes.*)

RC taught a lot of people about systematic oppression and how it operates in the larger society, including men's oppression. It's a little tricky in the world of pro-feminism to talk about men's oppression unless you're good at explaining how it's not equivalent to women's oppression at all because we live in a male-dominant patriarchal society. When men are socialized in the way we've been speaking about, they are hurt and isolated. It is out of that hurt and isolation (along with a sense of entitlement), that men's sexist behavior arises.

Charlie Kreiner was a leader and teacher active in RC and in NOMAS. I had my brother join me in an RC group and they called him the "maintenance man," because he kept everything contained. But after doing RC, when he was an engineer in a software company, he'd throw popcorn at the guys giving presentations, he wore pink shirts, he got really fun and liberated. It sounds like whatever was holding part of him back was reclaimed, the silly carefree part, so he may have gotten out of his own box.

What does the expression "the man box" mean to you? A "man box" would typically be, don't cry or you're a sissy; don't have sexual feelings for your own sex; be the breadwinner/protector; be in control of both emotions and the situation. These restrictions have shifted and softened in the last two generations and there's a new interest in shaking up gender definitions far beyond the binary, which is fascinating. Maybe down the road we won't have any boxes, we won't even be talking anymore about "masculinity," and "femininity," recognizing the myriad ways humans express themselves and their sexualities as the norm.

What's your current focus in addition to the Passion Test? I've been teaching at Southwestern College in New Mexico. I love their mission which is Transformation of Consciousness Through Education, looking at what wasn't working in old higher education models and pedagogy in general and trying to transform that. It's in process because I can see a lot of people are recovering from institutionalized learning oppression from the time we started in schools as little kids through higher degree programs and their demands. Those of us who became teachers very unconsciously pass on these unhealed traumas when we're not very aware of how we were hurt ourselves by the system. I've taught "Systems and History Of Counseling," "Group Dynamics," and "Career and Life," mostly with women from their 20s to late 50s. I've only had three guys as students at Southwestern; I always bond with these guys, of course. Understanding how gender oppression operates for both women and men has stood me in good stead for creating authentic and cooperative relationships with my students. And I get to be a student in disguise!

I talked to some men in Europe about how few American men show up in my Passion Test Facilitator Programs. They said, "American men are such wusses," because they're too afraid of their emotions to participate where they might have to talk about their feelings. They seem to be saying that in general Europeans are less afraid and more attracted to personal growth. My opinion is that we do have this hyper-individualist, make it on your own, nothing should be for free, society as a barrier to growth and these programs probably need to make a more compelling pitch to men. I did work with some MKP trainers to integrate elements of the Passion Test program with some of theirs, a healthy collaboration.

I think of Nordic countries as not being expressive emotionally. Janet Atwood, creator of The Passion Test, started living in Denmark because she found a whole new market in Scandinavia. There were men who were not afraid to step out and try new things and the same thing happened in a very patriarchal society in Japan. I became friends with Japanese professional men who were breaking out of the mold and going through the whole program. You don't get through a Passion Test program without getting in touch with your feelings using tools and processes.

This makes me think of male bonding that happens in Japan, England, and North America in bars after work drinking with men. But, it's not focused and intentional on how you were hurt as a boy and want to recover and become whole, is it? You don't usually ask these questions over a pint: "What was it like when you were an adolescent?" "What were your struggles as a young adult trying to make your way in the world?" "What is your fondest desire for yourself now?"

What are you writing about lately? For several years I wrote a dedicated men's blog, EveryMan's 21st Century Blog, about navigating manhood in this century. Now I write a monthly blog that's a bit whimsical and light, but deep, with accumulated wisdom and positive support for everyone going through these challenging times. It could be stories about how people use the Divine Dog and Cosmic Cat Wisdom Cards and Guide for self-discovery and their own daily "ah-hahs."

A recent story based on a true account was about a mother of an adult son who encouraged her son to take a look at the cards but he wasn't interested. He was facing a potential breakup with a girlfriend and it was beginning to dawn on him that he was part of the equation about why things weren't working. She asked him to take a quick look so when he pulled the card for Empathy, he said, "Mom, I get it."

Are you going to create another deck of cards? My partner is a biologist. We're very concerned about the accelerated extinction of life on earth resulting from the impact of one species, so we're thinking about creating a deck of cards of keystone species that anchor diverse ecosystems, like sea otters, for example. They're responsible for the stability of the Pacific Ocean marine ecology. That was not known until they were nearly made extinct by fur traders; the ecology of the Pacific Coast collapsed when their food source sea urchins over-populated and destroyed the kelp forest, which contained many species that also disappeared.

We feel that there needs to be messaging that can reach people where their hearts lie, not just a sciencey approach, though at one time I thought I was destined to become a marine biologist. Just as with helping people understand themselves and their own inner ecology, we want to instill a deeper sense of awe and belonging to the circle of life that supports us and all living beings.

If you were going to write another book what would it be? I was considering a family and child's guide to using the dog and cat cards. There's a free PDF called "Got Wisdom" with tips and tales for how to use the cards.[172] I've also thought about writing about the life story of Emmanuel Baya who leads the Magarini Children's Centre and organic demonstration farm in Kenya with his wife. It's such a miraculous and amazing life trajectory that led him to this point, as he was an orphan himself. Getting it in an e-book could be a fundraiser for the center.

How did you find out about the Centre? A good friend here who leads wilderness retreats formed a relationship with Emmanuel and saw his work in Kenya. I met Emmanuel when he came to visit New Mexico and we walked together on a trail in the Rocky Mountains. I realized that he had this amazing connection with nature and I felt an instant brotherhood with him, a very strong heart connection. He was trained by the UN as a peacekeeper and he worked to resolve some conflicts between the pastoralists running herds of animals where the people were trying to raise crops. Using very ingenious ways, he helped create some peace between those two groups. He's one of my great 21st century inspirations!

My hope is to visit the Centre, and you bet I'll be watching the boys there, as they learn to partner with girls while they all grow up learning how to grow their own healthy food and build a sustainable future. This is a model we could all learn from.

Boysen Hodgson
Communications Director of The ManKind Project

I was born in Hickory, North Carolina, January of 1971. I'm on the cusp of Capricorn and Aquarius. *You have Capricorn stability and Aquarian vision. Is that accurate for you?* A dreamer with a checklist?

Do you have siblings? I have six brothers. I'm either number two or number three depending on the time in my life. My father was married before he met my mother and had a son, my mother was married before she met my father and had a son, then they got together and I was their firstborn. They had two more boys together, and then my mother remarried again and had two more sons, so I grew up surrounded by male energy. I grew up with five brothers. I didn't meet one of my brothers until I was in my 30s, and I had two step-dads and three step-moms over the course of 15 years.

With all boys then, you're not as likely to get put in traditional roles like the boy mows the lawn and the girl washes the dishes? Very accurate and also in a split household, when my mom was a single mom for a period of that time. And often even when she was married, it felt like she was a single mom. Yes, it was a group responsibility for cleaning and cooking and I learned how to do my own laundry when I was under 10 years old. Whether we fought against them, that's another question but yes, we all had responsibilities.

That's translated well in my 16-year marriage. I'm the primary house picker-upper, vacuumer, cleaner, and dinner maker. My wife generally handles laundry, except for mine. *Do you work at home?* Yes. *And she works outside the home?* She did. But she has worked at home for the last year and a half-- also totally virtual. We're on Slack so we instant message each other even if we're on work phone calls.

What about kids? We're adoptive parents. We met our kids just about eight years ago. We have 17-year-old and 15-year-old siblings. We are a multi-racial, multi-ethnic, multi-orientation household. *How did that change your marriage to suddenly be parents of elementary school-aged kids?* Radically, since we were married for 10 years as dual-income no kids couple (DINKS). We traveled, had a grand old time, had a wonderful little house. We didn't plan on having biological kids, a decision we made fairly early in our marriage, which surprised both of us.

Then we went to India and something changed between us. We returned from India thinking that we would adopt a child from India and within a month or so of starting that initial conversation, we asked the question, "How many children are there within 50 miles of where we're standing who need what we have to offer?" So we started the process to become foster-to-adopt parents. We were thinking that we would be introduced to one child somewhere between the age of four to seven, but we got a phone call on a Tuesday afternoon that two siblings need a placement right now; can you work with us? We said yes. That was the beginning of our parenting journey. It's been intense and incredibly rewarding and very difficult. What a spiritual path; the learning that my wife and I have gone through has been unbelievable and continues to be.

Are they male or female or how do they identify? Both of our kids actually use "they/them" pronouns and identify as non-binary. They play, explore, experiment. What are roles? What is gender? That's been one of those learning experiences.

We made a clear strong decision as a family that we're going to affirm our kids and support them as parents. It continues to feel more and more natural and it's helped me in my men's work. I've been in men's work for almost 20 years and it helps me pull apart the cultural programming and socialization around this role stuff and all of this rigidity that we have around gender. It's fun and challenging.

What was striking to me about raising my son is I didn't give him guns, so he shot with a stick. It seems like our hormones and our evolutionary history so influence us. I love the new neuro-research that's going on around brain plasticity. I don't think that there's ever such a thing as a blank slate because from pre-birth, I was immersed in a culture and even the hormones we're exposed to in utero are influenced by our mother's environment, so we're influenced by multiple factors. And as soon as we emerged into the world, the expectations, the assumptions, and the beliefs about what a child is, boy or girl, what they're going to be like sets a course, based on what parts they have between their legs.

The more research they do about neurobiology, genetics, adaptation, and neuroplasticity, described by authors like Dan Siegel, Lise Eliot, David Eagleman, and Cordelia Fine, the more I can't separate the culture from that mix. The complex interplay of those things is just unbelievable. There's this incredible spectrum. *In chimp and human youngsters, testosterone seems to encourage more rough and tumble play and more aggressive behavior. There are gender spatial differences between mice and humans using different markers.*

How much do you think we are influenced by our physiology? We are some percentage influenced by our physiology, hormones, skeletal-muscular systems, and DNA. My belief is that most of what we experience as human beings is cultural, with our huge brains and the amount of neurodiversity and neuroplasticity that we have. Maybe 50,000 years ago that was far less true, but both the hardware and the software that we use as human beings are just so different than any other creature on the planet. *And we have self-awareness.*

What did you learn in your childhood about what it is to be a man? We talk about that in men's work and in the ManKind Project (MKP). The "Don't be a __" is one of the strongest policing forces. For me as a child, there was a lot of don't be a sissy and then in middle school don't be gay, with this degradation of things feminine. There was definitely a power hierarchy. *I'm okay because you're not okay.*

I grew up on a farm and my dad was the town veterinarian. My mom was a powerful woman. She was physically strong, breaking horses and working on farms since she was a teenager. She was mentally tough and had a lot of grit. She moved away from home when she was 17. She built multi-million dollar businesses, and she raised six sons. She taught me how to gut a room down to the studs, hang dry-wall, how to do roofing, how to use a hammer, so I didn't get a whole lot of "only men can do X."

I also have a beautiful sensitive emotional dad. I've been told that I was loved since forever and my dad has kissed me on the face my whole life. Some men have the experience of their dad never saying, "I love you," but I was totally immersed in being loved. He also loved sports, muscle cars, and bad jokes. For me, a lot of the "tough guy" cultural stuff was outside, what I saw on media, what I got from my classmates, my brothers, from teachers, and our pastor.

And the message was don't be weak, toughen up, *don't show your emotions.* Yes, the male programming mostly says it's okay to be angry and aggressive. There's a whole field of study called "contextual masculinity," exploring how masculinity is context-driven. So a father with his newborn child is allowed to express some tender qualities. This is true even in popular culture now when we see the hero who cries. *Like athletes such as Lionel Messi when he left his Barcelona team.* But, in general, the rule is you have to be invulnerable and tough, you can't show weakness to each other. That's enforced by men and women. *Yes, women told my little boy that big boys don't cry. I told him crying is good for you, it's a good release.* As a culture, we need to teach those relational skills and emotional management rather than emotional repression. And I see that as one of the strongest offers that men's support organizations like the ManKind Project offer through men's groups. [173]

What did you study in college? I did two stints in college, my first stint as a designer. I started drafting and designing houses when I was a teenager and so I went to Cornell's Design and Environmental Analysis School for

Interior Design. Being a young 19 year old, very naïve, and very much not prepared for the culture of Cornell, I dropped out of school after two years. I bartended and waited tables, a kind of school of social interaction that is unique to the restaurant industry. My career path has been largely in design and marketing and writing.

I came to Massachusetts and got my degree in English with a focus on American history and 20th-century literature and philosophy. I've always been a reader and writer. My mom was also a self-help junkie, so all the books that I know, Alan Watts, M. Scott Peck's *Road Less Traveled*, Robert Pirsig's *Zen and the Art of Motorcycle Maintenance,* and Edgar Cayce books, I started stealing those books from my mother when I was a teenager.

While we're talking about education, an issue is men aren't as likely to go to universities as women. Where are all those guys that used to be in college? Feminism happened, which I think is really good. Women have recognized for decades that the fastest way to achieve economic independence and increased social power is through education. Changes happened to the global economy. Farrell* talks about this in *The Boy Crisis* in a beautiful way, regarding the way that our economy has shifted so radically. It's still changing so significantly in that we need so-called "pink-collar" workers in service, health care, aging, etc.

Manufacturing is never going to come back to the US but we haven't reached a point in our cultural evolution where it feels good to a teenage boy to say I'm going into healthcare. *Unless he's a doctor.* Unless he's going to be in charge, right. We need more nurses but our culture hasn't caught up. *It's good for everybody when men go into women's fields because the pay goes up.* Wouldn't it be wonderful if we could erase that distinction?

Even in Scandinavia, the leaders in equal gender role opportunities, it's still true that workers in STEM fields are mostly men. There's beautiful research done about early childhood routing of girls away from STEM and boys into it, and overestimation of boys abilities in STEM and underestimation of girls abilities in STEM. These outcomes start as beliefs and suggestions. *When boys get erector sets and tinker toys for spatial learning, that sends you in a different path than playing with Barbie, who used to be programmed to say, "Math is hard."*

It seems like the biggest thrust in the men's movement today is in groups like yours that provide peer-led support groups to undo limiting role socialization. Social and emotional learning is part of the work that we do in our men's groups and training programs. We can create spaces for you to go back to when you were four and give you an experience of what it feels like to get affirmation, acceptance, grief, joy, play, or anger in a healthy way in a practice space.

The groups are our practice space where we get to go and screw up, try again and screw up, try again, and continue to improve. *Do you think that women don't need to do that because they got more training from their mothers and peers on how to be more fully humanly expressive?* I think there is some truth to the idea that women and girls are socialized to be more emotionally expressive and to communicate more fully, but I think women need just as much space to do the necessary grieving work, to do the rage and the anger work, to learn how to fully express feelings in that practice space. My wife needs shadow work as much as I do. *Every human does.*

In the consciousness-raising (C-R) groups in the Second Wave of the women's movement, we learned that our feelings of inadequacy or whatever were socially-conditioned sex roles. Several organizations, including Women Within--connected to the MKP--aren't as large, but similar C-R groups are definitely still doing some of that work. In our groups, we celebrate the differences between men. The guy sitting next to me can be extremely different than me: The inquiry is how I learn to accept and celebrate him without enforcing stereotypes on him. When I express myself, that I feel shame, or fear, or sadness, and all the hands in the room go up--this is a way we acknowledge that we "get it" with other men. We see that we share so much although we can be very different.

How do you handle differences in a group, like if a man says, "I want to be a man like Trump and be able to grab women's genitalia," and the other guy is repulsed? With difficulty, honestly, since that kind of divisiveness is out there. Over the last several years, this is an area of deep ongoing investigation because being able to be in a dialectic with others who have different opinions, values, and perspectives is beautiful but very hard to do. The double whammy is most of our work doing that kind of intensity is face-to-face where I can experience your feelings and then own my judgments and feelings--not blame you. I can take all the projections back to do my own shadow work around your opinions and beliefs. That is so much harder to do in a Zoom room.

A major theme in the men's movement is father absence is a key to men's problems. The MKP webpage explains that then they turn to the media and Rambo. What do you think boys learn from video games about being a man? It's about the micro-cultures that boys end up in on those platforms. I know teens who are gamers, who have a good time and don't end up in that kind of reinforced toxic swamp, and I know other teens who do. The research on the influence of video games on violent behavior does not show that it causes violence directly, but it does show that gamer culture does indeed shape boys' opinions and sensitivities.

Both of my kids have gotten into video games at different times, but we talk about it as a family, and both of them demonstrate a willingness to push back against that kind of culture. So, while playing games is not causative, it creates a normalizing effect for that kind of dominance-based masculinity--kill it, dominate it--and I think we have a responsibility to investigate it and keep it from being pushed into shadow.

The culture of video games can be a toxic, misogynist, sexist stew that keeps boys in that "don't be like a girl" box with all of the nasty words that you can associate with that-- don't be an effing "p" word if you're not competing hard enough. The video games reinforce competition and demeaning other others with slurs about women, gay people, people of color, and beyond. My kids have been called the nastiest names in those anonymous peer situations in the gaming world, really ugly micro-cultures.

I think that the dumbing down of culture is real. The lack of healthy male role models is a problem interconnected with so many other systems: our financial systems, the way we work, and our consumer-based culture. Everything is a transaction like, "I give you this if you give me that." You don't have to go back a long way to see a culture that is more deeply interconnected and communal. *For most of human history, we were cooperative hunter and gatherer bands.* Right, and we haven't been for a few thousand years now and it's very different than it was.

My dad is 78 and he certainly didn't get taught how to relate in a healthy way when he was a child and his father died in World War II. He had a stepfather who was present in his life but emotionally disconnected. *What I found in my 50/50 Marriage book is sometimes having a really negative example is just as propelling to do the opposite as having a positive example. Your dad probably said I'm going to be an affectionate dad because I didn't get it.* Yes, that's absolutely true. I don't like to pin it on father absence as much as we don't have models for healthy relational interactions between men and boys--and between women and girls in many ways also. We need high quality and quantity time seeing what healthy adulthood and healthy relationships look like. *If the parents are working two or three jobs and they're not there or they're tired?* Not a whole lot of space there.

How did you get involved in the MKP? My brother Jay, who's 18 months younger than me, did MKP's flagship training in 1997. He was in a place of desperation in his life and it blew his mind. He told me, "You got to do this," and most of the men in my family did and are still in some orbit around MKP. I was the holdout; I was in a huge spiritual bypass. I believed that I had it all worked out and just needed my brain and my books so I didn't need to connect and open up. For seven and a half years I was in a relationship that was not healthy, which I think we both knew for a very long time, but we were unwilling to end it.

After the relationship ended, I was seeing a chiropractor. After a particularly deep adjustment, I cried on the chiropractic table. After that, the doc came out into the hall with me, and he said, "Boysen, I can see there's a lot of change happening in you. Have you ever heard of the New Warrior Training Adventure?" I laughed at him and swore at him and then I signed up to do the training. So I did that initial weekend in 2004. My wife, who was then a girlfriend, went on to do a similar weekend process called Women in Power. We entered our relationship and our early marriage actively doing shadow work with each other and separate from each other, which I think has given us a really solid platform for our connection.

Niobe Way wrote a book about how teen boys are lonely and isolated because they had to give up their close buddies because they didn't want to be seen as gay. Peggy Orenstein also found boys didn't get talked with about sex. Yes, Dr. Judy Chu and Dr. Niobe Way have research-based books, long-term studies of boys reporting that the transition from pre-adolescence where boys have loving expression and close intimacy with other boys until it gets socialized out of them. By the time they're 15, they long for that connection and closeness but the only way that they can interact with boys is hyper-competitive kinds of stuff.

Guys give each other shit. *Farrell calls it humorous put-downs. It's a form of endearment that would make me cry if my friends said it to me, but guys laugh.* They laugh on the outside. In MKP, even in this kind of banter, we can get to a point where we say stop, bring it back down, reconnect, find a different expression for each other, and then we can go back to playing.

I think our whole culture is just an experiment. In the last 200, or 100, or the last 20 years, we're doing things that human beings have not done in our entire conscious history. It's a massive social experiment we're doing on ourselves. *The positive thing I see is that Gen Z and Y are very accepting of diversity.* Yes, I think that there are a lot of positives there, but maybe we're not having as many dialogues as we could. I have opinions based on being around a lot of teens right now where I see a lot of very polarized thinking, all good, all bad, so-called "cancel culture."

There's a lack of depth, a lack of paradox there. If you do something wrong, youth don't have enough nuance in their thinking to say, "That hurt me, that had an impact on somebody else, can we work with this?" The "clique" culture that I grew up in the '80s was very well documented in the John Hughes films for Gen X and still exists. Gen Z and Ys have deconstructed gender roles and sexual orientation, but they don't have a clear understanding of self-aware ownership of their emotional state, or projections, or detachment. They demand a level of purity from those around them that we only learn to work through with maturity and hard work.

Black and white thinking is probably fairly characteristic of adolescence in general. Totally, and that's a developmental step that religion and other communal experiences used to fill. Religion gave you an understanding of right and wrong and forgiveness and redemption, while now those values are kind of gone. *It seems what fills the vacuum is the media because youth spend so much time with it.* That's right. *I'm thinking of the young adult movies like* Hunger Games *and* Divergent *where they had a female heroine who fought for justice. Is the message of those movies that you stand up for justice even if you're afraid?* Yes, that's something that I see in pop culture. There are more female heroes, there's more gender diversity in what a hero looks like, there's more communal sharing. And that's all positive. We have the Avengers; you don't have just a single superhero anymore. You have a whole diverse group of people working together, which is certainly evolutionary. But it still teaches us that in order to do something you have to dominate and destroy the enemy.

I'm familiar with some of the young adult authors who do present more full understandings of what roles boys and girls and men and women can fit into. There are a lot more men crying in the movies and on TV than there used to be, such as "The Rock," Dwayne Johnson. He's a massive man and funny, silly, playful, emotional, soft, gentle with a range of characters. There's also the phenomenon of Ted Lasso. So I think kids are getting to see a much broader range of character in some popular media.

If we're positing that media is kind of the new religion, is the message you'll be happy if you buy a lot of things? I don't think I could point a finger and say it's just about consumption because I think it's everything. What I see watching my kids on TikTok is that morality is closely tied to choices. You can go down really ugly rabbit holes and get radicalized into whatever negative thing you want by your choice. The algorithms also will show you posts that are actually moral and educational and informative, providing cultural critique analysis. Choice is the religion.

An increasing number of teens in the western world are anxious and depressed, especially girls. Do you think that's just because boys can't talk about their feelings or if you think they're not as anxious and depressed? I think they're 100% as anxious and depressed and they express it in different ways. Girls tend to internalize so that anxiety is self-inflicted, self-harming behavior, while some boys externalize in violent misogynist banter on video games or actual violence in the real world.

Do the boys have men knocking on their door to say, "Hey, what's up?" Sitting down on the edge of the bed and not saying anything is the most effective intervention that I have with my kids. Sometimes they say, "Why are you bothering me?" And then they report interactions and I say, "How'd that make you feel?" You've got to have those people willing to sit on the edge of your bed and not lecture. Men's work has helped me learn to do this! To just be present. I think the quality of time that we spend with kids is way more important in many ways than the sheer quantity of time. *What I found is that the best time is driving in a car because there aren't any distractions and a lot comes up.*

Let's go to the history of the MKP. Three men started it, although they didn't know they were creating an initiation ceremony, in Wisconsin in 1985. What I get from two living founders, Bill Kauth and Rich Tosi, is that they wanted an adventure for men. They felt they were seeing men who weren't engaging life, weren't getting into their wildness--that Robert Bly kind of stuff, the mythopoetic stuff, really opening up and digging in. So they wanted to create an adventure and pulled ideas ranging from feminist encounter groups to the hard-edge military experience that Rich Tosi had, the therapeutic stuff that Kauth had, and all of the personal development work that they had collectively been doing.

And Native American rituals. Yes. Some of that, but much of that didn't come till later, after establishing some real relationships with a particular lineage in a Native tribe. They were doing encounter group stuff where you get right up in the face. That's a seed of what's in the New Warrior Training Adventure where we create a place where men can fully express authentically what's going on for them and who they want to be in the world.

It wasn't until years later that somebody said, "You guys are doing an initiation, like a hero's journey--Joseph Campbell's approach." They didn't have that in their minds when they were putting it together. *Maybe it's some archetypal need they were tapping into.* They didn't know what they were doing but something was speaking through them. *Thinking of initiation rituals around the world, a lot of times it involves something painful like circumcision to see if you're man enough to go through it. What does that tell us about archetypes?*

Frederick Marx, a filmmaker, released a book called *Rites to a Good Life: Everyday Rituals of Healing and Transformation* where he goes down very deep into that subject. He talks about the spiritual function of rites of passage. He's done a lot of work in the Zen Buddhist community, prison community, veterans' communities, and boys' rites of passage communities. He created films about veterans and their healing experiences--beautiful work.

A rite of passage, in the indigenous sense, gives you a very clear understanding of the boundaries of "us" and not "us." If you can't prove through ritual and ordeal that you can be a healthy contributing member of the community with these rules and these boundaries, you'll no longer be a part of the tribe. But now we have to expand our idea of what the community is to include the whole planet to help us survive as a species. *We can see that the smoke from our California fires caused by climate change came to you in Massachusetts.* We are all 100% interdependent, connected to a finite planet. I also recommend Charles Eisenstein's work, *The More Beautiful World Our Hearts Know Is Possible*. He speaks beautifully about being in a time between stories.

For so much of human history, we've had stories that seem to make sense, that ground us in a sense of place and sense of society, that we understand, mostly tribal, ethnocentric, or nationalist. MKP becomes a place where I can practice getting uncomfortable and trying to come up with new stories both personal and collective. *It's like that old saying, "Think globally, act locally."* Yes, I can't just be focused on the global problems because it's overwhelming. I have to be doing my personal work, starting with sitting and breathing and learning to be in healthy relationships.

Greek fraternities and sororities provide initiation rituals for some college students, as does boot camp for people who go into the military. There's also bar and bat mitzvah in the Jewish tradition. And *quinceañera/o* for Latinx teens. There are certainly also gang rituals for initiation that serve an important social function, but lack service to something bigger than myself or my tribe. Indigenous rites of passage had that bigger picture, that very big spiritual verticality that Robert Bly talks about. *There are also Masons and Elks.* Yes, they provide elaborate rituals and I know a bunch of Eagle Scouts who've done an initiatory process. *This indicates that initiation rituals are a basic need.* Yes.

Why is alcohol so important for male bonding as in when you go to college and are supposed to drink and be sexual? Is that because you can be uninhibited and is that an initiation process? I think for boys that has a lot to do with it. Men get permission to actually tell the truth when they're drunk. The football rituals, the sports rituals, provide identification with micro-culture, like the Boston Red Sox fan base who talk while watching the game.

In MKP there's an idea that men connect shoulder-to-shoulder. *Shepard Bliss says women do face-to-face and men do side-by-side.* Yes, but in MKP a lot of the work that we do is face-to-face, knee-to-knee work. *That's scary, right?* Yes, it is scary. But for men's work, that's the price! Get uncomfortable. Do that work so you can be a more alive contributor to healing yourself and your family. We create other spaces where we can do shoulder-to-shoulder work together. It's been said in the men's movement that if you put men in a room to make cookies together it's going to turn into a men's group if you bring men together with the intention of connecting. *It's easier than if we're sitting in a circle looking at each other?* It's harder and easier.

Bill Kauth said he wanted to create an alternative to the soft masculine that people blame feminism for and create "a sense of ferocity, a hard masculine." What's the difference between hard masculine and soft masculine? To me, the beautiful pieces of so-called traditional masculinity that MKP continues are integrity, one of our core values, along with accountability, respect, and authenticity. We practice goal setting and accountability and also personal reflection.

If I've got an interpersonal conflict with somebody in MKP, my responsibility is to look at my own shadow to see the data, judgments, and feelings. There's a hardness about what a tape recorder would capture, versus my judgments, which are just my stories, not about you, but about me. There's a beautiful ferociousness in men's love of one another. I had never been in a space except for MKP where men had open-throated yelling or crying, fully-embodied, somatic expression.

MKP creates a space where a guy who has been buttoned down like me with the mask always on, thinking I was doing the right thing, as someone who was and am gentle and soft. But in MKP we create a space where you can get as fierce as you want and then learn to contain it. We let you know that you can go there and still be safe and learn how to work with that energy. I think that a lot of men who go through the New Warrior Training Adventure that's a big pop they get. I thought if I allowed myself to feel, based on what happened to me from when I was a child, then I would kill someone or I would get lost in that feeling.

I've seen men bring up that energy full force 100%, to learn they're capable of choosing to express it or pull it back. Men can learn together in men's groups a kind of strength and resiliency that I don't see anywhere else, and least of all in the most common discourses we have on social media.

Grief is another huge emotion that we see with men, for both men and women there's so much to grieve. *If men are more lonely than women, then in some ways they have more to grieve.* Yes, there's so much to grieve. I was terrified that if I went into that grieving, and I see and hear this from a lot of men, that I will never be able to come back. If I start crying I will not be able to stop. It's very important for men to have spaces to get in touch with grief, as it is for women.

MKP reports that some men have been taught to be afraid of being with other men. If I'm in a circle of men, how do I learn not to be afraid? Yes, I'll tell a story of a beautiful man I know who has been in this kind of work for many years, James Arana. At the end of one of their training programs during their graduation, with their families there, everyone seated together, he said, "Turn to the man next to you and look him in the eye and hold that gaze for a moment and know that you don't have to be afraid. You no longer have to be afraid to deeply see another man." I come to know that the man next to me has experienced the same kinds of losses, same fears, carries the same shame, carries some wounding, and has within him a little boy who just wants to play and be loved. If I see every man on the street that way, it changes how I interact.

I used to think of it in terms of violence, some man is going to jump out from the bushes, but then it occurred to me that traditionally mothers said to children, "Wait until your father comes home!" to punish you. That's the ultimate bottom line for masculinity. If you don't do what I say, I will enact violence upon you. bell hooks in *The Will to Change* states the first act of the patriarchy is not men's violence against women but men's violence against themselves. Men are taught to annihilate the tender parts of themselves. If they are unwilling to do so, then other men will enact rituals of violence upon them to get them to fit in and from that emerges so much of the pain we see around us.

I'm thinking again of the hunters and gatherers. A book About the First People *reports that they didn't do violence to each other. They had initiation rituals like when girls first get their period. This indicates that our genetic makeup is that we're programmed to cooperate with each other.* We've survived as a species because we've cooperated with each other and because we have the capacity for empathy and connection from the moment we're born. *Mirror neurons connect us.* Yes, mirror neurons, offering and getting back. Reflections are what's allowed us to survive.

The New Warrior Training Adventure (NWTA) *happens over a weekend and it's staffed one-to-one?* More than one-to-one frequently. *The idea is to go through the hero's journey as Joseph Campbell spells it out, with descent, ordeal, and return. You're not supposed to talk about the details, but what could someone expect from that weekend?* Our graphic gives you a pretty good idea of the arc of the journey of the weekend.[174] What you can expect is that you're going to be frustrated, angry, feel confronted, and that you're going to feel joyful, and happy, and laugh. It is a once-in-a-lifetime kind of space. You're going to see more expressions of men's emotions than you've probably ever witnessed in your entire life. There are parts of it when you may just want to leave. At the beginning, we don't show you everything that we're going to do but we do ask you, "Are you willing to do whatever it takes to get what you came for?" For me, by Sunday afternoon, I felt like, thank God I hung around to get through the process. There are 50 or more different processes over 48 hours. It's packed, ritual, theater, emotive, playful and it's not a retreat.

What do you find is an optimal number where growth can happen? I love trainings with 25 to 30 participants, which means you'll have about 45 staff. We have a global certification process for leaders of the NWTA to keep it safe and properly managed. We provide small group experiences, team experiences, one-to-one experiences, journaling, visualizations, and individual process work.

Who is your typical participant and what does he want? Evolution happens when there's enough stress in the environment to push it. Most men approach the NWTA by getting a call, a quiet or loud message that says, "It's time to do something about this." Often they're motivated by pain and a sense of urgency: because I'm unhappy in my job, I'm starting a new relationship and I don't have the tools I need, my marriage is falling apart, or, I have no male friends, and I want community.

In any given NWTA weekend, there's going to be a few guys in their 20s, a bunch of guys in their 30s, and the bulk is going to be late 30s to mid-40s. *Midlife crisis time.* Yes, that's midlife transition point and that's a big deal for a lot of guys. Instead of going and buying a Corvette, they come to the NWTA. MKP started very white in Wisconsin and it's still very white, which is something that we have to continuously confront and work with over time.

You have the Gateway programs for specific groups like black, Asian, youth, or men with disabilities. Yes, our first gateway training was for GBTQ (Gay, Bisexual, Trans, Queer/Questioning) men, over 12 years ago. The idea is to make the minority the majority, to create a baseline of shared experience and culture so that a man can truly see himself represented. GBTQ men will understand the lived experience of other GBTQ men. Black men and men of color in the US will have a shared understanding of racism through lived experience. This is super important, especially when the men being served might have a deep lack of trust or traumatic experiences with other men. This kind of specialized space makes the work accessible to men who otherwise just wouldn't take the risk.

A guy in midlife is going to be looking for a different outcome from a process than a guy who's in his 20s. He's much more nomadic, less anchored, more about finding a deep generational connection, more about ego-building and building himself up. They have existed in digital culture since they were two so they see the world from a different place and have different masks that they wear than a 45-year-old married guy with kids. *How much demand is there for the young men's Gateway?* They've been around for less than 10 years and I think we've done six of them. We also have open men's groups for guys who have not experienced an NWTA and a bunch of online trainings so they can get some of the skills and the connection.

After NWTA, a man can join an I-Group? Yes, in the US we have around 750 ongoing peer-facilitated men's groups, called I-Groups, for "Integration Group." Globally, we have a thousand groups, supporting 8-10,000 men a week, with a presence in 25 nations. I've been sitting in a men's group since 2004, now in my third. *The prototype model for groups is that you do rounds, everybody goes around and checks in briefly, then we go around again with a focus on a few guys?* Yes, I think men like structure. We check-in, do some accountability work--how are you doing on your goals? How are you doing on your agreements? We do individual process work--what's going on for you specifically? A member can say, "I need 15 minutes to talk about what's going on with my kids that I'm really struggling with." We bless and affirm each other; how many men in their lives get blessed and affirmed on a regular basis? *If they have good partners they do.*

Yes, but it's really important for men to not put the burden of our emotional work on our primary partners. It's not my wife's job to carry my emotional burden or do my emotional work for me. A lot of men are actually taught that if you get married, your wife gets to carry all your emotional burden as well as the housework. Society has been giving you messages to stop connecting with men in an intimate way since you were five years old. Then you get with a partner and that's where you bring your emotion. Oh, but we're not going to give you any skills to do that! *And your main job is to make money.* Yes, to provide and be dad.

In our groups, we give you a place to do that emotional work and build skills so that you can actually do the hard conversations in your primary relationships in loving and open-hearted ways and take responsibility for your own shit. Yes, women initiate 70% of the divorces in the US, why the hell wouldn't they? If they're with partners who've never been taught to deal with their own emotions, who don't have skills for a deeper relationship and communication, and who have been taught to wear a mask of invulnerability all the time--not to show themselves. If I don't know how to have self-compassion and awareness, how can I be compassionate for my partner? Without these skills, we're stuck relying on your traditional role and don't go outside of that box. Most women I know these days say screw that, I'm not willing to be in that role. *Especially because they're working.* Yes, and they have to.

What I see in terms of women's anger is that the husband is on the couch watching the game and the woman is holding the baby, cooking the dinner, and says, "Honey, can I get a little help here?" There's a lot of anger over domestic sharing of work and when the woman is angry she doesn't want to have sex with him, an unbonding mechanism. With unhealthy power differentials, you end up with men who feel resentful, disrespected, unacknowledged although I go out and work hard. *Why, even when they're both employed, do studies report that women do more of the housework and childcare?* Gender roles that we've created over the last three or four centuries are slow to change, but they are changing and have changed. *No wonder women initiate divorce; they're tired.* Totally exhausted, and I would be too.

So we're telling men this system is unhealthy, telling you to work hard and sacrifice yourself, while "soft work" is not for you. I still see this in MKP, that men really struggle with the belief that you're less of a man if you're cooking, cleaning, and taking care of your kids. There's a whole movement out there of SAHD, Stay At Home Dad, daddy bloggers who are fighting against these stereotypes who get judged not only by men but also by women--like, "what's wrong with you?"

I think that we need to give guys space and cultural acceptance to do what calls to them because there are many men who find that being close to their children and being in an intimate, loving, nurturing, connected relationship to the home and nature is hugely important. Going away to work to put food on the table is a very new thing. An older pattern is the nurturing archetype of the farmer, digging your hands in the dirt, husbandry, stewardship. These are nurturing roles and such a beautiful opportunity for men to embrace more of who we are.

The mythopoetic movement that MKP evolved from is apolitical, compared to the women's movement's focus on the political--get the vote, get the ERA passed, elect people to office to change the power differential. The biggest branch of the men's movement is about doing men's work, which is inner work, and it's not about changing the political system. I think that has largely been true, and the mythopoetic work has changed also. There is a much wider examination of how "men's work" can't be removed from the context of systems at work in the culture.

As part of the society, we can't be outside economics, human rights, mental and physical health, the environment, diversity, and all forms of oppression and violence. We have to look at it because it impacts us all. We're also always working to raise our own awareness and create safety for other groups of men. This is inherently political, but not about political parties. There is also a large branch of the pro-feminist men's movement that has a critical focus on this kind of systemic change. *They focus a lot on violence.* Yes, and on patriarchal dominance-based masculinity, looking critically at masculinity.

It seems like the most political are the father's rights after divorce custody issues men, trying to get legislative changes. What I see of the Men's Rights, MRA, movement online is that there's a lot of energy toward blaming women and feminism in general. I'm personally suspicious of anything that is blaming, or that seeks to reinforce old ways and roles of being as "natural" gender roles for men and women.

The last couple of years we've seen divisiveness and polarity and attack in that conversation around masculinity, with the idea of "toxic masculinity." To me, those characteristics we often associate with men: grit, stoicism, striving, decisiveness, even aggression--they all have a place and a positive function, for men and for women. And some of these characteristics are like salt. It's good stuff, I need it, I love it. And do I put two tablespoons of salt in a glass of water and drink it every morning? No. That's toxic. If I dominate others, it's going to hurt them. So is extreme masculinity and this kind of hardness that Paul Kivel and others talked about way back in the '80s. Masculinity can include accountability, personal responsibility, integrity, service to others, and the beautiful strength and drive of a traditional masculine role. But, if you cut off the emotionality, softness, nurturing, compassion, and empathy, then you end up with men who are more likely to die five years earlier, five times as likely to commit suicide, multiple times more likely to end up in addiction, and multiple times more likely to commit violent acts. That's what happens when we rigidly enforce a dominance-based way of being for half of the human population of the world.

In the mythopoetic men's movement, there is an idea of asking what are the stories we're telling ourselves? Let's pull them apart and let's analyze them. In mythopoetics, there's an incredible opportunity for us now to reinterpret the mythology we've been living with for a long time that has gotten radically dumbed down in consumption-based cultures.

Do you agree that the peer counseling group aspect of the men's movement is the largest in terms of participants? Certainly, yes. *What are the other big organizations that do peer counseling for men?* There are many smaller groups all over the country and the world. Other groups deal with specific populations, like in the northeast an organization called All Kings is mostly men of color who work with men who have been incarcerated. There are groups working with new fathers, with men of color through barbershop culture, with veterans, sports teams, and even a growing movement in corporate environments to support growing emotional intelligence in the workplace.

There are also Christian men's groups. *Like the Promise Keepers?* I believe they were trying to make a comeback and then the pandemic happened. The Promise Keepers got men to connect with each other and with their emotions, and that's great. However, if your mission is to reinforce old gender roles or hierarchies, is that going to work for us in the long term? There are a number of other faith-based organizations working with men that I think are doing powerful work with communities and bring healing to men's hearts.

You wrote that movements fail because of the lack of mature bonding, the kind of connection that allows groups to overcome personal and psychological blocks, and resolve interpersonal conflicts in a way that's energizing rather than draining their efforts. How would you advise activist groups not to split into those kinds of factions? "No Mud, No Lotus" is a Zen saying meaning you have to get into the mud, you have to dig down. We call that shadow work, unconscious work, emotional work.

This is something I've seen in the nonprofit world and in the activist world. They care about other people but then they get them into the environment of the nonprofit world and find head games, power and control, and that demand for purity. If I can get honest and if I'm doing my own shadow work, then I ask what am I projecting onto you and then own it. Doing the deeper level of emotional, vulnerable work is the space of relationship, the space of connection.

I have been in the academic and the nonprofit world for most of my life and academics are so disconnected. It often feels like academics are in their heads much of the time. I get that, I'm like that, but I've come to believe that full integration of the mud, the shadow, and the aspirations have to be part of the conversation. Those are long, slow, often painful conversations that most of us are unwilling to do; I think that's what movements end up lacking. Claiming moral superiority from any side of the spectrum damages our collective ability to move forward.

Lee Mun Wah
Asian American Men's Group: Walking Each Other Home

I wrote this during the George Floyd incident:

Sometimes you can't believe it's happening when someone stands up and shares their story. At first, it surprises everyone and then you realize that what they're sharing isn't happening to just one person, but to lots of other folks who have been silenced or made to doubt themselves. The beauty of when it is finally spoken out loud is that it is so disarmingly honest. So real that you can't even touch it because it feels so fragile and rare. And when it is spoken purely from the heart, it resonates a certain kind of eloquence, because throughout history it has always been known by one word--truth.

I was born at 5:31 a.m. on October 25, 1946. When I see that date nowadays, it seems so ancient, maybe because it really was a long time ago. I came into this world the fourth oldest and the second youngest (just checking to see how good your math is) with five houses in Scorpio.

Before I was born, my parents came up with my Chinese name Lee Mun Wah, which means he who writes. How prophetic, because I eventually became a poet and writer. But, on the day I was born my parents wrote "Gary Lee" on my birth certificate. My father did so because when he came to his country from China and presented the immigration officials with his name: Lee Hoo Wah, they promptly gave him a supposedly easier name to pronounce: Richard Lee. My father was shocked but surmised that this must be because he needed an "American" name. What he did not realize until much later in life, was that this was a common practice by whites of anglicizing names from other countries outside of the US.

Up to the age of 38, I was known as Gary Lee until something dramatically occurred in my life. A good friend of mine, Spencer Brewer, invited me to a sweat lodge in Idaho. I had never been to a sweat lodge, let alone Idaho. It was one of the most excruciating and inspiring experiences in my whole life. When we exited the lodge, we formed a large circle led by a member of their tribe. He had each of us say our name and then the whole group would say it out loud in unison. When it came time for a young man to say his name out loud, he said, "David," but with a sadness in his voice and then everyone repeated it the same way. The tribal leader asked David to share why he spoke his name with such sadness. He replied that he hated his name and always wanted to be called Michael. And so the group said Michael and he was elated.

Hearing this birthing process, I wondered what would happen if I told everyone my real name. So, when it came to my turn, I said Lee Mun Wah out loud for the first time and then everyone repeated it in perfect unison. When I heard it out loud, every part of my body and soul responded with so much emotion and awe. From that moment on, I reclaimed my birthright and in doing so, my life changed forever.

In 1985 I created the only Asian Men's Group in the United States dealing with racism, anger, and leadership. I started this particular men's group because the men's movement consisted mostly of white men celebrating and studying primarily white archetypes. What was missing were authentic conversations around racism, classism and ethnic identity. I remember confronting Robert Bly about this omission and he responded that he didn't think there was a need. In some respects, he was right because there were very few men of color in the men's movement. However, it was his and many of his trainer's ambiguity and lack of curiosity as to why we were so few that I had difficulty with.

From my perspective, as a Chinese American man, the men's movement's only real representation of men of color was for entertainment at best. There was no pressing reason for whites in the men's movement to learn or talk about racism because there were so few men of color. As someone so aptly shared with me recently: "Not knowing how white privilege works, is how white privilege works." Even the men of color who were attending had long ago learned the art of 'blending in' with white culture or what I call "the art of accommodation."

I started the first Asian men's group not to counter the men's movement, but to offer an alternative, a place where Asian men could feel safe enough to be fully themselves, not having to imitate whites in order to be accepted. Many of the changes I created made my counseling supervisor nervous because they were often contrary to traditional therapy and counseling practices.

One major change was having the groups in my home. I have often thought that "white offices" often feel detached and lacking in any "cultural feel" to them. For many BIPOC [Black, Indigenous, and People of Color], seeing culture adorned throughout a room brings us comfort and a feeling of being welcomed and at ease. To me, if we are really truly multicultural, why don't Europeans display their cultures in their classrooms and offices. Why only BIPOC? It's as if the unspoken message here is that Europeans are already seen and accepted as the true "Americans" and don't need to have it proven or questioned. Whereas BIPOC, even we may be born here, are still seen as outsiders, aliens, and immigrants simply because the color of our skin is not white.

Having meals together: Ah, such a warm thought, isn't it? Then, why are we, as therapists, so shy to integrate it into our groups? To many BIPOC, food is connected to family and community. It's not just a "diversity celebration" but an expression of caring and sense of being a family. One of our rituals was to have dessert halfway through the session. Usually, someone brought a pie or something special for us to share. I don't how, but my son, Joaquim, always knew when it was the time for dessert because he was always there jumping up on one of the men's laps and opening his mouth waiting for a taste of paradise!

Another special ritual was our Acknowledgement Ceremony held at the end of each year. This was a special occasion where each man in the group could invite his parents, friends, and siblings to come acknowledge them for what they meant to them and for any changes/goals they had achieved as well as any obstacles they had overcome. I created this because I often felt (from my own experiences) that we overachieve because we feel inadequate, not good enough, or not successful enough. Usually, this comes from our childhood where we lacked support or praise and love was conditional. Another reason is that often when a person has passed away, we regret that we didn't share with them how much we loved and cared about them. So this was a way to afford everyone an opportunity to do just that.

As you might have expected, the response was overwhelming. One father, with tears, shared how he wished his father had done what he just did with his son who was in the group. He shared how he stayed at a job that he hated because it was prestigious in the eyes of his father. But his father never said anything so he got a bigger house and a new car every year. Eventually, his father died without him ever knowing if he was proud of him or not. In retrospect, why do we always wait until someone dies or retires before we let them know how much we appreciate and value them? So, what do you wish you could hear?

One of the major goals of my creating the Asian Men's Group was for the men to feel comfortable with anger. Part of our Asian culture frowns upon expressing our anger in public.

It's considered disrespectful and a reflection on our family. Unfortunately, in this Western culture, our lack of visceral and verbal anger as Asians is often seen as being passive, sneaky, hiding something, or lacking in assertiveness and leadership qualities. This is best exemplified in the surge of recent anti-Asian violence throughout the country and the myth that we won't or can't fight back. Hence, a perpetuation of our shame and feeling that we somehow lack the courage or physical fortitude to defend ourselves and those we love.

However, another interesting aspect of this story came quite unexpectedly when I started the group in 1985. I had expectations of talking about racism and the stereotypes we as Asian men faced, but instead, the men wanted to talk about their relationship struggles with their partners. Hence, a reminder to once again: Begin where they are, not where you want them to be. So, for the next two years, we dealt with the issue of anger in their relationships. Each of the men had a common thread to all their stories about their partners: Their partners were constantly angry with them and they felt victimized and threatened. Now, in reality, this was all true. But, there was another aspect to their stories--what ignited their partner's anger. In each incident, the more the men retreated from their partner's anguish, the more their partner's anger escalated. Hence, a vicious circle was created.

What none of their family counselors asked was: How much of this was cultural? You see, what we were faced with here was a conflict of cultures: Damned if you do and damned if you don't. For a long time, I struggled with how to approach this dilemma. One day I said to all the men: "You can't passionately say yes unless you have learned to say no." I'm not sure where I got this from, but for the moment I had all the men's attention! Their assignment was to practice saying no briefly and directly. In other words, I wanted them to practice being petty and self-centered, caring only about themselves. This is totally foreign in the Asian culture which trains us to be eternal caretakers. The problem with that philosophy is that we often put ourselves second. Another negative aspect of saying "no" is our fear of hurting the other person's feelings. This is the opposite of the Western male way of thinking, which is to always speak up for what you want or risk being viewed as less than a man.

With a lot of practice in the group and with their partners, a miracle happened. Their partners stopped getting mad at them. When we had our Acknowledgement Ceremony, their partners shared how they no longer had to be seen as the "angry out of control one" since the anger was balanced and their anguish was a shared responsibility. Also, no one died or was devastated from hearing "no," which gave them the opportunity to passionately say "yes" again.

Another important point needs to be made here. This American culture acknowledges Asians for being such wonderful "team players" and "trustworthy," but when it comes to promotions we are often seen as not aggressive enough or able to handle conflicts. This is called the "glass ceiling." We are trained to be docile and quiet because whites often whisper into our ears: "I'm so glad you're not like those people (usually referring to blacks) who are loud and troublemakers." In other words, we're loved as long we know our place. Once again, damned if we do and damned if we don't.

Another important step for our Asian group was to talk about and confront the racism that we had all experienced. This took a lot of practice and years to deal with. One day, I received an invitation from an all-white men's group that wanted to meet with our Asian men's group. I shared this information with the men in my group and there was a lot of hesitation. It took months of discussion back and forth about the conditions that needed to be agreed to before meeting. One of the conditions that our group insisted on was that they wanted to decide on what would make them feel safe being in a room with all whites since that was a privilege often only afforded white men.

At one point, one of the Asian men wanted the white men to wait at the door and only come in one by one when their names were called. He did this because he wanted the white men to experience what it was like to be alone and feeling powerless in a room with no one who looked like them. The second condition was much more painful. He wanted each white man to come in on their knees crawling, just like they had disrespected and demeaned his father. As he shared this, he couldn't stop crying. Eventually, he relented because he realized that he didn't want to do to them what had happened to his father. He wanted them to see by their example how whites could be welcoming and open to those who were different from themselves.

Needless to say, it was the process that was the most difficult: The first step always is. As I wrote in all my handbooks: "We are only one question away from being connected; from learning about one another's journey. And that one question only comes about when we are willing to be open to hearing another truth outside our own."

Eventually, word got out about our group and I was acknowledged by the American Psychological Association for my outstanding work in the field of diversity and group process. I later filmed a weekend with our group entitled: *Stolen Ground,* which won honorable mention at the San Francisco Film Festival. I facilitated the group for ten years, fifty weeks a year. I also started a Multicultural Men's Group.

From there, I went on to do many other films, the most notable ones: *The Color of Fear, Last Chance for Eden* and *If These Halls Could Talk.* Oprah Winfrey did a one hour special on *The Color of Fear* and its cast, viewed by over 15 million viewers. Since then its been viewed by over 30 million folks from around the world. Cornel West calls *The Color of Fear* the best film on racism in the 21st century.

Other useful StirFry Seminars and Consulting diversity materials are: *What Stands Between Us* (over 500 questions that whites and BIPOC are afraid to ask each other), *Let's Get Real: What people of color can't say and whites won't ask about racism,* and *The Art of Mindful Facilitation by Lee Mun Wah* (my experiences/case studies/exercises created over 25 years as a diversity trainer).

Owen Marcus
Co-Founder of EVRYMAN

I was born in June 1953 in Vermont and grew up in the Northeast. *Geminis often have many projects and like to communicate. Do you identify with any of that?* All the above. I have a lot of planets in Gemini and so I'm that way mentally. *What about your background and your master's in public health?* I'm not trained as a therapist but I did a lot of post-graduate training in therapy and I've trained therapists and psychiatrists.

I grew up not knowing I had Asperger's, dyslexia, dyspraxia (motor-learning difficulties), and ADHD, so part of what got me into all this work with men was first working on myself and healing the majority of those problems. *Greta Thunberg says that Asperger's helps her focus because sometimes they don't pick up people's emotions. How does that work in your work as a coach?* Traditionally, medical professionals misread a lot of it, as with so many things, but they're starting to get a little better. They thought that people with Asperger's were unaware and disconnected. We can be disconnected but, regarding being unaware, it's actually the opposite.

We're so hyper-aware that we get overloaded, which is part of the hyper-focus. For better or worse, I've always been aware of people's emotions. Through everything I've done in terms of homework, studying with some amazing people, and tens of thousands of hours of working with men, I learned to read people really well in a way that's non-judgmental. Because I was so dysfunctional, I have a lot of patience for others.

In what ways were you dysfunctional? In the traditional Asperger's and dyslexic ways, I was pretty checked out and I was very tense. I got into all this over 40 years ago because a roommate of mine in Boulder, Colorado had given up his law practice to move to Boulder to study to be a Rolfer. He argued his case so well that he convinced me to get Rolfed, which changed my life. I learned to be a Rolfer, spent four years studying Rolfing and a lot of other leading psychosomatic psychotherapies, starting out in Boulder in the latter part of the '70s. That ended up being the foundation of my healing and co-founding EVRYMAN.

Why do you think it is that way more boys are diagnosed with ADD, ADHD, Asperger's, learning disabilities--the whole gamut? Guys are much more physically based so getting the average boy to sit still can be torture, as it was for me. When we went into the industrial revolution, we trained people to work in factories and developed an educational system very similar to that. I don't think the system works for anyone and it certainly doesn't work for boys. Also, because fathers and uncles and other men left home, the family, the farm, and the community to work, women were left to raise boys.

As a consequence--and this is no conspiracy--boys picked up a more feminized model of emotionality. Most of us have been raised more by women; our teachers and therapists have been women, so we have this innately more feminine perspective on emotionality. It's not a bad one and it's not like a conspiracy that women are trying to take over, it's something that happened naturally. It's not that guys were trying to leave the home, they had to. So for me and for all these guys we work with, we find if we put a group of guys together, innately and without any training, they start training themselves.

My belief, and now my experience, is that instinctually we know how to connect, we know how to be emotional as men. When we put men together, guys get to learn and screw up and teach each other through the consequence of interacting in an authentic way. We teach each other how to be emotional as men. Inevitably, women love it because women are really good at telling us, "No, you're not getting it," but they're not as good at telling us how to get it right. They are good at telling us when we do get it right. After a couple of months, guys in our groups or coaching start to pick this up through interacting with other men. When they go home, they start to relax and open up because they're relaxed. Their relationships often turn around because the guy is being a guy.

You mentioned feminized emotional approaches. What's the difference? I would say it's 10% to 20% different. Many years ago, from working with guys and studying the research about men, I created the Masculinity Quotient test.[175] After working with men for years, I saw that there were emotional intelligence qualities that are more critical for men in order to succeed. The five qualities are on top of all the general EI qualities that started with Daniel Goleman, based on the work of Peter Salovey and John Mayer. Now that's changing as women enter the world that men have been dominating for years, but I think this is still more critical for men.

The quality that stands out the most for me is assertive vulnerability. I'm a huge fan of vulnerability, which is essentially what we're doing with guys. We allow them to be vulnerable by creating safe spaces and letting them work with each other or stumble through it.

What works for both men and women is the ability to be open, to be vulnerable, and at the same time take a stance. Often that assertive vulnerability shows up most powerfully in relationships. What clicked that trait for me was many years ago I was dating a woman who lived in Canada. "Sue" and I were talking on the phone and she kept ramping up her complaints about me and the relationship. My internal dialogue was, "I can't take this but if I say something I'm going to end the relationship," but I had to say something.

I said, "Look, Sue, this might be true for you but it's not true for me and I can't stand for this since in my part of the relationship it's not true," then I shut up. I thought that she was going to break up with me but she told me, "Honey, you melted me." She felt me standing up, not for myself, but standing up for the relationship, with the vulnerability of being open but taking a stance. However, many men don't know how to do it in a way that's not really hard or macho.

What are the other four traits? Being an emotional entrepreneur. I work a lot with entrepreneurs and find they're smart people who take smart risks. If something doesn't work, they change and learn as they go. When guys are able to do that emotionally, when we're able to take risks and learn from the feedback of the interaction, we really improve. This requires the ability to take the risk and be willing to make mistakes, but a lot of men are afraid to take the risk and also afraid to make mistakes because, unlike an entrepreneur, they don't believe they can recover from a mistake. The other traits are having a man's back, deep purpose, and holding space.

You make the point that our childhood is formative in developing our attitudes towards ourselves, so what was your experience with your father? My father was closed emotionally and didn't communicate. I knew he loved me but there was no real expression of affection, no "I love you." He traveled a lot so that added to the disconnection and now, looking back, he had insecure attachment because he didn't connect with me or my mother.

Jed Diamond thinks that our cells are different because yours are XY and mine are XX and women's brains are more empathetic as a general trend and men's more system-oriented. Do you agree with the importance of our physiological differences?* Yes, there's science that supports that. Some of it is biological and a lot of it is the culture. EVRYMAN found when we create a safe environment and give men some simple tools and support, they learn what is biologically instinctive in them. Be it in their genes or in the epigenetics, men can learn what was not taught to them or their ancestors pretty quickly when given the right environment.

What I think doesn't work is when we tell men how to be, because men don't like to do things that we can't win at, so a lot of guys give up. Now, they're giving up more and more because they sense that the program they were given doesn't work for them. We're getting two options; one is that we're hyper-masculine, we're macho, which fewer guys want to be as those archetypes are dying off. The other one, which has almost gotten too much support, is hypersensitive. I really perfected that years ago and it's safer but ultimately for most guys pretty unfulfilling, just as it is for most women. *You're saying that the five traits bloom when men are with other supportive men?* Yes, the fast track is finding the right kind of environment in which to meet. What happens is they take the best of both of the archetypical extremes, the sensitivity and assertiveness, and put it together as assertive vulnerability that works for everyone and creates empathy.

When I work with companies, I first work with creating a safe environment. I'm working with a lot of white men who everyone wants to change for obvious reasons, but what they miss is you can try to force change as we've been doing to men and it works for a short term, but it backfires as they resist directly or indirectly. I aim to make it safe for these white men to be vulnerable, to do the things you want from them for themselves rather than to perform. The research talks about how men are in a performance box or trap where we're reinforced and complimented on our ability to perform--but not in an emotional relationship way. Particularly when we're performing at something we're not good at, such as connecting to our feelings as a woman would, it's stressful and it creates a survival response, which shuts down our ability to connect.

Around 70% of divorces in the US are initiated by women, who often say he doesn't listen to me, he's on the couch, he doesn't do his fair share of family work. I think that's true on a symptomatic level but to borrow something from attachment theory of Emotionally Focused Therapy (EFT), most guys in the emotional realm are avoiders, they disconnect. What I teach is the application of attachment theory comes down to the survival response--fight, flight, or freeze. Most guys either check out or they freeze, which is another form of leaving. Then the woman gets more irritated and becomes the pursuer, so the guy backs away further and further. Then the woman pursues the divorce.

Often when a guy joins one of our groups or trainings or a platform, they come because they feel like they have a gun to their head, either they do this or therapy or they won't have a marriage or relationship. After a while, they're in there for themselves, so they're enjoying it and seeing all these secondary and tertiary gains. They go home to their partners and say, "Honey, let's do therapy together and this and that," and she asks, "What in the hell happened to you? Six months ago I couldn't get you off the couch and had to threaten divorce for you to do anything, while now you're pushing me?" And he answers, "Yes, I really want a relationship here."

What are your suggestions for how to keep romance alive in a marriage over time? The biggest thing is vulnerability. I often send my guys and their partners to EFT therapists so that they have someone to guide them and teach them. It's like giving someone a tennis racket and saying, "Go out and play tennis," but you have to train the person. We expect people to succeed in relationships although the only training we've had is models of dysfunction. Each person has to have a source of renewal in his or her own life as well as a source of renewal within their relationship, excitement that is not flat and consistent. Maintaining your physical health is crucial.

Sue Johnson, the founder of EFT, observed that the common pattern is the woman pursues emotionally and the man runs away. If someone is in a pattern like that, what can they do to get out of that vicious cycle? My partner is an EFT therapist and we teach the EFT workshop. My approach is to down-regulate because as long as you're in a stress response, you're going to see everything as a threat. What I tell people is that your individual survival strategy takes over and then your relationship survival strategy takes over like a virus. It's like we disassociate and our PTSD response takes over. We might understand it, but it's not going to change until we can down-regulate it.

What Sue and EFT therapists are really good at is getting people to feel and express their vulnerable feeling rather than the reactionary feeling. If I express my vulnerable feeling, immediately you're going to down-regulate because you instinctively feel that Owen's being vulnerable, so he can't be a threat. *In your book,* Grow Up: A Man's Guide to Masculine Emotional Intelligence, *what kind of strategies do you give men who don't have access to a group?* No man has to do it on his own; we literally have men from all over the world since our membership is really cheap.

I've met a lot of guys, including myself in the beginning, who couldn't feel their emotions, so the core of what I teach men is to feel your body. I was coaching a client who got it really quickly that if he could feel his physical response, he was set up to feel his emotional response. Most guys like me, if you asked me what I felt, I rolled my eyes, and asked, "What do you mean, what do I feel?" It's like you're speaking a different language. In a group when a more senior guy asks, "Joe, what do you feel with your leg?" "I'm tapping my foot." "You notice that? Great." "What do you feel with your hand?" "I guess my fist is clenching."

After a couple of minutes of getting him to feel his body, we ask, "What do you feel, emotionally?" He says, "I'm angry." Getting guys to feel their body is going in through the back door of awareness and I haven't met a guy who couldn't feel something in their body.

Do they shut down because they were trained not to act like women? I think that's part of it; it's often serial micro-traumas or stressful events that cumulatively have the same effect as a major trauma. Either way, what happens is when we can't fight or flight, we can't defend ourselves, our third instinctual option is to freeze. All mammals have this ability. As kids when we didn't have agency, and we couldn't do some form of fighting or running, we checked out or we froze. In some ways, the least of it is the feminine influence, but that adds to it, so you get all these compounding factors. The biggest is the trauma of childhood, growing up in a family where there's no secure attachment since having no real connection is traumatic for a kid.

This stress causes a man to disassociate and disconnect from his body and his emotions and move into fixing, doing, thinking, analyzing, and taking action. We get reinforced in a positive way for doing those things, for fighting the wars, being the grunt at the factory, figuring things out, and being stoic. We want to succeed, so we do those actions but we're not fulfilled; we're unhappy. We're conditioned to be disconnected and we're tired with stress, while the person we want to connect with is doing her thing. She's triggered by wanting us to be there for her, but we're not there, and it starts to disintegrate. Guys are lost, they don't have anyone to connect to, anyone to explain it to them. They feel trapped because they don't see a way out.

We provide global community calls every week or two with guys from all over the world, and we put them in little breakout groups on Zoom where they hear another guy has a similar problem. Every guy is blown away because that's how disconnected we are from other men in any authentic way.

It seems like the pattern is women are angry, the men are withdrawn, the women blame the men and the men withdraw more. Right, women are very angry, often for good reason, and men withdraw for good reason. Sue Johnson says the woman is protesting and the guy is withdrawing because he doesn't want to argue because when he does he loses. But as she feels him withdraw, she's more scared, and so it's a vicious cycle.

When we do couples retreats, we break off the couples into their separate relationship outside in private places. As I walk around, I say, "Great, let's unpack this." I see the guy is trying but getting more withdrawn and resistant because it's a no-win situation for him. I validate both of their experiences so they both start to relax and I remind them that you're both in survival response and relationship survival. Let's down-regulate it.

I may channel Joe and tell Sally what Joe is really feeling in a vulnerable way, like, "The first thing I hear when I come home is I didn't take the garbage out again, which deflates me, and when I try to say something you complain and that really hurts." I tell her, speaking for Joe, "Sally, I really want to connect," using some of the details of their relationship and she starts crying because she's hearing what she's always needed to hear. Sometimes, he's crying too because he's hearing what he's always felt. Then I say to Joe, "I want you to pick it up where I left it off. I'm going to help you. When you say it this way look at her and notice when you get it right she relaxes, but when you start to go back to your own pattern of withdrawal she tenses." That gives them hope.

Joe never learned how to communicate that way and when he's under pressure, he's certainly not going to learn. Me and every guy I know has performance anxiety because we don't perform well in a vulnerable way when we're under stress. The EFT therapists intervene, like I do, to unpack the cycle and help each partner speak in a vulnerable way and the other partner to hear it and give feedback in a vulnerable way. This creates new neural pathways, gives them a new model, and they start to literally feel the connection they had when they fell in love.

A friend of ours, Esther Perel, is probably the most popular therapist out there. She speaks nine languages and has written several best-selling books, such as *State of Affairs* talking about infidelity. She says we're really excited when we fall in love, but we want security and then when we get it, we get bored. She says the biggest cause of infidelity is boredom, so I try to use vulnerability to rekindle excitement and find that usually works--because in the beginning of a relationship you have vulnerability. In the beginning, I don't know if you're going to throw me out or what's going to happen, which is scary, exciting, unpredictable, a turn-on that keeps us engaged. She would say a lot of what we're dealing with is human nature, or we can call it biology, or psychology, or culture, but it's not pathology. She and I would say to this guy, "Go and have fun, look at kids having fun; if they're not having fun they do something else."

In my 50:50 Marriage *and* 50:50 Parenting *books, parents said after having kids, they had to go outside their home, even to a motel in town for a night, to make things interesting.* Yes, and more particularly with Covid when couples work together at home, there's a lot more strain on the relationship although every relationship needs some distance.

How does this emotional impingement on boys relate to the fact that now girls are more likely to go to university and graduate around the world? Young men are giving up because they've been told to behave in a way that is not natural for them, but they don't even know what is natural and how to be. You get someone like author Jordan Peterson saying that young men are lost. They listen. Young men are hungry for what they never got--models and direction.

Also, the whole educational system is being questioned, particularly now with Covid. Some guys are thinking I don't want to become a professional by spending all my time sitting behind a desk in school. Young women trying to date or to find guys who can match them have become in some ways more masculine than some men, which is confusing for both. I don't like to use the terms "femininity" or "masculinity" because they can be self-limiting and they change.

The men's movement grew on the coattails of the women's movement and now there's a new men's lib movement where men are rebelling in different ways, often more unconscious than deliberate. *So they're saying I don't feel good in the system so I'm not going to work hard to fit in.* Right, and I'm not going to date or get married. *I'm going to play video games.* Exactly, and hang out with my video games. *That's sad.* It is and it's like men are starving and they don't even know they are because we've been generationally starving for so long.

It's the water we've been swimming in has gotten worse as the water is draining out of the pond. When you give these men new experiences, it's like the first time they ever had a real meal. They feel now I have hope; we teach them how to do that for themselves and then with other guys, which it's actually fun, it's like their new video game.

In terms of youth issues, teens are increasingly depressed and anxious, especially girls. Is that because there's more permission for girls to talk about their feelings? Also, many teens are questioning their gender and sexual orientation. It's a bigger issue with the collective toxins in our culture from physical to environmental to emotional. Questioning the model of what it is to be human, let alone a man or a woman, accompanies the transformation of our institutions. Also, their parents aren't really there for them because they have to work so hard to make it and they're stressed out. We need to look at the chronic complex systemic issue. In some ways, this generation is canaries in the mine, showing how dysfunctional and toxic society is. Society's approach is: give it a diagnosis and give it a drug. *Yes, give the boy Ritalin and give the girl an antidepressant.* Right, the girl gets slowed down and depressed and the boy gets hyperactive.

Let's talk about the men's movement. Where does EVRYMAN fit in and how did you get involved with forming it? I did all this study and work on myself for decades. About 25 years ago, I turned the corner on a lot of my challenges but I wasn't having the kind of relationships I wanted with women. I've always been a guy who thought out of the box and I thought about being in a men's group. I didn't want to do that at all, but I thought that's probably a sign I should do it.

In 1995, I called up an old friend who knew about men's groups. I participated in a training and a group; neither was really impressive but it was enough. I helped start the first real men's group in Sonoma and Napa County in California. I moved to Idaho and 17 years ago decided to redesign the model, based on everything I've learned, to a group that's fun and different. I asked 11 guys and they all said yes, and for 17 years they've been my beta testers. We've had over 300 men through the group and have three ongoing groups in a town of 8,000 in Stanford, Idaho. I do it via Zoom with 40 guys. The groups have changed lives and saved men's lives. They did a documentary on us several years ago, *About Men*, filming a man saying if it wasn't for the group, he wouldn't be alive. It saved marriages and relationships, changed careers, and created a community for these men. Also, *The Work* documentary features Eldra Jackson, a brilliant guy. He has a great TEDx.[176] We've worked with men who do similar work.

I started getting requests to help other guys start groups and a little over four years ago, we started EVRYMAN. I keep refining the pedagogy about how we can help men, simply based on the physiology of our body, the physiology of emotions, and guys relate to it. Science backs it up and most guys say I can understand it, I can apply it. *It makes sense that starting with the body follows from your Rolf training, there's coherence to your development.*

Originally, there were four of us and now there are two of us. Lucas runs the organization as our CEO and I'm the mad scientist who comes up with the training and courses. Now we have a whole cadre of guys out training other men. I realized years ago in my clinic that most men will not do something until they're in so much pain that the pain is greater than the fear of relationships--either losing it or never getting one. They stay in the group because they like the brotherhood and life keeps evolving.

About how many men have been through EVRYMAN during these four years? Until Covid, we did live training of about a hundred groups around the world, maybe 50 trainings, and over 800 guys in our membership without any direct marketing. We also have guys join via phone calls and those who read our newsletter. Now we're pivoting to be a virtual company. I didn't think that virtual groups would be as powerful as they've proven to be with guys changing their lives. A man in his 50s who owns a successful business in New York City told me, "I'm telling guys I love them and I haven't told people in my family that." A lot of guys are hungry for connection so, with the right environment, most guys eat it up.

Do you see EVRYMAN in the lineage of Robert Bly's inner warrior work? No, although I've had training in that stuff. It's not that I'm against the archetypes because I've studied and even taught that stuff, but it tends to be top-down, while my approach has always been bottom-up, starting with the body, experience, and emotions. Rather than have your mind be the determiner, let experience be the determiner. Then re-frame that by taking all the pieces that were disconnected and giving them a new way to unify all the dissident pieces.

I put our lineage in somatic psychotherapy; one of my first teachers was Ron Kurtz who started Hakomi therapy.[177] Ron came out of the lineage of bioenergetics and Bowen. The aim is to have a body express emotions and Ron brought in mindfulness, which was new to that model. I was in his first professional training where one of us would stand up and he would ask a few questions. Sometimes within a minute or two, that person was sobbing on the floor because Kurtz knew the breathing in their body and what to ask to have that person connect to what they were disconnected from. He was like a shaman wizard and I didn't understand it and I slowly integrated it until I understood it.

My other main teachers were Peter Levine, Ph.D., who wrote the book on trauma and was originally a Rolfer; and Dr. Ron Kurtz of the Hakomi Institute; and Stephen Gilligan,

Ph.D., a lead teacher of Ericksonian hypnotherapy. It was 1980 when Levine first explained it and that became the core of everything I've done since.

Is there a profile of men who tend to be attracted to EVRYMAN? The last number I saw was 44 is the mean age. We tend to get guys in crisis with two inflection points. A guy gets out of school in his 20s and wants adventure until one day he wakes up and wants to settle down, have a real job, a real family, a real relationship--but he doesn't know how to do it. Until then his biggest source of education has been his peers, but they don't know how to do it either.

Guys at the other end of that cycle created their professional success but they come home one night and no one's there, sometimes literally but usually more metaphorically. They miss their children because they were working and now they feel remorse. They get to support the younger men, which is healing for the older men. Now, we get guys from different races and sexual orientations. We have a drop-in group for black men and one for gay men, but generally, it's heterosexual men from all over the world, but most of them are from North America.

I'm struggling to find young men who are interested in the men's movement and "gender liberation." Do you think that they're not in a place of being in a crisis so they aren't interested? Older men are applying our history and our prejudices onto these young men so they're not interested in a man's movement. They are interested in equality and diversity but not through the lens of the men's movement. They're not interested in being told what to do and that's a lot of what the men's movement was because men at that time thought that's what they needed.

Younger men want a context, a framework, and tools to figure it out with their cohort. One reason that EVRYMAN exploded was young men were hungry for it. They were bright, very successful, really happy in the way of being connected but not attracted to the other men's groups out there. They're doing everything that the men's movement would want them to do without thinking about it or calling it a men's movement.

It seems like a lot of the passion in the men's movement is father's rights after divorce as well as concern about father absence. What do you think has to change so that men can be more involved fathers? We can tell people what to do but that doesn't usually work; giving them the tools is better. It's hard for a man to want to be a husband, or let alone a father when he's never had any real connection to learn how to create it.

Guys tend not to want to do something if they can't win it or they don't believe that they can succeed at it. So by creating real connection in these groups, you give them a sense of contributing to other men through that connection. They feel I have support, community, my group, so I'm not alone in doing this. For most guys, the only source of emotional connection or support is their wife or their partner, which even in the best relationship is a burden. Their families look forward to the guy going every week because they get direct and indirect benefits.

In our groups, everyone checks in at a couple of levels, and then if one guy wants to work, he gets a chance to focus on his feelings. Guys need safety and a basic structure. Women need safety but they don't need the structure. *That's not true for me as a J" on the MBTI.* We say these are the rules and this is the structure and then the guys relax. A few times we brought in women in different capacities and they're blown away with how vulnerable these men are, how authentic they are. That's because it's safe, there's an agreed-upon structure.

We talk about logistical things, then we do a somatic meditation that gets guys to slow down into their body for about five minutes. It resets everyone and we get a big return on those five minutes. Each guy speaks about what he feels in his body, in his emotions, in two simple sentences that get things moving. The next round, every guy goes a little longer and gets to talk about what's happening with him. The first round is what's happening in that moment, while the second round is what's happening in our life. The third round maybe one or two guys get to do some work to get supported. The fourth round is a quick checkout round that completes the meeting.

I was in the NOMAS, which ran beautiful meetings because they were structured like that, with a timed agenda, check-ins at the beginning, evaluations at the end, and it worked beautifully. Yes, we create the external structure so that we can allow for chaos in the center of the meeting. Guys are able to bring all that because it's safe and we have a structure and they know that whatever happens a meeting stays in the meeting.

Any other thoughts about how we can help men be full human beings? Have compassion and patience for men because even when it looks like we're not trying to connect, we want to. Women often are critical of men because we're not doing it in the way that women expect. How we communicate vulnerability is not how women do it, but give a guy a little patience, and reinforce the positive. Telling him he's not doing something right doesn't work. Realize that in spite of how macho or how angry or withdrawn he might be, he's still sensitive. Even guys who look like they've given up, usually haven't given up. If they see hope and they get some simple tools, they'll show up and do their best to make the relationship work.

Do you know of any cultures that do a better job than we do of raising boys and letting men be full human beings? In general, the more primitive the culture, probably the better job they're doing. *Because they have initiation ceremonies and age groups?* They're more tribal, more connected in that the whole community raises the kids, which is how humans have been until the last few hundred years. In general, we tend to be disconnected in the West, while the more nature-based cultures tend to be more connected to nature and each other.

When I was in Cuba, a woman said to me, "You have so many material things but we have family, friends, we dance, we enjoy life." When guys get into a group, it becomes their little tribe and micro-community. Our ancestors used to go out on hunting parties, being together, and we need that. Statistics show that the older the guy gets, the more lonely he is and the fewer friends he has. The biggest suicide swath is guys in their 50s because they're so alone, particularly in rural communities, and it's a downward spiral.

College fraternities are like that tribal age group support system--are they helpful? Yes, but we've seen that there's a dysfunctional part to it too. Like the military provides community for men, as does the paramilitary like the fire department when they live together, and the police department, or sports teams, but most guys have no support groups, especially as they get older.

Eric Schneider, Germany
Sacred Sensuality, Adulthood, and Youth Leadership

I was born in Western Germany on the 27th of July 1971. I'm a Leo with a Sagittarius ascendant, and moon in Libra. I also looked at myself from other cosmological assessments like Mayan cosmology, which I sometimes find more useful for understanding my purpose on the planet. People call me chief and leader. A good Leo personality is like a good leader or king who really cares for the good of people. I've discovered that what is called a weakness of Leo is not a weakness, which is that Leo depends on people's opinion or feedback.

I wish all good mayors would do what they did in Curitiba or Porto Alegre, in southern Brazil, where the Communist Party said, "We are doing citizen budgeting because you know best what we need while we in the city center don't know." The citizens decided to put the funds into street lighting, garbage disposal, and 70% went into school education. It's much more difficult if you live in a totally messed-up society with lots of psychopaths after 5,000 years of empire where people are crushed. My Libra moon loves being in solitude where I get my visions and my creativity, especially for Europeans who are not masters of the feelings. I had to learn that it was very important to go into conflict and to assert myself.

Say a word about your educational and career path. Mine was a normal high school, spending my time doing sports, handball, volleyball, and fantasy role-playing like in the '80s. *When you were in high school, you felt constrained and rigid. Was it different for your son when he was in high school?* I think it has changed a lot since the '90s because now we see people dancing savagely without needing to go to dance classes. We have hip-hop and techno and everybody is throwing their arms and legs wherever they want. I think it's more acceptable to be silly, while back then it wasn't. Everybody comes up with a new stupid dance move on TikTok and YouTube.

My parents were both teachers so that meant I was going to become one as well. To improve my English, I went to the University of Western Australia where we had cockatoos and peacocks walking through the halls and everything was super relaxing. The whole year had sunshine and we walked barefoot to university. There were different colleges for the posh people, for the Asians, and for the country people, where I was. They were surfing and playing football and nature lovers. During the whole year, nobody ever talked badly about anyone--not behind their back, not publicly, which indicates it's a completely different universe than the USA and Europe at the time.

Living in Australia was a very strong initiation to the planet with magnificent nature, being out there with the animals. That's how I discovered the planet, making love with the female planet through this immersion in nature. There is also something masculine in the living universe but the queendom of nature is very much a feminine sphere. It really told me I didn't want to live a boring monotonous life of being a teacher for the next 40 years, holding back my feelings, and reducing my dreams.

Being in nature made me a much more beautiful man; women resonated to me better because I was not so boring; now I was this Indiana Jones person. So, it was very important for my personal evolution from a shy, timid boy hanging out with my boy friends, always with this longing in teenage years to have union with females.

I was shy, like all the Europeans there in Australia, but by the end of that year, the Aussies thought I was one of them. Europe is very different from the US. My teenage years in the '80s in Europe were totally easygoing, everything at peace, abundance, no ghettos, and everybody was wearing whatever they wanted without concern for brand or status symbols. Today everybody wants to be a Kardashian or a Steve Jobs, a billionaire. In Britain, 60% or 70% of teenagers say, "I want to become a celebrity." We were just being ourselves, relaxed mates with the girls.

If you go to countries like France or Italy, I found that they are unable to restrain their emotions and they lash out uncontrollably. For example, parents yell at small children and that's so hurtful. There's a reason that the Nordic countries are the most peaceful, prosperous, and gender-harmonious, nude-body relaxed, most chilled-out, with the most successful schools on the planet. They're more centered.

The next year I was in North America where I traveled with a Native American elder for one year, who took me as his final student. My love for nature transcended into a reflectful relationship with nature and then came healing and initiation ceremonies. *How did you find that elder in California?* I had really strong Native American dreams as a very little child that got reactivated there. I felt I'd love to meet someone who's still living that culture.

My travel buddy and I were in San Francisco. After three days, the buildings were so high I couldn't see the sky and I felt suffocated. I posted in a youth hostel looking for a ride anywhere and I got a call, "Hey, it's Tosh from Ireland, we're going north to Seattle." Everything glides into place with magical surprises all the time. It's not a typical white man's structured way, but rather a totally trusting feminine flow, which I didn't know at the time. We drove up north and the trees got bigger and bigger and I said, "Whoa! This is like in

Star Wars." I didn't know those trees were for real: There we were in the redwoods and I couldn't believe it.

Then the car stopped and this Native American came to the window saying, "You want to see some tall trees, huh? First, come in my teepee." Two Bulls told us the story of the spirit arrow over the door. I said to him, "I'm just a white guy, a student from Germany, and I believe I can learn something from your culture. Could you tell me where I could go, like a culture center or a reservation?" In his easy-going way, he said, "You can stay with me. I'm going salmon fishing in the realms in the clouds. I'm going to teach you to make fire without smoke."

He started telling me about the linear world and circular world--the traditional cosmologies. I learned to listen and almost not say a word for an entire year. During that first night in the teepee, I felt he had so much greatness, such grand power, a hardcore warrior, I wanted to be like him. Two Bulls said, "I'm going to de-program you from the industrial empire bullshit to something else." My inner voice said, "This is cool; I trust him completely."

I went back to Germany twice but I was always welcomed back. I unconditionally opened up to this wisdom-keeper to reprogram me, to go deeply into my psyche, my heart, and my worldview so I could grow. At the end of the year, he did some medicine ceremonies to get other stuff out of me, to have an expanded mind, with totem animal encounters. I was in communication with spirits when during the ceremony a real eagle appeared and swooped at arm's length over my head.

Later that day, I took a jump from a mound, driven by the wish to feel what an eaglet feels like when jumping off the parent's nest on a high cliff for the first time, opening its wings, trusting in faith that the wings will carry it. It was a great flight with a soft landing. . . into two-meter deep bramble bushes. As I opened my eyes, I realized that these brambles grow two-inch thick stems with murderous thorns. My Aussie surfer T-shirt was in tatters, my body scratched bloody. I stared in fascination at what looked precisely like a detailed drawing of a swooping eagle on my arm--the mark of the eagle.

I got a new taste of the Living Universe and animals have been supportive companions ever since. It makes good sense when animals (others call them totem spirit animals) make a sudden appearance in one's life, to study their medicine, their message for that moment. One doesn't only have one totem animal. That's new age nonsense, as one can have several, and they can appear at different phases of one's path through life.

Two Bulls' father was Lakota, his mother Inuit, in the lineage of the Sitting Bull family. His grandfather was a shaman. Like countless children, Two Bulls was taken from his family at age 12 to boarding school. When they spoke their language, they got their mouths cleaned with soap or a needle stuck in the tongue. Their teachers would kick them down the stairs and sexually abuse them. When Two Bulls saw this happening to kids, he grabbed a knife and said, "You ever do this to me, you better sleep with one eye open," and they never got close to him. Two Bulls was lucky his Uncle Goodheart taught him the traditions because by 1940 they were already pretty flattened out. After 50 years, the sun dances and dancing ceremonies were banned, so there was a lot that's been lost, resulting in alcohol, depression, and PTSD. To me, the North American Plains Indians are still the highest evolved spiritual culture on the planet.

Did you go to university in Germany after your year in California? I did study English and sports in Germany as a teacher then after some years, I went back to Australia in '95, then back to California, New Mexico, and Florida. In '97 I returned to Germany and completed my studies the next year, which was also the year my son was born.

During a medicine ceremony with Two Bulls, I had this revelation that the greatest gift in my life will be to see my son grow up. I wondered how I was going to ever find a woman to live with me and have a baby since I was like an extraterrestrial coming back to Germany. I felt like a deer in the middle of traffic but I was also badass because Two Bulls was a badass. The main thing he taught me was the warrior values. The warrior only takes what he needs and if you stand by that, then nobody can touch you. You are your only judge and you don't give a damn what anyone else says and that is super strong.

I ran into a girl five years younger than me. I'd seen her at my high school, the one with the colorful skirts dancing barefoot through the school, the crazy hippie girl. I ran into her by coincidence and then we became lovers and, half a year later, she was pregnant. Those were magical years when good stuff happened. We lived in a wonderful former horse ranch until the co-living broke up. Then we went to kind of a winter palace in the countryside until she wanted to live in the city because it was a long way to go shopping and see friends with the baby.

The Lakota carried and breastfeed the children for two years. When a Native American was pregnant, she would go for walks in the forest and sing songs to the trees announcing the birth of a hero. Through initiations into manhood, the boy arrives as a constant giver. You're not a taker; the richest is the one that gives the most. So, it's really a grand personality and the mother knows he's going to be like that. The teaching was to always be unconditionally loving, to never be angry, to never put the kid into a cage, to never let him cry. I was among the first generation of fathers who carried the babies in slings. I always treated him at eye level, as a complete soul from the first moment. He grew up in total harmony and he's like the most uncomplicated teen in Berlin, maybe on the planet. He's now 23.

In Europe, it is rare to hear anyone say, "It's so hard to raise teens," but I heard that from Americans. This is not normal, it's not natural or human. It's very bad if you perceive it as if it was a natural law, that that's how teens are. Leo was born in the summer of '98 and I graduated in winter '99. He slept in our bed until the age of 12. It was just so beautiful having the little baby on my chest breathing up and down. He never got a cold, he never was sick.

Why did you and Jenny get divorced? We weren't married in the first place because I didn't believe in white men's churches. We were good parents in terms of giving full-on to the child, which means we weren't doing the lover thing much anymore. We felt that after those two years we had lost ourselves. This wouldn't happen in the tribe because you would be so engaged with other members of the community, uplifting and loving so you get more nourished.

Jenny decided she wanted to go to some friends in Berlin and I worked at the Universal World Exposition in Hanover in 2000 for five months, which was the first time the sustainable development themes came up for me. That initiated me to my future mission. Then I went to Berlin thinking of myself as this Native American warrior, responsible father forever, and protector for her. But she said we had split up.

I was surprised and, at the same time, I simply respected it. That was also my native American warrior self; you're like a rock; you don't go into emotional stuff. Still today I'm one of her most trusted friends and we always appreciated each other as parents. We would do one week here and one week there. We lived in the same district, only ten minutes on foot. Everybody else was very surprised and admiring, saying that they've never seen parents that split up be so harmonious with one another. I understood that--especially since my initiations into feminism--required that I couldn't stay in that relationship forever. The spirit wanted me to go through many other experience fields.

Then came the greatest magic, my initiation into the feminine, encountering sacred women, shamans. One of my girlfriends, a temporary lover, said, "Eric, we are having sweat lodge ceremonies. It's a teaching by a female shaman because she's fed up with it being always guided by men." This was in 2005 before all the Yoni healing times had begun in Tantra, a big honor. I spent a year naked in the sweat lodge with women from 17 to 70 years of age, who discovered things about themselves. I was the little mouse, learning all this and experiencing all that.

That was a very important experience, not from the experience of the Native American or the Buddhist or the Hindu, which are more masculine. I continued this path of my initiation to the feminine through encounters with lovers on my path, a really great gift. When you fall in love, you are willing to go over limits for yourself.

I fell in love with a woman and then it fell apart when she went back to the guy before me. I had a dream, so intense, where she was like my soul mate; I had to be with her, waiting until the other guy would go. For three weeks, I would cry for five hours before I could get out of bed. As you know, this is not a common experience for a man or anyone but it definitely was some huge initiation that was happening as a spiritual experience in my emotional body and heart. There were so many things flowing out that had nothing to do with this specific experience, but something had exploded. When I was throwing up, I'd say, "I'm healing. It's great." It's like in the

Peyote ceremony when something bad is coming out and it feels great afterwards.

Then I encountered another super-magical woman. I was 37 and she seemed like 27 but she was just 19, a really mature, super-sexy being, the wild woman. This is an extreme mirror of experience for men to be in that presence because it constantly pulls you there magnetically. You want to have her but you can't, you meet her, its total bliss, things explode in you.

She was so sensitive that since she was a little child, she could close her eyes and feel the electric sockets in the room and she had lots of rashes and neurodynamic stuff. If we were in a mall, she would close her eyes, and say, "Go somewhere. I'm going to point where you are," and she did, 12 meters in that direction. I didn't know such beings existed on the planet. This also meant that in her sensuality, she lived on a different Venus planet than me.

In Mayan, I'm a blue eagle, so I see the world with this vision. My opposite is the red snake and usually, this opposite sign is your total nightmare, but you're meant to learn this in life, and she was this red snake. If you think about a snake, it totally feels the grass and the earth on the skin all the time--a total body person. It's not unconditional love like the eagle who forgets his body because he's up there and circling. The red snake is kundalini energy, sexuality, flint and tinder. She was totally that energy, an initiation into my opposite in the Mayan view. I got her out of her drug world to yoga and massage.

There were these Berlin Tantra greats, including a super-earthy stallion guy. Other men have no chance with certain females and he was that guy. She went into resonance with him because she could explore her levels of sensuality. He had a different woman in his bed every two days or so, just three or four times. With her, it was more often because she was really special. So, I was suddenly in this free love Tantra scene in Berlin, but I didn't want to become a student of that because my Native American smell sensed that it wasn't totally pure.

She left Berlin on a journey to North Africa and I felt this love thing but I couldn't connect with her on the sensual, so I wanted to learn it, doing yoga and massage, being super soft and rosy. At that time, I couldn't work on the computer; my body would refuse. I decided to get into this bodywork stuff and then I met her again six months later and had a great time. I was in love, I was fixed on her, so I didn't have any other relationships until I kind of gave up on her and I had several lovers per week. I had opened up all my spiritual skill of erasing myself and learned to be so sensual through these years since the sweat lodge. I adored all my beautiful sacred sisters in all their beauty and the joy, in our dance.

That's a very Tantric thing, to be in this adoration of the feminine and they the masculine. I found they're de-armoring themselves to be able to feel that again because brutish society closed it down. I made myself a gift so they can experience the sensual reality in the presence of a spirit in a masculine body when the others are too brutish or too robotic. The body knows how to do it, so I knew how to touch, what to do with my whole body as a musical instrument flowing into this rosy ocean with her and circling up into a heavenly experience.

I think the biggest key to harmonious gender companionships is that males get in touch with their sensuality. With all my awesomeness of being a warrior, I was a great giver, a beautiful person, but I didn't know sensuality. It's like a different universe because I couldn't feel and then in all these years, I was learning to feel my body cells, the soles of my feet and all. I did this journey from being a cardboard box to becoming an embodied human being who can feel myself, the blood running through my veins, and the heartbeat, and to surrender to the moment without a plan. Tantra helps the mental body understand what's going on, so it calms down.

To be mundane, how did you put food on the table during these years of exploration? Uncle Two Bulls said, "Great spirit will always give you what you need. You will never go hungry in Germany." I did a mix between doing little jobs on Saturdays, selling organic bread, or giving a workshop for international student companies, and doing video documentation. After one week I would have $9,000 and could hang out for six months because rent was $50 for a 40-square meter apartment, which is totally enough. Like Two Bulls taught me, time is money or money is time, so I was always able to live on very little money. I had a beautiful apartment with beautiful things I found in the streets. There were periods of being on welfare, which is really easygoing and pays your rent, plus health insurance, so that's how I was able to have a really good life.

How did you get involved in youth work and publishing Youth-Leader magazine?[178] You've written hundreds of pamphlets and led conferences and worked with the U.N. That started in the year 2000 when I was at the World Exposition for five months. I had just finished my university degree, so I wasn't in a hurry. I was there for five months going to conferences with changemakers and talks about sustainable development with global dialogues. I saw there are solutions for almost everything, talking about sustainable development.

I thought, "This has to go to the people and not just these small expert chambers. It has to go to schools because there are so many teachers doing global learning and green stuff." I decided I was going to do a positive news magazine for schools in the languages needed for all schools on the planet, which is 14 languages. I was going to do it like Wikipedia with online volunteers. Youth-Leader signed up with the United Nations' online volunteers to translate for free or write and I had 11,000 applications from 70 countries to write in 14 languages. Over the United Nations decade of education for sustainable development, I drew 11,000 volunteers because it's the coolest thing to write stories about solutions and heroes that will go into schools.

It started as a magazine and then in 2013, I made it known that we had this wonderful online magazine, available as PDF for downloads. The youth leader website provides a crash course like a guided tour with lots of videos. It's an enormous initiation to youth leadership. I realized that we needed print media, so the first was a card game with the story of the youth hero on the back plus a QR code linking to an online page with the story and videos. That's a lot of content on one little card, it's like a book. I have 50 heroes, 50 pages with a picture, plus you get more stuff online. It also exists as a 2017 book *The New Kids on The Planet: Tales of Teenage Change Makers*. I always have cards with me so when you're on the train and someone nice asks you, "What do you do?" I show them heroes.

We have posters because the card game is great in class but it's invisible, so you need something for a bigger presence. We experimented more in Germany because there's a lot of money in Germany and youth leadership doesn't exist in the whole of Europe. For example, there is not a single student club in France because they're banned, they don't exist.

In the US youth leadership is widespread, organized for 50 years, and even longer with the Girl Scouts for 100 years. Here in Germany, boys just do sports. I'm for actual youth projects over their demonstrations and strikes, like teens who do projects at an enormous scope, cleaning up rivers and raising millions of dollars for building orphanages for the super poor in India. They make water a human right in 30 cities, tangible rather than shifting responsibility for solutions to government or scientists.

Canadian Robyn Hamlyn was 12 when she learned of the looming water crisis in school. Troubled, she searched the internet for solutions and found a local solution composed by Maude Barlow and promoted by the Council Of Canadians, that city councils declare themselves a "Blue Community" by passing a three-pronged resolution: water stays public, becomes a human right, and bottled water gets banned in municipal buildings and events. Next week, Robyn met her mayor of Kingston, Ontario, spoke at the city council and they passed all three parts. That year, she spoke to 27 cities and all passed one, two, or three parts of the resolution. That's more than two towns per month when she was age 13. (*As a college student she wrote a book* Whose Water is it, Anyway: Taking Water Protection into Public Hands.)

Is there anything like a men's movement in Europe? There is in Britain. Men on Reddit lists make women responsible for all the bad in the world and plot to kill women. They feel rejected by women since they don't get sex from them. *InCels.* It also exists in Europe now because they are copy-pasting from the internet all the bullshit from America. It's a really sick wave from the past 10 years that Europe copies everything from America and it's worse than before. We've had all the American TV shows for the past 50 years and we read more about your president on our front pages than about our own politicians because they're always so outrageous. This had strong effect. I'd say that Europeans now practically identify as being American, and that's true for many people in the world, I think.

You're currently traveling around Europe. What projects are you working on and where are you headed? I am travelling Europe to activate youth leadership all over the continent, with special focus on starting Pan-European collaboration uniting fired-up youth crews, schools, civil society, and municipalities. Think of Cold War era West-East school partnerships for peace dialogue, but now to protect and restore natural and cultural heritage. The goals are to end the Mafia, child prostitution and trafficking, for sustainable development, and social entrepreneurship. Also for disconnected rural regions, with youth-led tour guides, small social businesses, etc.

I just spent two months in Sarajevo, Bosnia-Herzegovina, and am really surprised. It's like the '80s, with the music, and everybody's smoking. But also almost everybody is kind, healthy in the heart, sure of themselves. Western Europe has gotten really psychotic in comparison, where mental disease and distrust are omnipresent. It is true psychotherapy to be here in the Balkans and is a perfect space for Youth Leader Summer Camps for young changemakers. Pristine nature is still intact and urban and rural people are determined to protect it from Mafia-backed dirty industry invasion. Plus, of course, it's really affordable for people with euros or dollars in their pockets.

People here appreciate life and it is common that people buy an espresso and stay for two hours, no waiter bugging them to consume more, and owners don't care either, even cafes in the most touristy parts. People are HUMAN here. We are constantly told the West is so cool and healthy and the East so poor and Mafia, but it's the exact opposite and it is a veritable crime against humanity to be painting such false pictures. I plan to keep travelling for years, following invitations to activate regions for youth leadership. Youth leadership is needed and wanted everywhere now. That's exciting to see after all these years in the field.

George Simons
Exploring Male Identity Across Cultures

I was born in Cleveland, Ohio on January 12, 1938. Though I am not a fan of astrology, that makes me a well-grounded and hardworking Capricorn, or, as I would put it, a workaholic who loves what he does. I have shaped and edited over a hundred board and card games on values, customs, ecology, and social issues involving populations around the world. This diversophy® series is online so games can be customized according to the target group and the learning objectives of the user.[179] The games get people to share their stories and connect with each other. There are other ones at diversophy.com.

My latest game, *diversi*CASTE-RACE-SHUN is on toxic masculinity--if you say it fast, it's "castration."[180] I'm trying to get men not to slice away at their manhood, but rather to use traditional male virtues to expand their masculinity from its commonly limited emotional range. Also, the goal is to widen their sense of purpose from restrictively defined roles of honor, service, protection, and competitive hard work.

The game has five kinds of cards:[181]

1. CHOICE. Choosing behaviors that make you who and how you want to be. The cards offer choices about what actions are best to take for roles we wish to play. For example, one question reads: "You can use your male leadership values for social change by being a point man. True or False?" The answer says this is true if you are someone who points out injustices and directs yourself and others in safe and useful directions. It explains how the term originally designated cowboys who rode at the leading points of a herd to keep the animals from falling into an arroyo or other dangerous terrain. We can use the male value of alert leadership to guide, protect and choose better directions where needed.

2. GUIDE. Insights on masculine cultures, *e.g.,* a Japanese saying that lists the most dreaded phenomena in Japan: "Earthquakes, thunder, fire, and father." Such cards illustrate situations around masculine values. The underlying ideology of male dominance means that power and influence tend to flow toward the most abusive men in any given organization.

3. RISK. Situations you may need to deal with as a man, *e.g.,* "Your friend is angry and depressed. Over a drink, he confesses to you that demographics foretell a decline into minority status for white men. He fears that he and his sons are headed toward a social abyss." Risk cards ask, "If you're the person facing this situation, how do you react?"

4. SHARE. The players react by sharing their experience or in some other way on the topic presented, *e.g.,* "An example: "First impressions! Men size each other up. What are some of the automatic frames, criteria, or even biases that come to mind when you meet another man for the first time?" We need to know that masculine cultural values can be used well or they can be used in a deadly fashion.

5. SMARTS. Players respond to true/false or multiple-choice questions regarding facts and myths about men and masculinity, such things as suicide rates among young men, the fact that teachers give lower grades to male students, etc.

For over a year now we have played our games every Thursday night online with people from all over the world. I've also had face-to-face groups of up to 2000 people playing, employing a team of facilitators walking around the auditorium.

To go back to your origins. You were the child of immigrants surrounded by multiple languages growing up. We lived in northern Ohio, the Western Reserve, very much an Anglo-Protestant power system in which we were the "inferior" immigrants from central Europe. My maternal grandfather was a Polish blacksmith and factotum. Dad's father was a court tailor from Vienna who came to New York to study fashion and decided to stay.

My parents and grandparents insisted on not letting the children speak their native languages because we'd pay socially for it as an immigrant caste or perhaps be shunned for having an accent. When I was eight or nine years old, I asked my grandmother to teach me some German words and she did. Maybe the fact that it was forbidden made me curious to learn languages.

I got my primary education in an immigrant-safe parochial school. We had four years of Latin and two years of classical Greek in a prep high school, along with two years of German. I went to small Catholic colleges in Indiana and Ohio and majored in philosophy. As a freshman in college, I was inspired by a prof who made me love French literature and poetry. I actually memorized Charles Baudelaire's entire volume of poems, *Les Feurs du Mal* on my own initiative.

I earned a master's degree at Notre Dame summer school in the history of religious ritual and later a doctorate in psychology from Claremont with a focus on Gestalt theory and techniques. I didn't intend to be a therapist, but I wanted to focus on small-group learning and education, so mine was more of an educational psych degree. In Gestalt, you enter into conversation with yourself. Whenever we look at something, we tend to focus on the foreground or the background. Gestalt teaches us to move back and forth from foreground to background to digest and work with an issue.

Let's say you're having difficulty with your mother. We place two chairs facing each other. You sit down in one chair and talk to your mother as if she is in the other chair. Then you switch chairs and become your mom speaking to you. This is one way to widen one's perspective rather than being stuck in a single view. I later adapted some of these techniques in my first book, *Keeping Your Personal Journal.*

Do you still practice Catholicism? I've been living in France for the last 26 years, largely doing consulting and training, so I am not very active in religious circles, although the issues fascinate me both personally and professionally. I was a Catholic campus minister at Case-Western Reserve University and later at Oberlin College, where they offered me positions as a dormitory residence director and as a lecturer in the Human Development Program. I began to develop games for educating student staff there.

After about four years at Oberlin, I got a fellowship to do my doctorate at Claremont and thereafter was hired to create adult education materials for about three years in Santa Monica, California. At UCSD, where one part of my doctoral program took place, I met German students who invited me to Germany to lead small Gestalt groups. We lived on a big old farm, basically a hippie commune. There was only one bed for 30 people, a big, long table off the wall so people cuddled up to whomever they wanted to at night. I was based in Germany for about four years, leaving occasionally to lead communication workshops at Management Centre Europe in Brussels.

I went back to Ohio to pursue a career in management, and training and consulting, when Phil McCrillis, a priest from California, came to visit me in the early '80s, He was interviewing priests like himself who were exploring different lifestyles and relationships. *He had a woman partner in another town. He's on my men's roles video.* We discussed women's surging anger at men during what then seemed like the adolescence of the feminist movement. Guys were going crazy! "My wife doesn't love me anymore. I think my secretary wants to kill me. My daughters are critical of everything I do."

Phil and I decided to do research on how we could address these challenges, as men for men. At Phil's invitation, I moved to California, and we opened the Hidden Valley Center for Men, teaching "How to Love an Angry Woman" weekend workshops. To appeal to men, we took the approach of coaches rather than shrinks, demonstrating and practicing the "how to's" for bettering gender relationships. Later I co-authored a handbook, *Men and Women Partners at Work,* applying to the workplace much of what we did with the guys in our men's groups.

During this period, I connected with Warren Farrell,* author of *Why Men Are the Way they Are*, and with Gordon Clay* who was doing workshops on "Healing the Father Wound." One of the important how-to's was learning to give specific acknowledgment to women, like, "I really appreciate how you did X Y Z yesterday," complimenting behaviors rather than good looks. *Warren Farrell also emphasizes this today.* We also taught active listening, a relatively new technique back then, as well as giving simple advice like, "Mark your calendar so you don't forget your anniversary and her birthday."

Our men's groups underscored the importance of men having a safe place to share with men. As one of the guys in our group said, "It's great to talk about this stuff with men. I can't sit with a woman therapist and talk like I really want to talk." At first, wives and partners were suspicious of our men's groups, but they often became surprisingly supportive, as in "Don't forget, tonight's your men's group." "It's comforting to know a place where you're understood and supported--you can relax a little bit." *Owen Marcus* had the same observation.*

Did you see cultural differences in your work? In my men's workshops in Germany, it seemed the guys were much more dominated by women. At that time German women were often loudly insisting that men pee sitting down so they wouldn't make a mess and leave the toilet seat up.

What do you observe about French men's and women's interactions? French communication is a little different in the sense that we love to argue here, lots of words, more hand gestures. If you're not French, it's surprising, perhaps scary at first, but it becomes fun, and often you learn something new. Despite common biases, I don't see that the French are any more promiscuous than anybody else, but we haven't got a Cancel Culture here yet. In the US system now, there's no way for a person to repent of their sins and be accepted. One is scarred for life for indiscretions. It's a very strange phenomenon. There is no possible man's side to this #MeToo story open to discussion. The level of scandal is proportionate to the level of prudishness in the USA.

When you're training people to do business with China, what do you teach about cultural awareness? We have a game on the Chinese culture, but one of the best thinkers in the intercultural field now is a Vietnamese woman named Nguyen Mai. She's written several books using neuroscience to look at how we react and make decisions. Saving face in front of somebody else is important in Chinese and other Asian cultures, whereas in France we can argue it out with both bosses and buddies. *Guanxi* is a set of values about relationship formation and protection that you use to network in China to make things happen via those connections.

Business relationships differ around the world. Let's say that as a US American, I made a contract with you. When the contract expires, I may throw it open for bids. In several Asian countries, the assumption is that we've worked to create a relationship, so we'll work out how to continue the contract rather than opening it to strangers. In Brazil, if you show up at a negotiation with a team of lawyers, the Brazilians will wonder what they are doing in the room.

I teach negotiation a lot and one of the issues is: who is the decision-maker? That person may be in the room or 6000 kilometers away in their office. Another big issue is time: In France, you set a time and people may come 15 minutes or more later, depending on the nature of the meeting. *I taught workshops in Japan and a faux pas I made was sitting on a table in front of the classroom, which was considered rude.* I was in Central Asia where crossing your legs was considered rude.

To negotiate successfully, we need to make clear what the needs on both sides are--sometimes they are hidden or not made explicit. Teaching negotiation, I use a fun exercise, a 15-minute one-on-one negotiation where each negotiator puts 5€ in front of them. The rules of the game specify that at the end of 15 minutes one person must come away with all the money and the other person has whatever they have negotiated for. If there is no agreement, the 10€ goes into the George beer fund.

With college students, one of the most common outcomes is a deal where one person gets all the euros and in return the other cooks a meal for him or her. The hidden currency? Wanting to get to know the other person better!

We're always looking for the hidden currencies when negotiating. For example, a development bank rep was negotiating with a local government official. The bank rep thought he gave everything that was asked for, but there was no agreement. The deal was struck when the bank rep discovered that the official was running for office and made a new offer: "If you sign off, we'll broadcast to all the local news channels that you made this wonderful deal for building the bridge to improve the local infrastructure." The hidden currency was the official's unspoken need to get all the publicity he could, crediting him for this deal.

Do you see any gender differences in negotiating styles? We are likely to be brought up culturally to get what we want in different ways as women and men and this may affect how we negotiate until we learn more skills. Initially, men are more likely to talk more strongly, longer, and interrupt more frequently, while women frequently use deferential language and disclaimers ("I think...", "Perhaps...", etc.), thus appearing less forceful. At the same time, women may be more aware of non-verbal elements that are clues to next steps. Gender-sensitive negotiation training allows us to see and appropriately use each other's skills more effectively in a variety of contexts.

Another course I teach is called "Positive Power and Influence." Most of us have our set ways of persuading people, perhaps with logic, or maybe aggressively, or withholding approval, or even with a bribe. The most powerful approach, however, may be visioning. We align our motor neurons with a vision, a story of a shared successful outcome. This creates a kind of compatibility neurologically.

For example, I may start to connect with you by reminding you of our mutual interest in ecologically-sound food consumption, highlighting what we both do in this regard, thus aligning our shared thoughts, feelings, and common interests. Then I build this connection into a *vision*, a story of a future success we could create together. I could describe the two of us creating a delicious "eco-feast" for family and friends on a holiday or anniversary. We would present it in such a way that it opens their eyes to embracing similar ecological values and habits. I would then invite you to build on the story with what we could do to make this vision a success.

Also, if we share an artistic, poetic, or musical experience together, it is more likely that we can become inclined to work together more harmoniously. In US politics, Democrats, except maybe Obama, rarely tell stories well, while the country brims over with populist stories, both true and fake. Visioning is not manipulation if it is sincere and committed to results.

Men are telling me that women have superior verbal skills and are more able to deal with emotional conflict. Do you think that's because capitalism wants men to not feel so they'll work in stressful situations or is it something physiological? This is largely cultural, though culture activates elements of our genetic endowment. Of course, capitalism is one of the sacred unquestionable metanarratives of the USA and elsewhere. On the interpersonal level, however, the rich variety of men's feelings are often labeled as only anger by women who don't know how to explore them. What sounds like anger may be a cover for disappointment or rejection or other feelings.

When I got into men's work, I was stunned by the male deprivation that most of the guys I was working with had experienced growing up. I seemed to be a rare exception because I grew up with my dad working from home and my grandfather, who lived with us, building things in the basement. My other grandfather, the tailor, lived just down the street where I could easily find time with him.

I was shocked at how many men did not have any adult male companionship as boys. The "father wound," as Gordon Clay* calls it, is all about dad not being there for me because of the conditions of his life and work or due to a rupture in the family relationship. In the men's movement, one of the first things we told men was to bring your sons with you, whether we're going to the beach, or the sweat lodge, or on a hike, or volunteering for a social project. Though I had such good male support at home, like most in my generation, I never had a male teacher until I reached high school.

Have you had a long-term partner? No, I have traveled too much. I've been a rolling stone who's worked in over 60 countries and visited about 70. In one year, I checked my calendar to discover that I slept in my own bed for only 63 nights! Still, I have several wonderful woman friends who I work with and adventure with around the world.

You wrote Seven Ways to Lighten Your Life Before You Kick the Bucket. My best friend, Walt Hopkins, and I did this together. The seven ways emphasize shucking the useless stuff so you can really enjoy the tastiest part of the oyster and follow your dreams.

Are you optimistic that we're moving towards what Farrell calls "gender liberation?" In our current tsunami of political, pandemic, and ecological crises, our socially constructed realities are revealing themselves in naked abundance. If we pay attention, we can see the cracks and we can face the problems in the system. The challenge is how to create new and better stories to live by. I appreciate enormously what women have accomplished in the feminist movement, but an awful lot of women think that men's issues are non-existent. I lecture at a School of Applied Science in Finland and other universities, and, generally, at least half the students are from all over the world. What I see is that the guys are not doing very well. Men are not getting the same attention from profs as women are.

Also, young men face identity issues; for example, we're supposed to be providers, but women are making it on their own now. We are supposed to be protectors, but women know how to protect themselves much better than before. Our male sense of purpose is increasingly hard to identify and increasingly harder to realize. Gender liberation is for all. My motto is simple for both women and men: Onward together!

Jerry Tello
Co-Founder of The National Compadres Network

I acknowledge the creator and my ancestors because it's not about me; it's really about how I got here through my lineage and all my relations. I really want to thank all those ancestors who struggled, suffered, and were enslaved and raped, but didn't give up. They kept praying and working and dreaming for us. Because of their legacy, we're able to be a little bit better, to love a little bit better, to heal a little bit better. What we're trying to do one person at a time, one family, one generation at a time, is to reclaim our true Sacred self--just a little bit more every day

I was born in December 1952. *You're a Sagittarian. I wanted to ask you about education because I think of Julian*

Nava who ended up at Harvard, but when he was in school in LA like you, his counselors told him, "You should take shop classes, not college prep classes." You went to a private high school, why was that? We grew up in a neighborhood where my mom felt it was safer for me to go to private school; also my mom was Catholic and wanted the spiritual values part of it. It was also an all-boys school with mainly men teachers. I think since my Dad died when I was 13, she wanted me to have that guidance. In Spanish, *La Educación* doesn't just mean formal education but refers to the development of your character, your spirit. My mom was really concerned about making sure that I was taught about values and character.

I went to a Catholic school in Watts called Verbum Dei High School. The majority of students were African-American, with a small group of Mexicans. Because we were all black and brown boys, there was a strong component of telling us, "You guys need to succeed and get ahead for your people." They didn't necessarily teach me how to succeed, but they informed me, you need to take these classes.

Our problem was on the outside of the school, in the neighborhood. Many of my friends didn't do well in school because there was so much trauma going on in the home and the neighborhood, especially around the time that I was going to high school when the Civil Rights and Chicano movements were happening. As much as you want do good, all those things that are going on in society and in your community take your focus away and make it difficult for you to learn and study because sometimes it's just about survival.

What really helped me is there was a group of Mexican immigrant young men in my school who all played soccer; when they didn't have enough soccer players they recruited me. They taught me and really embraced me from a cultural standpoint. They called me *hermano* (brother). This was after my father had died and they became like older brothers. We realize that young men need other young men, but what I saw in my neighborhood is other young men were getting high, drinking, smoking, ...*gangs*.

On the other hand, because of all the inequities we faced, our team wanted to play soccer and wanted to win to at least enjoy a victory somewhere. I felt that in spite of everything I went through in the neighborhood, my ancestors helped me out by setting some people around me to affirm me. At least I had a safe place at least for a few hours, in contrast to many of my peers who never had a safe place. That consciousness of safety was a foundational element of my life.

The other major element that saved me was my family and culture. My father is Tap Pilam Cahuitecan and Mexican from the San Antonio area of Texas, a native lineage that goes back many generations there. My mom, Maria de Jesus Olague Ramos, was from Chihuahua, Mexico. They got together and had children, some of us born in Texas and some of us born in Los Angeles. I was raised from a small child in Compton in Watts, South Central Los Angeles, during the '50s and '60s. It was a tremendous time of consciousness.

I had just entered high school at the same time as the Watts Blowouts, or Watts Riots as some people call them, so I experienced a great upheaval as a young child. I saw a lot of injustice, a lot of mistreatment, not only of people who looked like me but my African-American friends and relatives who didn't feel safe. We had our problems of violence, drugs, and poverty and not feeling safe around police and even in school sometimes.

I recall walking to school and seeing a National Guard tank on the corner of my house. When my friend picked me up and we walked off the porch we heard a guard cock his AK-47. We tightened up and weren't sure if we wanted to go to school because we didn't want to leave our home. In school, I felt tight the whole day. Much later I realized tightness or inflammation was the norm in my body. That's the trauma or tightness of racism. I also saw my parents struggle to create balance between the values they were trying to teach us and the street life that we had to adapt to in order to survive.

We came home with some of that toxicity and those bad habits or disrespectful values and questioning my parents' values. My brother ended up getting locked up and doing time. My sister was pregnant at 16 and I saw a lot of upheaval, a lot of struggle for her. I think that's what built a consciousness in me, due to understanding trauma; we've been trauma-informed our whole life. We lived the trauma but no one else cared about our trauma and I'm not sure they do now.

How many siblings do you have? There are six of us. *How many went to university?* My older brother went to law school and became a lawyer. *The reason that you and your brother went to college and the others didn't is because you had a support group that encouraged you to study and go on?* My brother John is eight years older than me, but I call my brother George the warrior in our family, the gatekeeper. He and my sister Gloria took a lot of the wounds; he really struggled a lot and because of that, he shielded my brother who is a year younger than him from some of the problems.

George was the rabble-rouser who would fight everybody if they messed with us, protected us, so he got a lot of the wounds. He was also darker than my other brothers and that doesn't seem like a really big thing unless you live in racist society. My brother John is the lighter one who could be driving and George in the passenger's seat and the cops would stop him and go over to George and question him.

You have to know how you deal with your pain because my brother had to become a defender and a fighter and in this society that's not seen as a good thing. My other brother was a little bit more laid-back and liked to read, which kind of insulated him. He had perseverance and went to college and became a lawyer so I saw I had choices and I could do it. The other part is the ancestors' prayers, and the prayers of my grandma and my mom shielded me, plus hard work.

It's not coincidental that people of color, especially people living in impoverished and stressed neighborhoods, have health issues. Now with Covid, high rates of black and brown people are dying or sick. For generations, we've had inflammation as a result of stress and racial inequity that affected our well-being, our sleep, and lacking nutritional foods in our neighborhoods. We lack mental health resources that really understand us instead of locking us up, medicating us, putting us away, or deporting us and taking away our children, rather than creating a way for us to heal and deal with trauma. *Yes, in domestic violence cases they take the kids away if the mom doesn't have a proper home.*

That led me to try and figure it out. Why does my community have so many issues and so much pain? I realize now that when I went to school to become a psychologist, I was trying to heal my own family. I wanted to understand the wounds that I grew up with and was still carrying. Western society's way of looking at life is very racist, very misogynistic, very punitive. My professors taught me to diagnose and look at people in a very judgmental way, and in a way that I could control their lives.

With that power, based on my report, I could tell a judge these kids should not be with that mother, without even understanding what they're going through. I could say this kid needs to be locked up or say this person should be deported; they're a danger. It really bothered me because we were raised not to judge people and to be compassionate. I remember walking to the store with my dad when I was a young boy and seeing this man we called Mr. Joe outside the liquor store. I think he used to sleep there. My dad didn't call him the drunk or the homeless, but Mr. Joe.

I guess Mr. Joe had a hard night because his hair was sticking all up and I started laughing and my dad said, "What are you laughing at? Don't be laughing at people. You don't know what he went through last night. We could be like that someday; don't you dare be like that." That was the opposite of what I was learning in my clinical psychology classes, so when I came out of college I had to detoxify and undo that racist way of doing business. I understood the system wasn't really about healing or embracing our folks; it was about controlling them.

My partner and I have five children together and six grandchildren. That really is the reason why I do everything, trying to heal generations of wounds and wanting them to have less trauma and more blessings. As part of this journey, there's been a lot of teachings, a lot of challenges that have guided the trajectory of my life. Growing up in that South Central neighborhood I experienced how society doesn't look at you in a good way, doesn't value you, and makes you think you're not worth anything. When you also hear that message in the media and your school, it gets integrated in your body. I saw it in my own neighborhood with people hurting each other and killing each other in gangs; I saw it in their homes with domestic violence and I saw guys shooting at us.

As much as I was proud of my culture when I became a therapist most of the clients that we were getting were men who looked like me who were hurting our wives and children or hurting ourselves. That caused a big struggle in me, a big dilemma because I love my people and my culture. I realized that we need healing for our people, not just treatment, not just the criminal justice system. So some of us men got together because we knew it was the men who were causing the harm, to say, "Who wants to help build programs that would heal?"

In 1988, 19 men came together in Jolon, California in retreat. In our cultural way, we opened with prayer and asked the ancestors to come guide us, then we did what we call *conocimiento* or acknowledgment. "Who are you? Why are you here?" When it got to one guy, who was a therapist himself, he shared with us, "I'm going to tell you what's really going on with me. I'm hurting inside myself; I don't know how to love my wife; I don't know how to love my kids and even though I help other people, I drink too much."

Then he said, ``I'm going to share something deeper that I've never admitted to anyone. I was sexually abused as a kid and I've never told anybody and especially a man." He began to cry, almost one of those spirit cries where you could feel his spirit opening up. That was strange to us as men because we were taught not to show our feelings in public. But when he released it and he began to cry like that, all of the rest of us began to cry.

By the time we finished doing that acknowledgment of who we were, we realized even though we were the therapists, teachers, leaders, the lawyers--supposedly the successful ones, we were wounded. We had bought the lie that as long as you get your education, your degree, your house, your car, everything is fine and equal.

What we didn't realize is that we had generations of trauma that have come from generations of our people living in a racist society that has never been dealt with. It was in our bodies showing up in our liver and our kidneys and we were coping in negative ways by drinking or working too much and getting high or womanizing. As we sat there in each other's presence, we realized the most revolutionary thing we could do was to first heal ourselves, to heal the wounds of our fathers back to our great-great-grandfathers who were colonized, oppressed, and conquered.

We had to cleanse ourselves from all of those things to weed out the toxicity and had to recover and discover the sacredness of who we really were. We also made another commitment that we needed to bring other men into this healing path and make them accountable as well because if they were doing harm, we needed to do something; that's been part of our advocacy for over 30 years. We had to teach the next generation, so a lot of the work that I've done has been the rites of passage for young men who don't have fathers, or their fathers are deported, or are just as wounded as they are.

We're still healing because when you have 500 years of wounds you don't heal overnight. I co-founded The National Compadres Network to create healing communities, generationally from the elder to the young person and all the directions. We're expanding our Healing Practitioners Network. We have a strong women's division that works for women and girls healing all their relations, including those who identify across various gender identities.

I also have daughters and sisters and my companion who have taught me the trauma that women go through when they walk down the street or walk in a room and they don't feel safe either. They don't feel like they can say anything. There's a lot of fear all around and currently, we're seeing the rights of women taken away. We as men need to step up and support the women and support the feminine in this world because that's where the healing comes from.

When I look at my grandkids, the youngest one is three months old, a pretty, dark-skinned boy like his daddy. The first time I saw him, I picked him up and said, "Thank you, Creator, thank you, ancestors, for sending this special gift to us." Even though I just met him, I felt like I've known him for years. I said, "Welcome home, we're your family, I'm your *tata*, your grandfather, and I promise to make a commitment to you and the creator that I'll walk with you, love you, and feed you. When you fall to the ground, we'll pick you up. I'm not going to let you be alone, I'll teach you these ways but we're also going to make you responsible as well because we need you to guide that next generation that way."

As a middle-class Anglo, I grew up in West L.A. and I never had a day of fear. I think the scariest thing was when we teens snuck in at night to "pool raid" in a neighbor's yard. In the same city, our experiences were totally different. It was assumed my brother and I would go to college and my parents would pay for it. I still carry some of that fear in me because I saw people killed. I'd go to school and a friend wasn't there, they were deported or locked up. You never knew who was going to be there when you got home. That's a residual fear that doesn't go away, especially when it's still going on. *Yes, PTSD is hard to heal.* There's still this fear of systemic inequity and racism. *Like Trump saying the bad hombres come from Mexico and rape women.*

The other part is not recognizing our worth coming from a traditional, indigenous point of view. This world won't be at peace until we recognize that all people's teachings and medicine are necessary for this world to be whole. When you have a hierarchy of values and say to your kids and grandkids that, in order for you to be successful you have to act this way, talk this way, and give up certain of your ways, that's a destruction deep in the spirit.

As a young kid, I thought that because my grandma had never gone to school or couldn't read or write that she didn't know anything, that she was dumb, and I didn't need to listen to her. But I realized through the years that my grandma was so wise, the spirit who motivated us by her prayers at 4:30 in the morning when every day she would say prayers for all of us. She'd come in our room to give us all a blessing, the ones who were good in school, the stinky kids, the good-looking one, the ugly one, she didn't care--she blessed us all.

Her acceptance was my saving grace, but if you look at my résumé, it doesn't say my grandma's blessing was a significant element that got me to where I am, or doesn't mention my mother's unconditional love, or my father's hard work ethic. Do I heal from the challenges and use them as medicine? That's what I try to do. I share with people that you have a choice to transform the wounds or drown in them. Our social system doesn't offer that to people; we force them to do certain things. True healing is a journey. The question is how do we provide those resources and opportunities?

As a young boy, I didn't feel I could reach out or feel I should share my feelings. *What about your abuela or madre?* I'm talking about when I was in the neighborhood and boys weren't supposed to cry or express feelings or you'd be very vulnerable. Nobody told me that when you walk in your house you take that shield down; those are the kind of things that healing is about. Still today, I've got to tighten up, got to front up, going to act a certain way in certain places.

I went to college not because I wanted to be successful or get ahead, but to make my mom proud because I saw how hard she worked and I saw how much she wanted me to do that. However, I didn't like college at all. I got a scholarship to Claremont McKenna College, a full scholarship with room and board, books, everything. I went there for one year and then I got drafted. The Vietnam draft was going on and I was number one in the lottery. *I thought they weren't supposed to draft students?* I put in two requests for a deferment and they turned me down and I had to go. They turned down black and brown students ten times as often as they did whites.

Many of our people ended up in Vietnam on the front lines. I didn't want to go to but my mom said, "You're a man; you need to go to defend your country." I served my time and my scholarship was gone when I got back, so I had to go to Cal State Dominguez Hills for my bachelor's, and then I went to Loyola and got a master's in clinical psych.

Ashanti Branch in Oakland taught math in high school and now has a program for boys of color. In his experience, it's not cool to get good grades if you're a boy who's brown or black.* Yes, I see that attitude, and part of that comes from this indoctrination of who is smart in your history books and who are the successful people? Who are the inventors and the smart people? They don't look like you. Then you hear the negative narrative about we're criminals, gang members, and drug dealers. You see that in the media and all over the place, so in my neighborhood when you acted really smart, they said "Stop acting white." This educational system sets us up because education is about competition, being smart, and being the best.

But my culture wasn't about being the best or the smartest because that tends to separate you. In. fact one time I was playing with my cousins and we were bragging, "I'm faster; no you're not. I'm better than you." My dad walked by and said, "Hey, stop that, you're not better than anybody." I was like, "Dang, that's messed up," and then as he was walking away he said, "But you're just as good as anybody." I didn't understand the duality of that message until later on when I began understanding from an indigenous cultural point of view that we're not striving to be better, we're striving collectively to contribute in a good way.

Everyone has something to contribute and your medicine is not better than mine, it's just a different medicine. You're not more important because you graduated from high school than the elderly woman who didn't graduate. If you go to school and try to be better and smarter, your friends get mad at you, "Man, why are you acting like that? Why are you making me feel like you're better than me?"

If you grow up with society, media, and school saying you're not good, you're not smart, you're not anything, and then one of your friends acts smart, it triggers a whole lot. Friends say, "I won't play with you no more, go ahead smarty, get out of here." Schools make me feel that I'm not smart, especially in schools where the teachers aren't paid as well and we don't have the newest equipment. When I went to college, I didn't know how to type, while at Claremont guys walked in there with typewriters and also had money to pay somebody to write their papers.

For many professionals of color, we face the imposter syndrome. Are "others" going to find out that I'm really not that smart? All this because smart means white and we are not that. The problem is when it's ingrained in you when you grow up in a society that's paternalistic and you believe they gave you that credential, that degree, that privilege, which means the people in charge can take it away in a second. We see this often, so it's important for us to change the narrative that your people are brilliant, to my people are brilliant too.

My people invented things like the concept of zero, built pyramids, and did extensive farming. We have a genetic memory of traditions and customs that build spirit, faith, and interconnectedness. Sharing this with young people who are going through their rites of passage, we recognize that the world is sharing something else. One of my teachings that we share as a group of us across the country is a common narrative that sometimes gets challenged by the greater society and the system. The concept is they are sacred, come from a sacred people, and that all people have a sacred purpose--which is the opposite of racism.

Right-wing conservatives are passing state laws again teaching about racism ("critical race theory,") indicating we've gone backward. What happens sometimes is wounds get hidden underground, but the Trump Administration brought them out. Anytime you mention race it's a triggering point because of the historic injustices. *Especially because whites are becoming a minority, that really triggers it.* You can have people of color take on the very same values, the very same perception as the dominant culture.

In our community, we clamored for more African-American and Latino police officers and succeeded, but what we didn't understand at the time is they still went through the same training and indoctrination that other officers did. So now we have people that look like you who sometimes treat you worse. It's not as simple as just installing a person of color when a system has an ideology and a pedagogy that is still very inequitable, very oppressive, very negative, very traumatic, and very harmful.

In Texas, there are about as many Anglos as Latinos; in California, there are more Latinos. So why do we have Texas Governor Greg Abbott? Why did about one-third of Latinos vote for Trump in 2020? We have more women voters than men but get legislation that's very much anti-women. Numbers don't really dictate things since it's about the power structure and a mentality. There's a process of identifying with the oppressor. Let's say you want to be a tenured professor, but certain practices are unfair, racist, and inequitable, but you're not going to get tenured if you speak up. After a while, you begin believing in the system because now you want to maintain the status quo.

We live in a society that indoctrinates us to have a hierarchy of value for certain people who are seen as more intelligent, more progressive, more successful and other people are not. When you continue to hear those messages over and over, you begin to believe them. You also learn that in order to be successful you begin acting, walking, talking like the ones in power and that means sometimes you give up who you are.

Those are all these subtle things that I've experienced becoming a professional. I'm an award-winning author, including a whole series of children's books given awards by presidents and by governors of California. I speak to thousands and thousands giving large keynote presentations. To prepare for one of those, I walked in the room as people were having lunch and two women turned around and said, "Can you get me some more coffee?" I respect those people who serve others but these ladies looked at me and that's all they could see. That reverberates all those times when I got treated that way and saw my dad and mom treated that way, saw Miss Mosley treated that way, and saw Tyrone's father treated that way.

All those experiences were still in my body and I felt in that second that I'm going to kick somebody's ass. I was back in the neighborhood because I wanted to retaliate and of course, I had to breathe and learn how to deal with those traumatic reactions. I looked at the name tags of these two ladies and when I went to speak the keynote in the evening, after they read off all my credentials, I said, "Thank you and I want to acknowledge two women who greeted me when I got here today." I asked them to stand up and please give them a round of applause. That's my dad, a jokester, but the reason I was able to do that is because I've done years of healing and to recognize who I really am.

Talking about racism, culture, and inequity is not about making anybody feel badly, it's about dealing with the reality and the health of this country. When you don't deal with something it's a wound that gets worse, turns the anger, hate-- as we're seeing all across this country. Because of the Covid pandemic, isolated people don't have avenues to express and release, so you're seeing a tremendous amount of mental health issues, especially in children. We as people of color have been struggling with these issues all our lives. Sheltering in place is nothing new for us because the cops or immigration are around.

Is it a stereotype or are machismo and marianismo still valued? When you mention Latinos, we have different populations, and a lot of immigrants to the US these days are indigenous people from Oaxaca, from Guerrero, and machismo is always brought up. Let's talk about machismo because that's something I've had to deal with all my life. What many people don't know is that the true macho, the true honorable man, honors women, is responsible, is a person of his word, is compassionate and sensitive, and violence is not acceptable.

There are 12 principles but a lot of our families don't know that definition because what's been taught to them is the wounded sense of macho, which is not Latino but is patriarchy. We recognize that men, not just Mexican men but all men, have that indoctrination about masculine sense of control, superiority, thinking that you're smarter, stronger, and can be sexual with anybody.

I was one of the first people to work in the East LA Rape Hot-Line, the first male. I would go to a conference on sexual assault and domestic violence and they kicked me out just because I'm a man. Anytime I'd step in a room there was always the assumption that I was the enemy. If you talk to black and brown women of that movement, that was not their view, but the white feminists basically promoted that attitude. I think it's changed now somewhat, but for generations, men have been seen as the problem, the culprit, the perpetrator.

I don't want to take away the validity of what many women feel from violence, from the insensitivity, especially now when a woman in Texas can't make a decision about her own body and men making those decisions, with the support of some women. It's the same question of why sometimes black and brown people vote very conservatively.

By the way, domestic violence is not any higher in Latino culture than it is in white culture. Poor whites have as much domestic violence as poor blacks or poor Latinos. However, there's a whole other aspect of abuse with middle-class and upper-class populations, which is very high as well. If we really begin to understand the data, there's no more patriarchal, misogynistic, wounded behavior from one culture to the other. But more people of color are in the criminal justice and mental health systems because of poverty and racism.

When we talk about the true sense of being an honorable man, we talk about sacred manhood, which allows you to have elements of masculine in you and have the feminine too. You need to be nurturing and compassionate and also have the child spirit in you. You need to be able to laugh, play, act goofy and silly, as well as have the elder in you to be wise. So when we talk from an indigenous point of view, sacred manhood is having all of those qualities: the masculine, the feminine, child spirit, and elder's wisdom. The healed aspect of that sacred manhood gives you the flexibility to the dimension that is called for in your relations and circumstances.

Sometimes I need the feminine energy to be a nurturing grandpa or husband or father. If an earthquake happens, I need to bring the masculine out and say, it's going to be okay kids, and be courageous. When somebody's trying to harm my family I better step up aggressively. The true essence in our indigenous culture is that sacred manhood. Unfortunately when you're indoctrinated that you're true self is all those behaviors of the wounded macho, you begin to believe that's who you are, and that you only have these two choices. Rather than reinforcing the negative or giving up your culture for "success," you have to reground yourself in the sacredness of who you really are. We say that to men we work with who have issues with violence, drugs, and alcohol and we say it to young boys too, "Your sacred manhood--but also the wounded self is there too--so what will you choose to grow and develop?"

I'm not saying you can't be a hard dude and you can't protect yourself but know when to take that mad dog mask off. When you walk in your mom's house, take that down, be respectful. When somebody's hurting and you're feeling it, let it go, let the tears roll. Healing that wounded man is the work that we are trying to do to transform men and boys and also women, girls, and those across all gender identities as well. Now we have gender-expansive populations, the transgender, we need to consider it's not just binary, there's a whole spectrum of gender. We're getting transgender men in our group to explore and men who are raising children by themselves, or two men co-parenting.

The marianismo aspect meant that women should be protected, you should have a chaperone if you go on a date before you're married, you should be pure like Mary the virgin. The quinceañera *announces you're 15 and eligible for marriage.* I grew up with a strong mother, strong women, and my sister would kick my brother's butt. The stereotype is that Latina women are submissive, but no, not in my home. The Spanish conquistadores aimed to destroy the strongest so that they could conquer. The men would come out to defend the women because we recognize that the center of our families and cultures is the women. Women are the center; we're matrilineal; they have the wisdom, they give life, they're the nurturers, they are the healers, they are truly the leaders. We do not survive without the women.

My dad didn't want any of us to go out, but especially my sisters because of the thought of what could happen to us. I'm all woke and contemporary but I have a son and a daughter. When my son got to be 14, he could go and stay over at his friend's house and at 14 my daughter says, "Can I go out?" I feel my body tighten up and get afraid because I've seen girls raped and girls have come crying to me because it happened to them. I know that the woundedness of communities out there and there are some men and boys who are like that.

I have a 14-year-old daughter and my fear comes out in not wanting her to go. "How come Marcos gets to go? What's the difference?" My daughter really challenged me that way. The fear that's based in reality is real; if we don't talk about it and deal with it as a family then we end up doing things like saying no, you've got to stay here. So we heal together as a family and that transforms traditions.

Did you give your daughter a quinceañera? No, but we did do a ceremony. The quinceañera is the celebration, it's not the ceremony. In indigenous culture, there was a ceremony for boys and girls as preparation for their next stage of life, for adolescence. When the girl got her menses, the women have a council to guide them, you can go to your aunties. Your mom alone can't guide you, she doesn't have all the teachings and lessons. Sometimes, you're closer to the younger aunt who is two years older than you and takes you to the mall and other things. When you're upset, you're not going to talk to your mom but you may talk to her.

That was the true ceremony, surrounding young girls with women who love her and can guide and support her. There are teachings around life but the true aspect of announcing that she was 15 is saying to the community she's not a little girl anymore: You must respect her as a woman.

That got all twisted around when the conquistadores took away our ceremonies, our drums, our dances that built our spirit and our character. They said you can party and we'll give you all the liquor you want, as is going on today. Why is it that in poor communities a liquor store is in every corner? In a rich neighborhood, the ordinance says a liquor store is only every three miles. We know that part of addiction is access.

We did a ceremony for my boy, too, at 13. We prepared him, brought some uncles around. He had to speak to the family and give thanks to his grandparents, to his godparents, to all the people who helped him that far. I put him in the middle of that circle of around 100 people, and said, "Look at all these people who love you and care for you. You'll never be alone, you always have somebody as long as you reach out. Anything you do will affect them all good or bad, so be careful how you walk now that you're not a little boy." Now, unfortunately, when they take away your traditions, values, and customs, they say, "Hey man, you're 15, have a shot, smoke some blunt," or you have a dad taking his son to be with a prostitute, which is traumatizing. If you don't know your true culture and traditions, then you pick up the false harmful ones and pass them on to the next generation.

How have you institutionalized these values in organizations? We started The Circle of Hombres 33 years ago. Out of that developed the National Compadres Network. But all of these efforts are built on a philosophy, a way of life called La Cultura Cura. It means one's culture cures; it's the indigenous philosophy, the ideology for all the rites of passage and teachings, for the curriculum we've developed. The curriculum was developed to provide an invitation and a roadmap to teach other people how to work with young men for fatherhood, for men returning from prison, for doing healing circles, for working in schools.

We collaborate with other groups, such as the Brotherhood Of Elders Network in Oakland with the African-American population and other groups of color. It's about bringing together these wisdom keepers of healing practitioners from cultures across the country. We're building a network of healing practitioners across the country because we've realized--especially when the murder of George Floyd happened and then Covid happened--there's a lot of people who need support and healing. We're in the process of building that capacity in communities, really attempting to reestablish healthy, generational, extended kinship rooted in cultural and positive traditions.

Let's say a boy comes to you who's 16 and anxious and depressed and feels unaccepted by his peers. What's an example of a healing ritual that would help him find his center? We'll give him pizza, that's what helps. I'm joking, but in fact, I'm not. *Food is the best tool for organizing.* Yes, food says welcome, we will feed you, we'll take care of you. The most important thing is first acknowledging someone as a blessing. Our staff member Ozzie Cruz was 15 when we met him, on probation hanging out with gangs. He was a teen father and part of his probationary requirement was to go to a fathering class. We were running a teen-father group, based on all these teachings. He didn't want to go but in order to deal with probation, he went. Bobby Verdugo said welcome *mijo*, my son. Ozzie said that's the first time he ever heard a grown man call him "son" and all the men said *mijo*.

Ozzie went through the 12 sessions of the program and learned about fatherhood but really learning about manhood and about himself when he didn't have anybody else to teach him. After we graduated him he said, "Can I come for another round?" Then he said he will do a third time and I said, "Dude, you eat too much pizza here," so we had to hire him and Ozzie has been connected with us for 20 years. He's our senior training specialist, an amazing father, grandfather, husband, and one of the most powerful teachers that we have. We also have Mario Ozuna Sanchez, who was also a teen father, but through the years and teachings is an incredible leader. It starts with you acknowledging somebody as a blessing, you're embracing them and saying I will walk with you. That greeting is a ceremony saying welcome home.

It seems like the core of your work, EVRYMAN, The ManKind Project, and Ashanti Branch's program discussed in this book is they provide a circle of men who hold you accountable, care about you, give you undivided attention. That allows the man to develop in a way he can't in a circle of women. Yes, these are good positive examples, but you can have a circle of men who are not giving good teachings because they haven't done the personal work. You can have a circle of men who are very misogynistic and hard and we've seen that too. You have to have honorable men who are going through their own processes. I evaluate programs working with boys all across the country, and sometimes see the teachers are still being very misogynistic, still drinking, still getting high, still not being responsible.

The other part, that is essential especially for boys of color, is re-embracing your culture, your identity, learning to love yourself, and being able to separate from the oppressive ways you see in your family and community to follow your sacred ways. There's a lot of manhood programs that I've seen come and go that do great work but if you want it to be sustainable, you have to deal with the root, which is culture and identity. The opposite of that is racism and oppression. I've seen a lot of manhood programs that say we're going to make these kids accountable, we're going to get them to graduate and wear ties, which is all wonderful. However, if you're not dealing with historical trauma, generational oppression, and integrating their cultural roots, then it's not going to be sustainable.

There's a whole other women and girls division in NCN that is very powerful and very needed. I want to emphasize the need for building spaces and funding and developing avenues for women and girls to lead, guide, and heal. To develop all of that is as significant because we have to heal as a whole community.

Let's talk about your books, what are the themes in Recovering Your Sacredness? My latest book is a lot of what I talked about. We have to choose who we want to be as we move forward in a sacred way and that book gives practical ways to do that. *Cultura Y Bienestar: Mesoamerican-Based Healing and Mental Health Practice* was co-edited by Ricardo Carrillo and Maestra Concha Saucedo, including healers and practitioners who explain remedies to heal wounds. *Lifting Latinos Up: From Trauma-Informed to Healing* is similar.

Family Violence and Men Of Color was written by me and Dr. Ricardo Carrillo. We talk about the issue of family violence in the historical context of the oppressive values, attitudes, and behaviors that many men have developed as a result of generations of oppression and woundedness.

You did a book on Cesar Chavez for kids. Yes, this is part of a series of children's books you can see on my website (www.jerrytello.com). My first book was called *Trenzas Bonitos (beautiful braids) and the Barrio Bears*, my counter to Goldilocks and the Three Bears. In my neighborhood, there's nobody with goldilocks and I didn't know what porridge was, but I knew what beans and rice were so in my book she's eating beans, rice, and tortillas. I'm now writing a book on the philosophy, the teachings of the healing ways of La Cultura Cura, and several children's books with their own teachings.

What are the different branches of the men's movement in the US? They all have different intentions and some are more focused. If you talk about Men's Rights, you need to check out the behavior and the example of the men who are guiding them. Are they doing their own work? Is it really just about men or is it about all our relationships? From our philosophy, it always includes the women, the children, the elders, and various communities. In my 45-plus years of doing this work, I'm seeing more and more men who are healing, want to be good men in relationships, to heal, to contribute. They're also willing to learn and grow and we just need the support and the provide the resources for them to do that.

I would invite people to check out our podcast called "Healing Generations;" with about 60 episodes about the generational healing from generational trauma from different perspectives. I'll end with a Mayan teaching, *En Lak Ech*, which means "You are my other me." When you hurt, I hurt; when you heal, I heal; you are me, I am you; we are one. Let us go on the journey as a–universe to heal ourselves and all our relations, one person, one family, one culture, and community at a time.

Conclusion

We are limited by outdated gender stereotypes, both men in their lack of access to a wide range of emotions and caregiving and women in their limited access to leadership and power. It's in our best interest to move towards flexibility and being instrumental or nurturant as circumstances require. This means we stop telling boys not to cry or be like girls and stop telling girls to be nice little ladies. We need to encourage girls to go into leadership and STEM fields of science and technology and boys into caregiving professions, like many of the men in this book did as therapists, instructors, and heads of helping organizations.

The consensus of our experts is that boys and men are not permitted to show vulnerability, a word often repeated in this book. From the Netherlands, Stephan van de Ven, 32, said, "I don't know how to really express my emotions, not having had that many examples in my environment from men around me, from movies, from TV series, or anything." This prejudice shuts down even being aware of some emotions, which is why EVRYMAN and other men's groups begin with identifying body sensations.

Asking for help may require being vulnerable, which fits in the "threat to masculinity" danger zone. This fear of being perceived as weak contributes to men's health problems and a higher suicide rate. Being shut down emotionally also inhibits men's intimate relations with people they love, one of the reasons why women in English-speaking countries are much more likely to initiate divorce than men. Femininity is seen by sexists as weakening to precarious masculinity and can increase the fear of intimacy.

Divorce and poverty lead to an increase in single-mother households, which MIT Economics Professor David Autor links to worse outcomes for the boys than the girls with single mothers. This is part of the explanation of why boys are falling behind girls in higher education. This equation is shutting down boys' expression of human feelings leads to health and relationship difficulties, which is especially harmful to boys raised by single mothers. As Jed Diamond said, mothers can't teach boys what it means to be a man. The solution is to educate parents and teachers about how to encourage boys to be in touch with the full range of human feelings, as modeled in countries like Denmark.[182] As with other social and environmental problems, solutions are available but the will to implement them is lacking.

Why are some men willing to advocate for changes in male socialization and risk being seen as outside the norm of masculine interests? We've learned that it's mostly women who take men's studies college courses. Our changemakers, similar to men I interviewed for *50:50 Marriage* and *50:50 Parenting*, were influenced by a very positive or very negative role model, either a loving involved father (the minority) or an absent father due to death, divorce, or long work hours.

Many of our contributors felt that they didn't fit the masculinity standard as boys and were concerned about ways girls and boys were harmed by sexism. Gary Barker's female friends told him about forced sex, leading him to want to take action as a man: "This kind of manhood, with so much violence and anger, is not who I think I am." With feminist analysis, John Stoltenberg said, "I felt freedom from the cookie-cutter I was trying to fit into. I found it was possible to be who I am without constantly thinking about, am I male enough?"

Many of the contributors agree that schools need to accommodate boys' need for more physical activity, especially with many boys being developmentally behind girls. Boys of color act out their own versions of masculinity, which may include looking at school success as "acting white," as our men of color reported. Wanting improvement in gender liberation, changemakers organize men's groups, teach courses, research and write about gender socialization practices, and lobby for legislative change--particularly in child custody.

The common concern for gender liberation and equal opportunity doesn't mean these activists are united. Every progressive or liberal group I know argues over who is most politically pure and the men's movement is no exception. They debate who is most oppressed by traditional gender roles and if gender is more shaped by nature or nurture. As Michael Messner reports, "Those schisms between different groups run pretty deep and have been going on for many decades."

Men's rights advocates think men suffer more, while feminists think women suffer more from gendered power systems. The latter don't want to talk with the former, thinking problematically in a zero-sum game so that if I win, you lose. Daniel Ellenberg reported, "It's remarkable how many smart, professional people seem to think it's an either/or game. I think it's both/and. It tends to trigger a lot of vitriol from different folks. Until we change our mindset about it, we're still going to be at war." Some blame the peer-led men's groups for not being political and "getting stuck looking at our own belly buttons," as Barker said. However, many of our men have been part of men's groups.

What surprised me from interviewing these men of different ages, ethnicities, nationalities, religions, and ideologies is that some felt disadvantaged in relationships and in school, including young men like Tristan Glosby. (*I Hate Men* is the title of a recent book by Pauline Harmange, translated from French.) I was also surprised that young men still hear, "don't be a sissy." Some felt being male was under fire with the frequent use of the phrase "toxic masculinity."

Progress certainly isn't a straight line upward, as evidenced in the sexist cult led by Donald Trump. George Simons finds in international surveys that about one-third of men support gender equality. I'm hopeful because Generations Y and Z tend to not limit themselves in regards to their gender roles or skin color. They have models to emulate as they assume more political power, learning from Nordic gender equality programs, Danish emotional literacy instruction for children, research on boy's development (like that done by Andrew Smiler and Warren Farrell), and supportive groups for boys like those developed by Jerry Tello and Ashanti Branch. Promundo and MenEngage provide models of how to involve boys and men in activism for gender equality for all human beings.

Men's Studies Resources and Bibliography

Associations
The American Men's Studies Association (to advance the critical study of men and masculinities)
Canadian Association for Equality (CAFE)
Canadian Centre for Men and Families
Male Survivor: National Organization Against Male Sexual Victimization.
MenEngage Alliance
National Coalition for Men
National Compadres Network includes curricula
Many more organizations: https://xyonline.net/links#Acadorgs

Archives
Michigan State University
Stony Brook Libraries Men's Studies
https://guides.library.stonybrook.edu/mens-studies
https://www.academia.edu/444498/International_Encyclopedia_of_Men_and_Masculinities_2007_

Bibliography
https://xyonline.net/books/bibliography
https://libguides.ucmerced.edu/sprk001-toconis/masculinities
Diedrick Janssen, MD. *The Men's Directory: A World Directory of Research and Resources*. Men's Studies Press, 2009. Includes books, journals, guides, courses, organizations, etc.
Also see the EndNotes and short biographies for author books.

Initiatives
Global Initiative for Boys and Men: https://www.gibm.us/
Promundo: promotes gender equality and prevents violence by engaging men and boys in partnership with women and girls. https://promundoglobal.org/resources/

Journals
Gender and History

Fathering: A Journal of Theory Research and Practice about Men as Fathers
Journal of Black Masculinity
International Journal of Men's Health
Journal of Men, Masculinities and Spirituality
Journal of Men's Studies
Masculinities: A Journal of Culture and Society
Masculinities and Social Change
Men and Masculinities
New Male Studies: An International Journal
NORMA: International Journal for Masculinity Studies
Psychology of Men & Masculinities
Spectrum: A Journal on Black Men
Thymos: Journal of Boyhood Studies

Men's Studies Courses and Bibliographies
https://xyonline.net/content/curricula-men-and-masculinities-xy-collection
https://www.hws.edu/academics/mens/curriculum.aspx
http://xyonline.net/books/bibliography/2-best-reading-men-masculinities/best-texts (to 2019)
http://xyonline.net/books/bibliography/2-best-reading-men-masculinities/reading-beginner

Podcasts
Jed Diamond: https://menalive.com/the-blog/
Gayle Kimball, Interviews with Changemakers: https://anchor.fm/gaylekimball
Good Will Toward Men podcasts: podcasts.apple.com/us/podcast/good-will-toward-men/id1575596615
https://www.jackkammer.com/stay-tuned
ManKind Project: https://podcasts.apple.com/us/podcast/ManKind-podcast/id1555955858
National Compadres Network Healing Generations
Many more: See https://xyonline.net/content/podcasts-men-and-masculinities.

Support Groups
https://usmenssheds.org/find-a-shed/

https://goodmenproject.com/about/
https://www.themenslist.com/about-us/ (men's mental health directory)

Webpages and Blogs
Bettina Arndt #MenToo https://www.bettinaarndt.com.au/
Emotional Literacy Resources for Children:
https://childhood101.com/managing-big-emotions-best-resources-to-use-with-kids/
Menstuff (Gordon Clay) http://menstuff.org
https://www.strengthwithheart.com/
The Men's List website for mental health created by Dale Curd:
https://www.themenslist.com/about-us/
XY is a website focused on men, masculinities, and gender politics. http://xyonline.net/

Author Interviews with Young Men Internationally
Gen Y interview: Demi, 25, has lived in Israel, Greece, & Italy:
https://youtu.be/GgCKueSGWck
College Counselors Discuss Pressure Students Face Today:
https://youtu.be/GYO1C5lOwbI
Turkey 13-Year-Olds:
https://youtu.be/qbBzCcI5EOY
California Jr High students discuss school issues:
https://youtu.be/_39eeL31uo8
Chinese grad student in Finland's impressions:
https://youtu.be/emjKw24cciY
French Millennial Activist Discusses Protests in Paris:
https://youtu.be/3ykTa_ub3oI
Lanai (Hawaii) High School Students Interview with Alika and Rysssen: https://youtu.be/os6Oloc27FA

EndNotes

1 https://childhood101.com/managing-big-emotions-best-resources-to-use-with-kids/

2 https://greenlocalsolutions.wordpress.com/2022/01/07/biographies-and-contents-a-global-dialogue-on-masculinity-by-gayle-kimball/

3 https://sites.la.utexas.edu/utaustinsoc/2013/02/07/scouting-and-homosexuality-a-case-for-the-gender-policed

4 https://www.npr.org/2021/07/01/1012388865/boy-scouts-of-america-settlement-with-sexual-abuse-survivors-victims

5 Jordan Peterson. *12 Rules for Life*. Random House, 2018, pp. 330-332.

6 https://www.newyorker.com/magazine/2018/03/05/jordan-petersons-gospel-of-masculinity

7 https://www.cnn.com/2021/11/08/politics/josh-hawley-masculinity-video-games-porn/index.html

https://www.rollingstone.com/politics/politics-news/josh-hawley-masculinity-obsession-1254776/

https://www.theguardian.com/world/2021/nov/01/josh-hawley-feminism-men-pornography-video-games

https://www.theguardian.com/commentisfree/2021/nov/06/josh-hawley-is-right-that-men-arent-doing-well-but-its-because-of-toxic-people-like-him

8 https://www.psychologytoday.com/us/blog/men-crossroads/202008/learning-be-man-without-masculinity-0

9 https://www.businessinsider.com/tucker-carlson-falsely-claims-covid-19-does-feminize-people-2021-12

10 https://www.cnbc.com/2018/10/29/brazil-election-jair-bolsonaros-most-controversial-quotes.html

11 https://www.nytimes.com/2021/10/11/sports/football/what-did-jon-gruden-say.html?

12 https://www.businessinsider.com/trump-called-french-president-emmanuel-macron-a-wuss-guy-book-says-2021-10

13 https://www.ccs.neu.edu/home/shivers/rants/scum.html

14 https://www.cdc.gov/nchs/products/databriefs/db398.htm#section_1

15 https://tonicmasculinity.blog

https://www.centreformalepsychology.com/male-psychology-magazine-listings/a-tonic-for-the-toxic-narrative-on-masculinity

16 https://covid-19archive.org/s/archive/item/24027

17 This term was created by Paul Kivel and the Oakland Men's Project. Heilman, B., Barker, G., and Harrison, A. (2017). *The Man Box: A Study on Being a Young Man in the US, UK, and Mexico*. Washington, DC and London: Promundo-US and Unilever.

18 Sylvie Borau, "Female Robot are Seen as Being the Most Human," *The Conversation,* April 14, 2021.

19 V. Seehafer, "Evaluation and Revision of BSRI Trait Selection," 2018. https://digitalcommons.olivet.edu/cgi/viewcontent.cgi?article=1217&context=scholar_week_events

20 Andrew Kaczynski, et al, "Donald Trump to Howard Stern," CNN, October 9, 2016.

https://www.cnn.com/2016/10/08/politics/trump-on-howard-stern/index.html

21 https://whitehouseboysmen.org/BOARD-OF-ADVISORS-White_House_Council_Boys_Men.aspx

22 National Network to End Domestic Violence
https://www.nytimes.com/2021/09/30/opinion/gabby-petito-domestic-abuse.html?

23 https://www.cdc.gov/violenceprevention/pdf/2015data-brief508.pdf
Tables 9 and 11 re: physical violence, thanks to Robert Samery

24 https://www.bop.gov/about/statistics/statistics_inmate_gender.jsp

25 https://www.apa.org/workforce/data-tools/demographics

26 "Why Men are Lonelier in American than Elsewhere," *Paper Tribune*, January 7, 2022.
https://papertribune.com/economy/why-men-are-lonelier-in-america-than-elsewhere/

27 https://www.divorcemag.com/blog/why-do-women-initiate-divorce-more-than-men

28 Diana Bruk, "Marriage Experts Explain Why Women Initiate Divorce More than Men," *BestLife*, February 20, 2020.
https://bestlifeonline.com/women-initiate-divorce-more-than-men/

29 *JAMA*. 1999;281(6):537-544. doi:10.1001/jama.281.6.537
https://jamanetwork.com/journals/jama/fullarticle/188762

30 https://www.jchs.harvard.edu/blog/after-brief-return-young-adults-quick-move-out-parents-homes-pandemic-continues

31 Sean Massey, et al., "Feminsm's Legacy Sees College Women Embracing More Diverse Sexuality," *The Conversation*, April 28, 2021.

32 Scott South and Lei Lei, "Why are Fewer Young Adults Having Casual Sex?" *Socius*, March 1, 2021.
https://journals.sagepub.com/doi/full/10.1177/2378023121996854

33 Scott Galloway, "Young American Men Are Facing a Crisis," *Medium*, October 4, 2021.
https://gen.medium.com/young-american-men-are-facing-a-crisis-69e7233bc93e

34 Simon Usborne, "Sex isn't difficult any more': the men who are quitting watching porn," T*he Guardian,* September 6, 2021.

35 https://www.peggyorenstein.com/positive-sexuality

36 Harvard Youth Poll, April 23, 2021
https://iop.harvard.edu/youth-poll/spring-2021-harvard-youth-poll

37https://www.wsj.com/articles/gender-inequity-inequality-education-college-university-feminism-family-structure-11632079837

38 https://womensenews.org/2021/08/adhd-too-often-misdiagnosed-in-females/

39 https://www.nationaleatingdisorders.org/learn/general-information/research-on-males
Julia Taylor and Ara Groff Stephens, The COVID-19 Pandemic Increased Eating Disorders Among Young People, *The Conversation*, November 2, 2021.

40 https://economics.mit.edu/files/8754

https://www.wbur.org/onpoint/2021/09/27/education-college-crisis-among-american-men

41 ttps://www.census.gov/library/stories/2021/04/number-of-children-living-only-with-their-mothers-has-doubled-in-past-50-years.html

42 https://economics.mit.edu/files/8754, pp. 38-40.

43 Jon Marcus, "Why Men are the New College Minority," *The Atlantic*, August 8, 2017.

44 https://www.catalyst.org/research/womens-earnings-the-pay-gap/ https://www.census.gov/library/stories/2019/05/college-degree-widens-gender-earnin

45 https://www.vox.com/explainers/2018/9/27/17909782/brett-kavanaugh-christine-ford-supreme-court-senate-sexual-assault-testimony https://www.pbs.org/newshour/nation/more-americans-believe-ford-than-kavanaugh-according-to-new-poll https://www.usatoday.com/story/news/2018/09/28/brett-kavanaugh-christine-blasey-ford-assault-claim-gender-divide/1459557002/

46 https://www.forbes.com/sites/davidsturt/2018/03/08/10-shocking-workplace-stats-you-need-to-know/?

47 Colter Whitlock, "Modern Society Spits on Young Men," *Medium.com*, August 14, 2021.

48 Leslie Fiedler. *Love and Death in the American Novel,* 1960.

49 A.O. Scott, "The Death of Adulthood in American Culture," *New York Times*, September 11, 2014.

50 https://www.ru.ac.za/communicationsandadvancement/alumnirelations/theorunion/distinguishedalumniawards/2020recipients/robertmorrell.html

Johnny Clegg. *Scatterling of Africa* (Johannesburg: Pan Macmillan South Africa), 2021.

Malose Langa. *Becoming Men. Black Masculinities in a South African Township* (Johannesburg: Wits University Press), 2020.

Lisa Lindsay and Stephan F. Miescher (eds) *Men and Masculinities in Modern Africa* (London: Heinemann), 2003.

Robert Morrell (ed), *Changing Men in Southern Africa* (Pietermaritzburg/London: University of KwaZulu-Natal Press/Zed Books), 2001.

Kopano Ratele. *Liberating Masculinties* (Cape Town: HSRC Press)L Richter and R Morrell (eds), 2016.

Linda Richter and Roberet Morrell (eds). *Baba Men and Fatherhood in South Africa* (Cape Town: HSRC Press), 2006.

51 Johnny Clegg (2021), *Scatterling of Africa* (Johannesburg: Pan Macmillan South Africa)

Malose Langa (2020) *Becoming Men. Black Masculinities in a South African Township* (Johannesburg: Wits University Press).

Lisa Lindsay and Stephan F. Miescher (eds) (2003) *Men and Masculinities in Modern Africa* (London: Heinemann).

Robert Morrell (ed), Changing Men in Southern Africa (Pietermaritzburg/London: University of KwaZulu-Natal Press/Zed Books)

Kopano Ratele (2016) *Liberating Masculinties* (Cape Town: HSRC Press)

L Richter and R Morrell (eds) (2006) *Baba. Men and Fatherhood in South Africa* (Cape Town: HSRC Press).

52 https://etd.ohiolink.edu/apexprod/rws_etd/send_file/send?accession=bgsu1556039690313388&disposition=inline

53 https://equi-law.uk/boy-today/

54 Thomas Edsall, "It's Become Increasingly Hard for Them to Feel Good About Themselves, *New York Times*, September 22, 2021.

55 https://equalitycanada.com/project/momentum2021/

56 https://www.worldbank.org/en/news/feature/2013/02/26/are-gender-norms-changing-4-000-women-and-men-weigh-in

57 Shualshui Wang, "How 'Sissy Men' Became the Latest Front in China's Campaign Against Big Tech," *The Conversation*, September 10, 2021. https://www.nytimes.com/2021/12/31/opinion/china-masculinity.html

58 Choe sang-Hun, "The New Political Cry in South Korea," New York Times, January 1, 2022.

59 https://go.gale.com/ps/i.do?id=GALE%7CA381146825&sid=googleScholar&v=2.1&it=r&linkaccess=abs&issn=21640262&p=AONE&sw=w&userGroupName=anon%7E308399e4
World Bank, "On Norms and Agency, 2013. https://openknowledge.worldbank.org/handle/10986/13818

60 Pew Research Center, Gender Differences, December 5, 2017.

61 https://www.usatoday.com/story/news/nation/2020/06/09/what-terf-definition-trans-activists-includes-j-k-rowling/5326071002/

62 https://www.usatoday.com/story/news/nation/2020/06/09/what-terf-definition-trans-activists-includes-j-k-rowling/5326071002/

63 Davidson Nguyen Hang. *Redefining Masculinity*. Green Heart Living Press, 2021.

64 Stephen Whitehead. *Toxic Masculinity: Curing the Virus.* AG Books, 2021, p. 132.

65 #tedxrub2019 #embracetheunexpected #toxicmasculinity https://www.youtube.com/watch?v=Mi5TG3E4rnE

66 Todd Reeser. *Masculinities in Theory.* Wiley-Blackwell, 2010, p. 20, p. 49.

67 Maurice Berger, Brian Wallis, and Simon Watson. *Constructing Masculinity.* Routledge, 1995, p. 3.

68 Julie Moreau, "Nearly One in Five Young Adults Say They Are Not Straight," NBC News, June 9, 2021. https://www.nbcnews.com/feature/nbc-out/nearly-1-5-young-adults-say-they-re-not-straight-n1270003

69 https://www.nytimes.com/2021/10/11/fashion/the-end-of-gender.html?
https://www.nytimes.com/2022/01/04/t-magazine/altu-joseph-altuzarra-fashion.html?

70 http://www.raewynconnell.net/2011/09/interviews.html

71 https://robertbly.com/

72 https://goodmenproject.com/about/

73 https://usmenssheds.org/find-a-shed/

74 https://stirfryseminars.com/about-stirfry/lee-mun-wah/

75 Alyson Krueger, "A Fitness App Monlight s a Men's Support Group," *New York Times*, July 9, 2021.
76 Joan Meier, "Victims of Domestic Abuse Find No Haven in Family Courts," *The Conversation*, December 2, 2021.
77 https://greenlocalsolutions.wordpress.com/2022/01/06/steve-moxon-explains-the-origin-of-gender-roles-from-a-non-feminist-viewpoint/
78 Kevin Shafer, "Nurturing Dads Raise Emotionally Intelligent Kids," *The Conversation*, June 16, 2021. https://theconversation.com/nurturing-dads-raise-emotionally-intelligent-kids-helping-make-society-more-respectful-and-equitable-161395
79 https://www.voanews.com/a/usa_all-about-america_women-outnumber-and-outvote-men-they-dont-vote-alike/6205437.html
80 https://girlpowermarketing.com/statistics-purchasing-power-women/
81 Kevin Shafer, "Why Canadian Dads Are More Involved in Raising their Kids than American Fathers," *The Conversation*, July 27, 2021.
82 Darby Saxbe nd Sofia Cardenas, "What Paternity Leave Does for a Father's Brain," *New York Times,* November 8, 2021.
83 Tan Ting-ting, "Changing Practices on Fatherhood in Postmodern Sweden," *Journal of Literature and Art Studies,* May, 20217.
84 https://worldpopulationreview.com/country-rankings/happiest-countries-in-the-world
85 APA issues first-ever guidelines for practice with men and boys
86 https://nomas.org/songs-pro-feminist-mens-movement/
87 https://www.mensstudies.org/History
88 "APA Guidelines for Psychologcal Practice with Boys and Men," August 2018. https://www.apa.org/about/policy/boys-men-practice-guidelines.pdf
89 Judith Kegan Gardiner, ed. Masculinity Studies and Feminist Theory. Columbia University Press, 2002, p. xi.
90 Ibid, pp. 2-23.
91 https://userpages.umbc.edu/~korenman/wmst/programs.html
92 https://xyonline.net/content/curricula-men-and-masculinities-xy-collection
93 https://xyonline.net/sites/xyonline.net/files/2021-07/JSB280%20Engaging%20Men%20-%20Outline%20and%20readings.pdf
94 James Doyle and Sam Femiano, "The Early History of the American Men's Studies Association," 1999, www.menstudies.org/History.
95 https://www.hws.edu/academics/mens/curriculum.aspx
96 https://werklund.ucalgary.ca/masculinities
97 https://factuk.org/
98 Stephanie Leguichard, "Incel Terms Like Beta, Chad, and Thot Are More Dangerous Than You Think," *Medium,* March 11, 2021.
99 https://www.theguardian.com/lifeandstyle/2021/mar/03/incel-movement-terror-threat-canada
100 Lizzie Cernik, "'I Feel Hurt that my Life has Ended Up Here," *The Guardian,* October 18, 2021.

101 https://www.splcenter.org/fighting-hate/extremist-files/ideology/male-supremacy

102 Pew Research Center, "On Gender Differences," December 5, 2017. https://www.pewresearch.org/social-trends/2017/12/05/on-gender-differences-no-consensus-on-nature-vs-nurture/

103 https://marsvenus.com/relationship/make-peace-with-cave-time/

104 Carlyn Beccia, "A Brief History of Masculinity," *Medium*, September 12, 2021.

105 Annie Denton Cridge, "Man's Rights," Boston, 1870. https://digital.library.upenn.edu/women/cridge/rights/rights.html

106 Claire Suddath, "No Meaningful Differences in Male and Female Brains, Study Finds," *The Conversation,* May 13, 2021.

107 https://greenlocalsolutions.wordpress.com/2021/12/28/a-summary-of-the-male-brain-by-louann-brizendine-md/

108 https://www.youtube.com/watch?v=AwS7JaWB0x8

109 Ian Hodde, "Women and Men at Catalhoyuk," *Scientific American,* January 1, 2004. https://www.scientificamerican.com/article/women-and-men-at-atalhyk-2005-01/

110 Beronda Montgomery, "Plants Thrive in a Complex World by Communicating, Sharing Resources and Transforming their Environments," *The Conversation,* April 14, 2021.

111 https://globalyouthbook.wordpress.com/2014/04/25/top-4-responses-to-global-youth-survey/

112 June 2020 https://www.youtube.com/watch?v=SFAeayRauSM 33:29. 38:22

113 https://projects.theworld.org/every-30-seconds

114 https://www.statista.com/statistics/214869/share-of-active-duty-enlisted-women-and-men-in-the-us-military/

115 https://www2.ed.gov/documents/students/supporting-child-student-social-emotional-behavioral-mental-health.pdf

116 https://youtu.be/tYzF0b3qbTk

117 Lisa Tolin, "Women are Even More Burned Out in 2021," September 27, 2021. https://inshapemind.com/en/d/article/women-are-even-more-burned-out-in-2021-lean-in-report-finds

118 https://youtu.be/wnLmKmTdAgM

119 https://www.facebook.com/ watch/live/ ?ref=watch_permalink&v=1003655083068285

120 https://bi.org/en/articles/bi-men-are-not-considered-attractive-new-study-says

121 https://www.hansonrobotics.com/sophia/

122 https://www.4icu.org/ke/

123 https://www.simplypsychology.org/Bronfenbrenner.html

124 https://www.aecf.org/blog/more-children-living-in-single-parent-families

125 https:www.njr.nl/en

126 https://book.coe.int/en/
   https://edoc.coe.int/en/

[127] https://nhglobalpartners.com/maternity-marriage-leave-in-china/

[128] https://core.ac.uk/download/pdf/236407553.pdf

[129] https://promundoglobal.org/programs/international-men-and-gender-equality-survey-images/

[130] https://promundoglobal.org/promundo-axe-launch-first-ever-man-box-report/

[131] https://promundoglobal.org/wp-content/uploads/2015/01/Young-Men-and-the-Construction-of-Masculinity-in-Sub-Saharan-Africa-Implications-for-HIV-AIDS-Conflict-and-Violence.pdf

[132] https://promundoglobal.org/resources/the-cost-of-the-man-box-a-study-on-the-economic-impacts-of-harmful-masculine-stereotypes-in-the-united-states/

[133] See some of those results here: https://promundoglobal.org/resources/gender-transformative-couples-intervention-male-engagement-rwanda-randomized-controlled-trial/

[134] https://promundoglobal.org/resources/the-double-edged-sword-of-online-gaming-an-analysis-of-masculinity-in-video-games-and-the-gaming-community/

[135] Letter dated February 17th, 1923, to William H. Watson from the Calvary Baptist Radio engineer for station WQA0. American Baptist Historical Society, Call# 922.6 qst82P, Group #1075, Box 11, Folder e.

[136] See articles regarding this in The New York Times, September 13 & 14, 1926.

[137] Peggy Reeves Sanday, "The Socio-Cultural Context of Rape: A Cross-Cultural Study," Journal of Social Issues **37**, 4-27 (1981).

[138] See for instance, Domestic Violence, Abuse, and Child Custody, Legal Strategies and Policy Issues, Mo Therese Hannah, and Barry Goldstein, (eds) (Civic Research Institute; 2010).

[139] https://barrygoldstein.net/safe-child-act For more information about the Safe Child Act see Barry Goldstein, "The Safe Child Act: When a Parent Does More Harm than Good." Available at https://barrygoldstein.net/articles/the-safe-child-act-when-a-parent-does-more-harm-than-good

[140] Richard C. Kearney & Holly Sellers, "Sex on the Docket: Reports of the State Task Forces," 56(6) *Pub. Admin. Rev.* 587 (1996).

[141] Molly Dragiewicz, "Gender Bias in the Courts: Implications for Battered Mothers and Their Children" in *Domestic Violence, Abuse and Child Custody: Legal Strategies and Policy Issues*. (Mo Therese Hannah and Barry Goldstein, eds.) Ch. 5. (2010).

[142] Child Custody and the Politics of Gender, Carol Smart and Selma Sevenhuijsen (Eds.) (Routledge, New York, 1989), pp. 115 and 114, respectively, emphasis mine.

[143] J. S. Wallerstein and S. Blakeslee, *Second Chances: Men, Women, And Children A Decade After Divorce* (Ticknor & Fields, New York, 1989) at p. 187; and R. D. Felner and L. Terre, Child Custody Dispositions and Children's Adaptation Following Divorce," in *Psychology and Child Custody Determinations: Knowledge, Roles, and Expertise*, L. A. Weithorn (ed.) (1987) p. 106.

144 Mason, Mary Ann, and Ann Quirk, "Are Mothers Losing Custody? Read My Lips: Trends in Judicial Decision-Making in Custody Disputes—1920, 1960, 1990, and 1995," *Family Law Quarterly* 31(2)?: 215–36 (1997).

145 Joan S. Meier, Sean Dickson, Chris O'Sullivan, Leora Rosen, and Jeffrey Hayes, "Child Custody Outcomes in Cases Involving Parental Alienation and Abuse Allegations" (2019); https://papers.ssrn.com/sol3/papers.cfm?abstract_id=3448062.

146 Ibid.

147 Ibid.

148 J. S. Wallerstein and J. B. Kelly, *Surviving the Breakup: How Children and Parents Cope With Divorce* (Basic Books, New York, 1980); J. S. Wallerstein and S. Blakeslee, *Second Chances: Men, Women, And Children A Decade After Divorce* (Ticknor & Fields, New York,1989), p. 180; E. M. Hetherington, M. Cox, and R. Cox, "Effects of divorce on parents and children," in M. Lamb (ed.) *Nontraditional Families* (Lawrence Erlbaum Assoc., Hillsdale, NJ, 1982).

149 Nicholas Zill, in *The Impact of Divorce, Single-parenting, and Stepparenting on Children,* E. M. Hetherington and J. Arasteh (eds.) (Lawrence Erlbaum Associates, Hillsdale, NJ, 1988).

150 Peter G. Jaffe, David A. Wolf, and Susan K. Wilson, *Children of Battered Women* (Sage, 1990).

151 "Within the last year, 7% of women (3.9 million) who are married or are living with someone as a couple were physically abused, and 37% (20.7 million) were verbally or emotionally abused by their spouse or partner." Louis Harris and Associates, *The Commonwealth Fund Survey of Women's Health* (The Commonwealth Fund, New York, 1993), p. 8.

152 Booker T. Washington, An Address on Abraham Lincoln, February 12, 1909, Before the Republican Club of New York City

153 Beyond guilt: How to deal with societal racism, Lauren N. Nile and Jack C. Straton, *Multicultural Education* **10**(4), 2-6 (2003). Reprinted in *Lessons from The Color of Fear, Volume IV, Field Reports: Using The Color of Fear in the Classroom* Victor Lee Lewis and Hugh Vasquez (eds.) (Speak Out – The Institute for Democratic Education and Culture, Emeryville, CA, 2008), pp. 150-167.

154 https://pisab.org/our-history/

155 https://www.acf.hhs.gov/cb/report/child-maltreatment-2019

156 https://ninegates.org/

157 http://www.menstuff.org/

158 https://youtu.be/cca5QWdSTMQ

159 https://www.bbc.com/future/article/20190313-why-more-men-kill-themselves-than-women

160 https://www.ncbi.nlm.nih.gov/pmc/articles/PMC4089020/ https://journals.library.columbia.edu/index.php/bioethics/article/view/6008

161 France Moore Lappe, America's Killer Diet, *Common Dreams*, October 29, 2021. https://www.commondreams.org/views/2021/10/29/americas-killer-diet?

162 Mogens Nygaard Christoffersen, "An Investigation of Fathers with 3 – 5-Year-Old Children" (paper presented at the Social Research-Institute,

Ministerratskonferenz, Stockholm, Sweden, April 27–28, 1995), chart 2, "Parents Living Alone with 3- to 5-Year-Old Children."]

[163] https://www.thinkimpact.com/college-graduates-statist
https://www.simplypsychology.org/Bronfenbrenner.htmlics/

[164] www.warrenfarrell.com

[165] https://time.com/4753128/take-your-our-daughters-to-work-day-history/

[166] https://youtu.be/1Yar-jJSAwI

[167] https://www.brookings.edu/blog/up-front/2021/10/08/the-male-college-crisis-is-not-just-in-enrollment-but-completion/

[168] https://www.aei.org/carpe-diem/stunning-college-degree-gap-women-have-earned-almost-10-million-more-college-degrees-than-men-since-1982/

[169] Men Are Talking podcasts (audio)
podcasts.apple.com/us/podcast/men-are-talking/id1575596850
Good Will Toward Men podcasts (audio)
podcasts.apple.com/us/podcast/good-will-toward-men/id1575596615
Male-friendly Media YouTube vidcasts (both Men Are Talking and Good Will Toward Men in audio and video)
youtube.com/channel/UCrLW85qrmP5ezOvz1M--INw

[170] https://youtu.be/CykXo1Z7hbQ

[171] https://www.thepassiontest.com/about-the-passion-test

[172] https://enlightenup.biz/wp-content/uploads/2019/07/GotWisdom-TipsandTails.pdf

[173] https://mankindproject.org/

[174] https://mankindproject.org/wp-content/uploads/2016/01/Heros-Journey-Graphic-png.png

[175] https://owenmarcus.com/emotions/masculine-quotient-emotional-intelligence-test-men/

[176] https://www.ted.com/talks/eldra_jackson_how_i_unlearned_dangerous_lessons_about_masculinity

[177] https://hakomiinstitute.com/

[178] https://youtu.be/ibQtOkRN_wo

[179] https://diversophy.com/
Manhood 1
https://diversophy.com/collections/special-themes/products/manhood
Manhood 2
https://diversophy.com/collections/special-themes/products/manhood-2
Elderwise guys
https://diversophy.com/collections/special-themes/products/elderwise-guys-mini-game
diversiCAST-RACE-SHUN
https://diversophy.com/collections/special-themes/products/diversicaste-race-shun

[180] https://diversophy.com/collections/special-themes/products/diversicaste-race-shun

[181] https://diversophy.com/pages/how-to-play-diversophy

[182] https://www.theatlantic.com/education/archive/2016/08/the-us-empathy-gap/494975/